Cultures
of Modernism

Cultures of Modernism

Marianne Moore, Mina Loy, & Else Lasker-Schüler

Gender and Literary Community in New York and Berlin

CRISTANNE MILLER

THE UNIVERSITY OF MICHIGAN PRESS *Ann Arbor*

First paperback edition 2007

Published in the United States of America by
The University of Michigan Press
Manufactured in the United States of America
⊗ Printed on acid-free paper

2010 2009 2008 2007 5 4 3 2

A CIP catalog record for this book is available from the British Library.

Library of Congress Cataloging-in-Publication Data

Miller, Cristanne.
Cultures of modernism : Marianne Moore, Mina Loy, and Else Lasker-Schüler / Cristanne Miller.
p. cm.
Includes bibliographical references and index.
ISBN 0-472-11492-1 (alk. paper)
1. American poetry—Women authors—History and criticism. 2. Modernism (Literature)—United States. 3. Women and literature—United States—History—20th century. 4. Women and literature—Germany—History—20th century. 5. Lasker-Schüler, Else, 1869–1945—Criticism and interpretation. 6. Moore, Marianne, 1887–1972—Criticism and interpretation. 7. American poetry—20th century—History and criticism. 8. Loy, Mina—Criticism and interpretation. 9. Modernism (Literature)—Germany. 10. Sex role in literature. I. Title.
PS310.M57M55 2005
811'.509112—dc22 2004027418

ISBN 13-978-0-472-03237-2 (pbk. : alk. paper)
ISBN 10-0-472-03237-2 (pbk. : alk. paper)

Acknowledgments

Many individuals and institutions have been of crucial assistance in the composition of this book. Foremost I would like to thank the Alexander von Humboldt Foundation for funding a year and a half of research and writing in Berlin, for a summer stipend allowing me to read at the Schiller-Nationalmuseum, Deutsches Literaturarchiv in Marbach, and for funds to purchase books on Else Lasker-Schüler and Expressionism. Warm thanks also to Dr. Professor Heinz Ickstadt for enabling my affiliation with the Free University of Berlin, John F. Kennedy Institute of American Studies, under the Humboldt Fellowship, and for assistance with my translations of Lasker-Schüler's poetry. The National Endowment for the Humanities generously funded a year of research in Oxford, at the Rothermere American Institute—to which I am also thankful for yearlong support. Pomona College has been generous in granting leave time, funding research assistance, and helping with the considerable permissions costs for publishing this volume. Rafael Weiser at the Jewish National and University Library, Jerusalem, provided crucial help, facilitating my research at the library and my procuring of permissions. Evelyn Feldman, Michael Barsanti, and Elizabeth Fuller have exhibited great patience and knowledge in assisting me during my research visits over several years to the Moore archives at the Rosenbach Museum and Library.

Many friends have read parts or all of this manuscript. In particular, I would like to thank Linda Leavell for years of conversation about Moore as well as for her generous reflections on an early stage of the manuscript; Robin Schulze, for her ongoing willingness to share her thoughts on, and knowledge of, Moore; Maeera Shreiber, for astute comments about the conception of the project; Margaret Waller, for years of sharing manuscripts-in-process; Rena Fraden, for lively and generous response to a late version of the manuscript; Marjorie Perloff for astute commentary on the nearly final manuscript; Roger Conover for helping clarify certain facts about Mina Loy; and editor LeAnn Fields at the University of Michigan Press. Jerold Frakes has prevented me from making many embarrassing errors of fact and translation, read the entire manuscript more than once, and suffered through my anxieties of authorship. Such debts are acknowledged but not repaid.

My gratitude, also, to the following museums, libraries, presses, and literary executors who have given me permission to publish the following materials:

Mina Loy manuscript materials and photographs are quoted and reprinted with the permission of Roger Conover, Literary Executor of Loy's estate. The Man Ray photograph *Mina Loy in New York City* is printed with the permission of Roger Conover and the Man Ray Estate, © 2004 Man Ray Trust / Artists Rights Society (ARS), New York / ADAGP, Paris.

Else Lasker-Schüler manuscript materials, photographs, and sketches are quoted and reprinted with the permission of the Else Lasker-Schüler Archive, ARC. MS. V. 501, the Jewish National and University Library, Jerusalem; the Schiller-Nationalmuseum Deutsches Literaturarchiv, Marbach; ullstein bild Berlin; and the Bayerische Staatsgemäldesammlungen.

Marianne Moore manuscript materials and photographs are quoted and reprinted with the permission of Marianne Craig Moore, Literary Executor for Marianne Moore, and the Rosenbach Museum and Library. The oil painting *Marianne Moore and Her Mother* and the untitled sketch of Marianne Moore, both by Marguerite Thompson Zorach, are published with the permission of the Zorach Collection LLC.

Excerpts from *The Last Lunar Baedeker,* by Mina Loy (1982), Jargon Society Press, reprinted by permission of Roger L. Conover.

I am indebted to the following presses for permission to reprint published work by the three poets. Farrar, Straus and Giroux, LLC, for permission to reprint excerpts from *The Lost Lunar Baedeker* by Mina Loy. Works of Mina Loy copyright © 1996 by the Estate of Mina Loy. Introduction and edition copyright © 1996 by Roger L. Conover. Reprinted by permission of Farrar, Straus and Giroux, LLC, and Carcanet Press Limited. Simon and Schuster for permission to reprint excerpts from "The Hero" and "The Jerboa" by Marianne Moore. Reprinted with the permission of Scribner, an imprint of Simon & Schuster Adult Publishing Group, from *The Collected Poems of Marianne Moore* by Marianne Moore. Copyright © 1935 by Marianne Moore; copyright renewed © 1963 by Marianne Moore and T. S. Elliot. Simon and Schuster for permission to reprint "The Mind is An Enchanting Thing" by Marianne Moore. Reprinted with the permission of Scribner, an imprint of Simon & Schuster Adult Publishing Group, from *The Collected Poems of Marianne Moore* by Marianne Moore. Copyright © 1944 by Marianne Moore; copyright renewed © 1972 by Marianne Moore. Suhrkamp Jüdischer Verlag for permission to reprint excerpts from *Else Lasker-Schüler Werke und Briefe: Kritische Ausgabe,* 5 vols., ed. Norbert Oellers, Heinz Rölleke, and Itta Shedletzky (Frankfurt am Main: Suhrkamp Jüdischer Verlag, 1996–); and *Briefe von Else Lasker-Schüler,* 2 vols., ed. Margarete Kupper (Munich: Kösel Verlag, 1969).

Contents

Abbreviations

ELSE LASKER-SCHÜLER

DLA Schiller-Nationalmuseum, Deutsches Literaturarchiv, Marbach

WZ Sigrid Bauschinger. *Else Lasker Schüler: Ihr Werk und ihre Zeit.* Heidelberg: Stiehm, 1980.

MM *Marbacher Magazin: Else Lasker-Schüler, 1869–1945.* Ed. Erika Klüsener and Friedrich Pfäfflin. Marbach: Deutsche Schillergesellschaft, 1995.

Br *Briefe von Else Lasker-Schüler.* 2 vols. Ed. Margarete Kupper. Munich: Kösel Verlag, 1969. Cited as *Br* I or *Br* II.

WB *Else Lasker-Schüler Werke und Briefe: Kritische Ausgabe.* 5 vols. Ed. Norbert Oellers, Heinz Rölleke, and Itta Shedletzky. Frankfurt am Main: Suhrkamp Jüdischer Verlag, 1996–. Volume 1.1, *Gedichte,* cited as *WB;* all other volumes cited as *WB* and volume number (e.g., *WB* 3).

MINA LOY

BM Carolyn Burke. *Becoming Modern: The Life of Mina Loy.* New York: Farrar, Straus and Giroux, 1996.

LLB *Lost Lunar Baedeker.* Ed. Roger Conover. New York: Farrar, Straus and Giroux, 1996.

LLB82 *Last Lunar Baedeker.* Ed. Roger Conover. Highlands: Jargon Society, 1982.

MLWP *Mina Loy: Woman and Poet.* Ed. Maeera Shreiber and Keith Tuma. Orono, Maine: National Poetry Foundation, 1998.

MARIANNE MOORE

EP *Becoming Marianne Moore: The Early Poems, 1907–1924.* Ed. Robin G. Schulze. Berkeley and Los Angeles: University of California Press, 2002.

CPo	*Complete Poems.* New York: Viking, 1981.
CPr	*Complete Prose of Marianne Moore.* Ed. Patricia C. Willis. New York: Viking, 1986.
SL	*Selected Letters of Marianne Moore.* Ed. Bonnie Costello, Celeste Goodridge, and Cristanne Miller. New York: Knopf, 1997.

RESEARCH LIBRARIES

B	Yale University, Beinecke Rare Book and Manuscript Library.
JNUL	The Jewish National and University Library, Jerusalem.
RML	Rosenbach Museum and Library.

1 Situating & Gendering Modernist Poetry

"Paris, Capital of the Nineteenth Century."
—Walter Benjamin, 1935, *Reflections*

Berlin is the greatest purely modern city in Europe.
—Karl Baedeker, 1912, *Berlin: Culture and Metropolis*

More than any other city in the world, [New York]
is the fullest expression of our modern age.
—Leon Trotsky, 1916, *American Moderns*

In the composition, the artist does exactly what every
eye must do with life, fix the particular with the
universality of his own personality.
—William Carlos Williams, 1923, *Spring and All*

Paris, London, New York, Berlin—these great modern metropolises have long been regarded as central to the inception of modernism. As Raymond Williams asserts: "there are decisive links between the practices and ideas of the avant-garde movements of the twentieth century and the specific conditions and relationships of the early-twentieth-century metropolis."[1] In the characteristics frequently ascribed to "the" metropolis—crowding, speed, development of new technologies, extreme juxtapositions of wealth and poverty—these cities may be imagined as common ground, but in a multitude of particulars they differed from one another. In its history, national and local social and legal structures, demographics, architecture, and culture of literary production, Berlin did not function like London, nor New York like Paris. Moreover, the differences experienced by writers growing up and working in these cities were more extreme for women than for men. Early in the twentieth century, local and national infrastructures governing women's lives varied extremely from place to place, even in world cities like these.

This book looks at particular modernist writers in the context of national and local structures to argue that location significantly inflected modernist women's performances of subjectivity, gender, race, and religion in their texts and in their lives by making different subject categories available to them and enabling or preventing particular modes of expression. While, as Keith Tuma writes, "Situatedness, contextualism: these aren't new words or tactics," no study has explored how cultural and national context affects women's writing with attention to poetry, and no study has compared the literary and life strategies of the women most active in experimental modernism internationally.[2] Such examination shifts the locus of modernist studies from the individual as such to individuals and groups in particular places. At the same time, it demands that the local be understood in relation to gender and in comparison with other locations.

In comparing female poets internationally, this book argues that modernist cultures take distinctive and distinctively gendered forms from one place to another, and that to the degree that one recognizes women as significantly engaged in its writing and art, modernism appears less conservative, antithetical to religion, and divorced from personal life constructions than it has been portrayed. Situating and gendering modernist studies illuminates the cracks in theories of gender, popular culture, and aesthetics that see the universal in the (usually male) individual—to paraphrase William Carlos Williams—or regard a single place and moment as representative. This argument is based on analysis of the works of Marianne Moore, Else Lasker-Schüler, and Mina Loy, in the context of their shared and distinguishing life patterns in New York and Berlin. Characteristics of these poets that have been described in previous studies as individualistic or eccentric (and that indeed appear so when examining one writer in isolation) in fact recur in the lives of other female, and to a lesser extent male, experimentalist writers locally, and sometimes internationally. Hence these characteristics are significant not just for thinking about individuals but for thinking about the period. At the same time, the particular form of these characteristics is shaped by context. My argument, then, continually addresses the boundary between what may be generally stated in a gendered account of modernist production and what must be understood in terms of local or individual contextualizing factors.

Many modernist writers were conscious of the relevance of location to writing. Modernist narratives elevated various cities almost to the level of character: Virginia Woolf's London; James Joyce's Dublin; William Carlos Williams's Paterson, New Jersey; Nella Larsen's Harlem; and Alfred Döblin's Berlin. In their novels or poems, these writers assert the distinctive qualities of place. At a level approaching theory, Williams justifies writing about Paterson by quoting John Dewey's claim, "The local is the only universal."[3] Mina Loy writes enviously of the "fundamental advantage" carried by the "American poet wherever he may wander, however he may engage himself with an older culture"—namely the "shock of the New World consciousness upon life. His is still poetry that has proceeded out of America" (*LLB* 159). In contrast, more defensively, Ezra Pound claims that expatriation is necessary for Americans to become serious artists.[4] My interest, like Loy's and Pound's, lies less in what writers say about a place than in what specific locations provide that enables and influences their writing.

Unlike writers, critics more often write about modernism through the apparently universalizing lens of theory than the lenses of location, rarely acknowledging that theory, too, arises from particular circumstances. Failing to understand the locational basis of theoretical constructions leads to inappropriate generalization. For example, in an excellent analysis of commodity aesthetics, Laurie Teal uses the writings of Karl Kraus, Walter Benjamin, Otto Weininger, and Gustave Flaubert to demonstrate the depth of modernist misogyny, concluding that "all writings by women in modernity reveal traces of [the] misogynist paradigms [of modernist texts identifying modernity with prostitution] in their necessary negotiations of subjectivity and sexuality in the face of ideological reductions of woman to the body (the prostitute) and the relegation of mental endeavor to the masculine realm."[5] A modernist woman faced a "stalemate" in developing an identity as a writer: "there is simply no way, within these gender paradigms, to be both a woman and an artist, and there is no 'safe' way for a woman to (pro)claim her own sexuality without 'proving' that she is in fact a 'prostitute'" (Teal 104). Yet this conclusion does not hold for women in the United States, and it is misleading for many female expatriates. As I discuss in chapter 2, the prostitute is not an international figure for modernism or for the male artist, in part because the local positioning of modernist communities and of (especially middle-class) women in relation to both prostitutes and commodity culture differs enormously from city to city between the 1890s and 1930. Constructions of gender and sexuality similarly vary from place to place. Misogyny takes multiple national forms, as do women's responses to it.

Mina Loy, Marianne Moore, and Else Lasker-Schüler serve as examples of individuals whose work was inflected by the circumstances of their lives, respectively, as an expatriate in Europe and North America, in New York, and in Berlin. By the same token, these women were able to manipulate the local resources available to them in ways enabling their influential participation in their respective communities. A comparison of their and other women's lives raises the question of what constituted sufficient resources for such women and how their resources affected the forms of their art. In 1929, Virginia Woolf proposed that "to write *fiction* a woman needed a room of her own and 500 [pounds] a year" (emphasis added). On the other hand, Woolf speculated that only in "another century or so" might female poets be "born"; without a century of women's financial independence, access to rooms of their own, and the "habit of freedom and the courage to write exactly what we think," women's writing of notable poetry is "impossible."[6] In point of fact, many women published poetry during the late nineteenth and early twentieth centuries. As Celeste Schenck has argued, Anglo-American female poets were so popular that modernists attempted to marginalize the use of traditional form as feminine: they "willingly consigned poetic forms into the hands of genteel poetesses, keeping the 'new poetry' safe for the experimenters, the form-breakers, and the vers-librists—that is, the men."[7] The women who did break into the ranks of the "experimenters" were for the most part enabled by local and national patterns of earlier women's professionalism, enjoyment of legal, financial, and political rights, and access to the institutions producing aesthetic culture—as Woolf theorized they must be. Because such patterns varied from place to place, so did the ways women engaged in modernist writing and art and the numbers of women so engaged.

Of course, men's lives were also framed by access to education, sexuality, and degrees of marginalization from middle-class, racial, and ethnic norms. By the early twentieth century, however, middle-class men had approximately the same rights throughout Europe and North America, whereas women had widely varied legal, financial, and property rights, and cultural restrictions delimiting the boundaries of gender-appropriate activities, including education. The privileges of men did in fact vary according to race, ethnicity, and other factors—for example, of Jewish and Christian men in Russia or white and black men in the United States—but Jewish men enjoyed primary legal rights in all major European countries except Russia, and African American men in the United States had legal rights under federal laws, despite discriminatory state codes and practices.[8] Across Europe and North America, in contrast, even the rights of otherwise privileged white women were restricted to surprisingly various degrees. My point is not to minimize the effects of pogroms and racism or to claim women are uniquely affected by the conditions I discuss, but to point to widely differing conditions for women within countries generally seen homogenously as "the West."

This study claims neither that women have unique modes or concerns nor that location determines formal or topical patterns of writing and art but rather that an accurate understanding of modernism demands attention to the sometimes contradictory patterns of gender, location, and experimentalist poetics. Lasker-Schüler's, Moore's, and Loy's poetry and lives reveal multiple overlapping and contrasting patterns, which in turn reveal the trends and tensions of the literary communities and national cultures where they developed their distinctive oeuvres. Even a brief glance at their early poetry reveals some of the ways that location inflects their articulation and conception of similar concerns.

In 1910, Else Lasker-Schüler—already well known as a poet and notorious as a bohemian in Berlin—published "Leise sagen" ("Say It Softly") in the Expressionist journal *Der Sturm,* edited by her soon to be ex-husband Herwarth Walden. This poem of radical metaphorical juxtapositions and unreferenced pronouns was attacked by a local journalist as demonstrating "complete softening of the brain" *(Gehirnweichung),* initiating a libel case on the quality of Lasker-Schüler's verse and generally of Expressionism. In 1914, expatriate British painter and poet Mina Loy published "Café du Neant" in *International: A Review of Two Worlds*—the first poem of hers to appear in print. Later published as part of "Three Moments in Paris," "Café du Neant" uses Futurist techniques to explore gender relationships and the decay of communication in a mode laying the groundwork for the poet's reputation as a radical poet and feminist. In 1916, Marianne Moore—who had begun publishing in the little magazines of New York and London a year earlier—published "In This Age of Hard Trying Nonchalance is Good, And," a syllabic verse poem asserting the political and spiritual efficacy of conversational (or poetic) imagination and indirection over attack, through multiple formal techniques of indirection. None of these poems takes location, self-construction, or cultural history as a part of its focus, but each introduces aspects of these topics explored at greater length later in this study.

In the first stanza of "Leise sagen," the unexpected prepositional phrase of line 2 quickly removes the poem from any context of realism:

You took for yourself all the stars Over my heart.	*Du nahmst dir alle Sterne Über meinem Herzen.*
My thoughts curl I have to dance.	*Meine Gedanken kräuseln sich Ich muß tanzen.*
You always do things that make me look up, Wearing my life out.	*Immer tust du das, was mich aufschauen läßt, Mein Leben zu müden.*
I can no longer carry the evening Over the hedges.	*Ich kann den Abend nicht mehr Über die Hecken tragen.*
In the streams' mirror I no longer see my reflection.	*Im Spiegel der Bäche Finde ich mein Bild nicht mehr.*
You've stolen the archangel's Swaying eyes.	*Dem Erzengel hast du Die schwebenden Augen gestohlen.*
But I snack on the syrup Of their blue.	*Aber ich nasche vom Seim Ihrer Bläue.*
My heart sets slowly I don't know where—	*Mein Herz geht langsam unter Ich weiß nicht wo—*
Maybe in your hand. Everywhere it pulls on my tissue.	*Vielleicht in deiner Hand. Überall greift sie an mein Gewebe.*

(*WB*, no. 167)

The rapid juxtaposition of surrealistic metaphors (a heart with stars "over" it, curling thoughts, evening as a burden to carry, syrup one can eat from an archangel's stolen eyes) implies equally surrealistic consequences: apparently the speaker must dance because her thoughts curl, and "your" action makes her too tired to carry evening over the landscape. The compressed disjunction of these juxtapositions is echoed in the two-line, nonrhyming, unmetered stanzas. The poem provides no obvious system of order, only the speaker's responses as a reflection of a world going wrong. Lasker-Schüler's metaphors conflate romantic, spiritual, psychological, and physical realms of experience, suggesting desire, depression, and loss of identity while still affirming aspects of vital life: dancing, snacking on *Seim,* a syrup or honey, feeling an intimacy of touch as though a heart could—like the sun—sink into someone's hand, and feelings could pull on life's woven texture *(Gewebe)* of being. The speaker expresses radical alienation (even water no longer returns her reflection) but also the possibility of intimacy with an ungendered "you" and with all nature and spirit. In her universe of immediacy, the speaker's heart and stars share the same space, evening sets literally onto people's shoulders, and one can taste the sweetness of an archangel's eyes.

In a Berlin characterized by widespread artistic and literary innovation and bohemianism, by displays of nonconformity to public sexual norms, and by sharp divisions between institutions of high culture and avant-garde writers and artists, Lasker-Schüler's verse helped to establish a new sense of literary range. At the same time, the use of extreme metaphors skirting the sentimental and decadent (heart, stars, angels) and unidentified pronominal and deictic referents ("you," which thoughts "curl," which archangel) exemplify her own practice of disrupting norms. The only female poet widely respected during the period, and one of the few Jewish Expressionist poets, Lasker-Schüler had plenty of reasons for claiming that local streams (of thought, culture, or physical presence) did not mirror her: she could not look around and see anyone sharing the major defining categories of her life. The poem implies rebuke: "you" (a lover, society, God) selfishly take stars away from her orbit, wear her soul out. The speaker makes no mention of particular aspects of culture gone wrong, but there is a sense that the world has failed her. It no longer provides illumination (stars, archangel's eyes, the light of day); it does not allow her to see herself. "Leise sagen," like Lasker-Schüler's other poems, "soft[ly]" articulates a social critique with particular relevance to her life in Berlin.

The surreal is also an element in Mina Loy's "Café du Neant," although her tone is primarily ironic rather than desirous, and it expresses decadent ennui rather than alienation.

Little tapers leaning   lighted diagonally
Stuck in coffin tables of the Café du Neant
Leaning to the breath of baited bodies
Like young poplars fringing the Loire

Eyes that are full of love
And eyes that are full of kohl
Projecting light across the fulsome ambiente
Trailing the rest of the animal behind them
Telling of tales without words
And lies of no consequence
One way or another

The young lovers hermetically buttoned up in black
To black cravat
To the blue powder edge dusting the yellow throat
What color could have been your bodies
When last you put them away

Nostalgic youth
Holding your mistress's pricked finger
In the indifferent flame of the taper
Synthetic symbol of   LIFE
In this factitious chamber of   DEATH
The woman
As usual
Is smiling   as bravely
As it is given to her to be   brave

While the brandy cherries
In winking glasses
Are decomposing
Harmoniously
With the flesh of spectators
And at a given spot
There is one
Who
Having the concentric lighting focussed precisely upon her
Prophetically blossoms in perfect putrefaction
Yet   there are cabs outside the door.

(*LLB* 16–17)

The most striking effects of this poem are its lack of punctuation, unusual spacing within the line, Futurist capitals, and contrasting levels of diction. Whereas the difficulty of Lasker-Schüler's poem lies in connecting disparate metaphors of feeling and action, in Loy's the challenge is to follow the logic of sentences containing both extreme narrative juxtapositions and adjectives at odds with the connotative field of their subject: "perfect putrefaction," "baited bodies." Tables are coffins, eyes full of love are blackened with coal, lovers' bodies are disposable, life is indifferent, and the fact that both "flesh" and "brandy cherries" decompose "harmoniously" makes the former seem equally an item of luxury. If the "one / Who . . . Prophetically blossoms" at the poem's end can be read as the poet putting forth "her" poem, then even the poem arises from "perfect putrefaction."

Unlike Lasker-Schüler's poem, however, it is not clear that Loy's poem functions as critique. The sole contrast to this café world appears in the last line's "Yet," followed by white space and then "cabs outside the door." Although the "smiling" woman and buttoned-up lovers do not appear to seek to leave, the fact that the woman is challenged "to be brave" and observes the others' lack of communication suggests that cabs may indeed promise escape to some location where bodies are neither bait nor "hermetically" sealed and painted, and flesh might do something besides decay. This is, perhaps, the ultimate promise of the expatriate: one can always leave.

Loy probably wrote this poem in Florence, where she moved in 1906, thinking back on her art student and younger married days in Paris. Given that Florence was a provincial town in comparison with Paris, the poem may both satirize the life of stultified pretense she had left behind and express nostalgia for a past of sitting among bodies "Like young poplars fringing the Loire," focused in "concentric lighting," engrossed in the pleasures of satirical, distanced observation. Even while mocking the lack of communication and imagination in those young bodies, the speaker romanticizes their condition of extremity and transience. The latter may have been particularly attractive to Loy. A mother of two in an unhappy marriage, she may have longed for "cabs outside the door" and the anonymity of a crowded bar where at least decomposition is "perfect." Loy positions her speaker in this poem as an observer of the woman as well as of the scene, but she expresses sympathy for this "blossom[ing]" woman smiling "as bravely" as she can while apparently prophesying a future of further decay. The poem ends without event, without the possibility of connection between people; even the young have left "the rest of the animal" behind, expressing love only in blackened eyes. It offers no desire, no hope of change, no sign of life beyond the vaguely reassuring presence of those cabs.

Moore's "In This Age of Hard Trying, Nonchalance is Good, And" shares some elements of irrational juxtaposition and compression but nothing decadent. Instead it works through metonymies and paradox to tell a tale about the effectiveness of indirection and the folly of elitist indifference. Unlike either Lasker-Schüler's or Loy's poem, it makes a point rather than mapping a feeling or condition of being:

In This Age of Hard Trying Nonchalance is Good, And

"Really, it is not the
Business of the gods to bake clay pots." They did not
Do it in this instance. A few
Revolved upon the axes of their worth,
As if excessive popularity might be a pot.

They did not venture the
Profession of humility. The polished wedge
That might have split the firmament
Was dumb. At last it threw itself away
And falling down, conferred on some poor fool a privilege.

"Taller by the length of
A conversation of five hundred years than all
The others," there was one, whose tales
Of what could never have been actual—
Were better than the haggish, uncompanionable drawl

Of certitude; his by-
Play was "more terrible in its effectiveness
Than the fiercest frontal attack."
The staff, the bag, the feigned inconsequence
Of manner, best bespeak that weapon—self-protectiveness.

(*EP* 198, 200)

Syllabic verse, the quotation of outside sources, unaccented end and internal rhyme (not/pot, the/humility, wedge/privilege, taller/all/actual/drawl) construct a layer of surface difficulty in this poem that is mirrored by its syntax: everything seems to occur according to a pattern (numbers of syllables, positioning of rhymes, notes on the quotations), but the patterns don't obviously explain anything. The title functions merely as the poem's first line, providing the reader no explanatory theme and mocking conventions of reason. Its concluding punctuation and conjunction "And" also mock titular units by signaling the beginning of a phrase rather than the expected resolution. This flaunting of the unexpected is exacerbated by the fact that the poem's first two lines appear to interrupt the title's voice and logic with their peevish (quoted) insistence, "'Really, it is not the / Business of the gods to bake clay pots.'" In short, the poem does all it can to throw the reader off balance—not through bizarre or extreme metaphors but through the lower-key disruptions of tone, syntax, and form.

The poem's narrative, however, eventually clarifies the relation of title to opening quotation through an implied logic of progression. Unlike Lasker-Schüler and Loy, who proceed through soundplay and successive images, Moore proceeds through implied logical connections. The sequence of the poem's statements suggests that those gods who felt themselves to be above usefulness and "humility," spending their time obsessed with reflections on their own esteem, consequently lost their chance to wield "the polished wedge / that might have split the firmament." In apparent disgust, this potent tool "Threw itself away," accidentally conferring its "privilege" on a human "fool." The tale teller whose spiritual height can be measured only by "the length of a conversation" or act of communication appears to be this same "poor fool." Rather, however, than lapsing into godlike admiration of his worth, this talker uses the gift of his "wedge" to make up stories far "better" than any credo or doctrine—the "haggish uncompanionable drawl / Of certitude" characteristic of beings who assume their superiority to others. At the same time, his chatty fictiveness is also a kind of "axe," "more terrible in its effectiveness" than a direct attack. The poem's last lines return to the title: phonologically and semantically, "Feigned inconsequence" echoes "Nonchalance," which we already know is "good." The poet's change of focus from "effectiveness" to "self-protectiveness" similarly suggests that the gods' refusal to stoop to lowly activities of service and a "profession" (life career and stated claim) of "humility" weakens them.

Like Loy's poem, Moore's may contain a disguised self-portrait. A college graduate, voracious reader of texts of all kinds, active feminist campaigner for women's rights, and in every way a product of the U.S. Progressive Era's sense of possible reform, Moore celebrates an underdog. The gods are fallible and a "poor fool" enjoys a weapon of great power in his imaginative, inconsequential manner and wit. It is the fool, Moore suggests, who can survive his battles. The "nonchalance" she recommends is utterly absent from "Leise sagen" and "The Café du Neant," as is the sense of happy accident and come-uppance. While there is no neat tying of ends in Moore's poem, which remains disjunctive in any reading, there is nonetheless a sense of conclusion. The reader may not know what to do with the "staff" or "bag" proffered at the poem's end, but there is none of the suspenseful torment of Lasker-Schüler's pulled tissue or Loy's simultaneous transience and decay.

Marianne Moore, Else Lasker-Schüler, and Mina Loy are each the subject of substantial critical work. Moore is increasingly discussed as one of the primary poets of American modernism; a similar plenitude of studies examines Lasker-Schüler's poetry, fiction, drama, and life; Loy has inspired less criticism but is one of the female writers most often invoked in discussions of the avant-garde. For each, there are obvious omissions in the available scholarship as well as excellent resources. Moore is typically ignored by internationalist studies of modernism, as though her work did not intersect meaningfully with theoretical or supranational narratives of the period. Lasker-Schüler is similarly ignored in international comparative studies, at most appearing as part of a list of German poets or bohemians. Critical study of Loy places her conceptually within an international avant-garde but misleadingly as "American," despite the fact that she spent less than three years in the United States before 1936.[9] By examining her poetry as "American," such studies misrepresent the profound effects of her youth in London and expatriatism in Munich, Paris, Florence, New

York, and Berlin. Michel de Certeau and Luce Giard write that "living is narrativizing."[10] Through the private narratives of their self-naming, dress, religious beliefs, attachment—or lack of attachment—to places and propriety, and through the public narratives of their poetry and art, these women construct tales that illuminate the larger narratives of modernism.

To my knowledge, neither Loy nor Moore knew Lasker-Schüler's work, and she did not know theirs. In her few extant letters and notes, Loy makes no mention of meeting Lasker-Schüler or any other German writer or woman during her year in Berlin.[11] Moore could read German and would have seen Lasker-Schüler's name in a 1927 *Dial,* mentioned as one of the three poets "with a sense of the beat of the times" whose work Paul Hindemith had set to music—the other two being Christian Morgenstern and Rainer Maria Rilke.[12] Although Lasker-Schüler knew some English and had an exhibit of her drawings in London, she did not read poetry in English. Loy and Moore did know each other. Moore attended Loy's debut in Kreymborg's one-act play *Lima Beans,* and Loy sketched Moore twice. There is no indication, however, that the two women had any contact after 1921.

I have chosen New York and Berlin to demonstrate the significance of location in part because both cities had sizable, relatively stable innovative literary communities with at least some important contribution from female poets. Both were also similar in epitomizing modernity. Paris, often regarded as the paradigmatic center of modernism, even by critics whose theoretical frameworks are predominantly German, was not a location encouraging French women to engage in serious innovative writing, for reasons that become clear only in comparative analysis.[13] The primary factors determining the degree of women's participation in experimental writing and art appear to have been access to education, control of property and personal finances, and codes of social conduct. These factors differed radically in the United States, Germany, and France, as even a brief description of these nations attests.

Women in the United States enjoyed the most privileged circumstances on all three grounds of any middle-class women in Europe or the Americas. These privileges were in part the indirect result of the Civil War, which dramatically accelerated what was already a widespread movement toward women's wage employment and higher education. The surplus population of women after the war brought even conservative women into this movement. At the same time, the conjunction of Abraham Lincoln's 1862 land-grant program, establishing a coeducational state university system, and the burgeoning of women's colleges with high academic standards offered increasing numbers of women the opportunity to study for professional careers. According to the census of 1910, 10 percent of all receivers of a Ph.D. were women, and in 1920 15.1 percent of all Ph.D.s were women—a higher percentage than at any other time in the United States up to the 1970s.[14] Carroll Smith-Rosenberg claims that the effect of college education on women of this era can hardly be overestimated. In college, women were expected to succeed at a wide variety of endeavors utterly divorced from traditional notions of feminine occupation and in some cases directly violating Victorian norms—for example, putting a career before marriage or training a woman "to think and feel 'as a man.'"[15] According to Smith-Rosenberg, many female college graduates of this era translated this displacement from traditional gender norms into optimistic ambitions for altering national and international assumptions and laws (255). Because they were "quintessentially American," with their usually small-town and newly affluent bourgeois backgrounds, and because superior education offered them both economic autonomy and secure social status, they could "defy proprieties, pioneer new roles, and still insist upon a rightful place within the genteel world" (245). American women did not sacrifice social respect by rejecting traditional roles.

A striking number of the American women most prominently involved in writing and editing modernist literature—including Moore—attended college or professional school.[16] Among them, Gertrude Stein attended Harvard Annex (later Radcliffe) and then Johns Hopkins Medical School; Willa Cather graduated from the University of Nebraska in 1895; coeditor of *Poetry* magazine and poet Alice Corbin Henderson attended the University of Chicago from 1899 to 1902 and then because of her health moved to New Orleans, where she attended Sophie Newcomb College; coeditor of the *Little Review* Jane Heap attended the Art Institute of Chicago from 1901 to 1905 and studied mural design in Germany, while her coeditor Margaret Anderson spent three years at the Western College for Women in Ohio; playwright and Theatre Guild director Theresa Helburn graduated from Bryn Mawr and studied at the Sorbonne; Moore graduated from Bryn Mawr in 1909; H.D. attended Bryn Mawr; Djuna Barnes attended the Pratt Institute; Kay Boyle studied architecture at Parson's School of Fine and Applied Arts, also taking classes at Columbia University and (briefly) at the Cincinnati Conservatory of Music; Edna St. Vincent Millay graduated from Vassar in 1917; and Genevieve Taggard graduated from the University of California in 1920. African American women active in modernism also typically attended institutes of higher education: Georgia Douglass Johnson graduated from Atlanta University in 1893 and attended Oberlin Conservatory of Music 1902–3; Alice Dunbar-Nelson graduated from a two-year teacher-training program at what is now Dillard University in 1892; Jessie Fauset graduated from Cornell in 1905 and received an M.A. in French from the University of Pennsylvania in 1919; Zora Neale Hurston attended Howard University and then Barnard, graduating in 1928; Gwendolyn Bennett attended Columbia University and graduated from the Pratt Institute in 1924; and Anna Julia Cooper received her B.A. from Oberlin in 1884 and her Ph.D. from the Sorbonne in 1925.[17] This is a remarkable pattern, key to understanding the symbolic capital of this generation of women.

American women also enjoyed relatively early economic autonomy. With the Married Women's Property Laws of New York in 1848, 1860, and 1862, married women in that state gained substantial right to control their own wages, property, and inheritance. Similar laws in other states soon followed.[18] Hence, just as middle-class women by the turn of the century had access to an education equivalent, and in many cases superior, to men's, both single and married women in most states could also hold individual checking accounts, inherit and will property, and dispose of their income independently of male family members.[19] They achieved full national suffrage in 1920. Although they typically earned far less than men and dealt with gender discrimination at many levels, a striking number of American women wrote, published, and edited poetry, fiction, and drama, and founded journals, presses, galleries, art schools, and museums. Such activity was enabled by the conditions summarized above.

The very different trajectory of nineteenth-century German history led to different conditions for women. Not unified until 1871, late-nineteenth-century Germany was in the midst of massive change. By 1914, it was the greatest industrial nation in Europe and prided itself on its modernity and progressiveness. To some extent, this progressiveness extended to women's rights. In the new Civil Code of 1888, German women gained the basic rights of political equality: married women had full legal status, could initiate legal proceedings, conclude contracts, and had control of their own wages and income. Thanks to compulsory education laws of the 1820s and 1830s in the old German Confederation, literacy was nearly universal at the time of unification. According to Helene Lange, in 1887 29.5 percent of the students in

Prussian secondary schools were girls—a figure comparable to England's estimated 30 percent.[20] Girls were not allowed to take the university preparatory exam *(Abitur)* given in boys' *Gymnasiums*, however, until 1896, and they were first admitted to German universities in 1908.[21] Lasker-Schüler was typical in not finishing high school.

Despite its relatively liberal laws, German patriarchal traditions and a conflicting paragraph of the Civil Code undermined women's legal rights: paragraph 1354 gave the husband power to make all decisions concerning family life (Frevert 231). This contradiction mirrored general ambivalence in German society: on the one hand, since the middle of the nineteenth century there had been strong support for the liberalization of labor and property laws for women. On the other, the new state promoted ideals of masculine military heroism and the maternal, domestic woman. Further, because Germany could not begin to develop a nationally consistent system of public education or dispersal of printed matter until after unification, women were more isolated in the liberal or conservative trends of their local communities or families than in the United States.

The loss of male labor and lives during and after World War I forced German women into a wide variety of types of employment. With the founding of the Weimar Republic in 1918, women received full suffrage rights and, in 1919, full legal equality. Yet the weakness of the Weimar government, Germany's extreme political instability, and the financial turmoil of the years immediately following the war made it impossible to implement these new laws. Moreover, the patriarchal family law of the German Civil Code was not revised. With Hitler's rise to power in the early 1930s, the German government allied itself with a full-fledged campaign to reinforce legally and socially the old ideological bond identifying women as wives and mothers. Women in Germany, then, enjoyed some legal rights earlier than American women but had restricted ability to exercise them and less access to higher education. None of the German women prominent in literature or the arts studied at the university. Women were active in avant-garde art and literary circles, especially in the visual arts, but according to Christine Reiß-Suckow, *geistige Leben und die Macht* (spiritual/intellectual life and power) rested firmly in men's hands.[22]

A brief comparison of France to Germany during this period helps illuminate what is distinctive to the latter and gives a context for Loy's years in Paris from 1903 to 1906 and 1923 to 1936. Shari Benstock summarizes that at the turn of the century "Everything about [a French woman's] existence—from economic security to social status—

depended on the benign protection of a system created for and controlled by men." Class and status provided wealthy women some social freedom, but even these women were affected by restrictive social codes. In contrast, even impoverished expatriate women like Loy were not affected by these codes because French society was essentially closed to them—and indeed most Anglo-Americans showed little interest in it.[23] In this sense, Paris was the perfect home for British and American expatriates.

Education in France was strictly segregated. Until 1880, there were no high schools preparatory for the university for girls, and until 1914 the curriculum at girls' lycées was typically less demanding than at boys'.[24] It was several decades before women gained full access to French universities. Women's property rights were similarly restricted. The Napoleonic Code of 1804 declared that the husband ruled the French family: the wife owed her earnings to her husband and required his permission for employment outside the home; Article 213 required a wife's obedience to her husband. Thanks to the campaigns of French women's groups, divorce was legalized in 1884, and in 1907 and 1909 French married women gained some control over their earnings and family property. Other early-twentieth-century measures, however, ensured the continuation of the status quo, and Article 213 was not removed from the books until 1938. Women received the vote in France in 1944.

Political history helps to explain early-twentieth-century France's gender codes. From the time of the French Revolution in 1789, France was embroiled in decades of internal revolt and wars of aggression. With France's loss to Germany during the Franco-German War of 1871, the Third Republic made political and economic stability a priority. Indeed, from the mid–nineteenth century on, maintaining traditional gender roles was regarded by many conservatives and revolutionaries as key to national stability. Because of the low national birth rate, pronatalist programs encouraging women's pursuit of domestic, not public, authority were also increasingly popular in France early in the twentieth century, creating a situation of conflicting cultural expectations for young women.

Not surprisingly under these circumstances, few French women participated in literary and artistic innovation. Of the twelve painters Gill Perry discusses in *Women Artists and the Parisian Avant-Garde,* only five were French, and they for the most part stopped pursuing avant-garde techniques after World War I.[25] Even during their early innovative periods, these women tended to work on the fringes of avant-garde exhibiting groups, and those with strong access to such a group typically attained it through sexual intimacy with a more established male artist.[26] Even Surrealism, the historical avant-garde most often described as hospitable to women, became so only late in its development. Between 1924 and 1933, the period Susan Suleiman defines as the "most dynamic and 'ascendant' period of the movement," not a single woman was included as a member and even in the 1930s and 1940s, none of the (few) female writers was French.[27] Similarly, Benstock's twenty-two "Women of the Left Bank" includes only three Frenchwomen: Colette, whose fiction was innovative from its first appearance in the 1890s but never associated with an experimentalist group or movement; Anaïs Nin, whose first novel was not published until 1936 and who in fact spent her formative educational years (1914–24) in New York; and Adrienne Monnier, an important bookseller and supporter of experimentalist work, but not a significant writer. Suleiman summarizes: "there were no outstanding [French] women writers in the first half of this century . . . who had the tenacity to construct an oeuvre (much less the kind of innovative, rule-breaking oeuvre that can be qualified as 'avant-garde' and that requires the self-confidence of, say, a Gertrude Stein) until Simone de Beauvoir," who published her first novel in 1943 (31).[28] Given French women's relative lack of financial independence, access to higher education, and cultural support for autonomy in any sphere outside the home, the basis for these patterns is clear.

Moore, Lasker-Schüler, and Loy are in many ways atypical, like most significant writers, but their lives illuminate representative patterns enabling women's trajectories of success, and their poems illuminate patterns of modernist thought frequently overlooked in international modernist studies. As detailed in chapter 2, in some ways, their lives could not have been more different. Yet once each had committed herself to a life of artistic creation, she was devotedly and clear-sightedly ambitious in the pursuit of that career. Lasker-Schüler and Moore each felt herself to be both central to the circle of literary experimentalists of her time and an outsider to that circle—for reasons compounded of gender, life "style," and religious upbringing and belief. Committed more to social and sexual liberation and to her own independence as a designer than to a particular art form or craft, Loy was perhaps more a lifelong artistic entrepreneur than a poet; she did not devote her life to writing but had brief periods of remarkable creativity in various forms. Moreover, during her most artistically active years Loy apparently felt no significant division between her beliefs or life and those of her circle.

She was the avant-garde poster girl, seen in her work, her appearance, and her life to represent the arts, the movement, and the times.

Each poet created for herself a poetic style that was utterly distinctive and original while sharing important characteristics with other experimental writers and artists of her time; all were admired by fellow poets. All thrived in cities and in literary milieus that were predominantly male. Lasker-Schüler and Moore created styles of writing that combined traditional uses of poetic form with experiments in rhythm, line length, stanza form, and rhyme. These styles, in different ways, foregrounded dialogue, processes of communication, a conception of interactive poetics—Moore's "companionable drawl." Loy's verse from the beginning borrowed less from traditional forms and contained few illocutionary elements suggesting even a possibility for dialogue or communication: like the lovers of "Café du Neant," she wrote "tales without words / And lies of no consequence." All three poets painted or drew, and saw their poetry as associated with innovations in the visual arts at least as closely as with those in contemporary literature. Each woman also maintained close personal ties with individual artists, especially Lasker-Schüler with her *blauer Reiter* Franz Marc, and Loy with Marcel Duchamp and Man Ray. Moore knew many New York artists and was attracted to the *Blauer Reiter* concept of "spiritual necessity"—even purchasing a copy of the expensive *Blaue Reiter Almanac* in 1916. Loy's association with the more radically disruptive art of Dada fits with the more disruptive language and project of her poetry.

Loy, Lasker-Schüler, and Moore participated in the shaping of modernism in particular places, and their lives and writing were in turn partially shaped by those locations. The following chapters demonstrate both individual and collective patterns of influence and response characterizing these and other women's writing and art in the first three decades of the twentieth century. Chapter 2 examines sociological, cultural, and theoretical representations of modernity in Berlin and New York as a foundation for the more specific comparisons of the following chapters, with particular attention to the different structures of the experimentalist literary groups in these cities and a more detailed overview of all three poets' lives. Chapter 3 interprets the politics of self-naming, both as fluxional performance of an unconventionally boundaried self and in relation to the traditional speaking subject position or "I" of the lyric poem. Like numerous others across Europe and North America, all three women constructed a kaleidoscope of names for themselves, trying out aspects of identity and self-positioning, and breaking normative gender as well as other boundaries. Contextualizing this language performance within the urgent national discourses on gender illuminates ways that these performances both respond to local hierarchies and resonate differently at the local level than internationally. Chapter 4 examines the semiotics of performed embodiment, interweaving discourses of dress, the sexological science of the era, and literary forms. All three poets saw dress and life patterns as arenas for performance of identities and ideas parallel to those of their art. Similarly, although none of these poets was obviously lesbian, each benefited from analysis that placed her within a homosocial continuum. Just as self-naming and gender redefinition were endemic especially to female writers and artists of the period, so was the testing of ranges of sexuality.

Chapter 5 deals with the importance of religion, and particularly Jewishness, to modernist aesthetics, challenging the widespread critical assumption of modernist hostility to religious belief and practice. For these poets, Judaism (variously conceived) provided artistic grounding. In part through her concept of, or identification with, Jewishness, each also engaged popular tropes of orientalism, with Lasker-Schüler and Loy employing these tropes as a part of their shifting poetic and self-constructions. Unlike more widely discussed patterns of orientalism, these poets' engagement with the East provided an indirect route to active commentary on their own immediate worlds rather than fantasy or escape. The final chapter returns to poetry as such, asking what we can learn about reading these three poets' works from the historical and cultural explorations of the rest of my study. It serves, in effect, as a reminder of why these chapters may matter to readers of modernist poems.

2 *The Metropolis & Modernism*

Berlin and New York, 1900–1930

The city is one of the crucial factors in the social production of the (sexed) corporeality.
—Elizabeth Grosz, "Bodies-Cities"

It is male avant-garde artists and writers who signify most dramatically a sense of subjective instability in the face of the fragmentary experience of metropolitan modernity.
—Dorothy Rowe, *Representing Berlin*

In the early twentieth century, men's and women's responses to urban life were held to be dramatically different. As Rosemary Betterton notes, while "for male intellectuals the speed of modern city life—as well as flight from it into forms of primitivism—was a crucial condition for modernist subjectivity, in women it was popularly supposed . . . to induce deleterious results, even mental breakdown."[1] Women were regarded as psychologically frail, hence unable to withstand the pressures of urban excitation. By midcentury, male response was taken as a norm. Following Georg Simmel's lead, Raymond Williams writes of the shock effect of the modern city, to which artists and intellectuals responded with aesthetic distance.[2] Yet Betterton argues that German and English women did not respond with a "conscious stance of alienation" or dislocation (20), and Rowe depicts "subjective instability" as "dramatically" male. Similarly, Deborah L. Parsons writes that while "it has been a persistent masculine response to the crowd to define it as a brutal and engulfing mass," women of the period found "an external anonymity in the crowd," allowing them greater freedom to move through the city; what "seems threatening and disconcertingly unclassifiable to the observing male . . . is protective and usefully concealing for the urban woman." Women experienced the city's isolation, but they also made networks of connection that "act[ed] in reverse to the impulse towards interiorization that Benjamin defines as characteristic of the (male) bourgeois urban temperament."[3] Nonetheless, Parsons sees the structure and norms of the city as "all-pervasive in the texts of the most formally experimental" female urban writers (228).

Lasker-Schüler and Moore moved to their chosen homes as adults and never indicated a wish to live elsewhere, although Lasker-Schüler wrote an idealized portrait of Palestine before she was forced into exile there (*Das Hebräerland* 1937). Loy had no such loyalty to any city. She writes Mabel Dodge in February 1920 that "New York is the only city I have been grateful to" but in the same letter comments that "whoever cares for any city for long is merely attending his own funeral" (B ZA Luhan). Whether or not the city's forms are indeed "all-pervasive" in these or other urban poets' styles, a complex understanding of the *particular* cities in which Moore and Lasker-Schüler lived for decades, and in which Mina Loy spent significant time, illuminates the conditions to which they, and their peers, responded in writing and help to explain both the markedly different structures of their experimentalist literary communities and women's accessibility to positions of authority within them.

Although Lasker-Schüler is sometimes harshly critical of Berlin, she describes her exile as a divorce, implying that her longest, most important marriage was not to either of her husbands but to the city. In an untitled piece combining prose and verse, she writes:

> After my marriage I fell in love with Berlin:
> Under its linden trees I sat hours long
> Even furniture vans drove over asphalt like song.
> Where are you, Friedrich Street in Berlin?
> And you, my unforgotten Tauentzien?
>
> The divorce of my marriage was more comprehensible to me than my expatriation, violent divorce.[4]
>
> (*WB*, no. 444, ll. 4–9

Not a place of physical characteristics, Lasker-Schüler's city offers experiences of being: love, "song," betrayal. In the next stanza, Berlin "cut itself off" from her, initiating this "divorce"—and indeed, National Socialist politics aimed to eliminate Jews and bohemians. Her loss, however, is described in personal, not racial or political, terms: she loses daily relationship with unforgettable streets and friends.

A more finished poem uses the same metaphor: "Oh how the divorce from Berlin / Touched me—much closer than I knew":[5]

It took my breath,	*Ich verlor mein bischen Puste,*
Because I bet everything,	*Da ich auf das ganze ging,*
I was stuck on Berlin!	*Mich verrannte in Berlin!*
And had to flee.	*Und entfliehen musste.*
In the sorrow-train, late in the night!	*Im Wehzug spät in der Nacht!*

(*WB,* no. 445, ll. 7–11)

The pain of this separation is felt not just in its primary metaphor of divorce, but in the second stanza's increasingly brief and disjunctive phrases, moving from her love, to her forced flight, to the metonymic detail of the late night *Wehzug* or train of sorrow, pain, hurt. *Wehzug* compresses particular power in this line through its implied rhyming pun with *D-zug* (*Durchgangszug,* a train that goes through several small stations), suggesting that the city has become so violent and crazed that it now runs official *Wehzüge.* This is the only line that does not rhyme in a poem where all other rhymes occur at least twice. The *Wehzug* is out of harmony with the Berlin she married, as it were. Lasker-Schüler's connection to Berlin also appears in her rhymes, several of which play on the highly contrived, ironic rhymes of cabaret singers—playing off Berlin dialect and cultural parody. For example, in the first piece above, she rhymes *Allemente* and *Rente* with *Bekännte*—a coined word suggesting *Bekannten* or "acquaintances," and echoing her previous reference to "friends." Even in writing about the sorrow of leaving Berlin, the poet resorts to the language play popular there.

Moore never wrote with such directness about her feelings for New York—perhaps because she was never forced to leave it. She does, however, write about the extent to which "People's Surroundings" in general "answer one's questions." Not everything is significant: "In these non-committal, personal-impersonal expressions of appearance, / the eye knows what to skip," the speaker comments. Yet if one looks "with X-ray-like-inquisitive intensity upon" a setting, then "the surfaces go back; / the interfering fringes of expression are but a stain on what stands out . . . we see the exterior and the fundamental structure" (*EP* 269–71). In a poem called "New York," which she places immediately before "People's Surroundings" in *Observations,* Moore also mixes "the exterior and the fundamental structure," concluding that the city "is" "accessibility to experience"; it can be identified only as opportunity, not as the manifestation of any particular desire or historical or contemporary function (*EP* 107). Similarly, in "Dock-Rats," Moore writes from the perspective of her own nickname, "Rat," to claim the city as the natural habitat for all who resemble her—perhaps all poets: "There are human beings who seem to regard the place / as craftily as we do—who seem to feel that it is a / good place to come home to" (*EP* 245). Moore also identifies New York City with the possibilities of liberty—although such liberty may at times follow a "sojourn in the whale," as she called her 1915 trip to New York. An early poem referring to Jonah, "Is Your Town Nineveh?" leaves the speaker contemplating future desires and responsibilities "by the aquarium, looking / at the Statue of Liberty." A late poem on the Brooklyn Bridge, "Granite and Steel," begins "Enfranchising cable . . . / and Liberty dominate the Bay— / her feet as one on shattered chains, / once whole links wrought by Tyranny" (*CPo* 205).

Although Moore never uses a metaphor of romantic intimacy for her city, she imagines distance from it as "exile": as she writes in a 1952 letter to her friend, sculptor Malvina Hoffman, "Even death in New York would seem to me, preferable to 'exile.' I would clamber aboard a child's yacht drawn by a string if it could bring me into close proximity to 'art'" (*SL* 497). Similarly, in a collection of essays published as *Konzert (Concert),* Lasker-Schüler links Berlin specifically with art. The city is "strong and terrible, and her wings know where they want to go. That's why the artist always returns to Berlin; *here is the clock of art,* that runs neither slow nor fast."[6] With Max Tau, she might have said, "In Berlin we saw the center of the earth. Artists and arts exerted a magnetic force. People came from all over the world to take part in its intellectual/spiritual movements; it was a joy to live in that time."[7] While both cities were characterized by all the dirt, confusion, overcrowding, poverty, and vice that existed in any metropolis of the time, both were hailed as "the" centers of artistic and cultural energy for those seeking to become "modern."

Berlin was both extolled and excoriated as "the embodiment of the modern," "American" in its modernity, "uniquely among European cities, a paradigm of modernity."[8] Because of its public transportation system, advanced technology, and active cultural life, Berlin was regarded as "the quintessence of a modern industrial metropolis" (L. Müller 38). New York similarly asserted its claims to modern quintessence. Long the center of finance, foreign shipping, and business, by the turn of the century New York had surpassed Boston as the most important center of the arts and publishing, was surpassing Chicago in architectural development, and led the way in implementing new technologies (the subway, electricity, the telephone). Like Berlin, it was repeatedly described in terms of the rapidity of its growth and change, its materialism, and its entrepreneurial spirit.

Both cities were physically huge. In 1902 Berlin opened its first subway lines that, together with its extensive trolley system, linked the villages it had already overwhelmed, and in 1920 the city incorporated these communities.[9] With a population of 4.1 million, Berlin was Germany's largest city in population and area. In 1898, New York incorporated Brooklyn, Queens, the Bronx, and Staten Island, and in 1904 it completed the first section of its subway system. Like Berlin, it was the largest city in its nation with a population of 5.6 million. New York was already becoming "vertical," famous for the steel-framed skyscrapers that were to become the sign of American modernity. Both cities were upstarts—without the illustrious histories of Paris, London, or Rome. Neither began its rise to international prominence until the nineteenth century, and both attempted to make lavish spending and technological advancement substitute for their lack of historical grandeur.

Berlin and New York were immigrant cities. Beginning with the flight of six thousand Huguenots in the seventeenth century, Berlin was home to waves of immigrants from Holland, Bohemia, the Palatinate, Silesia, Pomerania, and Poland—joined in the early 1920s by three hundred thousand Russians (Brunn 18). Berlin was similarly characterized by religious diversity, with substantial populations of Catholics and Jews as well as diverse Protestant groups, from the early nineteenth century on.[10] Its population constituted a cross-section of Europe, not of Germany. Historically even more diverse, around the turn of the century New York City received immigrants in large numbers from Eastern, Central, and southern Europe and was a primary destination for African Americans out of the South and the West Indies, who played a major role in the city's modernity; the black population of New York increased 400 percent between 1900 and 1920.[11] By the early twentieth century, a majority of people living in both cities was not born there.

Both cities also gave rise to myths that figured prominently in their respective popular identities. Berlin (like Paris and London) was represented as a woman. Describing the modern metropolis generally, Andreas Huyssen sees "the political, psychological, and aesthetic discourse around the turn of the century" as "consistently and obsessively gender[ing] mass culture and the masses as feminine" and therefore also as threatening: "The fear of the masses in this age of declining liberalism is always also a fear of woman."[12] Yet the base of this representation of woman as dangerous is largely German—a fact typically ignored in studies of the city. Huyssen quotes from French, Italian, English, and some U.S. sources, but his primary examples stem from Germany or Austria—both from the predictable sources of this "powerful masculinist mystique" (Marx, Nietzsche, and Freud) and others. Simmel represents urban capitalism in terms of prostitution in 1907; Siegfried Kracauer and Walter Benjamin develop his (and Nietzsche's more general) line of argument, linking "Woman" specifically to mechanization, commodification, and metropolitan modernity. Such views—and especially Benjamin's analysis of Baudelaire—have been tremendously influential in modernist and urban studies associations of the city and the poet not just with woman but with the woman-as-prostitute.[13]

As Laurie Teal summarizes, to oppose bourgeois repression, men idealized female sexuality as primitive, hence theoretically capable of returning humanity (that is, they themselves, through their empathy with the sexualized feminine) to a past of meaningful and nondecadent physicality, to a "pure" sexuality that would coincide with and generate pure emotion or love. Yet the sexualized female body was also subordinated to male creative spirituality *(Geist):* "the modernist's alliance with the prostitute in opposition to bourgeois culture thus combines a moral liberalism with an aesthetic (and at times political) conservatism aimed at holding in place traditional aesthetic categories threatened by commodity culture."[14] Consequently, association of the masculine poet with the idealized "feminine" often coexisted with virulent misogyny. As David Weir puts it, the male writer's "self-idealization of himself as woman coupled with the negative fantasy of woman as the embodiment of all that is natural and therefore antithetical to the art he practices" rejected bourgeois masculinity but participated in patriarchy.[15] Such thinking is hardly exclusively German, but it is significant that Germans were among its foremost articulators, and that such theories arise historically from the institutions of German cities or German experiences of Paris after the turn of the century.[16]

It seems a simple step from the association of mass culture or urban modernity with the female to representation of the city as commodified woman, but this step did not occur everywhere, and took various forms where it did occur. While uses of the phrase "Paris is a woman" are legion, representations of Paris as female tend not to suggest that "she" is also a prostitute.[17] Representations of Berlin, however, were typically sexual. Dorothy Rowe argues that between 1896 and 1930, Berlin is "conflated with an image of a sexually voracious and devouring female who comes to symbolize the city's modernity" in ways specific to the conditions of imperial and Weimar Berlin.[18] In *Sodom Berlin* Yvan Goll personified Berlin "as a corrupt female body that posed a sanitary and moral peril" to the nation.[19] Döblin's 1929 *Berlin Alexanderplatz* associates urban sexual violence with women's new freedom and a kind of loose female sexuality in the city, as does G. W. Pabst's 1929 film *Pandora's Box* (from Franz Wedekind's 1905 play of the same title). Carl Zuckmayer describes Berlin as "the goal of [everyone's] desires. Some saw her as hefty, full-breasted, in lace underwear, others as a mere wisp of a thing, with boyish legs in black silk stockings. . . . All wanted to have her, she enticed all."[20] Hanne Bergius claims that Berlin's notorious reputation as "the Whore Babylon" constituted a major part of the city's appeal to artists and writers.[21] Grammatically, the tendency to represent European cities as female depends upon the gendering of nouns: *die Stadt, la ville, la citté, la metropoli, la ciudad* are feminine forms (whereas in German, for example, "state" is masculine and "village" is neuter: *der Staat, das Dorf*). The explicitness of language personifying Berlin, however, suggests that the association is not primarily grammatical. Berlin was perceived both as "a city of women" and as dangerous, unhealthy, and openly available to the desires of men.[22]

According to Patrice Petro, the obsessive association of Berlin with the commodification of women stems from German men who were distracted by the presence of women in public spaces—a feature of life unthinkable just a few years earlier. Marsha Meskimmon also notes that Benjamin's link between poet and prostitute resonates with the form prostitution took in the cities of the Weimar Republic, and with observations of female public presence.[23] Many young unmarried women moved to the city to find work; hence there was a higher percentage of young women in Berlin than in small towns. Modern forms of public entertainment, especially movie theaters, and women's more visible presence in the public workforce also made women a more obvious part of city life than they had ever been before.[24] The department stores designed to encourage women's shopping increased their presence on city streets—as did hotels, cafés, and reading rooms. Wilson points out that such spaces were both private and public, an intermediate zone in which the unchaperoned "presence of women created a special and ambiguous atmosphere" (59). In contrast, until 1908 German law had prohibited women even from attending public meetings (Petro 58–59).

Demographics in Berlin also fed national anxieties about declining birth rates, directly linked here (as in France) to anxiety about changing gender roles for women (Frevert 185–86). In the 1920s, Berlin had the lowest birth rate of any city in the world, the highest divorce rate in Germany, and probably the highest rate of abortions—although no reliable figures are available because abortions were illegal.[25] The high number of abortions and low birth rate caused some journalists to accuse middle-class women of staging a "birth strike": by 1933, 35 percent of all married couples in the city were childless—twice the German national average (von Ankum 5; Harrington 47). Commentators from the late 1910s and through the 1920s blamed the city's "moral chaos on the war and the inflation, but particularly on the New Woman. . . . A chorus of voices held the New Woman responsible for the break-up of the family, the epidemic of venereal diseases, illegitimate children, abortions, dancing, and cultural decadence" (Jelavich 133).

Female visibility in Berlin also related directly to prostitution. The prohibition of brothels and strict rules about sexual solicitation in Germany forced Berlin's active sex industry onto the streets. Moreover, it forced prostitutes to dress in a bourgeois fashion and solicit subtly, thus making it difficult—according to some observers—to distinguish between prostitutes and "proper" women, and giving the city's public spaces a "pervasive erotic ambiguity" (Haxthausen 80). Prostitutes' widespread practice of wearing widow's veils after 1918 and the slang reference to prostitutes as "war widows" heightened this erotic ambiguity: it both underlined the economic necessity making women turn to occasional prostitution and increased the embarrassment of men's guessing improperly. Prostitutes had to be visible to succeed, and for a woman to be visibly in public was to be suspected of prostitution.[26]

The erotic ambiguity of women's presence in public was a primary feature of German visual arts during this period.[27] Street scenes featuring women were a staple of Expressionist art—from Kirchner's elegant and ambiguously sexual strolling women to Grosz's repeated scenes of *Lustmord,* murderous rape. Both painters repeatedly title such paintings as though the women represented are identical to the streets. Kirchner titles paintings *Berliner Straßenscene* (1913), *Die Straße* (1913), *Der Potsdamer Platz* (1914) or *Friedrichstraße, Berlin, 1914,* although one can see little evidence of a street. Grosz's paintings of Berlin foreground commercial sexual exchange, often quite viciously, yet also have innocuous names like *Café* (1915), or *Berliner Straße.* Otto Dix's paintings present sexually available women with equal frequency.[28]

Not surprisingly, women did not represent Berlin as a seductive woman or regard the female prostitute as a paradigmatic cipher for modernity, and the prostitute was rarely a theme in women's visual or literary art. Exceptions, like Gerta Overbeck's 1923 painting *Prostitute,* which shows an unostentatiously clad woman in a chemist's shop purchasing a contraceptive douche, stress the daily experience and dangers of disease for women sex workers, not sexuality or eroticism.[29] Similarly in Irmgard Keun's *Das kunstseidene Mädchen (The Artificial Silk Girl),* the protagonist approaches her sexual commodification pragmatically, in relation to hunger, cold, and her own emotional needs.[30] As Meskimmon writes, "The prostitute acted as a symbol . . . within a male, heterosexual economy of meaning; the images and descriptions of prostitutes . . . signified the fears and desires of the male subject faced with the commodification, urbanisation and alienation of modernity" (27, 28–29).

It has never been recognized that the social conditions making the perception of prostitution nearly synonymous with the perception of Berlin did not prevail in the United States, and prostitution was not seen as a primary metaphor for the city or generally for modernity there, despite many shared cultural assumptions about gender differences and the popularity of literature about prostitutes in the second decade of the century—much of which was written by liberal men celebrating the prostitute as a rebel defying gender norms (Stansell 295). The prostitute was presented as a kind of working-class primitive, stimulating desire in the (male) observer and serving as a symbol of "modern female ambiguity," but not of the artist or modernist per se. Black women were written about using similarly primitivist sexual stereotypes—represented by Nella Larsen in *Passing* (1929) from the perspective of a black woman. The impetus of such literature, however, was often initially consciously feminist, despite its effective strengthening of patriarchal, heterosexual roles (Stansell 290).

The conditions in New York were even more different from Berlin's than the impetus of such (male) writing. By 1910 the number and visibility of prostitutes in the city had distinctly declined.[31] Various factors contributed to this pattern. Middle-class women were under little economic pressure to supplement their incomes through prostitution. Their movement had long been less restricted than that of German women, and hence their presence on streets and in public spaces was neither as titillating nor as shocking. Moreover, brothels were concentrated in a few districts, like the Tenderloin and Lower East Side. Skyscrapers and widespread use of the telephone also led to the replacement of streetwalkers by call girls, or women soliciting and working within a building. The 1896 Raines law had encouraged links between alcohol and prostitution by prohibiting liquor sales on Sunday except in hotels with ten or more beds. With a 1915 law prohibiting all forms of prostitution and the 1920 Prohibition amendment, connections between the control of alcohol and sex increased dramatically, and prostitution went further underground (Gilfoyle 299, 309). A general increase in premarital sex among middle-class youth also contributed to a decreased demand for prostitution (311). By 1917, prostitution had become largely invisible in New York, and during the "Roaring Twenties" procuring a prostitute required diligent effort (306, 307). Unlike in Berlin, in this city, during the late teens and twenties there was no ambiguity about a well-dressed woman's status on the streets, and the city was not perceived as dominated by women.

Typically, American cities are not gendered in popular discourse. When New York is gendered, it is more often masculine than feminine. For example, in Theodore Dreiser's 1901 *Sister Carrie,* Chicago and New York seduce women, not men. John Reed's 1910 poem "Foundations of a Skyscraper" identifies these buildings with the laborers who construct them: "Naked, a giant's back, tight-muscled, stark," and Lola Ridge's 1920 "Time-Stone" presents the seven-hundred-foot Metropolitan Life Tower as in phallic flirtation with the feminine moon.[32] In a 1911 lecture, George Santayana describes skyscrapers as "the sphere of the American man . . . all aggressive enterprise."[33] F. Scott Fitzgerald writes in "My Lost City" that, after having "lost" his "girl," he wants to return to New York because he "wanted a man's world" (22). And although Carl Van Vechten's 1930 novel *Parties* uses an occasional female pronoun—"perhaps it is more satisfactory . . . to instinctively feel the metropolis rather than to attempt to comprehend her"—most of his descriptions suggest the masculine: in the twilight, its towers look like "battling gangsters."[34]

New York's increasingly vertical skyline may have encouraged a phallic emphasis in representations of the city. The "straight" photography of Paul Strand and Alfred Stieglitz suggests this masculinity in images and in the photographers' sexually charged language claiming that the mastery of their work transforms objects into art.[35] Generally, visual art depicting New York focused not on women but on abstract angles and structures of architecture—for example, Stieglitz's *New York from the Shelton,* Strand's *The Court,* presenting one corner of a courtyard, or O'Keeffe's *East River from the Shelton,* depicting factories in moonlight. When people are present, they are often dwarfed by the city's architecture or infrastructure, and either male or without clear gender. John Sloan and other "ashcan" painters who represented New York streets through focus on women, identifiable through reference to street names or institutions as probably prostitutes, were an exception, and have been seen as influenced by French painters. Despite many similarities, in short, New York and Berlin were perceived by their inhabitants and by outside commentators as having different auras.

In his memoir, Carl Zuckmayer wrote, "Whatever sought to rise in Germany, Berlin pulled into itself with the force of a tornado. . . . Whoever had Berlin possessed the world."[36] In the years following World War I, the city was filled with wounded and beggars; the population was depressed and demoralized. Despite the hopes engendered by the founding of the Weimar Republic, many social critics feared disastrous consequences from Germany's continued underlying economic, political, and social instability. And yet, Zuckmayer writes, one could feel the "incomparable intensity . . . that made Berlin . . . the most interesting, exciting city of Europe. . . . Berlin tasted like the future."[37] This future was short-lived. On October 3, 1929, Chancellor Gustav Stresemann died, followed three weeks later by the collapse of the U.S. stock market. With the elections of 1930, the National Socialist party won six and a half million votes, and Hitler's rise to power accelerated. What had seemed unlikely a few years before began to look inevitable: the radical Right was coming to power through a combination of democratic process and ruthless manipulation of weak political structures and economic crisis. Artists and intellectuals began leaving Berlin.

In 1900, these events could not be anticipated. Innovative writers and artists in Germany faced the future with passionate critique and the enthusiasm of the consciously new. Expressionism (usually dated 1910–25) was the "first real urban art in Germany, and for that reason found its logical center in Berlin."[38] While there was no single category for innovative art movements in Germany, Expressionism was the most inclusive and hence functioned more like the umbrella term *modernism* than a strictly defined avant-garde. It was based broadly on hostility to bourgeois culture and an aesthetic that symbolized or enabled release from its norms. Often apocalyptic, Expressionists used violent images, convulsive emotions, and extreme juxtapositions to attempt to shock the modern world into social and spiritual renewal—goals simultaneously psychological and political. Many saw the antinaturalistic experimentalism of Expressionism as a sign of urban alienation; others saw it as responding positively to urban and technological change. Most artists associated with the term rejected "impressionist" beauty of surface and believed that capitalism was leading to the atrophy or mechanization of the human spirit. Each sought to release "the spiritual and psychological strivings of his time."[39]

Berlin Expressionism began with the organization of a number of small groups or communes. Among the most significant was Die Kommenden (The Up and Coming), initiated by Ludwig Jacobowski in the late 1890s as a series of weekly meetings. After Jacobowski's death in 1900, Ruldolf Steiner organized its recitation evenings and edited *Darbietung der Kommenden,* which printed Lasker-Schüler's early poetry. Walden and Franz Pfemfert developed the theoretical boundaries of Expressionism through their journals (respectively *Der Sturm,* founded 1910, and *Die Aktion,* founded 1911). Although many writers published in both periodicals, *Der Sturm* published more polemical statements and the "most cohesive group of Expressionists" published in its pages, sat with Walden in cafés, and participated in his evenings and exhibitions.[40]

At the state level, the Berlin art world was dominated by powerful institutions. At the level of groups or movements, it was dominated by powerful individuals with strongly defined philosophical, social, or aesthetic programs—like Jacobowski or Walden. As far as I have been able to tell, these individuals were without exception male. They invited individuals to join their *Stammtische* or cabarets and edited journals. Hence, alliance with a powerful individual could greatly increase one's chance of renown. Although individual women (like Käthe Kollwitz) made names for themselves, they were exceptions. Christine Reiß-Suckow describes a woman who left bourgeois women's occupations to pursue the career of artist or writer as existing in a "no-man's land between the sexes" (24–25).

This individual- and male-dominated structure was further complicated for a woman writing poetry by the extremely high regard in which Germans held poets. The poet was cultural god or king. Stefan Zweig writes of the word *poet* as "primeval-sacred," not to be confounded with "the looser and uncertain notion of author" (in Gay 64). This hierarchy is the same described by Pierre Bourdieu in France: the poet's position "by a sort of effect of caste, gives its occupants, subjectively at least, the assurance of an essential superiority over all other writers; the lowest of the poets . . . sees himself as superior to the highest of the . . . novelists."[41] Poetry was also associated with the purest and highest use of the German language, in a time when the language-purity movement had powerful public and academic appeal. According to Peter Gay, Germans raised the poet to importance above that of the philosopher or thinker because of the poet's supposed greater command of the essence of the language. Poetry remained the dominant genre of Expressionism until the midteens. Best known among the new poets were Gottfried Benn, Georg Heym, Jakob van Hoddis, Alfred

Lichtenstein, Georg Trakl, Ernst Stadler, Ernst Lotz, August Stramm, and Franz Werfel; Lasker-Schüler was the only woman even occasionally added to such lists.

Lasker-Schüler entered the Berlin avant-garde just as Expressionism began to develop. Growing up in a middle-class, partially assimilated Jewish family in the industrial town of Elberfelde, Else Schüler left high school at the age of twelve, and was then tutored at home.[42] Clearly romanticized, her stories of childhood at home with her parents and siblings are the happiest she tells. In 1894, Lasker-Schüler moved with her physician husband Jonathan Lasker to Berlin and began to take painting lessons. In May 1899, she published her first poems. In August, within a month of the birth of her son Paul, whose paternity she never revealed except in cryptic allusions to a foreign prince, she left her bourgeois marriage and entered fully into the life of bohemian Berlin. In 1902, she published her first volume of poems—*Styx,* perhaps suggesting a crossing out of her old bourgeois life. In one mark of this crossing, the poet refused help from her husband at Paul's birth, instead apparently paying for her hospital attendance by scrubbing floors in the days preceding her labor and allowing a medical class to witness the birth.[43]

It was probably at Die Kommenden's evenings of wild discussion and performance that the poet met many of her later friends, including Herwarth Walden, whom she married in 1903, and Peter Hille, one of the most influential figures in the Berlin avant-garde—although many of the same crowd were also associated with Die Neue Gemeinschaft (New Society). In 1901, Walden began Teloplasma, a short-lived cabaret (a venue for readings, music, and other types of performance), and in 1902, Hille organized cabaret evenings.[44] In 1909, Kurt Hiller founded Der Neue Club, which staged public readings under the name the Neopathetische Cabaret. Many cabaret evenings—like those organized by Walden, Hille, and Jacobowski—were small and idiosyncratic, and their programs were not widely publicized. Yet because of their loose organization and openness, they provided crucially important opportunities for writers to try out new work and they moved artistic ferment from private gatherings into the public eye.[45]

Given the structure of the avant-garde in Berlin, it is not surprising that Lasker-Schüler owed her early success in part to Hille's promotion of her work. Hille also encouraged the poet to take on a life like his, devoted to artistic endeavor and indifferent to the poverty a rejection of popular values would entail. Lasker-Schüler's career was also assisted through the collaborative avant-garde leadership she established with her husband Walden and, later, her publication in *Der Sturm.* Yet perhaps as a move toward independence from these male-dominated structures, by 1904 Lasker-Schüler had pulled back from defined groups and movements, relying instead on her network of friendships. And indeed Lasker-Schüler numbered among her friends some of the most influential artists and critics of the era—including Gottfried Benn, Viennese satirist and editor of *Die Fackel* Karl Kraus, founder of the Malik Press Wieland Herzfelde, art collector and editor Paul Cassirer, and Franz Marc.

While Walden is typically described as the more influential member of his and Lasker-Schüler's marriage, the success of their shared enterprises apparently stemmed from her energy and contacts as much as from his skills as impresario. Together they founded his Art Club (Verein für Kunst, 1904–9), and her reputation as poet helped establish the *Sturm* through her extensive publication in its pages.[46] M. S. Jones argues in particular that Walden's aggressive egotism and "unqualified confidence in his own abilities and judgments" were off-putting to cooperative work (10). Bauschinger notes that Lasker-Schüler shared performance opportunities with Wedekind, Rilke, and Gustav Mahler in the Verein für Kunst evenings, and that Walden ceased to hold these evenings after their separation (*WZ* 87).

Lasker-Schüler's circulation among several groups was made possible by the fact that they met in the open, porous environment of cafés, not private salons. No invitation was necessary to walk into a café. Public meeting places also offered women a more or less neutral space in which to meet fellow writers and artists.[47] Nonetheless, there were far more men than women in the cafés, and Lasker-Schüler is the only woman frequently mentioned as present who is not accompanying a lover or husband. Of all the cafés popular among Expressionists in Berlin, the most significant was the Café des Westens—a site of literary and bohemian gatherings from as early as 1901. Wieland Herzfelde writes that on his first trip to Berlin he went immediately to the Café des Westens to find Lasker-Schüler, whom he knew would be there. Frequently a stop for tourists seeking a glimpse of bohemia, it was widely known as Café Grössenwahn (Delusion).[48] When the Café des Westens decided to seek a more distinguished clientele, the avant-garde moved to the huge Romanisches Café, a few blocks away—a café also frequented by expatriate Americans, like Loy. Cafés were the site of serious work as well as of conversation. Table-hopping, heated discussion, and impromptu performances were the order of the day; the Café des Westens even provided its clientele with newspapers and reprint information about the latest publications (Bauschinger, "Café Culture" 80, 79). Drafts of poems, stories, plays, and essays circulated. Lasker-Schüler described cafés as "our stock exchange . . . where the deals are closed" (*Br* I 67). Allen describes Lasker-Schüler as "omnipresent" in such bohemian gatherings, and she read or performed at several, as well as frequently in Leipzig, Munich, Prague, Vienna, and Zurich (215, 216).

Despite the male-dominated structure of the German avant-garde, Lasker-Schüler was by no means alone as a woman. Other experimentalist female poets of the period include Emmy Hennings, Gertrud Kolmar, Margarete Beutler, and Franziska von Reventlow, as well as more traditional poets Ricarda Huch, Agnes Miegel, Lulu von Strauss und Torney, and Ina Seidel. German women writing feminist or modernist prose included Lily Braun, Hedwig Dohm, Annette Kolb, Gabrielle Reuter, Nelly Sachs, and Clara Viebig. Lasker-Schüler knew several of these women, and counted among her friends Marianne Werefkin, sculptor Milly Steger (who, like the poet, grew up in Elberfelde), and actress Kete Parsenow. Some of the better-known writers were too young to have provided companionship: Ilse Langner, Elisabeth Langgässer, and Vicki Baum moved to Berlin in the late 1920s; Gertrud Kolmar first began publishing in 1917; Irmgard Keun was born in 1905.[49] While there is no evidence that Lasker-Schüler provided assistance to these women, her stature must have facilitated their entrance into the literary avant-garde, and Dagmar Lorenz writes of the poet's influence on Kolmar.[50]

Although other German cities also enjoyed lively literary scenes, Berlin housed the most important presses and periodicals; between 1910 and 1920, thirty-two Expressionist periodicals were published there, and the city was home to the great commercial publishing empires of Mosse, Ullstein, and Fischer. Richard Brinkmann argues that this period brought about a new identification of publishers and presses with particular intellectual movements and authors.[51] Berlin was also a center for other arts. Die Brücke made its headquarters there from 1911 to 1913, Max Liebermann's Berlin Secession gathered visual artists from all over Germany for fourteen years, and Dada found a home there in the midteens. Mary Wigman formulated a theory of expressive movement that revolutionized modern dance in Central Europe, and eventually spread to the United States. American Isadora Duncan spent considerable time in Berlin, where she issued her declaration of dance theory in 1903, founded her first dance school (1904–7), and met Loy in 1922. In architecture and theater, postwar Berlin was especially progressive. Count Kessler wrote in 1930 that "where architecture is concerned London and also Paris are at least half a lifetime behind Berlin" (in Willett 132). Berlin had between 40 and 128 theaters—depending on how one counted small performance spaces—and three opera houses.[52] Moreover, Willett claims that because German society "had a special tradition of cultural decentralization and of strong public patronage with a Socialist slant," and because it "was in a sense a new society, with everything to rebuild after a disastrous war," it was more accessible than other cities to new ideas from both East and West (94).[53] It was during this period of extraordinary ferment and openness that Loy spent a year in Berlin.

By 1911, Lasker-Schüler had become one of the most widely noted writers of the time, author of three volumes of poetry, a book of sketches in memory of Peter Hille, another of stories and poems, and a play.[54] Gabriele Münter referred to the frequent imitations of Lasker-Schüler's style in *Der Sturm* as "lasker[ing] around [*herum zu laskern*]" (*WZ* 85, 94). Richard Dehmel, the most influential literary figure of the turn of the century, described her as "the only poet besides me who can write poetry" (*WZ* 316, 319, 64). In 1918, Kasimir Edschmid calls Lasker-Schüler "one of the greatest poets [of the day] because she is more timeless than the others. . . . The Lasker stands alone."[55] In his 1922 reissue of *Menschheitsdämmerung (The Twilight of Humanity),* Kurt Pinthus includes Lasker-Schüler as one of the few Expressionist writers who distinguished themselves from the crowd. In 1925, Zuckmayer describes the "top of the Berlin intelligentsia and society" as attending one of his premieres, then lists "Albert Einstein, Gustav Stresemann, Reneé Sintenis, [Max] Pechstein, [Hans] Poelzig, Else Lasker-Schüler, Brecht . . ." (445). Most significantly, Karl Kraus wrote in 1912, "I hold Else Lasker-Schüler to be a great poet. I hold everything else being stressed as new around her to be mere cheek [*eine Frechheit*]"; and in 1927, he concluded that Lasker-Schüler was "the most significant lyric poet in Germany today."[56] In 1932, she won the prestigious Kleist Prize.

Yet despite such recognition, Lasker-Schüler complained of feeling like an outsider in Berlin, one who didn't "speak the language" of her "land" ("Heimweh" ["Homesickness"], *WB,* no. 155). Her behavior, appearance, and art created controversy. Gustav Landauer speaks of this phenomenon as early as 1901, when inviting a friend to attend one of her readings: she "doesn't fit anywhere and certainly not in the milieu in which you will see her."[57] With the growing social conservatism of the 1920s, Lasker-Schüler felt herself to be increasingly isolated, admired as a spectacle rather than for her work. As she wrote to

Yiddish poet Abraham Stenzl in 1929, when he let her know that he had dedicated poems to her because this made it easier for him to get them published, "I have indeed already experienced that for one I'm just a ladder, for another a sensation, for another a lookout, for another an event."[58] Admiration of her work was far from universal. Because of anticipated protest, the Kleist Prize was divided between Lasker-Schüler and a nationalist, formally traditional, Christian male poet, yet even this conciliatory move did not prevent a storm of right-wing invective (both racist and antiexperimental) against Lasker-Schüler and the Kleist committee (*MM* 226–32).

Public disapproval also took more violent forms. Years before Hitler's rise to power in 1933, Lasker-Schüler was harassed by right-wing paramilitary bullies. The poet never writes about this persecution in detail, but her and her friends' letters and memoirs reveal that by the late 1920s she lived in fear and danger. Following a particularly violent attack in 1933, she fled from Berlin to Zurich—like many other Jews, hoping she would be able to return soon. Lasker-Schüler lived in Switzerland until 1938, when she was further exiled to Palestine. She died before the end of the war in 1945 and was buried on the Mount of Olives.

Lasker-Schüler's influence stemmed from her publications and her personal relationships with other writers and artists. Although she wrote no critical essays or formal reviews, she published dozens of sketches of writers, artists, actors, playwrights, and theater directors.[59] Similarly, she alludes to scores of writers and artists in her prose works—especially in the letters describing café life in *Mein Herz.* Such writing functioned similarly to a review in calling attention to a peer's work as significant, and it was characteristic of Lasker-Schüler's generosity to her friends in professional and private spheres. Similarly, while Lasker-Schüler "borrowed" money to support herself and her son (especially during the long illness that led to his death in 1927), she also frequently gave money to others in need. This was not financially pragmatic given her own poverty, but reflected her conception of life and art: one gives everything, holds nothing back—only in this way can art or people hope to transform both personal lives of suffering and cultures that breed such conditions.

Lasker-Schüler found in Berlin an environment that allowed her to make the most of her interests, minimal formal education, and ambitions. The public nature of artistic and social life and the leadership structured around individuals with whom she had significant relationships gave her full access to the most exciting minds and conversation of Central Europe. Her correspondence includes letters from Thomas, Heinrich, and Klaus Mann, Hermann Hesse, Arnold Schönberg, Magnus Hirschfeld, Freud, and Albert Einstein.[60] Martin Buber maintained a friendly argument with her for years over the present and future of Judaism. Although several of her poems present themes of loneliness and alienation, Lasker-Schüler was in fact part of an extensive community. She expresses this most publicly in an essay called "Ich räume auf! Meine Anklage gegen meine Verleger" ("Setting My Accounts in Order: My Charge against my Publishers"; 1925), written as a call to arms for fellow impoverished writers to speak out against the wealth of publishers. The essay charges three of her publishers with using the inflationary spiral of the early 1920s to cheat her out of earned income for her books, but many regarded it as a rallying cry for all writers, and it generated heated public debate.[61] Lasker-Schüler's letters from friends in exile also indicate the extent to which she represents important aspects of their shared experience of Berlin.

Moreover, to the extent that Expressionism valued fantasy as indicative of a work's imaginative power, it provided the perfect setting for her anti-intellectualist, antirealistic art. Ernst Bloch was among the most important theorists of Expressionist idealism. As he argues, the "utopian function" of art establishes the point of contact between "hope" or "dream" and the "objectively real"; as "the real forward tendency, toward the better condition" it is "the historical substance [*Geschichts-Inhalt*] of hope." The intensity of excess in the utopian function of literature causes a "mobilization of those contradictions inherent in the bad existence in order to overcome that existence, in order to bring it to the point of collapse."[62] Because the utopian is immediately linked to the historical, its content "changes according to the social situation"; the "essential function" of a utopia is "a critique of what is present."[63] Many Expressionists saw utopianism as politically more radical than socialism. Lasker-Schüler's linguistic and fictional experiments merging myth, religion, and fantasy participate in the kind of critique Bloch validates.[64]

While formally innovative artistic groups were already a factor of Berlin life in 1900, artistic innovation did not begin to gather momentum in New York until around 1910, despite the opening of Alfred Stieglitz's "Little Galleries of Photo-Secession" (later called "291") in 1905 and his publication of *Camera Work* (1903–17), the first American journal to print reproductions of European modern art.[65] During these early years, Greenwich Village was the undisputed center for the innovative arts, housing multiple theaters, galleries, salons, the Washington

Square and Provincetown Players, the Liberal Club, the Ferrer Modern School with its lectures, performances, and exhibits, Albert and Charles Boni's Washington Square Bookshop, and the offices of *The Masses*, the *Glebe*, *Trend*, *Rogue*, *Bruno's Weekly*, the *Chimaera*, *Others*, the *Little Review*, and other little magazines.[66] Dancer-choreographers Ruth St. Denis and Isadora Duncan (as well as, later, Martha Graham) frequently performed in New York. According to Scott and Rutkoff, thirty-four clubs or galleries presented more than 250 exhibitions of innovative art between 1913 and 1918, "making wartime New York a more important market for modern painting and sculpture than Paris" (45). The Village was called "the cradle of modern American culture."[67] Not coincidentally, it was also the last area of Manhattan to be affected by the grid plan, hence preserving its winding streets, old-fashioned community character, and cheap rents.

In the heyday of Village culture, it was dominated by journalists and artists who were political radicals, preeminent among them several feminists: among others, Floyd Dell, Crystal and Max Eastman, Emma Goldman (before emigrating to Russia and Berlin), Susan Glaspel, Ida Rauh, and Henrietta Rodman. During the teens, editors, artists, and writers like Stieglitz, Kreymborg, Lola Ridge, Eugene O'Neill, Robert McAlmon, Charles Demuth, Marguerite and William Zorach, Marsden Hartley, Millay, Georgia O'Keeffe, Loy, and Moore either held similar feminist views or were affected by their local prominence.[68] Linda Kinnahan argues that Williams's early poetry was distinctly influenced by the active feminism of the Village.[69] In *The New Woman: Feminism in Greenwich Village, 1910–1920*, June Sochen writes that the strong feminist convictions of so many of its artists and writers made the Village unique (7–8). There was no such feminist core associated with the avant-garde in Berlin or Paris in the second decade of the century, or in Florence, where Loy began writing her poetry.[70] Village radicals foundationally linked social and gender politics with art, moving New York modernism "away from narrow aesthetic concerns into an inclusive vision of modern life defined by social equality, feminism, socialism, and free love" (Scott and Rutkoff 75). By the mid-1920s, however, the Village was less of a radical cultural than a media-celebrated enclave, where the "new" appeared as much in "lifestyle" as in art or politics.

The feminist politics of the early Village no doubt contributed to one of the most striking and least often discussed aspects of modernism in the United States, namely, that by the mid-1920s, the central institutions supporting experimental arts and writing were dominated by women. This was not true before the Armory Show in 1913—despite the reemergence at the turn of the century of the popular myth of female cultural dominance.[71] Prior to the early teens, women in the United States had little power in institutions of culture. By 1930, however, they had assumed a leading role in public ventures associated with the new arts. In any new arts movement, a work must receive validation from some public source, typically constituted by exhibition, publication, reviews, or critical mention in a context of recognized authority.[72] The venues established by American women were widely recognized as providing such validation. In 1929, Frank Zorbaugh wrote of Chicago and New York, "It is the young women who open most of the studios, run most of the tearooms and restaurants, most of the little art shops and book stalls, manage the exhibits and little theaters, dominate the life of the bohemias of American cities"; in the early twenties, Genevieve Taggard wrote, "What's in the men nowadays—the *women* have the fire & the ardency & the power & the depth."[73]

This was certainly the case in New York.[74] According to McCarthy, in the visual arts women were more willing to take risks on the new art than men; they were not allowed access to already established institutional structures and hence had less than middle- or upper-class men to lose.[75] Abby Rockefeller, Lillie Bliss, and Mary Quinn Sullivan founded the Museum of Modern Art (MoMA) in 1929; sculptor Gertrude Vanderbilt Whitney opened two galleries in 1908, founded Friends of Young Artists in 1909 (which in 1918 became the Whitney Studio Club), and then in 1931 founded the Whitney Museum. Katherine Dreier founded Cooperative Mural Workshops in 1914; in 1917, she helped organize the Society of Independent Artists, and in 1920 she cofounded with Marcel Duchamp and Man Ray the Société Anonyme, the first museum of modern art in the United States.[76] Dreier later became president of the Société and ran it for over twenty years. Other women founding galleries or societies included Edith Halpert, Agnes Meyer, Jane Heap, and Marguerite Zorach. Frances Steloff founded the Gotham Book Mart in 1920, which immediately became an international literary haven and thrived until her death in 1989. In theater, the Neighborhood Playhouse—which Arthur Wertheim considers the "most important new little theatre on the Lower East Side" of the city (153)—was directed by Helen Arthur, Agnes Moran, and Alice and Irene Lewisohn. Edith Isaacs was associate editor of *Theater Arts* from 1918 to 1922, then editor until 1946; Theresa Helburn was according to some accounts the driving force behind the organization of the Theatre Guild, America's foremost art theater, and served as its executive director from 1919 to 1932; and Regina Anderson was one of four organizers of the Harlem Experimental Theatre (1927).

More pertinent to this study, during the teens and twenties women edited several influential innovative literary and cultural journals.[77] In 1916, Margaret Anderson and Jane Heap moved the *Little Review* from Chicago to New York. Jessie Fauset was literary editor of the *Crisis* from 1919 to 1926, and Gwendolyn Bennett wrote a weekly literary column for *Opportunity*, from 1926 to 1928.[78] In 1916, Pauline E. Hopkins founded and edited the *New Era*. Helen Hoyt and Mina Loy both edited special numbers of *Others*. From 1923 to 1926, Irita van Doren was literary editor of the *Nation*, and Freda Kirchwey was its managing editor from 1922 until 1937, when she bought the journal, and then edited it until 1955. Lola Ridge founded and edited the first two issues of the Ferrer School's *Modern School* magazine in 1912, was associate editor of *Others* until it closed in 1919, and U.S. editor of *Broom*. Moore began editorial assistance at the *Dial* in 1924, working with managing editor Alyse Gregory, then served as editor from 1925 until the journal ceased publication in 1929. Together with *Poetry* magazine, edited by Harriet Monroe and, initially, Alice Corbin Henderson in Chicago, and Amy Lowell's edition of three anthologies called *Some Imagist Poets* (1915, 1916, and 1917), these women were responsible for publishing much of what is considered canonical modernist literature today—including major work by Pound, Stein, Joyce, H.D., Eliot, Williams, Stevens, Alain Locke, Langston Hughes, and D. H. Lawrence, as well as by each other.[79]

Salons hosted or cohosted by women were also important to modernist organizing. Those of Stein and Natalie Barney in Paris are well known. In New York, influential salons were hosted by Mabel Dodge, Gertrude Whitney, Regina Anderson, Marguerite and William Zorach, Bill and Margaret Sanger, Elinor Wylie and William Rose Benet, and Walter and Louise Arensberg. Anderson also made the 135th Street branch of the New York Public Library a key gathering place for Harlem intellectuals. Equally crucial is the money women gave each other and their male peers. Agnes Meyer provided funding for Stieglitz's gallery, the *291* journal, and the Modern Gallery she cofounded with de Zayas; Dreier funded Duchamp for years. Peggy Guggenheim and Mabel Dodge were generous to many writers, including Loy. Charlotte Mason provided financial assistance to Harlem Renaissance writers including Hughes, Hurston, and McKay, and helped underwrite the Negro Art Institute and Harlem Museum of African Art. Moore was assisted financially by the novelists Bryher

(British) and Kathrine Jones, and she helped Djuna Barnes in her late years by soliciting money for her from a wealthy patron.[80] Loy was assisted financially by Natalie Barney as well as by Guggenheim and Dodge. Men also founded and edited presses, journals, galleries, and organizations and patronized writers, but these activities are both well documented and can be taken for granted in a way that women's similar activities cannot.

Just as women's professional success and feminism was a sign of the times, so was misogynistic resistance to it and general criticism of the New Woman—although such criticism was rarely as virulent in New York as in Berlin. Naomi Sawelson-Gorse points out ways in which male Dadaists trivialized conceptions of women and marginalized their female colleagues—prominently, for example, in the sole issue of *New York Dada* (1921).[81] Much has been written of Pound's desire to control selections of female editors and to claim greater influence than he in fact had.[82] In a 1920 editorial statement, Harriet Monroe quotes a reader of *Poetry* who accuses its "perverse" female editors of "stifling the 'vigorous male note' of verse."[83] Female editors had to face constant comparison with their often more illustrious male peers and with the (primarily male) artists and writers whom they promoted and with whom they worked. No doubt in part because of their numbers, however, they persisted, and we cannot today imagine Anglo-American modernism without their publications.

During the twenties, New York was home to Scott Joplin's ragtime, Charles Ives's dissonant tonalities, and the commercial development of the blues and jazz. Harlem rivaled the Village as a scene of cultural activity and dominated the field of popular music. The little theater movement was strong in Harlem as well as the Village, and by the mid-1920s New York had roughly eight hundred movie theaters—more than any other city in the world—although with the passing of the Prohibition amendment in 1920, New York's cabaret life had come to an end. At that point, illegal speakeasies, with their cheap liquor and musical entertainment, began to flourish.[84] Alcoholism became a problem for many associated with modernism. In "My Lost City," F. Scott Fitzgerald writes that by 1927 "most of my friends drank too much—the more they were in tune to the times the more they drank" (346). Many artists left New York for Europe in the early 1920s because of U.S. isolationism, xenophobia, prudery, and the low cost of living in Europe.

Moore began spending time in the Village in 1916 and welcomed its feminist and socialist attitudes. After a peripatetic early childhood in which she, her brother, and her mother lived with older male relatives (Moore never met her father), Moore spent the remainder of her childhood in Carlisle, Pennsylvania.[85] Although, like Lasker-Schüler, Moore in some ways idealized her childhood, the deaths of two close male relatives, the absence of her father, and the lack of a permanent family home until she was eight may partially explain the intensity of her bonds to mother and brother and her strong sense of the importance of community later in her life. By the time Moore graduated from Bryn Mawr College in 1909, she was well versed in contemporary literature and art, and confident in her own taste. For a variety of reasons, however, after a brief interval on her own, she returned to Carlisle to live with her mother, teaching English and business courses for part of this time at a local high school for Native Americans. While Mary Warner Moore and her son (John) Warner did not encourage Marianne's vocation as poet, once she had made up her mind, they supported her in it.

From 1916 to 1918, Moore lived in her brother's parsonage in Chatham, New Jersey, and spent most of her time in New York. In 1918, she and her mother moved to Greenwich Village, where she worked half days at the New York City Public Library. A nonsmoker, moderate drinker, and regular attender of Presbyterian church services, Moore enthusiastically embraced a life that included no sexual or romantic affairs, no work or public socializing on Sundays, and nothing markedly bohemian. In 1923, she declined Matthew Josephson's invitation to edit *Broom* and in 1925 became editor of the *Dial*.[86] By then, two books of her poems had appeared (1921, 1924), she had written significant reviews of many of her contemporaries, and she had won the *Dial* award (1924).[87] Linda Leavell speculates that "before the publication of *The Waste Land* in 1922, Moore was arguably the most esteemed of the modernist poets" (*Marianne Moore* 44). In 1917, H.D. writes that her poetry is "more rare, more fine than any modern I know" (August 29, 1917; RML V.23.32). William Carlos Williams considered Moore's poetry exemplary in its modernity—"the best," "a break *through* all preconception of poetic form and mood and pace."[88] Yvor Winters concludes a 1925 essay on Moore with the comment, "It is a privilege to be able to write of one of whose genius one feels so sure."[89]

Just as Lasker-Schüler was, in Moore's words, "hindered to succeed" by the structures of the Berlin avant-garde, Moore's patterns of involvement and success were shaped by the structures of New York's literary scene ("The Paper Nautilus," *CPo* 121). While in Berlin, and generally in Europe, each new aesthetic direction tended to distinguish itself by manifesto and name, in New York the literary and artistic groups were loosely defined: they claimed no identifying ideology, philosophy, or aesthetic beyond "making it new," or being "other" than the mainstream.[90] As a movement, U.S. modernism was also less politicized than that of Germany. Rita Felski observes that the explicit link of formal experimentation to social change in Germany (as well as in Russia, Italy, and France) played a minor role in U.S. (and British) modernisms (12, 23). Similarly, Peter Nicholls notes that the United States had no "powerful *academic* culture on the European model"; hence writers "felt little direct hostility toward art as an institution" (166). In fact, many U.S. modernist writers held college or university degrees. As a corollary, lines of influence and power were less clearly marked. Memoirs of this period mention endless parties and gatherings but no "movements" and no clear leaders.

The major exception to this rule was Stieglitz, whose galleries served in the first two decades of the century as a gathering place for those interested in the avant-garde. When first visiting New York as a poet, in 1915, Moore went to 291. Like Walden and Pfemfert, Stieglitz formally invited individuals to join his discussion circle. Yet Stieglitz organized his gallery and *Camera Work* to be aesthetically and theoretically inclusive, along the lines of the *Blaue Reiter Almanac*, published by Marc and Kandinsky. More characteristic of New York modernism was the role of Alfred Kreymborg, another son of German immigrants, who edited several little magazines. In the December 1918 *Others*, Kreymborg denied "that the contributors to *Others* . . . are members of a group, a school. . . . Collectively or separately, they eschew everything which approximates is-mism"; in *Troubadour* he later comments that in *Others* "a medium had arrived in which the diversified contributors, and not the editor, dictated the editorial policy."[91] Where Walden promoted the *Sturm* association and Expressionism as such, Kreymborg (perhaps too archly) denied the possibility of any group markings. Like *Others*, the *Little Review* and the *Dial* avoided aligning themselves with specific movements or principles. Moore remembers that "individuality was the great thing" at the *Dial*; "we certainly didn't have a policy, except I remember hearing the word 'intensity' very often."[92]

The closest thing to a European-style avant-garde in the United States formed in 1915–16, after an influx of French and other European artists into New York. Walter and Louise Arensberg's apartment became the site of gatherings three or four nights a week (the base of what was later called New York Dada) until 1918, when Marcel Duchamp and others returned to Europe.[93] Frequent attenders of these semiprivate salons included Francis Picabia, Man Ray, Charles Sheeler,

Katherine Dreier, Arthur Cravan, Wallace Stevens, and Loy.[94] Yet even the distinction between this group and the more amorphous meetings of other writers and artists held greater sway in the visual arts than in literature.

Moore was among the most significant American women of the period because she combined the infrastructural influence of a strong-minded editor and the aesthetic capital of an esteemed poet. As editor of the *Dial,* she selected what would be published, chose reviewers for new work, and suggested revisions on the manuscripts of her peers. Through her reviews and *Dial* "Comments" Moore also participated in developing the aesthetic criteria for judging modernist work, even though she did not call attention to her ideas as such by publishing editorial statements. Similarly, because her taste was more inclusive than that of many of her peers, its mark is less easily seen. She was as likely to read and review books on natural history, Chinese culture, theater, art, or fiction as on poetry, and she admired and published writers as different as Stein, Zukofsky, the Sitwells, and George Saintsbury. R. P. Blackmur speculates that Pound may have learned from Moore as much as she from him, and Pound urged Moore to take over *Poetry* after Monroe retired.[95] From 1925 until the end of 1929, while editing the *Dial,* Moore wrote no poetry. When the journal folded in 1929, she moved to Brooklyn and resumed writing poetry as well as continuing to review manuscripts and new publications. After her mother's death in 1947, she lived alone, increasingly lionized by literary and cultural circles until her death in 1972. By that time, she had published eleven volumes of verse, a play, and a translation of La Fontaine's fables, and she had won every major literary prize in the United States.

In contrast to the positioning of women in the American modernist literary scene, from 1900 to 1930 there were no major literary or art journals founded, run, or funded by women in Germany, and no presses founded and run by women. Similarly, no women of fortune commissioned work from or funded other women so that they could devote their lives to writing, although Lasker-Schüler was the beneficiary of several men and couples, and women did found a few galleries and cabarets.[96] With her husband, poet Maria Benemann founded the Horen Press, as well as a bookstore and exhibition space in Berlin, before World War I. Women also founded the Berlin Women Artists' Union in 1867; artist Alice Lex-Nerlinger and her husband Oskar founded *Die Zeitgemäßen* in 1924; and in 1927 Ida Dehmel founded the Society of German and Austrian Female Artists, which provided financial aid and exhibition opportunities to female artists (Meskimmon 4, 44). Female visual artists seemed more active in providing each other pragmatic support and generally in the infrastructure of modernism than were writers.

To my knowledge, no one has explained why this might be so. Perhaps financial structures are key: women controlled less money and had less access to private or institutional loans for capital outlay than men. It required more capital to found a journal than establish a society. Similarly, the greater prestige assigned to the word may have made editing more of a symbolic hurdle than founding an artists' union or cabaret. Theoretical assumptions, however, may also help to explain the difference. Literary Expressionism emphasized the exceptional artist or hero, implicitly defining the "individual" as male, and as superior, not just marginal, to society. As Huyssen summarizes, "Nietzsche's ascription of feminine characteristics to the masses is always tied to his aesthetic vision of the artist-philosopher-hero, the suffering loner who stands in irreconcilable opposition to modern democracy and its inauthentic culture" (194). New York's aesthetic individualism, on the other hand, was less firmly based on ideas of gender or class exceptionalism and was shared equally by women and men; hence it could more easily lead to cooperative planning and organizing, or to women's initiating roles in literature and the arts.

It is also difficult to know the extent to which German women initiated financial support for each other since such support typically came through a male partner or husband. Intellectual support may have been available in women's discussion circles, which were popular among bourgeois women, especially in the Jewish community. Lasker-Schüler participated in one around 1900, meeting at the home of Friederike Benjamin, Walter's aunt, and including feminist Lily Braun among its members (Reiß-Suckow 25). Such circles arose directly from the tradition of the private salon, many of which had been led by women.[97] Bourgeois salons, however, were isolated from the moving powers of the innovative arts. Moreover, because she had little formal education, Lasker-Schüler may have felt out of place in such circles. Reiß-Suckow speculates that the emphatic subjectivity of Lasker-Schüler's poems may have developed in part as a defensive strategy releasing her from the inevitable comparisons between her knowledge and that of her fellow poets, all of whom enjoyed more extensive formal education. Representing her poetry as a spontaneous production made it more difficult for others to criticize her ignorance: if creativity is "natural," it is out of the individual's control.[98] Whereas Moore competed in this regard by being more encyclopedic in her knowledge than any of her peers, Lasker-Schüler withdrew from such competition altogether.

Although Mina Loy spent less than three years of her life in New York before the mid-1930s and only one year in Berlin, these years were tremendously important to the development of her poetry. London, Paris, and Florence, however, provide the greatest influence on her early work. Mina Gertrude Lowy was the oldest of three daughters of Sigmund Lowy—a Jewish immigrant from Hungary—and Julia Bryan, a working-class English Protestant.[99] Loy described her London childhood as miserable. At seventeen (around 1900) she studied painting in Munich, returning to study further in London and then, in 1903, in Paris. In 1904, she married Stephen Haweis and began to exhibit under the name "Loy." In 1906, she was elected a member of the prestigious Salon d'Automne and then moved to Florence, where she also began to write poetry. According to her biographer Carolyn Burke, Loy was frequently depressed during her decade in Florence—in part because of ill health, in part because of dissatisfaction and infidelity on both sides of the marriage and her own lack of interest in mothering, and in part because of social isolation in Italy, although she was fluent in Italian as well as in French and German. Loy's financial dependence on her father's income and unwillingness to be or appear poor also complicated her life choices. Divorce from Haweis would terminate paternal support; remaining married allowed Loy to maintain a house (bought by her father) with cook and full-time care for her two children (a third had died on her first birthday). During these years in Florence, as also earlier in Paris, Loy suffered repeated nervous collapses, or periods of emotional distress, during which she took to her bed, sometimes for weeks. Later, she spent significant amounts of time in New York, Mexico, and Berlin as well as returning to England, France, and Italy. Without feeling localizing ties to parents, children, or community, she followed her sense of artistic stimulus across national borders and oceans. Where this would have spelt disaster for either Lasker-Schüler's or Moore's creativity, it seems to have stimulated Loy's. At the same time, there are clear patterns to where and when Loy engaged in the writing of poetry.

Loy wrote in spurts. While in Florence, she met Carl Van Vechten, became better acquainted with Gertrude Stein, and published her first poems. Both Van Vechten and Stein may have encouraged her to write.[100] After dabbling with Italian Futurism and affairs with F. T.

Marinetti and Giovanni Papini, she moved to New York in 1916, leaving her children with the nurse who was already primarily responsible for their care. During this first stay in New York, Loy published poems already written or drafted, wrote two brief one-acts, acted in a play by Alfred Kreymborg, edited one issue of *Others,* and collaborated in planning and writing articles for *The Blind Man.* It is hardly coincidental that the only period of her life in which she took on formal editing responsibilities occurred in New York, where so many women were similarly active. In 1918, Pound praised Loy's and Moore's work as "logopoeia" or "poetry that is akin to nothing but language, which is a dance of the intelligence among words and ideas."[101]

After her divorce from Haweis, Loy moved to Mexico to marry Arthur Cravan (January 1918). Cravan's disappearance after taking a trial sail off the coast of Mexico eleven months later sent Loy into an emotional tailspin from which she in some sense never recovered, although in 1920 she resumed painting and writing—traveling back to New York after stays in Buenos Aires, London, Switzerland, France, and Italy, where she left her and Cravan's daughter. In 1921 she rejoined her daughters in Florence (Haweis had by that time taken their son) and, in 1922, moved to Berlin, settling Joella (who studied dance) and Fabienne, with the nurse, nearby in Potsdam. When Loy returned to Paris in 1923, she was at the height of her fame. In 1926, Winters called Loy perhaps "the most astounding" of *Others'* poets: "Using an unexciting method, and writing of the drabbest of material, she has written seven or eight of the most brilliant and unshakably solid satirical poems of our time."[102]

In Paris, Loy published her first book of verse, *Lunar Baedecker* [*sic*], and then devoted her energy to manufacturing and selling collage-like lampshades and other decorative items, although she published an essay on Stein in the *Transatlantic Review* (1929). In 1931, after her son-in-law Julian Levy opened a gallery in New York, Loy became his advisor, eventually acting as a purchasing agent for several European and American artists living in Paris. During this time, she wrote no poetry and only sporadically wrote autobiographical prose. In 1936, because of the changing political situation in Europe and her increasing sense of isolation in Paris, Loy returned to New York for the first time since 1921. Initially she renewed a few contacts with friends, wrote poetry, and revised prose manuscripts begun in Paris. In the late 1930s, Loy also began painting again and launched a series of inventions, each of which she hoped to patent as a path to financial security. By the late-

1940s, however, she had turned primarily to the construction of collage sculpture made from objects found in the Bowery, where she moved in 1949. In 1953 she moved to Aspen to be near her daughters. *Lunar Baedeker & Time Tables* (1958), her second book, was greeted with acclaim. In brief introductory statements, Williams wrote that "the essence of her style is its directness in which she is exceeded by no one"; Denise Levertov celebrated Loy's "appetite for sounds," "dare-all contempt for falsification," and "electrifying truthfulness" with a value "indivisibly—technical and moral" (*LLB82* 1, 6–7). Later, Rachel Blau DuPlessis attributed the possible invention of the serial poem and the mixing of lyric modes with evaluative narrative to her 1915 "Love Songs" (*Genders* 55). In 1959, Loy received the Copley Foundation Award for Outstanding Achievement in Art for her "experiments in junk." For the most part, however, Loy had disappeared from the public eye. Far less directly affected by international politics than Lasker-Schüler and apparently less concerned about them than Moore, Loy's life pattern of response to the stimulus of an immediate creative environment and to passionate relationships left her increasingly bereft, as she tried to accept Cravan's mysterious disappearance, as the avant-garde groups she had known in Europe disbanded, and as she moved out of a cosmopolitan environment to Aspen.

Moore and Lasker-Schüler were attracted to the cosmopolitanism of New York and Berlin—the antiparochial, locally grounded internationalism characteristic of the metropolis. Moore called it "accessibility to experience"; Lasker-Schüler saw it as being "up to the minute" in art. In this sense, they lived in the same place—as did Loy in Paris, London, and Munich: they lived in the modern city. Each thrived on the stimulation of a lively, national and international community of writers and artists. On the other hand, Moore's greater infrastructural influence on modernism than either Lasker-Schüler's or Loy's was clearly enabled by the circumstances of her growing up in the United States and living in New York, where professionally minded women were already engaged in multiple pioneering efforts in the new arts. Similarly, Loy's peripatetic life habits may have been linked not just to her embattled family relationships but to her sense of London as too marked by British proprieties, too far removed from a bohemian avant-garde, to provide appropriate soil for her development. Throughout her most creative years, Loy traveled to remain with individuals supportive of, and in an atmosphere sufficiently stimulating for, her work. She never developed a relationship with a city or community of the kind that fed Moore and Lasker-Schüler so fruitfully for decades.

When Moore defines art, she does so in terms of the activity, motion, and cosmopolitan variety she found daily in New York. With her characteristic understatement, she writes that "complexity is not a crime" in "In The Days of Prismatic Color"—a poem declaring the superiority of a world containing Adam and Eve, or multiple points of view, to the crystalline purity of perspective possible only in an isolated garden containing "Adam alone" (*EP* 91). In "The Steeple-Jack," she similarly writes, "it is a privilege to see so / much confusion" (*CPo* 5). "Gusto" is among her most important defining characteristics for poetry and stands for the repeated unpredictable surfacing of the spontaneous, irrational, and idiosyncratic. David Kadlec describes Moore's aesthetic as contiguous, pragmatic, one of "accident" and "wayward semantic leaps."[103] Moore celebrates a nonhierarchical, intensely inquisitive engagement as key to the language and energy of poetry. For her, New York inspired passionate attention to the unexpectedness of daily life.

Lasker-Schüler predictably defines poetry differently. Living in a world that was itself far more chaotic, threatening, and unstable both personally and nationally, she celebrated not chaotic energy but intense intimacy, connection between individuals or between an individual and nature, or God. Uncharacteristically for German lyric of the early twentieth century, her poetry is frankly spoken, colloquial. "Komm, wir wollen uns näher verbergen. . . . Du, wir wollen uns tief küssen" [Come, we want to bury ourselves yet nearer together. . . . we want to kiss each other deeply], she writes in "Weltende" ("End of the World"; *WB,* no. 97). In "Heimweh" ("Homesickness") she writes "Ich kann die Sprache / Dieses kühlen Landes nicht / Und seinen Schritt nicht gehn" [I don't know the speech / of this cool land / and can't walk with its step], yet in her fantasy she is "ein buntes Bilderbuch / Auf deinem Schoß" [a colorful storybook / on your lap], sharing a kind of intimacy associated with parent and child (*WB,* no. 155). A repeated cry of the poems echoes in "O Gott": "O Gott, o Gott, wie weit bin ich von dir!" [Oh God, oh God, how far I am from you] (*WB,* no. 228). Perhaps in the instability of life in Berlin, Lasker-Schüler found intense personal and spiritual love to be the most powerful metaphor for art because love seemed so threatened, so fragile, so precarious.

Moore writes a poetry based on what she sees and reads, what can be observed with scientific as well as imaginative intensity. Lasker-Schüler bases her poetry and fiction on what can be imagined—fantasy figures, cities, worlds, and desired relationships. As I will discuss at greater length in the following chapters, Loy bases her poetic on static oppositions—the watched and the watcher, men and women, geniuses and common people—acknowledging only the occasional spark of (usually tainted) beauty. While no poetic comes from any single source, these poets' inclinations to write as they do were encouraged by the locations shaping their sense of private and communal potential, their ideas, and their sense of the (female, artistic) self.

3 *Gender Crossings*
Ova, Rat, and the Prince of Thebes

What's in a name?
—Shakespeare, *Romeo and Juliet*

Naming is a difficult and time-consuming process;
it concerns essences, and it means power.
—Jeanette Winterson, *Oranges Are Not the Only Fruit*

In the early twentieth century, the changes mandated by industrialism, capitalism, urbanization, and massive migrations of people within and across national borders called traditional gender roles into question, giving rise to new perceptions of sexuality, new professions and public roles for women, and generally to a disruption of previous assumptions about what constituted normalcy for individual men's and women's lives. This large pattern of disruption was inflected by multiple local and national differences. Both local and international patterns contributed to Loy's, Moore's, and Lasker-Schüler's self-formulations, performances of gender, and manipulations of the lyric "I." For all three poets, self-naming was allied to poetry both as an assertion of linguistic agency and as an opportunity for identity performance. Such opportunity results in part from traditional properties of the lyric poem: especially following the Romantic period's construction of the lyric as presenting a sincere speaker using the speech of common "men," lyric poetry was read with the widespread assumption that the poem's "I" reflected the author, if it was not simply interchangeable with an autobiographical "I." Poetic forms were read as transparently revealing authorial feeling: the love poem expressed its author's love for a particular person; an elegy expressed the poet's grief. Women were assumed to be especially suited to write a poetry of sincerity, often denigrated as occasional and sentimental, because of their supposed more emotional natures. Modernist poetry rejected both a clear speaking voice and the unquestioned relation of speaker to poet.[1] Just as visual artists experimented with representation, poets experimented with linguistic registers and "voice," resulting in Pound's *Personae* and juxtaposition of voices in the *Cantos,* or Eliot's early draft title of "The Waste Land" as "He Do the Police in Different Voices." In much modernist poetry, the lack of narrative and rational argument similarly undermined the positioning of the lyric speaker as the poet "himself." As part of this process, and despite his extensive expression of the personal in his own poems, Eliot argued for the "self-sacrifice" of the artist and the "extinction of personality" as crucial to "his" progress. Ideally, through depersonalization, art would "approach the condition of science."[2] As Lisa Steinman has argued, continued comparison of poetry to math, technology, and science assured the virility of poetry as well as its impersonal authority.[3]

According to Susan McCabe, H.D.'s, Stein's, and Amy Lowell's refusal of even the mask of depersonalization in their verse established contrary rules for the modernist poem.[4] To varying degrees, Loy, Lasker-Schüler, and Moore similarly eschew even apparent lyric impersonality. Like their male peers, they disrupt association of lyric language with a Wordsworthian "spontaneous overflow of emotion"; at the same time, they maintain strong illocutionary and suggestively autobiographical elements in their poems. Loy writes Carl Van Vechten that "to maintain my incognito, the hazard I chose was—poet," as though poetry constitutes disguise and disguise is risky, a "hazard," because it must reveal some construction of subjectivity even while it conceals others.[5] These poets reveal different formulations of selfhood in their poems; further, they manipulate the personal as well as the lyric "I" through experiments with naming, performing modes of subjective presence that simultaneously render fictitious and reveal desired or perceived aspects of their own psychic and social beings. Eschewing Whitman-like deictic markers of historical immediacy, they also disrupt conventions of the lyric speaker as universal. For them, as for other modernist poets, voice was constructed, not discovered or given. Its revelation of the poet was profound, but without confessional reference. Identity for them was historical and determined but also a matter of chosen alliances, hence always to some degree a matter of performance. Such constructed alliances functioned for them, as also especially for their female contemporaries, through self-naming in social relationships as well as within the texts of their poems.

In an essay on the nature of pronouns, Emile Benveniste contends that the first-person pronoun "is solely a 'reality of discourse,' and this is a very strange thing. *I* cannot be defined except in terms of 'locution,' not in terms of objects as a nominal sign. *I* signifies 'the person who is uttering the present instance of the discourse containing *I*.'"[6] Current theory on self-writing similarly declares that the autobiographical "I" is a fiction constructed to focus a particular narrative as life story. Claire MacDonald writes of the openly performative aspects of much autobiography as a staging of selfhood. According to Leigh Gilmore, gender is produced in autobiography "through a variety of discourses and practices that depict 'the individual' in relation to 'truth,' 'the real,' and 'identity.'"[7] The "I" of the lyric poem is even more performative in that a poem rarely names or describes its speaker but nonetheless asserts a subjective presence. A poem is a performative speech act. As Judith Butler, among others, has argued, one of the powers of discourse is "to produce that which it names"; gender constitution is one of the "subjectivating norms" preceding and producing the subject constituted by performative discourse.[8] In short, like a person in everyday performativity, a poem is an "active process of embodying certain cultural and historical possibilities" because its language (even if contradictorily) places itself in relation to normative discourse.[9] Lasker-Schüler, Loy, and Moore construct author figures through implied or stated positions of presence. Antje Lindenmeyer refers to Lasker-Schüler as inventing "biomythography," using a "'Penelope strategy' of creating and at the same time unraveling her autobiographical self, to stop it from becoming too fixed and unchangeable."[10] Alex Goody similarly writes of Loy's poetry as "auto-mythology," "which fundamentally refutes the transparent process of personal realization celebrated in the Romantic artist-hero."[11] Several critics write of Moore's animal poems as involving self-portraiture, and I have written about the colloquial aspects of her "personal/impersonal" poetic.[12] All three poets formulate subjective positions in their poems in ways consonant with the naming strategies of their private lives and with the public discourse on gender in the places they live.

In "At the Door of the House" (composed ca. 1915), Loy writes that "the nude woman / Stands for the world."[13] Although her immediate reference is to a card in the tarot pack, women generally in the poem seem to represent the world as naked integer—passed by, unfulfilled. The women of this poem passively wait for their future: the "eyes // Of Petronilla Lucia Letizia / Felicita / Filomena Amalia / Orsola Geltrude Caterina Delfina / Zita Bibiana Tarsilla / Eufemia" look "for the little love-tale / That never came true" (*LLB* 33–35). They are "riveted to the unrealizable." Notably, all names here are Italian. Loy could be suggesting that, in distinction to the expatriate Anglo-American women with whom she associated in Florence and who frequently orchestrated "love tale[s]," Italian women are captive to patriarchy. They make it no farther than the "door of the house." Yet the poem suggests that they are representative. The phonological structure of *Mina* resembles that of these Italian names with their feminine *-a*, *-ia* and *-na* endings, linking the author with her subject. Moreover, while a bourgeois daughter or matron might wait at home, a woman "at" a doorway also suggests solicitation, collapsing distinctions between women who repeatedly sell access to themselves and those who "sell" it only once, through the economic exchange of marriage. As the poem "Virgins Plus Curtains Minus Dots" puts it, "Nobody shouts / Virgins for sale," yet "Marriage [is] expensive," and women without *dots* (French for dowries) cannot marry. These "Virgins" live "behind curtains," throbbing, "Bait to the stars"; men, in contrast, "pass" by: "They are going somewhere" (*LLB* 22). The women's names in "At the Door of the House" do not function as author figures, but their sheer number suggests that waiting "at the door of the house" is the state of most, if not all, women in patriarchal culture.

Moore's perspective on women and gender bears little resemblance to Loy's. "Sojourn in the Whale," first published in the same 1917 *Others* anthology as "At the Door of the House," compares women both to Ireland and to the underdog heroes of fairy tales. Like fairy-tale figures who triumph over their harsh initial conditions, woman/Ireland has been forced to try "to open locked doors with a sword, threading / The points of needles, planting shade trees / Upside down" (*EP* 223). Addressing this composite figure, the speaker states:

You have lived and lived on every kind of shortage.
  You have been compelled by hags to spin
  Gold thread from straw and have heard men say: "There is a
      feminine
Temperament in direct contrast to

Ours which makes her do these things. Circumscribed by a
  Heritage of blindness and native
  Incompetence, she will become wise and will be forced to give
In. . . ."

(ll. 5–12)

Written shortly following the Easter Rising of 1916, Moore here uses the Irish revolt against British rule as a model for female emancipation.[14] Just as colonizers dehumanize the colonized through self-serving prejudice, men assume woman has an inferior "nature" that forces her to "give / In," or succumb to their wisdom and rule. The line break between "give" and "In" suggests the pressure or even violence required to enforce what men call the result of "Heritage" and "experience." The poem's speaker, however, indicates that the assumptions of the British, men, and by extension all who attempt to usurp the power of others are dead wrong: when "men say '. . . water seeks its own level,'" "you / Have smiled. 'Water in motion is far / From level.' You have seen it when obstacles happened to bar / The path—rise automatically." Adding science to the models of fairy-tale heroes and colonial uprising, Moore implies that in the physical order of things it is far more "natural" for women to "rise" to their own levels of competence and independence when facing "obstacles" than for them to succumb.

Like Loy, Moore represents women as trapped within patriarchal structures, but she represents the situation as temporary and concludes with a premonition of successful revolt. Moreover, where Loy's women are "sad" in their suspended animation, Moore's woman "smile[s]." Loy's poems reflect economic and class concerns: marriage is an economic arrangement between men, and the woman without a dowry is trapped behind "curtains." Moore's poem reflects the optimism of Irish nationalists, Progressive Era liberals, and the U.S. suffrage movement in 1917: given the forces in process, liberation across a number of spectrums seemed to her virtually "automatic." While events proved such optimism to be ill-founded, Moore does not change her fundamental belief that change is possible and that gender gives no group hierarchical capacity for knowledge, self-determination, or agency. Her concern is with political status, personal rights, and the discriminatory attitudes of any kind of prejudice. Loy's British-based, more class-conscious perspective is less optimistic about change: in her early poems one feels the psychological, social, and economic entrapment of women.

Where "At the Door of the House" foregrounds socially constructed spaces and "Sojourn in the Whale" evokes folkloric and political parallels, Lasker-Schüler's poetry typically stages its encounters in undefined or mythic realms, often outdoors. The early poem "Erkenntnis" exemplifies Lasker-Schüler's disruption of realistic categories of time and selfhood through an implied narrative of lawless desire. The word *Erkenntnis* translates as recognition or understanding, but it also alludes to the *Baum der Erkenntnis* or Tree of Knowledge. This poem's first stanza introduces not divine prohibition but "wild" human desire—"I naked! You naked!"—which in turn gives rise to "the original cry, Eve's song" [das Urgeschrei, Evas Lied], making Eve rather than Adam the original producer of language. In its central stanzas, the poem presents Eve's desire as both bringing about a fall from grace and as giving birth in a process independent of God and Adam, hence again usurping power not conventionally assigned to her:

Wilder, more impetuously, Eve, confess	*Wilder, Eva, bekenne reißender,*
The day you wrested from God,	*Den Tag, den Du Gott abrangst,*
That you saw the light too soon	*Da Du zu früh das Licht sahst*
And sank back into the blind cup of shame.	*Und in den blinden Kelch der Scham sankst.*
Gigantic	*Riesengroß*
Arises out of your lap	*Steigt aus Deinem Schoß*
At first timid, like fulfillment,	*Zuerst wie Erfüllung zagend,*
Then impetuously gathering,	*Dann sich ungestüm raffend,*
Creating itself	*Sich selbst schaffend*
God-soul	*Gott-Seele . . . .*

(*WB*, no. 103, ll. 14–23; ellipses Lasker-Schüler's)

This God-soul then "grows / Beyond the world / Losing its beginning / Beyond all time."[15] Eve's desire itself "was the snake." The God-like soul created from her transgression is a product of her snakelike desire and her *Schoß* (lap or womb). This is a truly virgin birth, and its offspring (like Jesus) is immortal but independent of God. Moreover, Eve has in some sense struggled with God and won "the day" from him, in the power of her impetuous desire. While the poem does not entirely cohere, its Eve is a model of self-creation, the expression of something that will outlast the shamed corporeal being. Later in the poem, the speaker says, "You are beautiful," and calls on Eve to "turn back" to Eden—not to give up her original claim to *Erkenntnis.* "Complete your blossoming, temptress" [Blühe aus, Verführerin], the poet calls, as though Eve herself is a tree that can bear fruits of knowledge.

That Eve continues "now" to flee Eden underscores the extent to which her position is constructed: if she feels shame, Eve will flee. The speaker works to change Eve's self-conception by reinterpreting her act and its consequence. Eve's temptation, in the speaker's eyes, is to challenge authority that would block her access to knowledge, perception, recognition, understanding, realization—all possibilities in English as translations of *Erkenntnis.* Eve evokes the desire for consciousness but also for stepping out of set patterns. Following this logic, the "you" with whom the speaker initially stands naked is linked to the speaker by desire, not by law or social categories. "We rip off our coverings," the speaker says in the introductory lines, yet what they reveal is nakedness itself, not gendered bodies. For Lasker-Schüler, the merging of physical bodies or of the self with anything beyond its boundaries manifests the instability of authoritarian limitations, including those of gender polarization, but she identifies no historical or social authority as responsible for such limitation, returning instead to an originary scene where Eve struggles directly with God. Unlike Loy, Lasker-Schüler provides no description of women's lives in the present. Unlike Moore, she constructs no historical or political analogies for gender revolution. While in their early poems Loy provides no way out of the impasse of gender relations and Moore suggests a perhaps too-easy solution, analogous to natural laws, Lasker-Schüler constructs a mythic model for change, suggesting both flaws in the grand cultural narratives of religion and "nature" or "essence" and possibilities for change in the ways women conceive their own lives in relation to them—for example, through heroism rather than shame, and through struggle rather than victimization.

As even this quick glance at three poems suggests, and although all three poets can be described as feminist, Loy, Moore, and Lasker-Schüler take different approaches to the lyric, and structure different kinds of relationship between a poem's speaker and performances of selfhood. Generally, in this period, ambitious female artists and writers demonstrated astute consciousness that both selfhood and gender were matters of display and artifice. Whatever they thought of "natural" qualities of male- or femaleness, they knew that they would be judged according to their willingness to perform cultural expectations of the feminine. Early theorization of the feminine as performed also begins in these decades. Joan Rivière's groundbreaking essay "Womanliness as a Masquerade" was published in 1929 and reflected the public and private experiments with self-formulation and costuming of the preceding decades.[16] Rivière concludes that "the essential nature of fully developed femininity" is artifice. Women masquerade as "women"; they do not express their "true" nature through manners, dress, or any other aspect of self-presentation. While few men or women in the United States, Germany, or Italy adopted this extreme view, one could not have read any newspaper of the period without being aware that traditional gender definitions showed serious strain. Women's movements were the primary institutions responsible for such changing views, and to varying extents all three poets of this study position themselves in relation to the movements with which they were most familiar.

The women's movement in the United States fought for political, legal, and economic equality between the sexes through legislation and broad-based institutional change. This movement manifested itself in multiple women's associations and reform movements, many of which came together in the late nineteenth century in support of suffrage.[17] Because of the long tradition of women's participation in reform campaigns, the twentieth-century women's movement conceived of its legal and moral goals within the context of reform, hence as possible without violent rebellion or the rejection of most middle-class values. This is one of the reasons that women's suffrage associations in the United States resorted to less radical extremes than parallel organizations in Britain. In England, "suffragettes"—the militant wing of British suffrage—favored "tactics of guerilla warfare" such as disrupting political meetings, provoking their own arrests to gain publicity, and attacking members of Parliament with whips (Smith 396). Such tactics were admired by some feminists in the United States. For the most part, however, the women's movement was consonant with progressive middle-class women's ideas of reform.[18]

According to Nancy Cott, by 1910 women's associations were moving away from nineteenth-century essentialized definitions of gender and instead stressing the diversity of women's experiences and seeking legal and intellectual equality with men while remaining "loyal politically and ideologically" to women.[19] The goal of such thinking was to degender both women and men rather than to redraw the lines of distinction. Unlike late-twentieth-century feminism, then, early feminism saw gender neutrality as liberating. The contemporary ideology of professionalism (linked to increasingly widespread higher education for women) similarly promoted the forging of a "human sex." Professions claimed to be "sex neutral" (Cott 216). Women who educated themselves "like men" theoretically stood an equal chance of advancing within them.

The first self-described American feminist movement got its start in Greenwich Village. Emma Goldman edited *Mother Earth* from 1906 until 1917 and strongly supported women's right to sexual autonomy and reproductive freedom—as did Margaret Sanger, who founded and edited *Woman Rebel*, beginning in 1914. Several women in the Village met weekly in a feminist discussion group called Heterodoxy.[20] Beginning in 1910, the Equality League organized annual suffrage parades in New York, in which thousands of women marched "with immense dignity before awed and enthusiastic crowds" down Fifth Avenue (K. Smith 396). These parades had a huge effect on public consciousness of women's issues. On March 3, 1913, feminists staged a similar parade in Washington, D.C., in which bystanders heckled the eight thousand marching women while police stood by—despite the fact that the organizers had obtained a permit and requested police supervision. On February 23, Marianne Moore wrote her family from Baltimore that she had studied "the Woman Suffrage program" and planned "to march with the authors and artists" (RML VI.10.03). It appears from the ensuing correspondence that she did not join the march, but she pasted several clippings about it and the ensuing calls for a national investigation of the police into a scrapbook.[21]

After 1920, a backlash developed in the United States against both feminism and radical reform politics. Having obtained the vote, women's groups were split about further directions for the powerful political lobby they had developed, and younger women had little interest in joining their ranks. The new generation was more interested in a lifestyle feminism of individual privileges and sexual reform than in broadly based legal and institutional change, and they saw homosocial organizations as old-fashioned, preferring to identify themselves politically, socially, and personally with men. Such attitudes resulted directly from other transformative developments in American culture, in particular the commodification of heterosexuality, and the increased significance assigned sexuality generally as a defining aspect of life.[22] This turn to the personal as political significantly widened the boundaries of women's lives but weakened the core of women's political organizing. Rayna Rapp and Ellen Ross refer to the 1920s as a period of "heterosexual revolution," in which consumerism allied itself with heterosexual conceptions of romance and family, implicitly labeling all female-centered concerns as deviant (56). Themes of female independence were also co-opted through movies, popular literature, and fashion (59). Consequently, women coming of age in the 1920s had a different sense of themselves and of feminism from those coming of age earlier in the century.

Moore articulated feminist arguments in her college letters and was active in suffrage campaigning after college. In New York, she and her mother distributed leaflets supporting a female candidate at the polls in 1919.[23] Moore writes in "Marriage": "experience attests / that men have power / and sometimes one is made to feel it" (*EP* 120); her definition of marriage as an "institution" or "enterprise" rather than a holy bond indicates her critical eye toward gender institutions generally.

Such thinking meshed well with the broad-based social and legal goals of early Village feminism. Loy's feminism, in contrast, was focused on economic, psychological, and sexual liberation at the level of personal freedoms.[24] Her relative isolation from educational or social contexts encouraging political activism may explain this focus in part: from the age of seventeen, Loy lived primarily outside of England and attended only art schools. Even as a child, Loy was educated at home by governesses, except for three years in a progressive school in Hampstead. Hence, even in her childhood, she was not in daily contact with girls her own age; Burke describes "her first attempts at friendship" as occurring when she was about twelve (*BM* 32). The Anglo-American community in Florence was not noted for its political activism.[25] While Moore was finishing high school, majoring in politics, economics, and history at Bryn Mawr, and teaching at the Carlisle Indian School, Loy was primarily concerned with gaining independence from her family, the sexual politics of various art schools, groups, or relationships, birthing children, and establishing herself as a painter. Consequently, it is hardly surprising that for Loy feminism took the form of insistence on women's sexual and economic independence from marriage.

Significantly, when Loy arrived in New York in late 1916, she moved into an apartment on the Upper West Side near the Arensbergs, not into the Village, and her closest ties were with the European French speakers of the Arensberg circle. The location of the Arensbergs' apartment marked its political as well as its geographical distance from the Village. Because Duchamp spoke little English upon his arrival, this group was relatively closed. Fluency in French and familiarity with Paris provided a clear demarcation of who was in or out, and Loy had the credentials for joining the inner circle—although, according to Burke, she felt some discomfort with its often misogynistic prestige and power games (*BM* 214–19). By the spring of 1917—less than half a year after her arrival in New York—she was deeply involved with the English-Swiss Cravan, whom she would marry in January 1918. In short, in New York—as in Paris and Florence—Loy spent much of her time with expatriates.

Loy was critical of reform and of organized women's movements, in a mode resembling that of militant British suffragettes. Her 1914 "Feminist Manifesto" begins "The feminist movement as at present instituted is ***Inadequate*** . . . NO scratching on the surface of the rubbish heap of tradition, will bring about ***Reform***, the only method is ***Absolute Demolition***. Cease to place your confidence in economic legislation, vice-crusades & uniform education. . . . Professional & commercial careers are opening up for you—***Is that all you want?***" (*LLB* 153). In the same year, in a letter to Mabel Dodge, Loy refers to her manifesto as a "fragment of Feminist tirade," continuing: "I feel rather hopeless of devotion to the Woman-cause" (*LLB* 216). Loy's upbringing in Britain and years in Munich, Paris, and Florence gave her no ties to the ideology of rights articulated by American feminists or to a history of female leadership in reform; but the highly publicized antimale attitudes of British suffragettes would also not have appealed to her in these years of her own intense heterosexual negotiations. Consequently, it is not surprising that Loy felt "hopeless of devotion" to organized feminism.[26] Instead, her interest was in liberating female sexuality and the language of female desire from Victorian double-standards and prudery.

In Germany, conceptions of gender essentialism were stronger than in the United States or England. Both the bourgeois and the proletarian women's movements advocated women's economic gains and educational rights, but also saw women's maternal qualities *(Mütterlichkeit)* as natural.[27] Modeled on the National American Women Suffrage Association, the Federation of German Women's Associations (1894) was made up of several smaller organizations; the Jewish Women's Federation was founded in 1904.[28] The federation sought to expand the range and improve the conditions of women's lives, not radically redefine female roles or activity. In contrast, the proletarian women's movement emphasized economic equity, convinced that emancipation for women could only follow the socialist reorganization of all property (Frevert 146; Kolinsky 10–11). Their focus was the "liberation of proletarian women from Capitalist economic oppression," not achieving greater status for "feminine" labor or curtailing male domination through reform (Frevert 147). Both groups, however, believed in the uniqueness of women's experience. Even novelist and radical feminist Lily Braun, who moved from the bourgeois to the Social Democratic Party women's movement, believed that "to choose not to have children was a violation of one's femininity."[29]

The most prestigious feminist association in Berlin was the General German Association of Women Teachers, founded by Helene Lange and her colleagues in 1890, which by the turn of the century, was the largest professional association for women in Germany, with sixteen thousand members. Associations of women workers also first came into being in Berlin, in the 1880s. In 1895, Lily Braun edited *Die Frauenbewegung (The Women's Movement)* with Minna Cauer, who continued editing it until 1919. In 1908, Jewish feminist Alice Salomon founded the Women's School of Social Work. Lasker-Schüler was involved in no women's organization and rarely manifested explicit feminist concerns. In 1911, she spent time with women's rights campaigner Eliza Ichenhäuser in Munich (*MM* 82) and in the same year published a sketch in *Der Sturm* praising Franziska Schultz—a social worker and founder of a Berlin home for unwed mothers and infants. In a letter to Jethro Bithell, however, the poet writes, "I'm always free as a bird—not free in the sense of women's rights advocates."[30]

Even more than in the United States, in Germany the 1920s brought a less favorable climate for feminist organizations. Katherina von Ankum writes that the liberation of women was increasingly represented in the German media as a foreign idea (French or American), and not just women but women's movements were blamed for urban degeneracy; maternal women were idealized as the potential "redeemers of modernization."[31] Here, too, during the 1920s, younger women rejected what they saw as women's rights associations led by "old" and single women. The heterosexual focus of movies, advertising, and fashion made prewar women's issues seem dull. Young modern women felt trapped between the politics of "old-fashioned" feminism and popular pressure to manifest a clear "biological conscience" through becoming a mother.[32]

Expressionists had little to do with feminism. While supporting some platforms of national women's associations, they enthusiastically essentialized definitions of gender, marking "genius," and especially poetic genius, as masculine. Barbara Wright explains this inclination in relation to the German intellectual tradition: the long history of philosophical emphasis on *das Wesentliche*, the nature or essence of being, gave rise to repeated examinations of the nature of the masculine and the feminine. As Wright points out, many Expressionist writers had a background of studying philosophy or law.[33] Additionally, Expressionism defined itself as "manly" in contrast to the "effeminacy" of Art Nouveau and Impressionism. Coupled with antibourgeois attitudes and the general association of bourgeois values with femininity, emphasis on *das Wesentliche* led male Expressionists to support the liberation of women only insofar as such liberation provided men greater sexual access to women: there was, for example, widespread support for the campaign protesting Germany's antiabortion law (paragraph 218).[34] Especially in the early 1910s the exploration of women's mysterious nature was a favorite topic, and most essays articulated views directly or implicitly in opposition to the goals of women's movements (Wright 587).

Expressionists were not unusual in these views. According to Gerald Izenberg, (German) male anxiety about threats to masculinity generally took the form of opposition to women's emancipation movements: "The vast majority of men opposed these movements," he wrote, "and there is plenty of evidence showing that many men were terrified by them far out of proportion to their size or the threat they realistically posed to male prerogatives in education, politics, or the arts."[35] Theoretical physicist Max Planck, for example, wrote in 1897 that it could "not be stressed enough that Nature herself assigned to women the role of mother and housewife, and that to ignore natural laws is to invite great damage which will in this case be inflicted upon coming generations"; in 1907, Emil Hannover wrote that "Manliness is one of the first requirements of art."[36] Izenberg's *Modernism and Masculinity* explains these attitudes as a result of cultural history. As he summarizes, from 1885 through World War I, "manhood in jeopardy" was a repeated theme of European high modernism. This period coincides exactly with the rise of strong women's movements and with increasing criticism of bourgeois ideals of both gender and culture. At the same time, Izenberg sees a deep ambivalence toward masculinity, especially for artists, within the German bourgeoisie (8). Masculinity had long been defined as that which was specifically not feminine; women "were" emotional, physical, passive; hence men were rational, spiritual, and active. Yet in general terms culture and religion were associated with the feminine (6–7). This contradictory association created a dilemma for artistic men: to be creative required the realms of art and spirit, which were identified with the male individually but with the female socially and culturally. While similar ambivalence existed in the United States, the crisis in masculinity took a less virulent form and had a smaller impact on innovative literary production there, perhaps because of women's and feminists' roles in developing early American modernism.

Late-twentieth-century gender theory emphasizes the contextual performance of gender in ways useful for understanding the interplay of particular framing milieus with women's creativity and lives. Social definition varies according to time and place and occurs cumulatively. Consequently, changes in such definition occur slowly. Virginia Woolf writes of women's need to develop a "habit of freedom and the courage to write exactly what we think" over a period of generations (117). Bourdieu writes of the habitus as a concept of agent free from both idealistic subjectivity and mechanistic causality: the habitus is a "set of dispositions which generates practices and perceptions," inculcated over a period of time and, once formed, lasting throughout a lifetime.[37] As

Judith Butler puts it, the habitus is a site wherein social conventions animate bodies "which, in turn, reproduce and ritualize those conventions as practices."[38] Habit and habitus are both formed in a historical location and themselves become formative. Butler emphasizes the linguistic aspects of this process. As she summarizes, the habitus "generates *dispositions* which are credited with 'inclining' the social subject to act in relative conformity with the ostensibly objective demands of the field" (116). Both this inclination and the cultural field's demands occur in part through language, and particularly through performative speech-acts. Butler writes that "to be hailed or addressed by a social interpellation is to be constituted discursively and socially at once"; hence, "the social performative is a crucial part not only of subject *formation,* but of the ongoing political contestation and reformulation of the subject as well" (120, 125). The language of naming and address both generates subject formation and may expand or contest conformity in the subject's social production. In more metaphorical terms, Monique Wittig theorizes similarly about the role of language in changing social norms: "Humankind must find another name for itself and another system of grammar that will do away with genders, the linguistic indicator of political oppression"; "language casts sheaves of reality upon the social body, stamping it and violently shaping it."[39] By implication, to change language is to reshape the social body. Whether radical or subtle in their degrees of difference from social norms, the names one calls oneself and by which one is called, the descriptors associated with one's physical being, and the grammar through which one expresses one's presence all mark both the social body and subject formation.[40] Self-naming may be an intensely political act.

Although without the benefit of articulated theorizing, early-twentieth-century female writers were as a group exceptionally conscious of the politics of naming and gave great attention to what they called themselves and how they were publicly named. Many famous authors have changed their names: Samuel Clemens adopted the pen name Mark Twain, and Jósef Teodor Konrad Korzeniowiski anglicized his name to Joseph Conrad. Among the more famous examples of women's name changes early in the twentieth century are Russian Anna Gorenko's self-naming as Akhmatova and American Hilda Doolittle's abbreviation of her name to H.D. and publication under a variety of names, including Delia Alton, Rhoda Peter, Sylvania Penn, and John Helforth. French Sidonie-Gabrielle Colette abbreviated her name to Colette. German photographers Grete Stern and Ellen Auerbach worked together under the names Ringl and Pit; Italian Futurist

Eva Kühn Amendola published as Magamal, and Belgian poet Marie Closset as Jean Dominique. British Winnifred Ellerman changed her name to Bryher. Russian Zinaida Gippius published under several male pseudonyms, most frequently as Anton Krainy. Other examples of self-naming include Russian painter Marevna (born Maria Vorobëv); Australian George Egerton (born Mary C. Dunne); New Zealander Katherine Mansfield (born Beauchamp); French Vernon Lee (born Violet Paget), Claude Cahun (born Lucy Schwob), and Marcel Moore (born Suzanne Malherbe); Irish Lola Ridge was born Rose Emily. In Germany, Ida Dehmel was called Frau Isi; Ricarda Huchs published as R. I. Carda and Richard Hugo; Gertrud Kolmar was born Chodziesner; Anna Seghers was born Netty Reiling; and Henriette Hardenberg was born Margarete Rosenberg. British writers include Jean Rhys (born Ella Williams), Renée Vivien (born Pauline Mary Tarn), Gluck (born Hannah Gluckstein), Radclyffe Hall (born Marguerite Radclyffe-Hall), Rebecca West (born Cicily Isabel Fairfield), and Harriet Weaver, who published as Josephine Wright and was addressed by friends as Josephine or, in her Communist period, Comrade Josephine. In the United States, Katherine Ann Porter was born Callie Russell Porter;[41] Djuna Barnes published as Lady Lydia Steptoe, and Jane Heap as "R" and Garnerin; Janet Flanner wrote her "Letters from Paris" for the *New Yorker* under the name Genêt; Edna St. Vincent Millay published caustic magazine sketches as Nancy Boyd; Henrietta Walter Stettheimer published as Henrie Waste; Laura Reichenthal legally changed her name to Riding; and Willa Cather went by Will or William in her youth and college years.

Several female writers who published under their own names engaged in intimate nicknaming, often well-known within their circle of friends: Stein was "Baby" to Alice B. Toklas, and Djuna Barnes and Thelma Wood called each other, respectively, Momma or Junie and Papa or Simon; Natalie Barney called herself and was painted by Brooks as "the Amazon."[42] Among other names, Bryher called H.D. Horse or Kat, while H.D. called Bryher Fido; Radclyffe Hall went by the names Peter (as a child) and John. Amy Lowell called Ada Russell, her longtime companion, Peter or Mr. Pete, and within her family Edna St. Vincent Millay was called Vincent. Modernist men also used pseudonyms, code-naming, or changed their names. Famously, Ford Maddox Hueffer became Ford Maddox Ford, Emmanual Radnitsky became Man Ray, and T. S. Eliot was Possum to friends; less famously, Pound published as Bastien von Helmholtz, William Atheling, and B. H. Dias, among other names. The practice was, however, far more marked among women than among men. Name changes may provide psychological escape from prohibitive familial circumstances, greater freedom of expression, or independence from an array of limiting social conditions; to change one's name is to generate at least the potential for new subject formation. As is obvious from the list above, for women regendering played a significant role in such changes, even when the adopted name was not explicitly masculine. H.D., for example, was assumed to be male by her earliest reviewers because men, not women, presumably went by initials (as also patronymics). Literary men did not use pseudonyms or nicknames to cross gender.

Nicknames for private use function differently from names adopted publicly and professionally. The former cannot influence public perception of the individual. On the other hand, the inclination to adopt alternate names signifies a self-determined, and in some cases a fluid, sense of identity. One way in which women responded to the challenge of entering the male-dominated literary profession was by understanding the self as constructed, hence capable of change. Lasker-Schüler puts this defensively: "I myself can't be found, so can't be destroyed except by myself."[43] Whether or not the world knew of these parallel or layered performances was relatively unimportant. As Emily Dickinson wrote in the 1860s, when she rejected "The name They dropped opon my face," she "stopped being Their's"; previously "a half-unconscious Queen," the speaker claims the "Will to choose, / Or to reject" when she declares her independence.[44] Her choice of "just a Crown" at the end of the poem does not distinguish her visibly from her previous "half-unconscious" royalty, just as the substitution of one female name for another does not openly mark social disruption, but the individual knows the self-authorizing involved in such change.

Early-twentieth-century women's renaming, however, needs to be distinguished both from nineteenth- and from late-twentieth-century patterns and theories. Modernist name change was not primarily a matter of disguise or pseudonym, as it was for the Brontë sisters or George Eliot. Name change was typically just one of the many manifestations of modernist women's gender and cultural politics. At the same time, women like Loy, Lasker-Schüler, and Moore were uninterested in a trickster-like conception of indeterminate fluidity, in which endless self-transformation makes the individual into a cultural prankster—mythic or mischievous, or both.[45] Theirs is not an Irigarayan concept of the feminine as endlessly multiple, by nature unfixed. Instead, their naming disrupts particular historical and gendered structures while participating in other local and international prejudices and structures of their times; it has a definite and positioning as well as a destabilizing function. Like many of their peers, Loy, Moore, and Lasker-Schüler assigned themselves a variety of names over a period of several years. Through these appellations and through the self-portraiture and linguistic strategies of their poems, they construct assertive performances of gender and selfhood illustrative of the local and international patterns previously described.

Loy/Ova/Goy

Mina Lowy began to exhibit under the name Loy around the time of her marriage to Stephen Haweis in January 1904. By taking the name "Loy," she rejects not only the expected use of her husband's name but her father's name—perhaps to avoid its Eastern European and Jewish look.[46] If so, in distancing herself from her ancestry, she follows her father's implied lead: he reputedly called her "Goy" when she was a girl, stamping her non-Jewishness paradoxically, insofar as the term *goy* has meaning only within a Jewish environment. Loy is the only name under which the poet published, and the timing of her choice indicates that it represents a declaration of independence; as Dickinson says, Loy, although married, had "stopped being Their's." In 1917, upon obtaining her divorce from Haweis, Loy legally adopted this professional name.

Loy also took a variety of given names. In Munich as a teenager, she was playfully called Dusie because of her confusion of the pronouns *Du* and *Sie.* While living in Florence, she refers to herself in letters as Minna Levi, Minn Lowey, Minna Loy, and Jemima, and in correspondence with Mabel Dodge, she signed herself "Doosie" or "Doose" (addressing Dodge as "Moose").[47] In poems and prose manuscripts, Loy constructs figures of selfhood called Gina ("The Effectual Marriage or Insipid Narrative of Gina and Miovanni," 1915), the anagrammatic Nima Lyo, Anim Yol, and Imna Oly ("Lion's Jaws," 1920), Ova ("Anglo-Mongrels and the Rose," 1923–25), Maraquita ("Preceptors of Childhood, or the Nurses of Maraquita," 1921), Daniel ("Hush Money," n.d.) and even returns to the name Goy ("Goy Israels," n.d.).[48] These figures mythologize the author as "insipid[ly]" feminine (Gina), archetypally female (Ova, the reproductive egg), the prodigal son (Daniel), gentile within a Jewish family (Goy Israels), and unstably multiple (in the anagrams). In "Giovanni Franchi" (1916), the speaker also refers to "the threewomen," who are something between independent entities and a conglomerate self. Unlike Lasker-Schüler's and Moore's names, Loy's do not function in any single way or reveal a particular pattern.

Critics have associated Loy's repeated renaming with a desire to cover her tracks or remain anonymous in the public eye. Roger Conover reports rumors in 1920s Paris that Loy "was not a real person at all, but a forged persona." She encouraged such response, he suggests, through her construction of "deliberately camouflaging demonstrative and theatrical first-persons behind inscrutable selves" (*LLB82* xviii, xvii). Susan Gilmore similarly describes Loy's poetic of "impersonality" as imposture. Certainly in the period between 1914 and 1919, Loy wrote out a number of automythologies, suggesting that her early poetry emerged partly in response to her shifting formulations of selfhood. Virginia Kouidis calls this early work "poems of the female self," commenting that Loy grounds "spiritual autobiography in uniquely female experience."[49] Some of these author figures play so transparently on the poet's name that they hardly function as camouflage; at the same time, the disruptive structures of language in the poems disrupt a reading of historically voiced or realist subjectivity, calling attention to the word as artifact and the poems as made. Maeera Shreiber links this aspect of Loy's art to Futurist collage, understanding Loy's writing as aggravating states of separation.[50] To my mind, Loy constructed these and other self-formulations to write out the logical consequences of particular attitudes or types of behavior that she had observed among women, could imagine for herself, or had herself in some form enacted. The poems are not autobiography. Through name-play, however, they invite the reader to link their narratives with the author. It is significant that she constructs most of these poetic automythologies in Florence, where she was both most socially isolated and living in the most patriarchal general and avant-garde culture she was to know.[51]

Loy's poem "Lion's Jaws" (composed 1919) is a poetic roman à clef summarizing the poet's reflections on her years in Florence. In this poem, "the 'excepted' woman" escapes from the "lion's jaws" of masculine sexual and intellectual domination. Representing the Futurists as "flabbergasts," Loy depicts three male characters (recognizable as Italian nationalist Gabriele D'Annunzio and Futurists Filippo Marinetti and Giovani Papini) as attended by the "myriad-fleshed Mistress," and as seeking "every feminine opportunity" for their competitive sexual amusement. For them, manifestos and creeds function as "fashions in lechery," such that "new schools" of thought can hardly be distinguished from "new courtships." In particular, the two "flabbergasts" compete against the popular D'Annunzio and against each other, while the "'excepted'" woman's "cautious pride" in being the exception who is accepted contrasts with her sense of "betrayal / of Woman wholesale / to warrant her surrender / with a sense of . . . Victory" (*LLB* 47–48; ellipses Loy's).

This poem condemns both the egocentric lechery of political and literary masculinity and the complicity of women who acquiesce to it, feeling simultaneously chosen or victorious and like a conquered people, traitor to themselves and to "Woman wholesale." Near the end of the poem, Loy introduces "Nima Lyo, alias Anim Yol, alias / Imna Oly / (secret service buffoon to the Woman's Cause)" as the sender of "duplicate petitions" to "Ram" and "Bap"—reductive nicknames for the flabbergasts—offering "to be the lurid mother of 'their' flabbergast child." "As for Imna Oly . . . She is not quite a lady," the speaker later comments. Yet because the comment comes in the form of agreement with "Mrs. Krar Standing Hail"—a ridiculous figure and a pseudonym for a woman who had an affair with Haweis—its irony is underlined (*LLB* 187). Who would want to be a lady in a world where men manipulate even their political and artistic ideals into aphrodisiac advertising? As she comments in "There is No Life or Death," "tame things / Have no immensity" (*LLB* 3). Moreover, while there may be self-parody in Loy's allusion to her own affairs with both Marinetti and Papini in Oly's "duplicate petitions" to motherhood, one might indeed see her poetry as in some sense the product of her affair with Futurism. Loy's poetic "child," however, is fully her own. In 1914, she writes to Carl Van Vechten, "If you like you can say that Marinetti influenced me—merely by waking me up—[but] I am in no way *considered* a Futurist by futurists" (*LLB* 188). By 1919, Loy had left Futurism's manifestos and posturing behind. Futurism did, however, seem to trigger her early poems, with their extreme gender-consciousness and aggressive womanly assertion.

Loy's first publication aligned her with the Futurists, even to the point of promoting "the tremendous truth of Futurism" in masculine pronouns: "THUS shall evolve the language of the Future THROUGH derision of Humanity as it appears— / TO arrive at respect for man as he shall be," referring to the Futurist as "HE."[52] Later the same year, however, she writes an answering "Feminist Manifesto" (first published in 1982). Perhaps with reference to the restricted choices offered women of her generation, Loy asserts that women must choose "between ***Parasitism, & Prostitution***—*or Negation*" (*LLB* 154). In its outrageousness, this representation of the gender economy both counters the negativity of Futurist sexualized representations of woman and satirizes the social purity arguments of some feminists. At the same time, this manifesto and several early poems continued Futurist emphasis on the sexual. For Loy at this point in her life, liberation of the spirit was inseparable from the body. In their enthusiasm for the machine, Futurists associated the body with mortality and projected both mortality and materiality onto the female, demonizing women's bodies while conceiving their own as phallic cores of masculine energy.[53] Loy both asserts positive, independent female sexual energy and mocks masculine posturing in "Lion's Jaws," "The Effectual Marriage," "Three Moments in Paris," "Sketch of a Man on a Platform," "Giovanni Franchi," and "Human Cylinders."

"The Effectual Marriage or The Insipid Narrative of Gina and Miovanni" is perhaps Loy's bitterest poem on heterosexual conventions. Here Miovanni "kindly kept" Gina in the kitchen. "So," the poem's speaker speculates, "here we might dispense with her":

> Gina being a female
> But she was more than that
> Being an incipience a correlative
> An instigation of the reaction of man
> From the palpable to the transcendent
> Mollescent irritant of his fantasy
> Gina had her use
>
> (*LLB* 36)

Gina is so inchoate, so spiritually and intellectually unformed as to be a mere "incipience"; her "use" is to irritate "his fantasy," like sand in an oyster shell. He "was magnificently man," and she "insignificantly a woman who understood" but never "thought." At the end of the poem we learn that this woman "with no axis to revolve on" save the monumentality of her man is "mad"—as, Loy implies, a woman must be to submit to such a dehumanizing relationship.

Women are never independent of a heterosexual and sexist economy in Loy's "Feminist Manifesto," hence: "Men & women are enemies, with the enmity of the exploited for the parasite, the parasite for the exploited. . . . The only point at which the interests of the sexes merge—is the sexual embrace." Further, full personhood demands sexual expressiveness: "the woman who is a poor mistress will be an incompetent mother—an inferior mentality." To achieve liberation within this heterosexist economy, Loy reasons, it is necessary to destroy the "fictitious value of woman as identified with her physical purity" or the commodification of virginity. Loy satirically calls for "surgical *destruction of virginity*" at puberty, to put women on an equal basis with

men in the pursuit of sexual pleasure.[54] Further, Loy asserts that sexuality must be detached from emotional commitment: "women must destroy in themselves, the desire to be loved—" (*LLB* 154–55). Early in her manifesto Loy calls on women to "deny" the "pathetic clap-trap war cry ***Woman is the equal of man***" and "leave off looking to men to find out what you are ***not***" (152–53). Anticipating theorists like Luce Irigaray, she insists that woman's fulfillment must come from her own experience, not from definitions based on man's—although for her the key experience seems to be heterosexual. Even breathing takes heterosexual form in "Ignoramus," where "You can hear the heart beating / Accoupling / Of the masculine and feminine / Universal principles / Mating" (*LLB82* 65). She writes to Carl Van Vechten in 1915, "I know nothing but life—and that is generally reducible to sex. . . . I'm trying to think of a subject that's not sexy to write about . . . & I can't in life" (*LLB* 189–90).

Indeed, Loy's early poems revolve around the critique of patriarchy and sex. The poem "Parturition" juxtaposes a woman's painful labor with her husband's dashing upstairs to another woman's apartment, singing. The speaker then comments: "The irresponsibility of the male / Leaves woman her superior Inferiority / He is running up-stairs // I am climbing a distorted mountain of agony" (*LLB* 5). "Superior inferiority" describes well the ambivalence underlying the angry energy of these early poems. As the anagrammatic self-positioning in "The Effectual Marriage" implies, these poems also manifest Loy's coming to terms with her own authority as poet: the figures Gina and Miovanni transparently allude to Mina and Giovanni Papini. While the poem is not about their relationship, Loy imagines in it an extreme but logical outcome of any hierarchical and essentialist conception of the sexes. "Songs to Joannes" (1917) also apparently written in response to her affair with Papini, similarly presents its lovers as representative (*Giovanni* is the Italian form of *Joannes* or *John*).[55] In this thirty-four-section song cycle, the speaker's linguistic display suggests in verbal form the passionate intensity no longer available in the love affair giving rise to the poem's observations: "shuttle-cock and battle-dore / A little pink-love / And feathers are strewn" (*LLB* 56). At the high point of the relationship, "When we lifted / Our eye-lids on Love," the poet synaesthetically imagines "A cosmos / Of coloured voices / And laughing honey // And spermatozoa / At the core of Nothing / In the milk of the Moon" (IX). Masculine sperm and feminine milk mix in a "honey" of conversation, laughter, and intercourse. At the end, however, the poet comments, "The moon is cold / Joannes" (XXXI) and "Love" is a "litterateur" (XXXIV)—a professional writer, suggestively equipped with all the clichés of the profession: Cupid, "once upon a time," and moonlight. In contrast, the speaker is a poet, and the poem she writes in "Songs" distinguishes itself in multiple ways from popular love stories. In particular, the poet's manipulation of multiple registers of language provides her a way out of both fairy tales and spermatozoan narratives of romantic desire. "Songs to Joannes" may be read as Loy's working out an escape from the patriarchal love-plot in a world "hostile to love."[56]

After arriving in New York, Loy seems no longer absorbed by the anger fueling her initial poetic output, and indeed she apparently stops writing poetry for almost two years once she has finished the revisions for "Songs": according to Burke's and Conover's accounts, Loy writes no new poems between 1917 and 1919, although she does write two very brief plays and a few Dada sketches. This hiatus is significant in thinking about Loy's positioning within Anglo-American modernism. As Robert von Hallberg writes, avant-garde groups were not closely in sync with the concerns of Anglo-American poets. Even Pound, who lived in Paris during the height of Paris Dada (1920–22), "did not expect great poetry to come from the Dadaist effort, only a momentary clarity"; "Dada was for him not a movement capable of producing serious art."[57] Loy's participation in the Arensberg circle from late 1916 through 1917 marks her philosophical and social affiliation with America's closest approach to a modernist avant-garde. Her definition of the artist in "In . . . Formation" echoes Futurist and Expressionist antiacademicism: "The only trouble with *The Public* is education. // The *Artist* is uneducated" and strives for "pure, uneducated seeing" (*LLB82* 285). A 1919 poem refers to "forebear's excrement" and presents "Our person" as "Choked with the tatters of tradition" ("O Hell," *LLB* 71). The assumed hostility of the artist to the public and to disciplined, historical ways of seeing runs in direct contrast to Moore's, Pound's, Eliot's, Lowell's, H.D.'s, and Williams's conviction that one may see one's own time and condition more clearly through understanding other times, cultures, languages, or bodies of knowledge. Loy publishes narrative collage, not poetry, in New York's Dada journals. She aims to subvert "the Real (the obvious, the observable)" by "'break[ing] the power of facts over the word.'"[58] Yet Loy apparently swings between affiliations with groups just as she changes genres of artistic production and cities of residence. Similarly, Loy writes little poetry in Paris between 1923 and 1936.[59] On her return to New York in the spring of 1920, the Arensbergs were on the verge of leaving the city and Loy moved into the Village, this time finding her primary contacts among Heap, Anderson, Ridge, Barnes, and other women there.[60] Between 1919 and 1923, while traveling and living in both the Village and Berlin, Loy also produced a significant number of new poems.[61]

Loy's automythologizing takes its fullest poetic form not in the Florence poems but in "Anglo-Mongrels and the Rose" (1923–25), where Ova is a composite of English and Hungarian, Anglican and Jewish, lower-class and ambitiously bourgeois parents—without clear identity boundaries and in conflict with most parts of her world (see chap. 5). A part of the conflict has to do with her mother's restrictive manifestation and practice of gender conventions: the mother is an "English Rose" of "arrested impulses / self-pruned / of the primordial attributes . . . simpering in her / ideological pink" (*LLB82* 121, 124). The poem stresses that this conception of femininity is "an Anglo-Saxon phenomenon"—foreign to the "Oriental" (Hungarian Jewish) suitor who becomes Ova's/Loy's father; there is nothing natural in gender as the young girl is encouraged to practice it. Although the daughter has conflicts with her father as well, "Anglo-Mongrels" presents the archetypally female Ova as completely alienated from her feminine "Rose"-mother.

According to Shreiber, Loy repudiates the concept of an autonomous self, and her identity is sustained through social relations, including that of mother and child: the "reproductive relation is central to Loy's poetic enterprise" ("Negative Aesthetics" 159, 148). In my reading of Loy, reproductive capacity and relationship are key to Loy's poetic only insofar as they contribute to confirming adult female subjectivity: there is little sense of fulfilling relationship in these poems. Instead, they protest patriarchal definitions of the feminine without constructing alternate possibilities for female expression and power—perhaps because, to Loy's knowledge, no such cultural models existed.[62] Loy's life changes, however, in 1917–18, when she throws all forms of status and stability to the winds in an affirmation of sexual and spiritual fulfillment with Cravan. In league with other factors, this experience seems to have altered Loy's sense of what provides an adequate basis for identity formulation and her poetic itself.

Gator/Fangs/Rat

While Loy's most important name changes were her permanent adoption of an Anglicized last name and the construction of self-figures in her poems and prose, Marianne Moore's name-play was primarily familial and involved the adoption of animal names and features. All Moore's family names were masculine, and she frequently took names interchangeable with her brother's: for example, in their teens, both she and Warner were called Weaz (for Weasel), Basilisk, and Bruno. Before 1914, Moore's most frequent family names were Launcelot B. Fangs, Hamilcar Barca, and Gator—suggesting power and ferocity as well as, in the former two cases, social status and resistance to the ruling order (Barca was a Carthaginian opponent of Roman imperialism). In 1914, when the poet was in her midtwenties, the family read Kenneth Grahame's *The Wind in the Willows* and adopted names from this children's story for themselves. The mother became the homebody Mole, following in their tradition of assigning her the weak, feminine, or small animals (Bunny, Fawn, Mouse); Warner became the mischievous Toad or Badger; and Moore became the poem-writing Rat. Until her death at the age of eighty-five, Moore signed herself and was addressed by her family as Rat (or other animal names), and styled herself her brother's brother.

This construction of an intrepid masculine selfhood was not limited to her family. In college letters, Moore sometimes refers to herself as male, expecting friends to "acknowledge me a man" or commenting with satisfaction that a friend "talks to me as man to man."[63] Some of her friends go by male names—Frances Jackson is "Jack," and Margaret Morrison is sometimes called "David" (February 12, 1907, RML VI:13a:03). After college, a few friends address Moore in letters as George, and one calls her Gillespie.[64] In a 1942 poetic anagram for Hildegarde Watson, "The Wood-Weasel," all characters are implicitly male: "he is / determination's totem," she writes of Hildegarde; "this same weasel's playful, and his weasel / associates are too" (*CPo* 127). Although convention regarded the masculine pronoun as grammatically gender-neutral, the consistency of Moore's self-reference as masculine and her friends' similar play with masculine names suggests greater significance. Moore and some of her friends found a range for assertive self-formulation within masculine identities that were not available within the feminine.

Once this naming pattern is known, Moore's poems appear surprisingly self-referential in the same generalized way as Loy's poems constructing author figures. For example, "The Jerboa" features a (male) desert rat that is "not famous . . . lives without water, [and] has / happiness" (*CPo* 13) because it can live without enslaving or oppressing others and without exploiting its environment, qualities Moore admired. In "The Hero," the (male) hero has "the feelings of a mother— a / woman or a cat," and one model for the hero is a female hobo (*CPo* 9)—a use of the masculine pronoun in conjunction with female characters or qualities that elides gender boundaries as marking essential difference. "We" are the hero, and "we" are not all, or not simply, male.[65] Moore's self-naming in letters often borrows from the poems on which she is currently working, another indicator that she stages versions of selfhood in the masculine and animal portraits of her poems. Additionally, she writes several (mostly early) poems about the animals for which she most frequently names herself. In addition to "The Jerboa," she writes "Dock-Rats," "To an Intra-Mural Rat," and "Holes Bored in a Workbag by the Scissors" about the rat, and seven poems featuring various forms of lizard, playing off her early names of Gator and Basilisk and her lifelong enthusiasm for chameleons and dragons: "The North Wind to a Dutiful Beast Midway Between the Dial and the Foot of a Garden Clock," 1915; "To Disraeli on Conservatism," 1915; "You are like the Realistic Product of an Idealistic Search for Gold at the Foot of the Rainbow" (1916, retitled "To a Chameleon" in 1924); "Sun," 1916; "The Plumet Basilisk," 1932; "His Shield," 1944; and "O To Be a Dragon," 1957.

Lizards attracted Moore because of their ability to adapt to their circumstances. In "O To Be a Dragon," Moore takes her admiration for such flexibility to an extreme, claiming that her one Solomon-like wish is "to be a dragon, / a symbol of the power of Heaven—of silkworm / size or immense; at times invisible" (*CPo* 177). The power she desires can manifest itself as tiny or stupendous, invisible or aggressive. This poem suggests that Moore admires not the chameleon's modesty but its ability to choose its mode of attack or retreat. While this, like most of her animal poems, does not topicalize gender, the fluid boundaries it celebrates suggestively reflect Moore's naming patterns of masculine femaleness or feminine masculinity. She chooses not to "be" one thing, but to choose. It is also a telling feature of her cultural context as a white, Protestant woman in the United States that self-identification as an animal causes the poet no psychic anxiety: such identification for an African American woman or for a Jew in Germany would resonate with prejudicial stereotypes from which Moore is free.

Moore's identification with unfeminine and socially scorned animals like lizards and rats may also relate to the popularity of the comic female performer, who typically staged her humor on self-mockery, or what Susan Glenn calls the "comedic sacrifice of normative femininity and beauty."[66] Moore, too, rejects normative stereotypes in order to assert her own values. The 1917 "Roses Only" is the closest Moore comes to defining her feminism. Like Loy's "Feminist Manifesto," Moore's poem takes on the cultural identification of women with sexual accessibility to men, but her poem promotes female independence from heterosexuality rather than their liberated sexual circulation. Taking as her foil the carpe diem poem urging a woman to relinquish her virginity before her beauty fades, Moore addresses women as roses and tells them that "in view of the fact that spirit creates form—we are justified in supposing / That you must have brains"—however women might try to hide or disguise them. Similarly, the poet counteracts the misconception that a rose's petals are her best feature by distinguishing mere beauty from "brilliance." The poem concludes that not petals but "your thorns are the best part of you"; they do not protect against "mildew" or other natural and temporal threats, but they guard against "the predatory hand." If women valued their brains and used them to secure their independence against predation, Moore implies, they might live up to their capacity for brilliance. Through the poem's address, Moore accuses women of complicity in valuing conventional beauty over the characteristic that distinguishes them from other flowers and protects them: namely, thorns, which allow them to enjoy their full bloom in their own time.[67] Women should not hide their petals: they are not to cease to be lovely or feminine. Yet they should value the thorniness that is equally a part of their nature.

"Nature," for Moore, gives all creatures qualities or characteristics in order that they use them. Not to use them is to be unnatural. Femininity, as culturally defined, is unnatural and leads to women's victimization. Yet, as seen in "Sojourn in the Whale," Moore also problematizes the idea of nature. "Peter," a 1924 poem about a cat, exemplifies such problematization. The first four stanzas of "Peter" admire the cat for typical behavior—sleeping, looking, springing—concluding with the observation that "to sit caged by the rungs of a domestic chair would be unprofit- / able—human" (*EP* 93–94). "What is the good of hypocrisy?" the speaker then asks; "It is clear that he can see / the virtue of naturalness." A cat should do what cats do, and not what humans want. The conclusion to Moore's sentence, however, anthropomorphizes the cat by extending this "virtue" to authorship: "It is clear that he can see / the virtue of naturalness, that he is one of those who do not regard / the published fact as a surrender." To be natural is to stand by one's principles; this cat/poet regards publication neither as inevitably right (hence requiring the reader's "surrender") nor as the author's surrender to public taste. These lines are immediately followed by the poem's conclusion, suggesting, through juxtaposition, that publication is also akin to confrontation: "As for the disposition"

> invariably to affront, an animal with claws wants to have to use
> them; that eel-like extension of trunk into tail is not an accident. To
> leap, to lengthen out, divide the air—to purloin, to pursue
> to tell the hen: fly over the fence, go in the wrong way—in your perturba-
> tion—this is life; to do less would be nothing but dishonesty.

For a cat not to use its claws would be "dishonesty." For a woman not to use her brains is equally dishonest. As typically in Moore's animal poems, by the end of "Peter," the boundary between feline and human psychological qualities is no longer distinct: people also, the poet implies, have "claws" and should "use them." More importantly, it is "life" to "go in the wrong way," to make mistakes, be impetuous, live honestly as one understands it at each moment. Yet if humans and cats are not by nature different, the poem's apparent goal—to describe the catness of a cat—loses its point.

The argument of nature—as Moore knew from her own contacts with those regarding women as naturally unsuited to higher education, professionalism, and creative power—can be dangerous.[68] In Moore's hands, however, nature is as "slippery" as a cat. "Peter," like most of Moore's poems, contains detailed information about the animal under observation, but this information is interwoven with similes and metaphors linking that animal to several others—just as every object or being Moore describes "is" also something else: a glacier is "An Octopus / of ice"; the opening lines of "Black Earth" compare the elephant to a hippopotamus and alligator, and its skin to a coconut shell and glass. "Peter" the cat resembles or reminds Moore of stories about a katydid, porcupine, seaweed, snake, prune, alligator, eel, mouse, frog, and elephant—as well as implicitly resembling the poet herself, in her "disposition to affront" when facing "the published fact." In its very nature, as Moore sees it, the cat resembles a whole menagerie of animals in addition to a plant and a fruit. To be human is to resemble several animals and some plants. To live honestly is to use all characteristics one can imagine oneself as having in analogy to other things or beings in the world, not to find in one's self some single essence. By observing a rose and a cat, Moore gathers information about her (or female and human) thorns and claws. Honest behavior, for Moore, is limited by a conjunction of physical qualities (like the "shadbones regularly set about" Peter's mouth) and by imagination, not by social dictates. Similarly, aesthetic beauty depends on dignity, proportion, a sense of purpose or use, and contiguities of inquisitive, imaginative association, not a preconceived standard of prettiness or perfection.

Although she never calls herself an elephant, elephants were among Moore's favorite animals; "Black Earth" (1918), in which Moore celebrates the hardihood and sensitivity of the elephant, is one of only two animal poems she wrote speaking as the animal itself; significantly, the other is "Dock-Rats," spoken by a rat. "Diligence Is to Magic as Progress Is to Flight" (1915) presents the elephant as a proper mount for a woman. Here Moore places the nursery-rhyme lady "'with rings on her fingers and bells on her toes'" on an elephant instead of a cock horse, because this smart woman "knows":

> That although the semblance of speed may attach to scarecrows
> Of aesthetic procedure, the substance of it is embodied in such of those
> Tough-grained animals as have outstripped man's whim to suppose
> Them ephemera,
>
> (*EP* 190)

Continuing her rhyme highlighting what the woman "knows," Moore concludes that elephants are "prosaic necessities—not curios." This is precisely the model Moore sets for herself: she will not be a "curio," an exotic, a pedestaled ideal or spectacle, but a "tough-grained" "prosaic necessity"—a rat or lizard—and as such she will outstrip "scarecrows / of aesthetic procedure" who are hobbled by the definitions of "man's whim."

Moore identifies with animals of cut-throat urban survival skills (the rat), cold-bloodedness (the lizard), aggressiveness, and power. These identifications contradict in every way the usual descriptions of Moore by those who did not know her well and who perceived in her poems and behavior only propriety, decorum, and a tendency to excessive modesty. Moore was called "Miss Moore" in all public circumstances—unlike Loy, who was frequently referred to by both given names, Mina Loy, as though the conventional titles of social and marital status were inadequate or irrelevant. For Moore, the spinsterish and proper "Miss" seemed to fit—in complete contrast to the character of her self-naming. As I will discuss in the next chapter, Moore encouraged this conception of herself through the tailored decorum of her appearance and through her enthusiasm for many kinds of propriety. Yet the title "Miss" revealed only part of the poet's range. The rest is revealed in her intimate naming patterns and poems about an array of animals whose behavior is antithetical to feminine decorum. Randall Jarrell describes Moore as sending "postcards only to the nicer animals," and omitting from her poems "the brute fact that works . . . the whole Medusa-face of the world."[69] None of this bruteness is, in fact, missing from Moore's poems, but it is presented indirectly, through implication rather than through naturalistic emphasis on raw, unvarnished detail. To return to the analogy of "Roses Only," Moore will give up neither the petals of feminine decorum nor the thorns of idiosyncratic, intelligent, and aggressive independence. For her, both are consistent with womanhood, although not with the socially feminine. For her, the masculine and the feminine are not polarities but modes all reasonable individuals choose to combine.[70] She remains both Miss Moore and "Rat" without an apparent sense of inner contradiction throughout her adult life.

In her life as in her poems, then, naming for Moore constitutes an implied political statement about qualities of being. As Victoria Bazin argues, "the task of poetry [for Moore] is not to mirror what is already there but to change it."[71] Names, like other kinds of identifying information, both assert a particular kind of agency in their bearer and indirectly intervene in the social system that assumes that only a narrow range of classification is appropriate (or possible) for the being under consideration. This same implied agency inheres in other aspects of Moore's language use, as suggested earlier in the chapter. According to Moore, not only is social and cultural change possible, but language can effect such change; poetry is "language in action" (Bazin 436). Bazin develops this idea according to Kenneth Burke's 1930s theory of the (admirable) inefficiency of art, which in turn resembles Russian formalist theory of defamiliarization as social practice. Burke argues that the aim of art is to "'throw into confusion the code which underlies commercial enterprise, industrial competition, the 'heroism' of economic warfare'"; through its impeding of the communicative process, poetry disrupts the symbolic code that reinforces a capitalist economy (Bazin 438).[72] Robin Schulze develops Moore's concept of the poet similarly, as serving "the social function of actively releasing those oppressed by habitual and deadening thoughts."[73]

Moore's construction of a poetics of oppositional resistance aligns her with Lasker-Schüler, through her (Bloch-like) notion of "hopeful" literature as a more effective counter to contemporary political problems than realist sociological critique.[74] Ernst Bloch's reminder that fairy tales are an ancient form "filled with social utopia, in other words, with the utopia of better life and justice" calls attention to the political function of Moore's reference to fairy tales—in "Sojourn in the Whale" but also in "The Hero" (1932), "The Frigate Pelican" (1934), and "Spenser's Ireland" (1941). "The Hero" even echoes Bloch's definition of hope as "the opposite of security . . . the opposite of naïve optimism . . . hope is not confidence."[75] Moore writes that the hero is "tired but hopeful— / hope not being hope / until all ground for hope has / vanished" (*CPo* 9). By disrupting stereotyped understandings, Moore attempts to change individual attitudes that, in her view, are responsible for both conceptions and patterns of history. These interventions are directly transformative in her poems written before 1924, the period when she (like Loy) is most critical of patriarchal gender relations: "Roses Only," "Sojourn in the Whale," "Those Various Scalpels," "Silence," "Marriage," and "An Octopus." This is also the period in which Moore writes several poems protesting militarism: for example, "To Military Progress," "To Statecraft Embalmed," "Isaiah, Jeremiah, Ezekiel, Daniel," "The Bricks Are Fallen Down, We Will Build with Hewn Stones . . . ," and (less clearly) "The Fish" and "Reinforcements."[76] Moore uses difficult poetic surfaces and initially puzzling descriptions to construct implied self-portraits and commentary on the politics of modern life.

The Prince of Thebes

Of the three poets in this study, Else Lasker-Schüler engaged in the most extravagant and distinctive name-play, both in the fantasy of the names themselves and in her adoption of their characters in published work, dress, and correspondence. Moreover, Lasker-Schüler seems to have seen the act of naming as radically synonymous with an artistic life, renaming not just herself but many of her friends. Within her first few years of entering Berlin's bohemian circles, she adopted the name Tino of Baghdad. Although "Tino" is gendered female and is often called a princess, Peter Hille attributes "Tino" feminine, masculine, and neuter gender, addressing letters to *Liebe Tino, Lieber Tino,* and *Liebes Tino.* By 1910, Lasker-Schüler was shifting from this Asian (usually) feminine persona to the Asian and Jewish masculine Jussuf, Prince of Thebes—although she continued to call herself Tino at times and friends write to her in 1944 as "Tino-Jussuf."[77] The poet had referred to herself as a prince as early as 1902, and her shifting between genders continued for several years. On occasion, she also referred to herself by other names—"Knabe von Jericho" in a 1909 letter to Jethro Bithell (*Br* I 47) and the Blue Jaguar in later letters, in affiliation with the "Blue Rider" Marc.[78] She signs letters with an anagram ("Onit") or as "Your very sad stalking bird Pampa."[79] Generally, however, by the early teens she identified as Prince Jussuf, and it was under the princely title that she was known among the German-language avant-garde. Lasker-Schüler's contemporaries addressed her as Prince Jussuf. There is apparent biographical precedent for the poet's adoption of a male persona based roughly on the biblical story of Joseph in exile, although Lasker-Schüler did sometimes fictionalize stories of her past. The poet claims to have identified with the biblical Joseph from childhood and to have worn boy's clothes on outings with her father because he preferred boys to girls.[80] This early cross-dressing and the fact that her hair was short well before bobbing came into fashion suggest that a masculine role suited her. At the same time, Lasker-Schüler idolized her mother and traced both her love of poetry and her lineage as poet through her maternal side—claiming her grandmother was a poet.

Critics speculate that Lasker-Schüler shifted from the name Tino to Jussuf either to adopt a more androgynous self-fiction or to assert self-sufficiency after her divorce from Walden. Given social constructions of gender in Germany, the latter would certainly be reasonable. The poet begins her 1912 epistolary novel *Mein Herz* as Tino and concludes it as Jussuf. Yet both *Die Nächte Tino von Bagdads* (1907) and *Der Prinz von Theben* (1914) abruptly change narrative strategies from one story to the next—from first to third person and using narrators who may be male or female, Jewish or Arab, and old or young, suggesting that no single tale, description, or name is conclusive.[81] Neither in her fiction nor in daily life did Lasker-Schüler perform a single, conventionally circumscribed identity.

As Sonja Hedgepeth reviews, many of the poet's contemporaries described her work as *männlich*—manly or masculine (83–88). Karl Kraus called her "the only masculine presence in German literature today"; in 1912, Eduard Engel wrote that the poet was "the only remarkable [female] poet who stands under the influence of the *männlich* Sublime"; in 1916, Alfred Biese claims she "strives . . . equally with the most serious *männlichen* poets for a great, noble art."[82] Lasker-Schüler encourages such association through her Jussuf persona but also through remarks like "I am not a woman / like the others."[83] Given the typical belittling response of critics to *Frauenlyrik* and the initial association of Lasker-Schüler primarily with women's writing, such comments both distinguish her from "poetesses" and participate in the prejudice assuming that serious art and genius are masculine. Lasker-Schüler, however, may mean that she is unlike other women in being double-gendered, not masculine. In 1919, Camill Hoffman interprets Kraus's pronouncement in this way, suggesting that among Expressionist poets only Lasker-Schüler can balance gendered elements in her writing: "The whole group is all too manly, all too boyish—Werfel, Hasenclever, Ehrenstein, Wolfenstein, Becher, even Klemm. . . . But Else Lasker-Schüler remains the only feminine poet of today (not because but in spite of being a woman)."[84] Lasker-Schüler makes the same point in her Zurich journal: "The true poet, dear reader, cultivates self-division . . . The poet displaces his or her two-part condition in the Primitive being . . . Adam and Eve were originally *one* being . . . Their soul would experience all possibility and impossibility as doubled and only after the Fall did they step apart, detached from each other."[85] The poet returns to her or his own ancient Adam-and-Eve doubleness to write, while also conscious of the division.

In her fiction, the poet assigns Jussuf masculine and feminine characteristics in a male body; in her poems, she frequently collapses gender distinction altogether. Not primarily interested in erotic mythologizing or androgyny—the popular modes of gender-blending in Wilhelmine and Weimar Germany—Lasker-Schüler typically represents indeterminate gender in the form of gender doubling, foregrounding artifice as much as nature. In letters and poems, she imagines the two genders as alternate and coexisting possibilities for self-formulation rather than as bisexual wholeness. She frequently signed letters as Jussuf and Else (or Lasker-Schüler)—names in parallel, substantiating each other. Precisely this composite quality made Lasker-Schüler's self-naming as Prince Jussuf so striking: it was ostentatiously artifice. Lasker-Schüler never attempted to appear male.[86] She was openly a Jewish-German woman bearing the name of an Asian man and occasionally donning some elements of male Arabian clothing. Her friends responded to this doubleness in the poet's assertion of identity by addressing her as male, understanding some elements of her work as masculine, and acknowledging her as a woman. No doubt by many considered a mere fantasy, the figure of Jussuf manifested the poet's ability to blur the boundaries both of binary gender divisions and of imagination and pragmatic being, or art and author. This is the epitome of life as coincident with art, and of both as performance.

Lasker-Schüler's naming of others was as striking as her self-address. The poet is assumed to have given her husband Herwarth Walden his name: originally Georg Levin, this entrepreneurial composer began to call himself Walden at around the time of his marriage to Lasker-Schüler and kept the name in his second marriage.[87] She suggested that Wieland Herzfeld change his name to Herzfelde—which then remained his professional name. In letters, Martin Buber was "the lord of Zion" [Der Herr von Zion], Karl Kraus the Cardinal or Dalai Lama from Vienna, Kete Parsenow the Venus from Siam, Tilla Durieux the Black Panther, and Oskar Koskoschka the Troubadour or Giant. In *Der Malik,* Franz Marc became "Ruben," her "brother"—and he in turn addressed the poet as "his highness, Jussuf" and as his "sister," following the poet's lead in gender doubling. In the same novel, Johannes Holzmann is Prince Sascha (in letters, Holzmann is Senna Hoy), and Gottfried Benn is Giselheer the Barbarian; Milly Steger appears as Milila or Milli Millius. Many poets received representative names of nobility or honor: Hans Ehrenbaum Degele was Tristan; Georg Trakl, the Knight of Gold; Franz Werfel the Prince of Prague; Paul Leppin was Daniel Jesus or the King of Böhmen; Richard Dehmel, a forest prince; and Peter Hille, Saint Peter.

While the poet's performed gender varied, the gender of her friends remained stable, with the exception of a few of her female friends. In the poem taking her name, Marianne Werefkin is both a baroness and a boy: "I named her the noble streetboy. / Rogue of the Russian city."[88] Like Lasker-Schüler as Prince Jussuf, Werefkin is woman and youth, noble and common. Moreover, in this poem her nobility lies in her "unruly heart" and competence among radical artists on the streets, that is, in the characteristics that lead Lasker-Schüler to call her a boy. In "Milly Steger," the cross-dressing sculptor has a "Gulliverin Hand"—or a hand like a female Gulliver, a play whereby the poet marks her friend as both female and like a (fictional) man.[89]

Given the persistence of "Prince Jussuf" in the poet's self-naming, it is surprising that he does not feature openly in her poetry. Perhaps this is because Lasker-Schüler associated the lyric directly with self-formulation, hence not requiring supplementary fictions. Or perhaps several poems are in the voice of Jussuf but because the genre does not require a described speaker, Jussuf is no more apparently masculine than the poet is feminine. More important than gender categorization in her poetry is immediacy of address and spiritual urgency. In the context of a literary tradition dominated by philosophical discourse, the direct colloquialness of her tone was as unusual in Germany as were Moore's and Loy's "logopoeic" poems in the United States. Lasker-Schüler's "I" is aggressively present. Much like Dickinson, Lasker-Schüler often constructs a spoken presence revealing the emotions of a particular moment without providing a contextualizing frame, taking full advantage of the ambiguities of the lyric present tense and "I" to leave her speaker scene-less. Moreover, and also like Dickinson, Lasker-Schüler often layers unrelated metaphors or metonymic structures, destabilizing any single direction of interpretation. Encouraging the performance of engaged but undescribed agential presence, lyric poetry provided Lasker-Schüler with a formal structure bypassing narratives of conventional selfhood and binary gender exclusions.

In her early poems, Lasker-Schüler reflects specifically on the shifting boundaries of gender formation. The poem "My Drama" ("Mein Drama," 1902), for example, suggests in its title that love is dramatic and staged. Writing her own "Drama," the speaker exclaims, "I don't believe any longer in Woman and Man." Although the speaker makes this claim in the context of suffering brought on by unrequited love, the brief mapping of that love suggests both that she has a masculine element and that her lover has "Eve's blood"; she identifies a "pale angel" as crying inside her: "Hidden—I think deep in my soul, / It [he] fears me." While *Engel* is masculine in German, the context of gender rejection and doubling suggests that the poet also engages in gender play here. The poem then ends with the exclamation, "my soul would never learn . . . to know Eve's blood / as in you, Man!" (*WB*, no. 67).[90] The gender difference between the enticing lover and unhappy speaker is elided through her angel and his "Eve's" blood—or her understanding of her own femininity "in" him. Moreover, the statement that she doesn't "believe" in woman and man represents gender as constructed.

In another early Eve poem, the surreal "Urfrühling" ("Original Spring," 1902), Lasker-Schüler constructs a more complex elision of gender boundaries by blending a third-person portrait of Eve with a speaker who is ambiguously Adam, a female lover, and the poet herself:

She wore a snake as belt And Paradise-apples on her hat, And my wild desire Raged on in her blood.	*Sie trug eine Schlange als Gürtel Und Paradiesäpfel auf dem Hut, Und meine wilde Sehnsucht Raste weiter in ihrem Blut.*
And the primitive sun-fears The melancholy of embers And the paleness of my cheeks Also suited her.	*Und das Ursonnenbangen, Das schwermüt'ge der Glut Und die Blässe meiner Wangen Standen auch ihr so gut.*
It was a play of fate One of her riddle-things . . . We sank our glances trembling In the fairy tale of our rings.	*Das war ein Spiel der Geschicke Ein's ihrer Rätseldinge . . . Wir senkten zitternd die Blicke In die Märchen unserer Ringe.*

I forgot my blood's Eve	*Ich vergass meines Blutes Eva*
What with all these soul-cliffs	*Über all' diesen Seelenklippen,*
And the red of her mouth burned	*Und es brannte das Rot ihres Mundes,*
As if I had boy's lips.	*Als hätte ich Knabenlippen.*
And the evening red glowed	*Und das Abendröten glühte*
Snaking itself around heaven's hems	*Sich schlängelnd am Himmelssaume,*
And from the tree of knowledge	*Und vom Erkenntnisbaume*
The blossoms smiled, mockgood.	*Lächelte spottgut die Blüte.*
	(*WB*, no. 46)

Logically the speaker of a love poem to Eve would be Adam; the poem describes Eve as Adam might first have seen her, evoking desire. Yet the speaker of this poem seems also to be part of Eve: the speaker's desire rages in Eve, and the paleness of her cheeks suits Eve. The line "as if I had boy's lips" indicates that "I" does not in fact have them, hence is female, and "I forgot my Eve's blood" makes the speaker descended from Eve. The repeated first-person pronouns and metaphors also make the speaker seem to be the poet, just as (despite the past-tense verbs) the intensity of the passion makes the scene seem present.

In this poem, any romance or marriage (that "fairy tale of rings") apparently resembles the "Ur" or original "spring" of desire, temptation, and betrayal, but here the betrayal seems to be nature's or heaven's. Eve's snake-belt and the speaker's glowing or burning desire are miniscule versions of the emberlike sunset reds "snaking . . . around heaven's hems." Further, the apples of desire belong to Eve as decoration rather than to God's tree, and the "tree of knowledge" blooms with deceptive mock goodness. Like the annual return of spring and the repeated scene of human desire, there is a repeated blooming of knowledge, which not only allows one to differentiate good and evil but is itself satirical, mixed, *spottgut.* In a world where even divine knowledge takes compound and contradictory form, it is less surprising that there is no heterosexual imperative and that one's desire or being might also mix supposedly discrete categories, like male/female, mythic/real, and past/present.

Lasker-Schüler does not call herself "Eve" in this or any other poem, but here as in "Erkenntnis," the speaking perspective is aligned with Eve. Particularly the phrase "my blood's Eve" suggests that Eve lurks in the twentieth-century poet. The poem's paratactic syntax (like its unusual compound words—mockgood, soul-cliffs, primitive-sunfears) contributes to the conjoining of the poem's subject and the poet.

The blank connector *and* provides the only logical link between several of the poem's lines, and hence between one category of being and another. For example, in lines 2 through 4—"And paradise-apples on her hat / And my wild desire / Raged in her blood"—the repetition of "And" makes the relationship between the phrases seem parallel, while in fact the first "And" is a simple additive, but the second "And" stands in for the entire imagined relationship of the speaker to Eve that is at the crux of the poem.

Here and in other poems, Lasker-Schüler invokes the loss of strict ego and gender boundary.[91] Her doubling of the feminine and the masculine entails direct alignment with Eve, for Lasker-Schüler the embodiment of rebellious desire. As I discuss in chapter 4, sexuality is a figure for intimacy and knowledge for this poet: in several poems, her speaker metaphorically enters into landscapes, the bodies of others, or God. Intimacy involves intersections of the corporeal, the emotional, and the psychological. In "Dem Prinzen von Marokko" (1911), the speaker sees her lover's "face" as "my palm garden," and claims: "In your face all the pictures / Of my blood are enchanted."[92] In "Abel," Lasker-Schüler describes mythic figures through embodying metaphor: "Abel's face is a golden garden, / Abel's eyes are nightingales. . . . But through Cain's body run the sewers of the city" (*WB,* no. 181).[93] She addresses "Prince Benjamin" as having a voice that "wakes up my colorful heart"; "Your voice scatters itself always-blue / Over the path"—reifying voice and air, and personifying her own heart (*WB,* no. 233).[94] In "To God," the speaker longs to "eavesdrop on your [God's] heart / To substitute myself for your most distant nearness" (*WB,* no. 214); and in "Zebaoth," the speaker addresses a young poet-God: "Lonely, I drink from your scents // The first flowers of my blood long for you" (*WB,* no. 218).[95] In "Full Moon" ("Vollmond"), "Lightly the moon swims through my blood. . . . / Slumbering tones are the eyes of days" and the poet seeks the "far-away city" sensually, by its "consecrating scents" and "lips" (*WB,* no. 175).[96] City, time, moon, and poet share common properties of embodiment, and the poet experiences each as a visceral aspect of her being. Sigrid Bauschinger refers to this mingling of the fields of art, nature, love, and religion as the closest thing to Lasker-Schüler's Weltanschauung (*WZ* 206).

The general collapse of distinctions between the physical boundaries of bodies in these poems are mirrored in the poet's prose, letters, and drama by a splitting of the self. Most famously, her late unpublished play *Ichundich* begins with the narrating poet's claim, "I have split myself into two halves," the *IandI* of the play's title, doubled but undifferentiated by the spaces that would normally separate one "I" from the other.[97] In *Concert,* the poet writes that "each true prayer is a concentration . . . I and I. And out of this combination with oneself comes double the strength."[98] In *Mein Herz,* the poet uses wordplay to assert the relation of language to self-formulation: "I will no longer say anything without pay, except conjunctions—if I could only find one that would join [connect] me."[99] Meike Ningel writes that Lasker-Schüler's "masquerades show her consciousness that, as Nietzsche remarked, every word is a mask and even the 'I' is a mask that hides others, and from which one can never recover the original [I], which in turn only bears the signature of unreality."[100] Lasker-Schüler's rejection of reified selfhood or assumed "realities" like gender identity, however, is not nihilistic, as her insistence on community suggests. In writing of the poet's cultivation of self-division, she identifies this doubleness as love: "The poet's poetry springs from this deep, most internal ancient and everlasting feeling [*Gemüt*] of the double-love of his soul"; double being signifies the presence of love-for-another (Adam and Eve) as the soul's deepest, most primitive source of creative being; to be split is also to be doubled.[101] The split self recombines in multiple forms; each "I" is more and less than a single selfhood; words assert embodied and subjective presence as much as they reveal the slippage between imagination and being and the alienation of the speaker from her present circumstances. The radically split and doubled self-formulations of Lasker-Schüler's writing, like its radical metaphors and language play, function as social critique: through language disruption, the poet rejects the anti-Semitic, nationalistic, and materialistic environments of Wilhelmine and Weimar Germany, attempting to establish an alternate reality of loving care, where even the physical boundaries of personhood would be permeable to multiple kinds of reality. In this attempt, although not in any of its techniques, her poetry comes surprisingly close to Moore's. The Russian formalist concept of defamiliarization or *ostranenie* was extremely popular in early-twentieth-century German avant-garde circles and—like the utopianism theorized by Bloch—took diverse forms. By disrupting illusions of realism and naturalism and thereby preventing automatized perception, both poets reveal the troubling contradictions of their respective and shared worlds.

Lasker-Schüler's poems and life-fictions push beyond realism in asserting imagined truths about the human heart and mind. Although her appellations assign her social status as royalty and Jussuf would appear to give her the additional status of masculinity, the names are so patently constructed as to be laughable to those unwilling to participate in their fantasy. In my view, then, these names do not seek to assert social empowerment or substitution. The poet constructs Asian male royalty as one of the life possibilities she can live through as a way of signaling that she will not be bound by others' notions of what an impoverished, aging, Jewish woman may be or do. The empowerment is spiritual and psychological—as are most of the self-formulations practiced by women of this period. Like Eve with her snake-belt, Lasker-Schüler tempts others by example to challenge social constructions that would limit one's ambition, vision, or behavior.

Mina Loy assigned herself a professional name early in her career that became synonymous with her legal and daily being. For the most part, however, she, Moore, and Lasker-Schüler used names not to alter a legal denomination or disguise themselves but to expand formulations of potential selfhood or characteristics of being. They allowed names to proliferate. Names performed additional and simultaneous possibilities of being—not an exclusive or substitutive one. Similarly, through a variety of poetic strategies varying from the relatively transparent construction of author figures to suggestive manipulations of grammar, metaphor, and diction, these poets engaged in a critique of fixed cultural structures of value and power. The playfulness or satire of their poetic constructions assert the problematic nature of current gender relationships and institutions of exchange, both through defamiliarizing language practices and through critique or alternate formulations of being and exchange. As Tino, the Blue Jaguar, or Prince Jussuf of Thebes, Gator or Rat or Basilisk, and Imna Oly or Ova or Goy, these poets formulated terms of address more compatible with their poetic ambitions and aesthetic independence than their given names alone could be, and perhaps thereby facilitated their productivity as poets in careers that demanded the assertiveness and invention implied by exotic male royalty, rats or alligators, and the chutzpah demonstrated by declaring one's non-Jewishness in Jewish idiom. Here one sees the usefulness of both comparative and locally attentive study: self-formulations through renaming were common among female (and familiar among male) writers and artists across Europe and North America early in the twentieth century, although the forms and significance of such self-performance varied according to location. Not all women who engaged in code-naming or multiple performances of selfhood produced art of notable quality or art engaged in explorations of gendered identity. Nonetheless, it is instructive to note that among the most significant female writers of the early twentieth century were many who did engage in such self-naming and exploration. Moore, Loy, and Lasker-Schüler chose unusual names and wrote exceptional poetry, but their practice of self-naming as a mode of gendered identity performance was shared with many literary and artistic women of their generation.

4 *Sexology, Style, & the Poet's Body*

To emphasize the word behavior indicates that the body is the primary, fundamental, support for the social message proffered . . . it is a blackboard on which is written—and thus rendered legible—the respect for codes, or the deviation from them, in relation to the system of behaviors.
—Pierre Mayol, "Propriety," in *The Practice of Everyday Life*

Apart from face and hands . . . what we actually see and react to are, not the bodies, but the clothes of those about us . . . indeed the very word "personality," as we have been reminded by recent writers, implies a "mask," which is itself an article of clothing.
—J. C. Flügel, *The Psychology of Clothes*

Men are quick to say that mere beauty is not enough—
(. . . I notice that beauty is the without which
nothing of their interest in the intellect).
—Marianne Moore, conversation notebook

In the late nineteenth century, gender and sexuality were not for the most part differentiated: sexual object choice became linked to definitions of "sexual inversion" only later in the century and after a period of definitional murkiness.[1] When the word *homosexual* was first introduced to U.S. readers in 1892, it was defined to mean persons whose "general mental state is that of the opposite sex."[2] Clothing, hairstyles, mannerisms, and career choice were the primary attributes signifying "inversion." For female writers and artists, whose careers placed them in a professional sphere gendered masculine, choice of dress and manner assumed great importance as a strategy for manipulating spaces of public agency.[3] Such choices were also frequently read as intersecting with their literary style.

During the first decades of the twentieth century, expectations for women's wear altered dramatically, giving women a wide range of choice among styles all more or less readily available. Whereas in the 1880s, a middle-class woman's daytime dress was hand-sewn, ankle-length, full-skirted, and assumed a bustle and multiple layers of underclothes, by the 1920s it was ready-made and included the possibility of knee-length sheathlike dresses, suggesting "natural" contours rather than corseted bodies, or even trousers.[4] In Germany, choice of fashion had distinctly political connotations: rejection of French haute couture was promoted as a sign of nationalism during World War I, and during the 1920s U.S. fashion was understood to unite "the cult of functionalism with the promises of social equality," although all international design was seen as leading to a homogenization of peoples that threatened national or "folk" distinction.[5] In the United States as well, dress constituted a political language of signs, placing a woman along the era's spectrum of modernity and sexual politics.

Modernist poets, like other women, were "read" as bodies. Mary Warner Moore calls attention to this metaphor in a reading notebook, where she quotes from J. C. Flügel's *The Psychology of Clothes:* "It is not so much that clothes make the man. . . . They are like writing on his body, explaining what he is, for the world to decipher if it has the key" (VII:03:07).[6] Flügel's "if" is telling: while the world assumed it had the key to reading women's bodies, women themselves experimented with coded inscriptions that were not always easy to "decipher." Moore herself earlier took nearly twelve pages of notes on Frank Alvah Parson's *The Psychology of Dress* (1920): "A man's clothes . . . like other reactions to his needs . . . are his material response to a demand for them & by the results he must stand or fall whether judged commercially, socially, artistically, ethically or by a simple standard of common sense" (VII:01:03).[7] In another notebook, Moore writes, "I am as uninterested in dress, as a human being could be but I have managed to *make* myself interested"—as though she saw this as necessary (VII:03:11). Flügel's book was published by Leonard and Virginia Woolf's Hogarth Press, and indeed Woolf, like Moore, understood that whether or not a woman attended to her wardrobe, she would be "judged" on the basis of her "material response" to the need for some kind of dress—as would a man.[8] In Germany, Georg Simmel's 1919 essay "Die Mode" concluded that "fashion gives woman a compensation for her lack of position in a class based on a calling or profession"; yet fashion dissolves the old distinctions only "to introduce new ones based on its own definition of boundaries."[9] In 1930, Siegfried Kracauer's *Die Angestellten* asserts the importance of clothing, fitness, and other aspects of embodiment for men and women in obtaining work and advancing professionally.[10]

In short, writers of the early twentieth century understood style to raise issues of social interpretation. As Leigh Gilmore summarizes, assumptions about gender, ethnicity, or class are "projected onto the body's exterior and then read as proof of an interior [universal] truth."[11] Pierre Bourdieu describes the body as "a form of engagement with the world," constructed in mutually formative relation with its cultural fields.[12] Body is a text performed and a page on which social scripts are inscribed. A 1913 *Life* cartoon reveals this translucence of the physical in representing a dissonance of vision in the United States: while feminist "Militants" imagine themselves in the noble form of saints or goddesses, they are seen by patriarchal lawmakers as monstrous and satanic, with no hint of femininity (fig. 1). The bias of the cartoonist is evident in his portrayal of the women "as they are": here they look old, unkempt, mean or unhappy, and masculine. His drawing implies that social reformers, feminists, and women active in politics cannot inhabit attractive or young feminine bodies: they "are" unappealingly masculine. Some female poets were represented as attractive and feminine, but most were imagined on the model of the "Militants" in the cartoon. Individual choices about style may reflect defensive reactions to such negative stereotypes as well as more affirmative self-formulation.

In Sandra Gilbert and Susan Gubar's words, for many women poets fame was "as theatrical as it was literary," and response ranged from adulation to scorn: Amy Lowell and Edith Sitwell were reportedly besieged by fans and curiosity seekers; on the other hand, Pound ridiculed Lowell's poetry through her weight by dubbing her a "hippopoetess."[13] In a 1924 essay suggestively titled "Gallantry and Our Women Writers," Joseph Collins writes that Edna St. Vincent Millay "is like a beautiful woman who has a varied, attractive wardrobe"—the peculiar "like" suggesting that Millay is not in fact beautiful or well dressed but gives this impression through her poetry. According to an early biographer, the popularity of Millay's poetry made her "the It-girl of the hour, the Miss America of 1920," "the unrivaled embodiment of sex appeal"—phrases that do not suggest an intellectual or aesthetic presence. Reviewer Harold Acton commented about British poet Anna Wickham that "her poetry [was] as unfashionable as her person"

(Schenck 236). Randall Jarrell continued this pattern in the 1950s, commenting, "One feels about most of [Muriel Rukeyser's] poems almost as one feels about the girl on last year's calendar."[14] Men read women's poetry as revealing the feminine body—as sexual or grotesque, or both.

"The poetess" was typically imaged through sexual degradation or lack. In a long passage eliminated from *The Waste Land,* Eliot represented modern depravity through the figure of Fresca, a prostitute complete with female "stench"; Fresca writes in half-consciousness and boredom: "When restless nights distract her brain from sleep / She may as well write poetry, as count sheep."[15] Educated women fare worse than prostitutes, according to these stanzas: "Women grown intellectual grow dull, / And lose the mother wit of natural trull." In 1915, Maxwell Bodenheim writes a polemic personifying "rhymed verse" as a "girl"; as "Bluebeard," he then entices that girl into his "dim chamber of poetic-thought. Suppose I took the little knife of rhyme and coolly sliced off one of her ears, two or three of her fingers, and finished by clawing out a generous handful of her shimmering, myriad-tinted hair, with the hands of meter": the conventional poem is indistinguishable from the female body.[16] Ernest Hemingway mocks female poets in a brief poem called "The Lady Poets with Footnotes," which reduces each poet to the object of a sexual, marital, or reproductive relationship; the poem suggests that "lady poets" are distinctive only for their unsatisfactory sex and reproductive lives.[17] In *Miss Lonelyhearts* (1933), Nathanael West presents men "childish[ly]" satirizing women writers, commenting that what "Mary Roberts Wilcox, Ella Wheeler Catheter, [and] Ford Mary Rinehard" "all needed was a good rape." West here suggests it would be normal for men disillusioned with "beauty and personal expression as an absolute end" to imagine that women write out of unfulfilled sexual need.[18] In the brief sketch "A Poetess" (1922), which Carolyn Burke regards as "most likely a prose portrait" of Loy (*BM* 294), Robert McAlmon describes a "malnutrite saint politician, bitter through never having realized purification." Dissatisfied with her own songs, she is chilled by her "cold purity of understanding," "vicious," and incapable of simplicity; she "reaches out spiritual talons . . . groping and grasping, starvedly." In contrast, in *Post-Adolescence,* McAlmon's Djuna Barnes character laments that the "male editors I want to sell special articles to try to feel my figure, or comment on my shape, when I go to market with my literature."[19] Similarly, in Germany, as Sigrid Bauschinger summarizes, the "poetry-writing woman was apparently seen as such a rarity that her sex provided the first and most important literary-critical perspective for observing her work"

(*WZ* 311). Paul Remer describes female lyricists of the first decade of the century as laying bare the "uncovered nakedness of their souls and sense," praising in contrast those few who "have again found veils and shame" (1905–6); Theodor Klaiber criticizes the many poetesses "who fall into overheated sexual and maenadic perversity" (1907).[20] The poetess was a woman gone wrong: a prostitute or harpy, sexually voracious or dissatisfied—or both.[21]

While some women (like Millay) encouraged the association of their poetry with heterosexual desirability, others strove to prevent it. Public cross-dressing and other more or less explicit claims of masculinity short-circuited the logic linking female sexuality with artistic production. In his study of dress, Flügel asserts that "sex distinction in dress" stems from both the "desire to utilize every opportunity of heterosexual stimulation, and the need to guard against the possibility of homosexuality." Those who depart from clear sex distinction in dress symbolically "express nonconformity in social and political thought"—as indeed many of the women of this period did (203, 207).[22] Women cross-dressing in England and France included Una Troubridge, Radclyffe Hall, Vita Sackville-West, Gluck, Romaine Brooks, Thelma Woods, Natalie Barney, Colette, Renée Vivien, and opera singer Emma Calvé.[23] In the United States, Amy Lowell was infamous for smoking cigars; Edna St. Vincent Millay was photographed in "butch-suits"; Willa Cather showed up for college at the University of Nebraska dressed as "William"; Gladys Bentley made her tuxedo and top hat a regular feature of her performance; and Georgia O'Keeffe wears a man's suit and hat in some of Stieglitz's photographs.[24] In Berlin, Milly Steger and Renée Sintenis wore men's clothing, and painters Grethe Jürgens, Lotte Laserstein, and Hanne Nagel dressed in mannish or androgynous styles. Many women wore what was called a *Herrenschnitt*, a "men's" cut shorter than the popular *Bubikopf*, literally "boy's head."

During this period, transvestism—like sexual inversion—was not typically linked with sexual object choice, although some women did cross-dress to signal lesbianism. In 1913, Havelock Ellis reported that there were more instances of heterosexual cross-dressing than of homosexual, and that many instances of aesthetic inversion were performed by individuals uninterested in the question of sexual choice.[25] Man Ray's well-known photograph of Duchamp as Rrose Sélavy *(eros, c'est la vie)* plays on concepts of the real more than on sexual politics: Duchamp eroticizes himself as feminine (borrowing clothing, makeup, and even Grace Ewing's hands) for the purpose of the collaboratively staged performance; this is art as event, a staple of Dada practice, crossing the ephemeral moment with the iconic form and the popular with the elite (presumably only French speakers would get the pun).[26] In a more openly political performance, the German expatriate Baroness Elsa von Freytag-Loringhoven walked through the Village with Kewpie dolls attached to herself or a bird cage complete with live canaries around her neck, or a bustle with a tail light—each element of costume a satire on bourgeois femininity: woman as doll, as caged bird, and as sexual property. As the baroness's outrageous costuming demonstrates, there were many modes of mocking gendered propriety besides transvestism. Generally, women's transvestism had a more open and conflicted political basis than men's, although factors like frequency of cross-dressing, social privilege, and segregational behavior affected its semiotics. Transvestism could also signal misogyny or self-contempt, a denial of allegiance to womanhood and hence reinforcement of patriarchal distinctions.[27] Similarly, the increased range of female fashion by the twenties undercut the force of cross-dressing, per se. Nonetheless, throughout the teens and twenties, women signaled a desired liberation from feminine cultural restriction through fashion. Moreover, in this period of still relatively fluid sexual definition, dress allowed the expression of more complex performances than straight or lesbian.

Given their emphasis on philosophical concepts of essence and on binary gender distinctions, it is not surprising that Germans and Austrians produced the earliest theories of sexual inversion.[28] Among the best-known theorists at the turn of the century were Richard von Krafft-Ebing and Magnus Hirschfeld in Germany, Sigmund Freud and Otto Weininger in Austria, and Edward Carpenter and Havelock Ellis in England. In 1886, Krafft-Ebing's *Psychopathia Sexualis* founded the science of sexology, codifying all nonprocreative forms of sexual activity and quoting articulate individuals who represented themselves as sexually inverted in lengthy case histories. Krafft-Ebing's text helped other men name their own preexistent sense of sexual difference, hence liberating inverted constructions of sexual identity even while it categorized inversion as degenerate.[29] Weininger's popular *Sex and Character* (1903) similarly substantiated popular essentialist views with some ambivalence.[30] Weininger states that the pure or simple man and woman do not exist: women have some masculine aspects, as men have some feminine. He also, however, conflates the masculine and feminine with not just man and woman but men and women. Basically, Weininger distinguishes M *(Mann)* and W *(Weib)* as consisting respectively of mind or spirit and corporeality. Woman's "whole being, bodily and mental, is nothing but sexuality itself"; "prostitution is as organic in woman as the capacity for motherhood."[31] Moreover, although women can "become masculine by becoming logical and ethical," "the virtues of the man are sicknesses" in woman (340, 31). Among other of Weininger's more extreme claims are that "M lives consciously, W lives unconsciously" (130); the absolute woman has no ego (*kein Ich;* 240); and "Woman possesses no free will"—in fact, she has "ganz und gar keine Seele," absolutely no soul (340). Himself a homosexual and Jew, Weininger links both sexual inversion and Jewishness with woman, arguing in particular that the Jew was incapable of reason and autonomous action: "The real Jew like the real Woman both live only in the species, not as individuals" (437).[32]

According to Peter Nicholls, Weininger's text functioned virtually as an Expressionist manifesto (152). In one of the many contradictions of the period, however, German Expressionists (many of whom were Jewish) also promoted the decriminalization of homosexuality. One of Weininger's strongest supporters, Karl Kraus writes that "'acquired homosexuality' is the sign and right of ethically and aesthetically superior men."[33] Such support can in part be explained by a split among sexual theorists in Germany. Where reformers like Hirschfeld saw homosexuals as a "third sex," arguing that congenital difference was natural and should not be punished by law, others saw gay males as "the most manly of men," celebrating male-identified bonding modeled on an idealized Greek homosexuality and classic male beauty. This group perceived a continuum between homoerotic and homosocial experience that stressed the spiritual joining of men in intense erotic friendship, with no necessary physical manifestation of feeling.[34] Not all Expressionists were pleased with the fluidity of masculine homosociality. Stefan Zweig writes with disgust of "made-up boys with artificial waistlines" who "promenad[e] along the Kurfürstendamm."[35] On the other hand, Thomas Mann was preoccupied with homoeroticism, as revealed in *Tonio Kröger* (1903) and *Death in Venice* (1912), and his son Klaus Mann wrote plays featuring lesbianism and fiction revealing his homosexuality in the 1920s. Stefan Georg was the center of an openly gay group of writers, and Robert Musil, Franz Wedekind, and Bertolt Brecht also published work dealing with homoeroticism or homosexuality. There were gay and lesbian periodicals, clubs, bars, and hotels; the first gay film was produced in Berlin, in 1919; and Berlin boasted a gay theater from 1921 to 1924.[36] In *Berlin's Third Sex* (1904), Hirschfeld emphasizes the pervasiveness and normalcy of the behavior of "inverted" men throughout the city and across class lines.[37] By 1930, the city's gay and lesbian life had become so notorious that guides were published to underground Berlin. Curt Moreck's modishly illustrated *Guide through "Scandalous" Berlin* (1931) informed tourists and Berliners where they could go to observe inverted behavior—and indeed Berlin's gay and lesbian balls and nightclubs attracted straight participants and spectators.[38] In Hirschfeld's view, only London potentially surpassed Berlin in the open activity of its homosexual men.

Greenwich Village in the 1910s was home to New York's first visible middle-class gay subculture.[39] By the 1920s, the Village was characterized as frequently for its sexual inversion as for its artistic culture: Malcolm Cowley reports that letters to the *Broom* were sometimes addressed to "45 Queer Street" rather than King Street, and many newspaper articles and cartoons referred to the Village's long-haired men and short-haired women (Chauncey 230). The feminist club Heterodoxy welcomed its many lesbian members, and at least twenty restaurants and tearooms catered to lesbians and gay men in the early 1920s, many sponsoring poetry readings, musical evenings, and discussions (237–38). In 1929, a conservative Greenwich Village paper charged that sexual inversion was so popular in the Village that "the majority of [bohemian women] manifestly endeavor to create a third sex" by "do[ing] their best to appear like men" (229). Following World War I, Harlem became equally (in)famous as a mecca for gay life in New York, reputed to be livelier and more open than the Village. Among the prominent gay New Yorkers of the early twentieth century were Marsden Hartley, Charles Demuth, Hart Crane, Carl Van Vechten, Horace Mann, Countee Cullen, Alain Locke, Wallace Thurman, and Claude McKay. In a 1914 poem, Williams debates the proposition that "it is the woman in us / That makes us write," and in an essay he writes that "there's no sex."[40] Typically, however, American male modernists stressed the virility of the new poetic: as Rachel Blau DuPlessis puts it, they supported a "pro-female (possibly pro-feminine) but anti-effeminate position" for the artist; their promotion of a "third sex" blending of the genders found its limit in reflection on their own sexual expression.[41] Whereas Berlin Expressionists tended to be progay but not feminist, American modernist men were apt to sympathize with feminism but emphasize the heterosexual masculinity of their profession.

In 1895, Havelock Ellis speculates about why "inversion" was less noted in women than in men. Perhaps men were indifferent to women's homosexuality, or society allowed "a much greater familiarity and intimacy between women," making inversion "less easy to detect"; or perhaps society assumed "the extreme ignorance and the extreme reticence of women regarding any abnormal or even normal manifestation of their sexual life" (Behling 65). The construction of lesbian sexuality generally lagged about thirty years behind that of male homosexuality. In 1871 in Germany, homosexual activities were prohibited by law and defined as performed by men; lesbians were not recognized by German law until 1910.[42] Lesbians were also publicly less visible than gay men because they depended more on family structures, enjoyed lower wages (hence had less disposable income), and had more restricted access to public spaces like street corners and bars.[43] Perhaps because definitions of sexual inversion for women seemed more indistinct than for men, women's professional roles were more directly related to perceived inversion: intellectual and professional women were depicted in popular media and scientific journals as inverted; male artists were held to be effeminate but not inverted. Both in the United States and Germany, conservative thinkers linked women's rights associations to sexual aberrance and blamed them for the apparent rise in sexual inversion among women.

In Germany, political radicalism may have been associated with inversion because several leaders of the German women's movement were lesbian, although the movement did not support gay rights (Meskimmon 204). On the other hand, according to Richard Dyer, many straight women accepted a female-identified concept of lesbianism parallel to male-identified gay bonding, stressing notions of femininity. In this view, lesbianism was a "typical and profound experience for women, neither deviant nor a 'mere' phase," founded on the powerful mother-daughter bond and continued in the attachment of students and teachers.[44] Similarly, androgynous fashions would seem to signal at least the acceptance of mannish women. For the most part, however, inverted women as such were more feared and scorned by popular culture than inverted men, perhaps because they more directly threatened patriarchal family structure. Because lesbianism was not outlawed and hence did not involve the same degree of public danger, there was also less political support for lesbians than for gays in Germany.

German lesbian life did not extend along a social continuum to the extent that gay male life extended ordinary male activities. German *Frauenkultur* was organized largely around institutions: family, church, sports and fitness clubs, children's education, and social work. Unlike in the United States, there was no tradition of women's leadership in reform movements or of women's colleges providing opportunities for bonding parallel to men's in political organizations and the university.[45] Moreover, in German urban life, most nonfamilial socializing took place in public venues; this structure discouraged regular female gatherings for precisely the same reason that it enabled women's access to male gatherings: given the questionable propriety of unescorted women's appearance in public venues not designated for a specific sexually neutral purpose (like a fitness club), bourgeois women did not make a practice of gathering in public spaces in the evening. During the Weimar period, young unmarried urban women did enjoy extended homosocial bonding and use of public spaces: they frequently shared housing, were fascinated with bohemian and to some extent lesbian lifestyles, and were the target of fashion advertising that encouraged androgynous styles as a manifestation of femininity. Women-only clubs and cafés provided these women with a comfortable and safe environment. These women rebelled, however, primarily against their parents, not heterosexual values. They assumed that their flirtation with alternative lifestyles was temporary, looking forward to marriage, motherhood, and, generally, return to the provinces.[46]

In understanding the simultaneous lively gathering and relative isolation of lesbians in Germany, then, one must hold in mind the whole complex of alliances defining women's public space. To summarize: women's-only spaces proliferated in Berlin, appealing to both lesbians and an emergent culture of young urban women; women's fashions promoted superficial androgyny for all women, but *Frauenkultur* remained structured largely along bourgeois and patriarchal lines. According to Lavin, "for the most part lesbian life [in the 1920s] and earlier was marked by invisibility and silence," at least outside openly lesbian circles; sexual ambiguity prevailed (198). Oscillating gender identity could be read both as liberating and as part of a consumer control mechanism to link fashion to femininity. Female Expressionist writers may have been more guarded in gender politics than women in other arts. According to Meskimmon, lesbian nightlife provided a haven for straight and gay actresses, singers, dancers, and artists (207). To my knowledge, however, women in Expressionist literary circles participated far less actively in this scene.

In the United States, there was no clearly defined majority discourse distinguishing middle-class, socially approved female homosocial bonding from sexual inversion during the early modernist period, despite popular sexological and medical discourse.[47] As in Germany, this lack of definition was based on contradictions within popular culture and on differing norms even within mini-environments like Greenwich Village. George Chauncey documents the accepted liveliness of gay and lesbian life in the Village; Nina Miller, in contrast, argues that in the 1920s modernist female poets felt social pressure to define themselves heterosexually.[48] Both are right: depending on their age, upbringing, and social circles, women of the Village perceived more or less of a spectrum of acceptable modes of female performance; at its least clearly defined, this spectrum constituted what Adrienne Rich has called a "lesbian continuum," or lack of categorical distinction between forms of "primary intensity between and among women."[49] This continuum offered women the opportunity to develop a range of life-patterns within a relatively open interpretive field. While some women in Berlin experienced similar social interpretive fluidity, German women by and large did not.

Perhaps as a result of this fluidity, relatively few of the American women active in modernist cultural production lived in conventionally heterosexual relationships. Such relationships offered distinct advantages to men: the woman was assumed to provide full domestic services and emotional sustenance, and if she was also professionally active, she no longer necessarily needed economic support in return. In fact, male artists and writers were frequently at least partially supported by their spouses. The man in a heterosexual partnership, however, less often gave domestic or psychological support to his partner or considered her work as important as his. Consequently, those female writers and artists who did marry typically also developed strong nurturing relationships with women.[50] Many American women associated with modernism were lesbian or bisexual: Margaret Anderson, Djuna Barnes, Natalie Barney, Sylvia Beach, Gladys Bentley, Romaine Brooks, Willa Cather, Janet Flanner, Frances Gregg, H.D., Jane Heap, Amy Lowell, Ma Rainey, Bessie Smith, Gertrude Stein, and Ethel Waters. Despite her heterosexual styling, Millay was widely known to have had lesbian lovers, and radicals lionized her and Mabel Dodge's multiple affairs, as well as Isadora Duncan's affairs and unmarried maternity.[51] Like Moore, Harriet Monroe, sculptor Malvina Hoffman, and Florine Stettheimer lived alone or with mothers or sisters. Few innovative American women writers or artists had children. During an era when almost 90 percent of the population of women in the United States married, this pattern is extraordinary.[52] Women found both conventional marriage and motherhood incompatible with the production of avant-garde literature and art, and so adopted life-support patterns that were more compatible with such production, usually involving active, daily relationship with other women.

In contrast, the majority of women in German-speaking Europe associated with innovative arts and literature were married or engaged in significant heterosexual relationships, although few had children. These include Lou Andreas-Salomé, Sophie Taeuber-Arp, Margarete Beutler, Lily Braun, Ida Dehmel, Claire Goll, Emmy Hennings, Ricarda Huch, Käthe Kollwitz, Hedwig Lachmann, Berta Lask, Gabrielle Münter, Anna Seghers, Ina Seidel, Reneé Sintenis, Clara Viebig, and Lasker-Schüler. Some lived unconventionally: Hannah Höch was bisexual; painter Elfriede Lohse-Wächtler was married briefly, then lived highly unconventionally, including a period with Gypsies and, reputedly, female partners. No well-known writer lived openly as a lesbian. Gertrud Kolmar, Annette Kolb, Jeanne Mammen, Milly Steger, Lotte Laserstein, and Nelly Sachs never married. Höch, Hennings (who married Hugo Ball), Taeuber-Arp, Claire Goll, Paula Ludwig (who had a lengthy affair with Goll during his marriage to Claire), Charlotte Berend-Corinth, Gabrielle Münter (who lived with Kandinsky), actress Tilla Durieux (who married Paul Cassirer), and Lasker-Schüler were among the many women who had significant relationships with prominent male artists or writers.[53] At the same time, many of these relationships involved unconventional negotiation about domestic responsibilities and emotional support.

Jeanne Mammen's and Hannah Höch's lives shed interesting light on the complex currents of sexual negotiation in Berlin. A financially successful illustrator and painter, Mammen was well known for painting women and lesbian locales, and the titles of her paintings indicate her sense of gender as performance—for example, *Masked Ball* (also titled *She Represents: Carnival Scene*) and *Putting on Make-Up,* or *Boring Dollies,* where two modish, masculine women share space with a carnival doll.[54] In 1930, Mammen had a one-woman show in the Galerie Gurlitt, which then commissioned her to illustrate a luxury volume of prints based on the popular 1890s lesbian love poetry of Pierre Louÿs. She had completed seven of the proposed twelve lithographs when the project was terminated, immediately following the elections of 1933. Mammen never married and kept her private life private; no evidence reveals her sexuality. The popularity of her illustrations and her commercial success, however, indicate the vogue of lesbian styles and the open depiction of lesbian images coincident with sexological and mainstream condemnation of masculinity in women and female inversion.

Hannah Höch, the most gifted artist of Dada Berlin, developed the art of photomontage together with Hausmann, with whom she frequently collaborated (Hubert 228). Höch and Hausmann's relationship was stormy. Hausmann refused to leave his wife and children but lectured Höch frequently in letters about the need for women—and Höch in particular—to liberate themselves from theories like Weininger's. His liberal theory of women's freedom of mind and body, however, was compromised by the way he manipulated it to keep both his wife and mistress, while Höch wanted an exclusive relationship (Hubert 289–90). By 1922, Höch had left Hausmann. In 1926, she began a nine-year lesbian relationship with the Dutch writer Til Brugman. Neither, however, was active in homosexual organizations, and Höch had "no public identity as lesbian" (Lavin 189). In 1935, Höch married Kurt Matthies. Although these shifts in sexual partnering are not reflected in her painting and photomontage, from her earliest Dada work Höch deconstructed binary gender conception—pasting women's heads on men's bodies and men's on women's, or otherwise constructing ironic and androgynous or double-gendered images in her art.[55]

As these patterns indicate, despite similar parameters of changing gender and sexual norms, Moore and Lasker-Schüler would have been encouraged to conceive of relations between their bodies, art, and lives differently. While the patterns of behavior and attitude around them did not determine their choices, they do help to explain those choices in terms that go beyond idiosyncrasy or individual proclivity. In New York, Moore would have been broadly within the norm of fellow modernist writers (although not the population at large) as an unmarried, female-oriented, masculine-dressing woman. In Berlin, Lasker-Schüler was similarly within an Expressionist norm as a heterosexual woman dressing with bohemian extravagance. On the other hand, broadly normative assumptions may prevent scholars from hearing the lesbian suggestions in some of Lasker-Schüler's work and encourage interpretation of her cross-dressing as bohemian rather than "inverted." Similarly, Moore's mannish style has been read primarily as apolitical and asexual. The fact that Loy is the most sensitive of these three writers to heterosexual imperatives of self-fashioning has to do with the norms of the expatriate communities in which she spent her early years and with economic pressure to remain at least legally within the bonds of her unhappy first marriage. The remainder of this chapter turns to verbal and visual portraits of these three poets, and to their own manipulations of sartorial, life, and poetic styles.

Portrait of the Artist I: The Asexual Sensuality of Marianne Moore

Moore, Loy, and Lasker-Schüler were photographed, painted, sculpted, and sketched by multiple artists and written about in reviews, newspaper articles, and memoirs. Each poet largely constructed the ways she would be seen, through manipulation of the figure available to the photographer, painter, or audience. Sartorially, Moore adopted a style of dress that rides the line between masculinity and femininity, Loy designed clothes that manifest the feminine, and Lasker-Schüler occasionally dressed in men's clothing in a way signaling exoticism rather than masculinity. Moore's mannish but female clothing reflects her self-positioning on a continuum of intense friendships with women. Loy moves from identification of womanhood with reproductive heterosexuality to a rupture between performed femininity and ungendered aesthetic spiritualism. Lasker-Schüler positions herself as intensely female but not feminine, achieving something like the performance of a protosexual desiring subject that suggestively echoes lesbian and gay narratives of the period. There is greater consonance among patterns of Moore's dress, life, and poetic than for either Loy or Lasker-Schüler, perhaps because of the greater political stability of the United States and emotional stability of her life with her mother. Moore's radicalism is decorously clothed. Perhaps partly in response, her peers described her in terms suggesting both uniqueness and only marginally human or adult qualities, as though she lived almost literally outside her body and world.

The only body part of Moore's frequently commented on was her red hair, tightly braided and wrapped in a crown around her head. Kreymborg describes her as "an astonishing person with Titian hair" who awed "every man" through "a mellifluous flow of polysyllables."[56] In 1923, McAlmon describes both Loy (Gusta Rolph) and Moore (Martha Wallus) at some length in his autobiographical *Post-Adolescence.* The Loy character has a "straight Greek profile" and "must have been wonderfully beautiful a few years ago." The Moore character looks like "a Dresden doll thing with . . . Chinese eyes," a "wisplike body with its thatch of carrot-colored hair," and "half-boyish clothes."[57] In 1923, Matthew Josephson contrasts Moore to "heedless womanhood," seeing in her poems a "refinement" that is "almost oppressive"; Williams takes the tendency to characterize Moore in asexual terms to an extreme, writing that "Marianne was our saint."[58] Gilbert Snow in 1925 writes of Moore's "aesthetic shrinking from the present industrial ugliness"; in 1935, R. P. Blackmur declares that "no poet has ever been so chaste"; and in 1969, Randall Jarrell imagines Moore's poems as "entirely divorced from sexuality and power, the bonds of the flesh." By deflecting attention away from her embodiment, Moore sent her observers to the opposite extreme: they elevated her to a pedestal of unworldly purity and thereby to some extent dismissed her as knowing nothing of the world, sexuality, or its "power."

Photographs of Moore show a slender woman wearing a large dark hat, a straight-cut suit jacket, white blouse, scarf or necktie, a skirt of mid-calf length, and holding gloves. The effect is masculine and yet, because of the gloves and complex hairstyle, femininely decorous. Around 1920, Loy sketched Moore twice, suggesting a plain, slightly masculine woman through the spare lines of her face, lapels, and hat.[59] In Marguerite Zorach's 1925 oil painting, the blocky modernist brushstrokes of the large-cut purple jacket make the poet's chest appear flat (fig. 2). A Zorach sketch from approximately the same date elegantly caricatures this look: Moore sits in masculine pose, wearing a blocky suit jacket, collared blouse, and hat (fig. 3).

Moore's suit and hat constituted her professional costume. As Patricia C. Willis writes, "When [Moore] sat for her portrait she composed a persona which became an equivalent of her poetry" for more than fifty years.[60] A 1922 Marjori studio photograph presents Moore dressed in this style (fig. 4); a 1924 Sarony photograph presents a nearly identical image (fig. 5). Other depictions show a more relaxed look, suggesting that Moore regarded this costume as professional, not an essential marker of selfhood. In 1918, Alice Dewitt Little, editor of *Modern Art Collector,* paints the poet in a light dress with a relatively low-cut V-neck bodice. In a 1921 photograph, Aimé Dupont depicts Moore smiling, wearing a long-waisted black dress, with pleated skirt and white, crocheted collar. In a Doris Ullmann 1928 photograph, the poet wears a black velvet dress with a lacy collar and no hat.[61] A 1920s Alice Boughton photograph presents Moore as modish, looking over the high fur collar of a coat with a matching felt hat, pulled low—but the modishness is strikingly ungendered, despite the feather that softens the hat's sweep (fig. 6). In contrast, scores of late and famous photographs stress the poet's idiosyncrasy: she stands with an elephant, or parakeet, or wearing a tricorn in front of the Brooklyn Bridge, almost invariably dressed in her trademark suit or cape and large, dark hat.[62]

Moore did not follow fashion. She writes, "Fashion can make you ridiculous; style, which is yours to control individually, can make you attractive—a near siren" (1958; *CPr* 503); "'Fashion may be at the mercy of whim. Style is basic and does not change with the year" (1965; *CPr* 596). Numerous letters to family and female friends attest that Moore sought to combine fine fabrics and quality craftsmanship in a low-key masculine but elegant look. In 1907, a series of letters to her family describe her search for a suit, concluding that her final purchase "fits perfectly and as it is not like every other blue one, but rather longer in the coat and more manly in cut than the pony jacket effect every one's wearing, I shall like it greatly" (April 22; RML VI:13a:05). In January 1908, she briefly worries that the hat she has bought is "perhaps . . . too much in style" (*SL* 29). That Moore perceived her costume as gender-crossing is also indicated by a story Bonnie Costello relates from the late 1940s, when Moore "walked into a milliner's shop and asked to be fitted as Washington Crossing the Delaware."[63]

Moore wrote with frequency about fashion, pronouncing on the most attractive kinds of shoes, hats for men, cuts of armholes in blouses, how much of one's bosom or shoulder appropriately shows, makeup, and the relation of style to weight.[64] In letters and essays, her descriptions of clothing have the same extraordinary detail as descriptions of plants and animals in her poems, and in various formulations she asserts that "Dress . . . should conform with behavior" (1965; *CPr* 597). Indeed her own dress and behavior mix elements conventional to both genders, suggesting decorous restraint and assertive confidence. Moore's poetic forms show similar balances.

Moore's best-known poem on female appearance was first published in 1917.[65] "Those Various Scalpels" parodies the traditional desirable female poetic subject (cheeks like roses, lips like berries) by addressing a different kind of woman: "your hair"

> . . . the tails of two fighting-cocks head to head in stone—like
> sculptured scimitars, re-
> Peating the curve of your ears in reverse order: your eyes, flowers
> of ice
>
> And
> Snow sown by tearing winds on the cordage of disabled ships; your
> raised hand
> An ambiguous signature: your cheeks, those rosettes
> Of blood on the stone floors of French châteaux, with regard to which
> the guides are so affirmative—the regrets
> Of the retoucher being even more obvious: your other hand,
>
> A
> Bundle of lances all alike, submerged beneath emeralds from Persia

And the fractional magnificence of Florentine
Goldwork—a miniature demonstration in opulence—a collection of half
a dozen little objects made fine
With enamel—in gray, yellow, and dragonfly blue; a lemon, a

Pear
And three bunches of grapes, tied with silver: your dress a magnificent
square
Cathedral tower of unbelievably uniform
And at the same time, diverse appearance . . .

Moore then asks, are these elements of style and dress "weapons or scalpels? Whetted / To"

Brilliance by the hard majesty of that sophistication which is su-
Perior to opportunity, these things are rich
Instruments with which to experiment. We grant you that, but why
dissect destiny with instruments which
Are more highly specialized than the tissues of destiny itself?
(*EP* 261–62)

Moore's question indicates that to her mind this aggression is not justified by the circumstances. Although her photographs suggest that she, too, knows how to take advantage of opportunity, here the "hard majesty of sophistication" goes too far. Reading a woman's appearance should provide more than a sense of how well armed she has become or how sharply she can dissect. Moore's own "manly" suits could not provide a greater sartorial contrast to this representation of female dress. The poem's tone of detached description similarly distinguishes Moore's understated feminist critique from a more glamorous mode of feminine attack.

Like her dress style, Moore's life-patterns balanced the decorous and unconventional. She was influenced in these patterns by three primary cultural environments, none of which presented heterosexuality as a norm: her family, her college years, and her friends. For years, her mother maintained an intimate friendship with a local unmarried woman: Mary Norcross frequently spent the night at the Moores, and letters suggest that their intimacy became passionate during the years when Warner and Marianne were in college. The young poet could hardly have failed to associate her mother's intimacy with Norcross with her own intense feelings for female friends. At Bryn Mawr, she participated enthusiastically in the college practice of "crushes." The normalcy of these feelings in the perspectives of

Moore and her family is clear from the openness and frequency of their discussion in letters. As the young poet reports, Bryn Mawr even published a "Bird News" which "deals with all college crushes and comes out daily on the bulletin board" (*SL* 27). Around half of Moore's college peers did not marry.[66] In adulthood, many of her closest friends were lesbian or lived with female friends or family members, including H.D. and Bryher, the sisters Frances and Norvelle Brown (friends from Bryn Mawr), Elizabeth Bishop, Louise Crane, and Katherine Jones and Marcia Chamberlain. Although Moore had an extensive network of friends, many of whom did not fall into this category, Hildegarde Watson was the only of her long-term intimate female friends to be conventionally married, and even she had an independent professional career as a musician. From this background, Moore constructed for herself a markedly homosocial and asexual personal life.[67]

Spinsters have been portrayed in literature as repressed or filled with unsatisfied sexual desire—typified by Eliot's and Hemingway's lampoons of the poetess, or William Faulkner's Rosa Coldfield in *Absalom Absalom.* Moore does not fit this stereotype. Her poem "Black Earth" (1918) indirectly asserts her comfort in her own skin by exploring the relation of soul to embodiment that is constructed but not "made-up" on the model of female fashion. Speaking as an elephant, Moore opens the poem with a declaration of independence from public opinion:

Openly, yes,
With the naturalness
    Of the hippopotamus or the alligator
    When it climbs out on the bank to experience the

Sún, I do these
Things which I do, which please
    No one but myself. Now I breathe and now I am sub-
    Merged; . . .

(*EP* 237)

The speaker "sub / Merge[s]" and reveals herself at her own whim, but her indifference to judgment is far from antisocial. "This elephant skin / Which I inhabit [is]"

    . . . cut
Into checkers by rut
    Upon rut of unpreventable experience—
    It is a manual for the peanut-tongued and the

Hairy toed.

One's body instructs others of one's species (for an elephant, other "peanut-tongued" and "Hairy toed"): experience writes the body, and the body is then read as a guide enabling others to cope with similar experience. Following the analogy of the poem, Moore's experience-marked "skin" or readable appearance serves as a "manual" for other female poets, or women. Not only the toughness of its hide but its environmental context is legible:

> . . . The sediment of the river which
> Encrusts my joints, makes me very gray but I am used
>
> To it, it may
> Remain there; do away
> With it and I am myself done away with, for the
> Patina of circumstance can but enrich what was
>
> There to begin
> With.

Local conditions, the "Patina of circumstance," do not construct the embodied subject, but "do away / With it" and nothing recognizable as an "I" remains. Clothes, appearance, the embodied performance of self is both only a "crust" and the only "I" available.

As in "Peter," "Sojourn in the Whale," "Roses Only," and "Those Various Scalpels," here Moore raises the question of how nature relates to appearance. The elephant's skin provides a "manual" of "unpreventable experience," not of nature or spiritual essence. Moreover, what "please[s]" an elephant will in part determine what it experiences: by analogy, if Moore pleases to attend college or edit a journal, these choices will give her "unpreventable" experiences different from those of a woman who "pleases" to devote her life to the domestic sphere. In this sense, the will is indeed author of the body. While some aspects of experience have to do with breathing or other physiological functions, much is self-determined or social. To make sure we have not missed the point, Moore uses the word "history" to describe what is "cut" into the elephant's back: this "back / Is full of the history of power." As elephant, she is literally powerful. As female poet, she may have "cut" into her skin a "history" of her confrontations with others' power. At the same time, Moore identifies power with inner reserve. The philosophical emphasis of the poem lies in the poet's assertion that manifest power must be balanced with "spiritual poise" and receptivity. The elephant's skin is "translucent" as well as "thick"; it resembles "black glass." Its "depth" results in part from the "Beautiful element of unreason" under its hide. Due to this sensitive openness and "unreason," the elephant gracefully as well as confidently inhabits its body.

For Moore even indirectly to portray herself as a black elephant collapses stereotypes of masculinity, femininity, and heterosexual attractiveness. Hogue reads Moore's poetic generally as revealing this process of "taking things out of their original contexts and putting them in new ones," thereby "construct[ing] a new lyric subjectivity as well as question[ing] discrete epistemological categories that . . . order gender identity."[68] Yet the poem ends with a question stressing a social reading of one's "skin" rather than isolated self-formulation: "Will / Depth be depth, thick skin be thick, to one who can see no / Beautiful element of unreason under it?": what will the elephant (or poet) "be" to the observer who cannot read its manual of experience and appreciate the idiosyncrasies or soul of its being? The end of the poem reiterates—typically, for Moore, as question rather than statement—that being and interpretation cannot be fully distinguished. Moore speaks as elephant performing naturalness in order to construct a "manual" written in the "Patina of circumstance" by which people learn a manner of being different from that of current stereotypes. Yet, to return to Flügel, such reading is possible "for the world to decipher [only] if it has the key."

The body, for Moore, did not determine life's choices. The post-Freudian world, however, seems to have lost the key for deciphering her conception of a fulfilled physical life. Moore had read Freud, and she talked with her friends about the significance of the physical.[69] On April 18, 1921, she writes to Bryher:

> What you say is true; the physical is important as well as the spiritual and I don't doubt that a thousand derangements are the result of our misunderstanding of the physical. Freud says his object is to substitute a conscious for an unconscious—a normal for a pathogenic conflict and we must do this if we can. A knowledge of abnormal conditions is a help in understanding normal conditions but as Freud says, our capacity for transferring energy from one field to another is almost infinite and the adjustments of one need to another, involve so many things that it is no easy matter to be absolute as to what course of action we are compelled to adopt for our all round best good. (B, GEN MSS 97, Box 37, folder 1357)

Moore's poems are full of enthusiastic pleasure in things of the world; as her lifelong identification with animals and love of sports also suggests, she relished physicality.[70] This letter to Bryher indicates that in Moore's balance of multiple desires, she did not feel the sexual to be the strongest; she adjusted "one need to another," for her own "all round best good."

Moore's correspondence is full of the pleasures of looking, hearing, touching, smelling, eating, and being with friends. To Louise Crane, she writes, "Another psychologic miracle, Louise. You know how much I care about my appearance just now; yet these shoes are such masterpieces, fit me so well, remind me so exactly of my pleasure in seeing you" (August 29, 1946, RML V.13.02). Katherine Jones, who like many of Moore's friends, delighted in sending her small extravagances, receives the following thanks:

> This masterly cheese—would any other word exist—is a thing of mystery to us—the thickened surface like the rind of tropical fruit . . . The Indian Chutney! It shall be an ornament for a *long long* time . . . . the magic skin cream performed a miracle this very morning, altering me so that I could appear civilized & needfully delicate at a little talk which I gave to Brooklyn College Eng students today. (March 19, 1942, RML V.30.45)

Another letter to Crane demonstrates as well the permeability of borders between Moore's physical being and her pleasure in language: "I had a letter from Elizabeth [Bishop] a day or two ago which I am thinking of having tattood on me—in which she talks of Mrs. Almeyda's identifying certain little dark specks in a white bowl, as 'Them's Lizard'" (February 14, 1940; RML V.12.27).

The extravagant language of Moore's poems, like that of her letters, expresses intense pleasure, not renunciation, repression, or lack.[71] Similarly, the embedding of colloquialism, wit, and whimsical assertion in the ostentatious artifice of her syllabic stanzas and complex syntax demonstrates subjective agency; the poems celebrate "gusto" in forms of ardent curiosity and intelligence. John Emil Vincent analyzes these qualities as the "erotics" or "orgasmics" of her verse. Eliot muses in his 1935 introduction to the *Selected Poems* that each of us chooses the "subject-matter" that allows us "the most powerful and most secret release"—implying, as Vincent argues, that Moore's detailed descriptions provide exactly such release for her. Because she often deploys her lyric "I" unemphatically, however, Moore gives the impression of distance or disembodiment at times: the speaker gets lost in the poem's detail. Vincent sees precisely this willful embodiment and disembodiment of Moore in her poems as "erotic oscillation," a key factor in her "queer poetics" (99, 119).[72] The dense aural patterning of her poems and their relish of even the shortest syllable as the basis for a rhyme or smallest detail as topical point of interest suggest Moore's tactile pleasure in language as well as in the physical world. Moore did not need a sexual relationship to experience eroticism or write a poetry that is attuned to embodiment.

Moore's words also resonate with historical and cultural significance. The title "Black Earth" suggests not just the "Patina of circumstance" encrusting the elephant and the elephant's strength but translates into English the Greek name of the religious reformer and philosopher Philipp Melancthon, which is in turn a translation of his German name, Schwartzerd—thereby referring both to Melancthon's reforms and to a practice of self-naming among early-sixteenth-century German philosophers who frequently translated their names into Greek. Moore's words foreground connection with political, social, and cultural fields, even while asserting the arbitrariness of sound and form. Balance is the key word of such a poetic. Moore brings together apparently contradictory elements to assert that opposites do not cancel each other out; one learns about one's own capacities through attentive study or observation of the world; and both poetry and life invite visceral engagement. Moore's decorous self-styling in dress and photographs provides a provocative counterpoint to her animalistic and unruly name-play, illuminating the hide-and-seek quality of embodiment in her poems. She challenges the reader to enter a poetic and lived realm where the boundaries distinguishing masculine and feminine, sexual and asexual, intellectual and embodied experience are replaced by continuums allowing dynamic interplay of sensuality, intelligence, and art. Until both Moore's aesthetic and life can be understood within the context of early-twentieth-century American gender, sexual, and social continuums, however, it will remain difficult to read the politics or erotics of the poetic "manuals" she has left behind.

Portrait of the Artist II: Designing the Feminine, Mina Loy

Loy's attitudes about gender and sense of herself as female poet contain greater contradictions and tensions than either Moore's or Lasker-Schüler's. Loy does not share Moore's conviction in the possibilities of change or Lasker-Schüler's belief in what Bloch calls the "militant optimism" of utopian fantasy. Her poetry is grounded in a critique of the present at times both more direct and astute than theirs and less historical in its concerns. At the same time, while Loy presents herself within the conventions of feminine heterosexuality, her poetic asserts a power divorced from gender—in this sense resembling Moore's different route to a similar end.

If Millay was the "It-girl" for modernity, Loy was "it" for Futurism, Dada, and the radical edge of modernism. Kreymborg describes Loy as an "exotic and beautiful . . . English Jewess" and comments that "her beauty interested some observers more than her poetry."[73] Harriet Monroe, who disliked Loy's verse, ascribes to Loy "Beauty ever-young" and "charm which will survive a century"; Sylvia Beach claims that Loy and her daughters "were so lovely they were stared at wherever they went"; McAlmon claims that "many of the famous stage beauties . . . would have come off decidedly second" in a comparison with Loy, "not only for wit but also for looks and style" (*LLB82* xx, xxi). In a *New York Evening Sun* interview, Loy is the exemplar of "the modern woman" with her poetry, stylishness, and striking good looks. Williams refers to "Mina's long-legged charms," and Moore describes Loy as "beautiful," "very clever[,] and a sound philosopher" (*BM* 222). According to Susan Dunn, Loy was among the most frequently photographed women of the period.[74]

Man Ray took two famous photographs of Loy. In a photograph of the poet with Djuna Barnes, Loy appears feminine: her top hat emphasizes the curve of her hair and dangling earring, and the lighting calls attention to the relaxed oval neckline of her dress and choke-necklace (*BM* 368ff.). Even Loy's top hat, with its rounded top and matching the color of her dress, suggests rakish sexuality rather than masculinity. Photographed alone, the poet strikes a rhapsodic pose—head upturned, eyes apparently closed, hair unruly (fig. 7).[75] The delicate ear and graceful eyebrows stand in marked contrast to the angular thermometer earring dominating the profile and casting a straight shadow across the curves of her bare breastbone and shoulder. This photograph seems curiously indifferent to the individuality of its subject, instead representing simultaneously a thermometer-adorned "modern" woman and classic woman-as-rhapsode.

"Dusie," a 1905 Haweis photograph of Loy smoking, also depicts the poet with closed eyes, head tilted up—suggesting the subject's mystical state, not least because the cigarette falls down across her relaxed lips as though she has forgotten to smoke it (frontispiece *BM*). In another Haweis photo, Loy holds a Rodin sculpture and looks slantwise at the camera: her lips are parted, her hair loosely pulled back so that one strand escapes in curls (fig. 8). Loy does not look at the sculpture but appears in juxtaposition to it, almost as herself another icon of the modern. A livelier snapshot shows Loy standing between Jane Heap and Ezra Pound, who looks at Loy (fig. 9). Loy looks directly at the camera, hitching her ankle-length fur coat up to one side to reveal both her ankles and the outline of slender legs and hips. In a 1920s George Platt Lynes photograph, the poet looks directly at the camera and smiles, looking alert, windswept (*MLWP* 265). Here again, Loy plays to the camera to totally different effect than Moore, emphasizing romantically unfocused feminine rhapsody or alertly self-conscious (heterosexual?) challenge. In a self-portrait (1905), Loy looks soberly and directly at the viewer but appears altogether feminine, in her large flowered hat and loosely coifed hair (fig. 10). Similarly, while in 1907 Moore was already admiring the "manly" cut of a jacket, in a 1905 photograph Loy wears a long flowing dress with lacy sleeves and leans forward in a feminine pose (fig. 11).

Burke claims that Loy wrote "for the most part in a deliberately unmarked or asexual poetic voice"; in contrast, Loy's presence was far from asexual.[76] Loy approached appearance from the perspective of both dress designer and model, alert to changes in fashion and to making the most of her own looks.[77] Although Loy's designs ranged from bathing suits to evening gowns, most combined art-nouveau and geometric patterned material with nonconfining formfitting styles to suggest natural (uncorseted) feminine sexuality and abstract forms.[78] They were not for the factory worker or career woman but were playful, theatrical, as were her doodling designs. Loy's interest seems to be in the posed female figure: one page of doodling shows only outfits that are extremely short (perhaps bathing suits?) or formfitting, and emphasize or expose breasts (fig. 12). In late manuscripts, Loy also writes about fashion in ways that suggest the importance of attractive stylishness. "Goy Israels" repeats as part of the litany of blame against Mrs. Israel that she dressed her daughter only in clothes that were ugly and didn't fit (B Box 2, folders 28 and 29). In a long page of prose on the possible spiritual effects of an evolutionary "extension of the normal gamut of vibrational reception," Loy mentions that an unanticipated "increase of nervous tension on behalf of vibratory acceleration" results from "fashion[']s apparently diabolical contrivance that that part of [the office girl's] body subjected to the wear & tear of constant locomotion, be encased in gossamer film" (B Box 7, folder 187). Fashion, this implies, may have unwitting spiritual consequences; the materials draping a moving body affect the pattern and development of its vibrations. Loy indicates the seriousness of this claim in another "note": "Death is a horizontal current running counter to the vibration of vitality." Although these notes were written decades later, their ideas may have developed from the dress reform movement Loy witnessed in Munich and subsequent years of designing her own clothing, beginning around 1904. Loy's initial designs in Paris preceded Pierre Poiret's famous revolution in women's fashion and, Alex Goody speculates, may have influenced "the trend towards simplicity" marked by his styles and associated with the "modern" woman (269).[79] Burke repeatedly asserts Loy's extreme concern with her appearance in the years before 1917.

In tune with her sartorial style, Loy's "Feminist Manifesto" implies that women should appear feminine: "the women who adapt themselves to a theoretical valuation of their sex as a *relative impersonality,* are not yet *Feminine*"; and "Woman for her happiness must retain her deceptive fragility of appearance" (*LLB* 154, 156). To base women's happiness on the fiction of weakness or fragility apparently echoes the heterosexual imperative, but Loy's statement emphasizes the deception involved. In this emphasis, she seems to play on cultural stereotypes of femininity as "the privileged marker of the instability and mobility of [all] modern gender identity."[80] Loy's stylishness is allied to the decadent production of self as aesthetic artifact, capitalizing on looks and on objects of consumption—even though Loy consumes what she herself has made. Moore and Lasker-Schüler, in contrast, use unconventional appearance to deflect attention from female embodiment.

Unlike her dress, Loy's poetic contains no hint of this play with feminine deception: there is nothing "fragile" in the Latinate complexities, juxtaposed condensed phrases, dense puns, or jarring referential shifts of her poems. Moreover, Loy's later poems leave behind the gender narratives of her early work. While Loy's costumes suggest delight in sartorial style, her poems suggest a distrust of language and tight control—even in the midst of extravagance. Her metaphors and diction include extremes of fantasy, neologism, and other wordplay, but the overall effect is of concision, a paring down to essentials. Her words reverberate not with historical association but with the concrete qualities of language as such. Phrases and individual words are isolated in short lines, often containing line-internal white space and irregular indentations and lacking punctuation. Words are suspended in the space of the page. Language, Loy writes, should attempt to emulate the "gorgeous reticence" of sculpture or painting, at the same time that it can have an explosive power like radium, beyond that of visual art ("Brancusi's Golden Bird," "Gertrude Stein"). Earlier than her peers, Loy uses the visual resources of the page.

"Songs to Joannes" (1917) demonstrates the way Loy's language combines "wild" and compressed elements. The poem's first section emphasizes this contrast, with its

Spawn of   Fantasies
Silting the appraisable

Pig Cupid his rosy snout
Rooting erotic garbage
"Once upon a time"
Pulls a weed white star-topped
Among wild oats sown in mucuous-membrane

I would an eye in a Bengal light
Eternity in a sky-rocket

(*LLB* 53)

Yet, in contrast to the fireworks of orgasm (the "eye"/"I" of pleasure), the speaker calls these "Spawn of Fantasies" "suspect places," and claims "I must live in my lantern / Trimming subliminal flicker / Virginal to the bellows / Of Experience." The rest of the poem makes clear, however, that this speaker has not been "Virginal" and does not desire a return to isolated enclosure or trimmed light. Rather, her distrust of a culture that promotes the sowing of "wild oats" merely as an exercise in spreading "mucuous-membrane" prompts her to draw back, to harness feeling and language more precisely in order not to lose the energy, pleasure, and light she herself maintains.

At the level of narrative, this poem relates an affair begun with sexual pleasure and hope, leading to Joannes's abandonment of the speaker, the speaker's apparent pregnancy and miscarriage, and concluding reflections on love.[81] As love story, the plot is mundane. The language of the poem, however, makes this plot of "Shuttle-cock and battle-door" far from transparent and shifts the interest of the poem to itself (sec. X, *LLB* 56). This focus is demonstrated near the middle of the poem, when the speaker suggests what might have been: "Let us be very jealous," she begins, "Or we might make an end of the jostling of aspirations / Disorb inviolate egos":

Where two or three are welded together
They shall become god
- - - - - - - - - - - - - - - -
Oh that's right
Keep away from me Please give me a push
Don't let me understand you Don't realise me
Or we might tumble together
Depersonalized
Identical
Into the terrific Nirvana
Me you—you—me

(sec. XIII, *LLB* 58)

At its best, sexually expressed love may "depersonalize" lovers, "disorb inviolate egos," knock down the boundaries ordinarily differentiating "you" and "me." It may even make the lovers "Identical": there are no roles, no social mannerisms, no man or woman in the "Nirvana" of sexual "understand[ing]" or "realiz[ation]"—"Me you." Each "I," by this logic, exists as an "orbed" ego until two egos are "disorbed" or "welded together" through the heat of intercourse. There is no fixed individuality, just fear of trespassing apparently "inviolate" boundaries of self. Through its equalizing of the partners in intercourse, insistence on female sexual agency, and unapologetic depiction of sexuality as key to self-formulation, "Songs to Joannes" shocked its readers.[82] As Kreymborg recalls, it was regarded in the same scandalous class as Margaret Sanger's sexual-reform pamphlets, and was most shocking because written by "a woman who dressed like a lady."[83]

By juxtaposing language of religion, fairy tale, myth, romantic metaphor ("eternity in a sky-rocket"), anatomical science, and other fields of diction, this poem indicates that being and "Experience" are constructed; language mediates perception; embodiment is a product of many registers. In the late 1920s, Loy links this aesthetic of constructedness with gender in a poetic portrait of British heiress and poet Nancy Cunard. Like Moore's "Those Various Scalpels," "Nancy Cunard" plays off the form of the *blason*:[84]

Your eyes diffused with holly lights
of ancient Christmas
helmeted with masks
whose silken nostrils
point the cardinal airs

The vermilion wall
receding as a sin
beyond your moonstone whiteness,

Your chiffon voice
tears with soft mystery
a lily loaded with a sucrose dew
of vigil carnival,

Your lone fragility
of mythological queens
conjures long-vanished dragons—
—their vast jaws
yawning in disillusion,

Your drifting hands
faint as exotic snow
spread silver silence

as a fondant nun
framed in the facing profiles
of Princess Murat
and George Moore

(*LLB* 103)

Loy's poem departs from the conventional *blason* through a defamiliarization of language so extreme that it removes Cunard from the realm of visibility—a striking move in the portrait of a renowned beauty. Conventionally, eyes reflect the soul and are bright; Cunard's eyes are "diffused" by "lights" of memory or ritual and "helmeted with masks" that call attention to nostrils and "cardinal airs"—a phrase that could suggest songs of "ancient Christmas" or the affectations of social prominence ("airs"), but that in any reading distracts attention from Cunard's eyes. Similarly, a scarflike "chiffon voice" resembles a lily "loaded" with sugary "dew" of "vigil carnival." This voice is contradictorily wispy, sweet, mysterious, and alertly watchful (vigilant?) in its rule-breaking festivity. Like avant-garde painting, Loy's portrait rejects representation.

Cunard, in this portrait, exudes ancient rites and the commodities of empire: silk, moonstone, chiffon, silver. Both its exoticism and aristocracy suggest romanticized femininity: this is the queen for whom dragons were slain. Deception or disguise, however, lurks in every stanza: the face is helmeted and masked, the voice mysterious, the dragons disillusioned and still alive, and the portrait as a whole is "framed"—falsely presented in conspiratorial silence by two mysterious "profiles." As Conover explains, George Moore had an affair with Cunard's mother and may have been the poet's father. Women named Murat were linked with Surrealism and Dada, and another artistic Murat was a houseguest of Peggy Guggenheim (*LLB* 206). Such framing gives no sense of Cunard as poet, editor, woman, or friend. It presents a subject that cannot be seen except as mask, recession, carnival, disillusion, or silence. There is undeniable beauty in her eyes, voice, skin, and hands, but the poem tells us that this beauty reveals nothing. It is made up of Western civilization's myths of the feminine, constituting a "framed" portrait of Woman.

In contrast, Loy's "Apology of Genius" (ca. 1922) thematizes problems of embodiment, suggesting by its title that the poem's "we" are geniuses and that "you" "watchers of the civilized wastes" cannot understand *us* (*LLB* 77–78). *We* are "ostracized with God"—marginalized, but in obviously creative company, thereby suggesting that *we* are artists. Although all are "lepers of the moon / all magically diseased," *we* are "innocent / of our luminous sores." As the poem later asserts, "You may give birth to us / or marry us" but "we" bear a distanced relation to such contact. In "Black Earth" Moore claims that experience cuts legible marks in the skin; in contrast, Loy imagines the scars of experience as detached from the being of geniuses. Moreover, while Moore's elephant constitutes a living "manual," Loy's geniuses are cut off from their "watchers": their "wills are formed . . . / beyond your laws"; watchers misinterpret even the armor or "cuirass" of *our* souls. Most importantly, the "imperious jewelry of the Universe" that *we* forge out of "the dusk of Chaos" is "to your eyes / A delicate crop / of criminal mystic immortelles" waiting for the "censor's scythe." Both the lives of geniuses and their creations are visible to others only as corroded or criminal. "Watchers . . . reverse their signals on our track": signs do not mean the same thing to *you* and *us*. What "feed[s]" "sacerdotal clowns" can only appear as romantic fantasy or "pulverous . . . poverty" to the rest. Like her fellow Dadaists, Loy sees art as opposed to public institutions and the artist as both marginal and exceptional—a "genius." Moreover, to the extent that genius is "innocent of" physical being, sex and gender are irrelevant to the production of art, a conclusion substantially different from her portraits of patriarchy in early poems like "The Effectual Marriage or the Insipid Narrative of Gina and Miovanni." As this analysis implies, Loy's creative work during her brief stays in the United States do not make her an "American" poet conceptually.

In fact, Loy's notion of genius resembles the German concept *Geist*, with its blend of intellect, creativity, and spirit, except that it is not gendered masculine. The subject portrayed in "Nancy Cunard" reveals no *Geist;* the poem functions in part to demonstrate that beautiful, cultivated surfaces do not reveal what lies beneath the "helmeted" mask. In "Apology of Genius," however, we are allowed behind the mask, as it were, to see what mere "watchers" cannot. Loy's verbal portrait "Gertrude Stein" similarly presents *Geist* rather than the "deceptive fragility" of traditional femininity. This "Curie / of the laboratory / of vocabulary" crushes "consciousness . . . to extract / a radium of the word" (*LLB* 94). This is undisguised power. Stein is female but her science of the word is ungendered. Like Loy, she makes all language seem foreign, transforms it into an element different from speech.[85] In these poems, Loy imagines a poetic energy constructed from materials of the world but obliterating all traces of its historical embeddedness, leaving its sores and even consciousness behind. Appearances are irrelevant to, or block, understanding, these poems suggest, a remarkable conclusion for a poet who attempted to support herself through dress design.

"Nancy Cunard," "Gertrude Stein," "Apology of Genius," and several of Loy's other poems also suggest the isolation of the artist. In "Apology of Genius" the speaker uses a first-person plural to mark artists as a group ("we" are marginalized), but the poem's focus is on the gulf between artists and a broader community. Such a stance is typical of Loy's life as well as of her poems. Loy had many friends, and she is remembered in several memoirs with warmth and admiration. Most of these memories, however, stem from a relatively brief period of time: Loy apparently did not maintain correspondence for more than a few years with friends at a distance. Her friendships, unlike those of Moore and Lasker-Schüler, depended on proximity, and Conover describes them as "guarded" (*LLB82* xxxiii). Moreover, Loy herself defined her primary intimacy as (hetero)sexual. When asked in a 1929 *Little Review* questionnaire, "What has been the happiest moment of your life?" she answered "Every moment I spent with Arthur Cravan." For "The Unhappiest?" she answered, "The rest of the time." Similarly, she notes that Cravan alone gave her that "one other intelligence to converse with" that she craved (*LLB82* 305–6, lx). In this same interview, Loy also described her strongest characteristic as "capacity for isolation."

Loy's later writing bears little thematic resemblance to her early poems of heterosexuality or her middle poems of isolated genius. In the story "Street Sister" (n.d.) Loy writes about her sympathy for a Parisian street woman who at first appeared "deranged," with eyes "totally unoccupied, for whoever had once looked out of them, having been too long rebuffed by the world of the exterior, had drawn in so far they had lost focus."[86] Yet when Loy tries to help by buying her food and they are both thrown out of a café, the "common defeat established [them] on the footing of absolute equality which seemed to warm her." Soon, "a perfectly normal human being, with light in her friendly eyes" looks out of what had been holes in a derelict face. Sisterhood, as Loy's title suggests, brings a "street" woman back to life. Such communion between women appears in none of Loy's poems written in Florence or during the early 1920s.

Loy's early writing proclaims sexual freedom for women while also writing out personal depression, grief, and anger. In her poems of the twenties, Loy steps away from the conflicted freedoms of an explicitly sexual politics to map what is problematic in both embodiment and language as modes of intimacy and communication. Beauty suggests the sugary tradition of constructed femininity and gives no sense of spirit and power; masculinity may founder on its own strength. In

"Joyce's Ulysses," Loy describes the novel she admired as "impaled upon the phallus" (*LLB* 88), or pierced by myths of male cultural/sexual power. Meanwhile, leperous sores may coincide with spiritual greatness. Ordinary language, she implies through her poems, is inadequate, but the poet's disjunctions, juxtapositions, multilingual puns, and grammatical wrenching function less to relay information or feeling than to approach the Stein-like crushed consciousness that releases a pure "radium of the word." Shreiber comments that Loy sees language as disconnective ("'Love Is a Lyric'" 148). Indeed, where Moore might be seen as a poet of the sentence or stanza, forms of connection, Loy seems a poet of the word. She does, however, appear to see hope as well as loss in this disconnection. Loy wrenches sign from signifier in an attempt to generate a level of communication beyond language's message-bearing function.

For Loy, there is a chasm between spirit and skin. Her deceptive appearance of femininity is not reflected in the nongendered speaking voice and radical linguistic structures of her poems. These contrasts represent the two types of lingua franca available to her in all the cities she temporarily called home. As an attractive and stylishly feminine woman, she received a degree of attention not granted most of her poetic peers. Femininity was a known coin. At the same time, within the avant-garde in Paris, Florence, and New York, an antisentimental, language-focused, gender-neutral (or masculine) poetic style was the coin of value.[87] Loy was not following fashion. She was a shaper of the free verse language of intellectual abstraction and concision that would become synonymous with Anglo-American modernist poetry, publishing poems more radical in style than anyone but Stein in 1914 and 1915. Perhaps especially because of her peripatetic traveling, the simultaneous maintenance of a modish feminine appearance and a decisively anti-sentimental, anti-traditional, anti-bourgeois use of language may have simplified her self-positioning and acceptance among Italian Futurists, expatriate Anglo-Americans throughout Europe, expatriate Europeans in New York, and modernists everywhere. Neither Moore's nor Lasker-Schüler's self and poetic styling would have traveled as effectively as Loy's.

Portrait of the Artist III:
The Double Gendered Sexuality of Else Lasker-Schüler

Like Moore, Lasker-Schüler encouraged nonfeminine conceptions of herself in daily exchanges and as poet. Unlike Moore, sexual desire had for her a foundational, almost Whitmanian centrality, expressing love but also the desire for immediate connection with others that grounds her sense of spiritual being. Unlike Whitman's, however, Lasker-Schüler's articulation of loving did not focus on the experience of a particular body.[88] Even in her love poems, Lasker-Schüler often enacts desire without gendering the body. Like Höch's photo-montages combining men's and women's body parts, Lasker-Schüler's poems blur gender lines.

Descriptions of Lasker-Schüler also foreground the exotic and sexual. Because Expressionist prose is generally highly metaphorical, some of this foregrounding may be generic. Nonetheless, there is a marked charge to contemporary descriptions of her poetry and readings. In 1903, Hans Benzin characterizes Lasker-Schüler as having "an exalted, unartistic style. . . . similarly a gypsy-like, erotic sensitivity" (*MM* 46); in 1904 Peter Hille characterizes the poet's style through almost a full-body portrait: "With little delicate brown sandals she wanders in deserts. . . . Her poetic spirit is a black diamond that cuts into her forehead and hurts. . . . In the night of her hair, winter snow wanders. Her cheeks are fine fruits, burned by the spirit." Some experienced titillation in the poet's masculine dress: Wieland Herzfelde describes the poet at a reading as wearing "wide pants, silver shoes, a kind of loose jacket, hair like silk, deep black"; "at times wild then again sensually soft . . . Jussuf was so completely a woman, she was so beautiful."[89] After a reading in 1912, the poet was described in racial clichés as having "a face of oriental sensuality, her body suggested something snakelike."[90] Eduard Plietsch, in contrast, found Lasker-Schüler without "feminine erotic appeal"; the "wretched body of this poor soul was given over to torture by the demon of sexual irregularities."[91] Similarly, a 1912 newspaper review reported that "the fog of symbolism, mysticism, and a strong voluptuousness fluttered through her verses" together with a tendency toward the "eccentric, unnatural, even ugly"; Walter Benjamin admired her poetry but wrote to a friend in 1914 that the poet's "manner is empty and sick—hysterical."[92]

Visual representations of Lasker-Schüler also manifest a range of responses, although paintings typically present the poet as Jussuf, while photographs show her in female dress. Most famous is a 1912 oil by Karl Schmidt-Rottluff called *Die Lesende (The Reader)*. Its flat planes, dark reds, greens, and browns, and angular surfaces obscure its subject's features, while suggesting her dark hair and striking eyebrows and eyes. Although the painting's title suggests that its subject consumes literature and her eyes look down, the poet stands upright and holds her book high; her mouth is open. The "reader," in short, appears to be reading aloud—perhaps her own poetry. The humor of this play between consumption and performance is echoed in the mixture of bright and dark colors emphasizing the poet's red lips, hence perhaps sexuality as well as agency. Schmidt-Rottluff also published a sketch of the poet as *Prince of Thebes* in *Der Sturm* (1912), standing in profile with raised arm and highly stylized face, hair, and clothing.[93] Its rough outlines suggest the poet's strong face (echoed in the power of the raised gesture), the cropped thick hair, and (in another double gendering) female clothing: a low-necked blouse with patterned, curving bodice, and open jacket with high buttons.

Jankel Adler's 1924 oil of Lasker-Schüler is realistically but roughly blocked—heavyset, with an old-looking, strong-featured face, looking to the side or shiftily toward the viewer (*MM* 174). The poet's indistinctly defined pants and flat slippers suggest domesticity rather than exoticism or rakish masculinity. On the other hand, long hair, a lightly draped head cloth, and large hips mark the figure as female, and its large contours suggest strength. Christian Rohlfs's 1920 watercolor, *Die Dichterin. Ein Bildnis Else Lasker-Schüler* presents a rhapsodic poet, with head back and hands crossed on her breast. As in several Loy photographs, here the "poetess" communes with herself.[94] Franz Marc's 1913 *Sitzender gelber Frauenakt (Seated Yellow Female Nude)*, painted for and mailed to Lasker-Schüler, presents a woman with eyes closed in sorrow. Perhaps taking Lasker-Schüler as spiritual model, Marc places this nude next to a swan, possibly alluding to Hille's review calling her a "black swan of Israel" and suggesting her closeness to nature.[95]

Lasker-Schüler was her own most frequent portraitist, and sketched or painted Prince Jussuf hundreds of times. All depictions of the Prince are recognizably related to the poet in having ear-length black hair, a prominent straight nose, protruding eyebrows, and piercing black eyes. A 1912 photograph of the poet (fig. 13) shows striking resemblance to her own 1913 *Selbstbildnis als Prinz Jussuf* mailed to Marc (fig. 14). Lasker-Schüler's sketches of Jussuf are highly stylized: he wears brightly colored Arabic clothing, and often appears in a city of mosques or with a city resting on his arm. He is young, slender, tall, Jewish (sometimes marked with a star of David), and active—often positioned in a lanky stride, as in the watercolor where Jussuf and his companions walk toward Irsahab "in dance step" (fig. 15). A 1910 photograph shows Lasker-Schüler costumed as Jussuf, wearing loose pants with a long matching jacket and stylish heeled boots (fig. 16).[96] Most photographs of the poet, in contrast, show a woman in standard dress. A newspaper 1905 photo shows Lasker-Schüler sitting in a long, full-skirted dress and small hat at a table in the Café des Westens (*MM* 51); in a 1906 photo, she wears the same hat, a necklace, and a white blouse with lace under a velvet jacket with trim (fig. 17).

Lasker-Schüler dressed as the Prince for public events. Bauschinger claims that the poet was indifferent to her appearance as prince: the costume made a political, not a fashion statement (*WZ* 146). Indeed, Lasker-Schüler seems to have been indifferent to fashion: she never moved toward "modern" short skirts, tunic-style dresses, or other popular styles. According to Hallensleben, Lasker-Schüler presented her readings like an actress, complete with defamiliarizing props and costume, music, a darkened room, and multilingual recitation (26).[97] In a 1910 letter to Jethro Bithell, she describes her dress for an *Indianerfest* (probably a cabaret): "my nails are dyed with Henna and I've tattooed my forehead full of stars. Red satin jacket, white shirt, black pants with Indian fringes. 5 wild necklaces, feather belt, feather bracelets, ring of foot-feathers" (*Br* I 52).[98] Herzfelde describes a performative reading as "singing, ecstatic, eternally resounding, like the magic prayer of an oriental prophet" (Hallensleben 26). Whereas bourgeois Jewish women were encouraged to dress and act modestly to prevent any appearance that they were outside the cultural norm, Lasker-Schüler was outrageous.[99] Oskar Kokoschka describes Walden, himself, and Lasker-Schüler as traveling around Europe in 1910 to advertise *Der Sturm*, all dressed in "comic-elegant" clothing, the poet "as Prince of Thebes in wide breeches, turban, and with long black hair," smoking with a cigarette holder.[100] Extravagant costuming was common among bohemians, and oriental dress and tropes were common within the lesbian circles of Berlin.[101] To name, sketch, and dress herself as Asian was to ally herself with marginal communities and the avant-garde.

Descriptions by the poet's contemporaries suggest that she stood out even when not cross-dressing. Summarizing her appearance in 1952, Gottfried Benn wrote, "The whole world stood still and stared at her: extravagant wide skirts or trousers, outrageous shirts and jackets, neck and arms festooned with ostentatious costume jewelry, necklaces, earrings . . . servant-girl's rings."[102] As Benn's comment suggests, rather than heightening Lasker-Schüler's beauty or femininity, her appearance emphasized antibourgeois difference. Given the dissonance between cultural norms and her persona and dress, it is remarkable that Lasker-Schüler was not more frequently described as "unnatural" or lesbian in the contemporary popular press. Even in late-twentieth-century scholarship, Ulrike Müller in 1997 is the first to address the topic seriously and argue against her assumed hostility to women.[103] Lasker-Schüler indeed made disparaging remarks about women with bourgeois tastes and concerns. There is substantial evidence, however, that women were significant to the poet's life.

Müller provides a long list of the women Lasker-Schüler knew in Berlin and with whom she corresponded. In addition, the poet often includes women in her address when writing to male friends or professional acquaintances—a thoughtful and feminist as well as friendly gesture.[104] In *Gesichte* and *Konzert,* Lasker-Schüler writes admiring sketches of a number of women. More significantly, she wrote poems dedicated to or about Steger, Werefkin, Parsenow, Paula Dehmel, Hedwig Wangel, Durieux, and Charlotte Bara, and she dedicated her play *Die Wupper* to Helene Soutzo as well as a chapter of *Gesichte* to painter Lene Kainer. One copy of *Hebrew Ballads* contains an inscription to Lucie von Goldschmidt-Rothschild, "Yes, you are the only true living princess in the land and are just like / my sister, that's why I love / you."[105] "The Queen," a poem to Kete Parsenow, claims that "the nights of lovers awake from your countenance"; a later poem to Parsenow states, "I give you . . . my heart" (*WB,* no. 154, no. 408). In a note left among her papers in Jerusalem, the poet writes to her friends in Berlin, beginning the letter with the names of the women she misses: "Elfrieda and Hedwig you two nightingales / Mariaquita and Wally and Elisabeth and Kete and Enja / and Margarete," turning afterward to her male friends.[106] Like Moore, Lasker-Schüler maintained decades-long friendships. Moreover, the intensity of feeling expressed toward women in some poems suggests that the poet's gender doubleness also took a bisexual form—even though her "love" for women cannot necessarily be taken any more literally than that expressed for men.

Critical neglect of Lasker-Schüler's friendships with women partially explains the neglect of potential bisexuality in her poems. Possible reasons for such neglect are multiple, beginning with her own dismissal of femininity and followed by assumptions that female artists and writers are of less interest than male. Little is known about most of Lasker-Schüler's female friends. Early biographers may have seen the poet as isolated from other women as a sign of her seriousness. During her own day, reviews associating Lasker-Schüler with *Frauenlyrik* (as nearly all early reviews did) tended not to discuss her work in relation to experimentalism or take it seriously; Samuel Lublinski, for example, praises Lasker-Schüler as a great poetess but focuses on what is and is not *weiblich* in her poetic.[107] An association with lesbians would only have increased the tendency to isolate her from the avant-garde. As

Weininger makes clear, association with women conferred no authority. It could also be that Lasker-Schüler short-circuits any association of herself with lesbian or straight women through the exoticism of her Prince Jussuf persona, which marked her foremost as alien. Similarly, given stereotypes of the Jew as effeminate, the poet's Jewishness may have interfered with readings of the poet as either masculine or inverted. As I will discuss in chapter 5, Lasker-Schüler was so strongly identified as Jewish that perhaps other forms of unconventionality seemed peripheral in comparison, particularly by the late 1920s.

As seen in the last chapter, the radical synaesthesia of Lasker-Schüler's poems functions semiotically to challenge fixed categories of gender. Through the insistent apostrophe and address of her poems and through radical metaphors of bodily interpenetration, she also suggests the breakdown of categories separating individuals from each other or from any biological sexuality. This occurs most obviously in Lasker-Schüler's love poems addressed to Giselheer, her name for Gottfried Benn, in 1913–14.[108] These poems suggest intercourse in the intensity of the lovers' contact, although the interaction is not explicitly sexual. Instead, bodies break through each other's surfaces in ways that degender both parties. Each body penetrates the other, but not as phallus; each receives or is invaded by the other, but not as vagina or womb. In "Die Liebe," for example, the speaker asks to be hidden in the lover's "sweet-blood" (*WB*, no. 161). In "Das Lied des Spielprinzen," the speaker sits "on your hard forehead . . . as on a gable / And in your chin's cleft / I build myself a robber's nest / Until you've eaten me up."[109] In "To Giselheer the Tiger," the speaker uses the metaphor of scalping to describe intensity of desire: "I always carry you around / Between my teeth," the speaker exults, like a cat with its young, but "I can no longer be / Without the scalp-play. // Your knife paints red kisses / On my breast— // Until my hair flutters on your belt."[110]

In "To the Barbarian" ("Dem Barbaren"), each body covers and opens or cuts the other:

I lie in the nights On your countenance.	*Ich liege in den Nächten* *Auf deinem Angesicht.*
On the steppes of your body I plant cedars and almond trees.	*Auf deines Leibes Steppe* *Pflanze ich Cedern und* *Mandelbäume.*
I dig without tiring in your breast For the golden joys of Pharaoh.	*Ich wühle in deiner Brust* *unermüdlich* *Nach den goldenen Freuden Pharaos.*

But your lips are heavy, My wonders don't set them free.	*Aber deine Lippen sind schwer* *Meine Wunder erlösen sie nicht.*
Oh lift your snowy sky Off my soul—	*Hebe doch deine Schneehimmel* *Von meiner Seele—*
Your diamond dreams Cut my veins open.	*Deine diamantnen Träume* *Schneiden meine Adern auf.*
I am Joseph and wear a sweet belt Around my brightly colored skin.	*Ich bin Joseph und trage einen* *süssen Gürtel* *Um meine bunte Haut.*
You delight in the alarmed murmur Of my shells.	*Dich beglückt das erschrockene* *Rauschen* *Meiner Muscheln.*
But your heart lets in no more seas. Oh you!	*Aber dein Herz lässt keine Meere* *mehr ein.* *O du!*
My heart howls over your rough plains And banishes my radiant stars.	*Mein Herz heult schon über* *deine rauhen Ebenen* *Und verscheucht meine seligen* *Sterne.*[111]

(*WB*, no. 179)

The speaker digs in her lover's body; his dreams open her veins. She lies on his face's nights, and his sky suffocates her soul. Her heart ranges wolflike over his plains, thereby banishing the stars from her own sky. Both are sky, both are earth; both are captive, both are powerful—and both are men. The "you" is associated with "Pharaoh," and the speaker is either male ("Joseph") or double gendered (Joseph/Jussuf/Lasker-Schüler). Yet their passionate interaction makes the distinctions of conventional sexuality irrelevant. These lovers are more like spiritual forces metamorphized into primitive elemental nature than embodied humans.

The speakers of Lasker-Schüler's love poems are sometimes explicitly masculine. In "To Giselheer the Boy" (*WB*, no. 205), the speaker claims to be "your Prince," and says "we play King and Prince"—that is, two powerful men. In the poem "Höre!" ("Listen!"), the speaker threatens: "In the night I will rob / The roses from your mouth / That no woman can find drink" (*WB*, no. 229)—perhaps suggesting no *other* woman, but perhaps again speaking as male.[112] Lasker-Schüler—like Moore—may enact personal agency within a social and sexual continuum, but her continuum is gay. In his journal, Werner Kraft reports Lasker-Schüler as saying, "I think that if I were a man I'd be homosexual."[113]

Yet Lasker-Schüler also addresses women as lovers. As seen previously, the poems "Erkenntnis" and "Urfrühling" address Eve, the latter openly in the context of its female speaker's desire: "the red of her mouth burned / As if I had boy's lips" (*WB*, no. 46). In "A Song of Gold," the speaker not only gives her heart (to Parsenow, the dedication implies) but longs to lay it "in your golden lap . . . be your golden plaything"; she concludes by calling the actress "my golden night / Gold-syrinx."[114] More strikingly, in "Our Love Song" ("Unser Liebeslied"), the speaker wanders with a girlfriend or lover (*Freundin* was slang for lesbian partner).

Under the melancholy of the ash trees My girlfriend's eyes smile.	*Unter der Wehmut der Esche* *Lächeln die Augen meiner Freundin.*
And I must weep Wherever roses bloom.	*Und ich muß weinen* *Überall wo Rosen aufblühn.*
We don't hear our names— Always nightwanderers among the multicolored boys.	*Wir hören unseren Namen nicht—* *Immer Nachtwandlerinnen* *zwischen den bunten Jünglingen.*
My girlfriend juggles with the moon Shocked listeners follow our star play.	*Meine Freundin gaukelt mit* *dem Mond* *Unserm Sternenspiel folgen* *Erschrockene nach.*
Oh, our revels intoxicate The streets and squares of the city.	*O, unsere Schwärmerei berauscht* *Die Straßen und Plätze der Stadt.*
All dreams eavesdrop behind the hedges It can't become morning—	*Alle Träume lauschen gebannt* *hinter den Hecken* *Kann nicht Morgen werden—*
Oh, and the silky night was slung A thousand times around our throats	*O, und die seidige Nacht uns beiden* *Tausendmal immer um den Hals* *geschlungen.*
How I must turn!	*Wie ich mich drehen muß!*
And my girlfriend giddily kisses the rosy dew Under the dusk of the mourning tree.	*Und meine Freundin küßt taumelnd* *den Rosigtau* *Unter dem Düster des Trauerbaums.*

(*WB*, no. 177)

The suggestively misplaced kiss and the women's difference from the city's "boys" suggest romance. This suggestion is intensified by Lasker-Schüler's use of the courtly love trope of dawn song, or *Tageliet*—the hope that morning never come to interrupt them. The presence of this trope marks the poem as explicitly echoing a tradition of romance. Unconcerned with the city's other inhabitants, these women focus only on each other in the present moment.

While some poems, like "Dem Barbaren," present lovers as playing virtually interchangeable roles, others present only the speaker as active—reversing assumed subordination of the feminine to the masculine, to the extent that the speaker can be identified with the poet herself. In a second poem titled "Dem Barbaren" (*WB*, no. 178), the speaker leans on her lover's "night," teaches his stars to play, "walk[s] singing through the rusty gates / of Your holiness," "wear[s]" his "proud heart," covers him with her soul, and loves him "like after death." The object of the speaker's love does not act. Here love crosses even the boundary of life and death; it mingles the sensual, corporeal, emotional, and spiritual, and concludes with a question clarifying that this desire is the speaker's: "We want to kiss / Don't we?" [Wir wollen uns küssen / Nicht?]. If the beloved agrees, then she speaks for him, announcing what "we" want. If he doesn't, the speaker has nonetheless demonstrated the penetrating intensity of her own desire and love.

While the love she most often depicts as crossing multiple boundaries is erotic, for Lasker-Schüler all love involves intense spirituality and the collapse of ordinary divisions. In "To My Child" ("An mein Kind") memorializing her son after his death, the poet writes that "my love of you is the likeness / That one may make of God"—or, loosely translated, my love of you looks like God.[115] The late poem "Prayer" begins with the lines: "Oh God I am full of sorrow. . . . / Take my heart in your hands."[116] Similarly, in "To my friends," she laments the many dead and wishes to be with them again in her parent's house, where they sweeten each day with kisses. Life is love: life is "Not the dead quiet / I love so to be in breath. . . ! / To be on earth with you already heaven."[117]

Lasker-Schüler's presentation of sexual embodiment is radically unstable. Given the predominance of love in her poetry and the gender essentialism of most Expressionist work, this is an extraordinary feat. She writes about the power of loving, the joy and pain of emotional abandon, and intense sexual desire without anchoring them in consistent gender positioning. Again, the slipperiness of the lyric "I" may be relevant: to address a love poem to Giselheer, the name of a naive hero in the famous medieval German epic the *Nibelungenlied*, was patently for the female poet to address a man, whether or not the reader linked this name to Benn. Consequently, presenting herself as male within the poem, thereby also enacting her Jussuf persona, did not disrupt parallel readings of the speaker as female and the poem's desire as heterosexual. And yet making her speaker both female and male radically equalized heterosexual and homosexual love, and a woman's love with a man's. Such ambiguities of gender and sexuality suggest precisely the fluidity of feeling underlying Rich's lesbian continuum and much German homoeroticism of these decades. Lasker-Schüler's erotic love poems overturn cultural hierarchies through personal connection. Albeit indirectly, they assert aggressive female presence in ways contradicting every one of Weininger's claims about woman's lack while also frequently making use of the discourse of male (homo)sexuality to underplay suggestions of feminine coquetry, lesbianism, or titillation in their expressed desire. In a way almost opposite to Moore, then, Lasker-Schüler eschews the sensual pleasure of daily living for the wildness of desire as a figure for gender equality, intimacy, and spiritual belief. Both poets understand the mixed gender and sexual continuum of their lives and art as rejecting previous limitations on the authority and expression of women.

Moore's attempt to erase gender and sexual hierarchies through mannishly female dress and self-positioning along a homosocial lesbian continuum is consonant with the environment of her primary defining communities, including the Village. While it would be simplistic to identify the feminist authority of her experimental forms with any single factor, the confident stability of her life patterns and her conviction of their basic acceptance within her family and circle of friends must have contributed to Moore's assurance as editor and poet. In contrast, both Loy and Lasker-Schüler had more conflicted relationships with their communities. Loy protested the patriarchy and sexism of bourgeois and avant-garde cultures but maintained a strongly heterosexual, gender-defined perspective. For her gender was not significantly fluid or multiple, although other aspects of identity were. Her friendship and public alliances with lesbians in Paris and her conflicted relation to motherhood—leaving her children to a nurse's care for most of their upbringing and seeming to need care as much as they did—are two ways in which she acted out a rejection of traditional gendered strictures.[118] They did not, however, bring her an alternative or stable sense of identity or belonging. Lasker-Schüler similarly enacted some and rejected other dominant patterns for her cultural milieu, but those patterns themselves were contradictory: she was a hetero- or bisexual woman calling herself and addressed by her peers as Jussuf, and in her poems expressed erotic desire between men, between women, and between ambiguously gendered beings. The fact that her contemporaries like Mammen and Höch were so private about their sexual lives makes it less surprising that little is known about this very public woman's sexuality beyond what she writes.

In their poetics, Moore and Lasker-Schüler write out of the conscious and accepted decisions of their life patterns, in conflict not with themselves but with dominant cultural values. Again, Moore voices a more assured exuberance than Lasker-Schüler, often expressing even her critique of American gender distinctions or consumerist materialism and egocentricism through celebration of its opposite. Lasker-Schüler's poetry reveals the emotional extremes, anxieties, and passionate desires of her life in a location and time of great cultural instability and eventual personal danger. The metaphors and narratives of her poems frequently express immediate or feared loss, homelessness, and desire rather than fulfilled pleasure, although there is also affirmative power in the intensity of the desire and in the poet's only rare expression of despair. Loy, in contrast, seems less conflicted and more radical in her poetic than in the patterns of her life. In her poems, she seems able to crystallize her concept of a spiritually transformative aesthetic mode while sharply interrogating or appreciating the subjects of her focus. Loy does not voice desire or the idiosyncrasies of immediate feeling. Hers is a poetry of judgment, reflecting aspects of her experience or feeling but not focused on them as such. In this sense, her poetic comes closest to the dominant Anglo-American model of an apparently impersonal, critical, iconic poetry, although the poems carry a powerful emotional charge in their satire or critique. In all three poets' work, one sees primary evidence of the murkiness of sexual definition during the period. Each addresses questions of embodiment in relation to a heterosexual imperative and along a female homosocial continuum, variously conceived. Each determines a sartorial and behavioral style that allows her the freest circulation given her cultural location and psychic limitations. Each constructs a poetic that enables the articulation of her choices about selfhood and embodiment within a modernist paradigm pushing formal qualities of language to enable new possibilities of understanding in a rapidly changing world. While in no way simply representative, each reveals effective modes of biographical and aesthetic response to the conditions of her time and place.

5 *Self-Orient(aliz)ations & Judaism*

All poets are Jews.
—Marina Tsvetayeva, "Poem of the End"

Lincoln was Egyptian, Red Indian, of impressive stature.
—H.D. ("Sylvania Penn"), "I Sing Democracy"

Religious discourse and cosmopolitan multiculturalism are typically conceived as antithetical in discussions of modernism, and orientalism is represented as Eurocentric. For Lasker-Schüler, Moore, and Loy, however, religious and Asian discourse extend the boundaries of tolerance, supporting their cosmopolitan and international poetics rather than marking its exclusions. As with gender and sexuality, these three women understand Judaism and orientalism in ways both congruent with and reacting against dominant cultural understandings. Not surprisingly, cultural responses to Judaism differed enormously from one country to another in the early twentieth century, just as an understanding of the "Orient" has always depended on the writer's orientation. Similarly, Christian affiliation is more nuanced and various than is frequently acknowledged, even among those identifying as Protestant; only an understanding of denominational history reveals what it means for Moore to call herself Presbyterian in New York, or for Loy to practice Christian Science in Florence, or (for example) Eliot to become Anglican in London. Moore, Loy, and Lasker-Schüler perceive Jewishness in ways marked by multiple aspects of their experience. In part, each uses explicit praise for a religious culture different from that of her upbringing to rebel against cultural parochialisms. Lasker-Schüler rejects contemporary orthodox and secular Judaism and Zionism to identify herself with the ancient Jews, while also insisting on the common foundations of Judaism and Christianity. Moore uses ancient Hebrew poet-prophecy (as read through liberal Protestant scholarship) to develop a model of the poet as urgently ethical speaker but distinctly not an inspired diviner of the future or American "Jeremiah." Loy portrays the artist as "mongrel," at home nowhere and relying on revelation, while associating artistic capacity and intellect with the "Jewish brain."

These orientations are striking in part because it has become a truism of modernist studies that the literature of the era was averse to religious belief. Major Jewish and Christian thinkers contribute to this perception—for example, Marx, Matthew Arnold, Nietzsche, and Freud. As Andrew Kappel summarizes, it is widely assumed that whatever is religious in a work creates tension with "modern" aspects of that same work.[1] Yet the era as a whole was distinctly interested in spiritual matters. William James's explorations of spiritualism, W. B. Yeats's of the occult, and H.D.'s psychic spiritualism stand at one end of this interest; widespread fascination with Madame Blavatsky at another.[2] Rosemary Betterton suggests that modern women in particular turned to spiritual representational practices—a useful speculation for considering ways that patriarchal institutions may have provided liberating tools for spiritually minded women.[3] This chapter instead argues that the example of consonance between religious affiliation and formal literary innovation in these writers' poetry may illuminate similarly unexplored avenues in the work of other men and women of the period.

In Germany, Jews were regarded as and often considered themselves Asiatic. In 1897, Walter Rathenau referred to Jews as an "Asiatic horde," and in 1911, Werner Sombart wrote a series of essays arguing that the Jews are an unassimilable nomadic Asiatic clan that subverts the culture of native Germans.[4] In his 1912 essay "German-Jewish Parnassus," Moritz Goldstein notes that while "we" Jews think of our style as German, "the others call it Jewish, they detect the 'Asiatic' element."[5] In contrast, paradoxically, around 1914 the French began referring to everything decadent or pernicious associated with orientalism as German—*boche, munichois*—after a period of highly fashionable orientalism spurred by the Russian ballet.[6] In the United States, transcendentalism identified America with the East as an ancient and superior culture in contrast to Europe and to its own materialism, not as its reflected and primitive "other"—an association that continued into the twentieth century.[7] Lasker-Schüler and Moore associated Judaism with biblical Hebrews and saw it as providing a model for poetic intervention in the public world that is congruent with Christianity. Such orientation is notable in a genre and era noted for secular and anti-Semitic exclusions—for example, Gottfried Benn's 1933 essay listing Expressionists who are "pure German" as proof that modern art is not "degenerate."[8] The links between fascism, anti-Semitism, racism, and modernism have been discussed at length. As Jonathan Freedman accurately summarizes, according to some critics anti-Semitism was simply "the price to pay for admission into the club of Modernism" with its attendant cultural authority.[9] This is a price none of the three poets I discuss paid.

Judaism provided anchoring identity categories for many early-twentieth-century Europeans and Americans. As Freedman's *Temple of Culture* reviews, constructions of the Jew become the "prime means by which nineteenth- and twentieth-century cultural critics, anthropologists, philosophers, and philologists sought to define the nature and limits of their own discourse and culture"—primarily because Jews did not fit into any of the major emerging cultural categories: nation, race, or language (31). The resistance of Jewishness to compartmentalization made it seem both foundational to the process of categorization and subversive. Lasker-Schüler, Moore, and Loy understand Judaism as a useful tool for disrupting such compartmentalization. For them, Jewishness and the ancient traditions of Jewish poetry structure a relationship toward the world both foreign and familiar. In contrast to standard explications of primitivism and orientalism, these poets bring the foreign within; the alien or exotic aspect of the poetic speaker or self is that which enables social commentary and poetry. They turn to early Judaism, ancient Hebrew prophetic poetry, and stereotypes of Jewish sensuality and intellectualism not as a route to escapism or an originary relationship to nature but as an authorizing historical precedent and, in Lasker-Schüler's and Loy's cases, empowering myths of personal origin. Given the taxonomies of the era, such orientation had distinct political resonance, which they were also to some extent choosing—as were other Jews and liberal Christian writers of the period. Hence the patterns observable in their manipulations of orientalism foreground an aspect of its attitudes more widespread than has been acknowledged, just as they foreground a concern with religion.

To my knowledge, neither Judaism nor orientalism has been understood as a route to political engagement in modernist poetry. This is no doubt in part because none of the canonized modernist poets identified positively with Judaism—the conceivable exceptions being Gertrude Stein, who was at best ambivalent about being a Jew, Paul Celan, who was not born until 1920, and Lasker-Schüler herself—although she remains virtually unknown outside the fields of German and Jewish studies. It is also in part because orientalism—while political in and of itself—is rarely understood as a form of intervention into contemporary Western politics.

Until recently, modernist poetry and "modernism" itself have been seen as hostile to public, political, and social engagement, as well as to religion. Like many critics tracing modernism from nineteenth-century French beginnings, Peter Nicholls describes a severed connection between "poetic vision and social transformation" and regards the historical avant-garde, in contrast to modernism, as attempting to return art to the political arena (*Modernisms* 10, 11). Critics of Anglo-American modernism have begun to see the split differently. James Longenbach regards "the social effectiveness or responsibility of poetry" as a central concern of the period.[10] Mark Morrisson argues that British and American modernists manifested their belief that "art must have a public function" through their commentary in social and political magazines like *The Freewoman* and *The Masses*.[11] Suzanne Churchill argues that even what Morrisson calls "purely literary" magazines like *Others* and *Poetry* attempted to restore a public function to poetry, using the manipulation of formal elements of verse and structures of publication to re-form social conventions—particularly, she argues, of gender and sexuality.[12] I concur. Like many others, Lasker-Schüler, Moore, and Loy articulate social concern at the level of the individual poem. Far from locating themselves as peripheral to the political debates of their eras, they demonstrate that there is no necessary dichotomy opposing formal, religious, and political concerns, and no necessary conjunction of formal and religious concerns with fascism.

Lasker-Schüler and the Politics of German Orientalized Judaism

Whether or not Else Lasker-Schüler's poetry was political was hotly debated by her peers long before the National Socialists revoked her German citizenship in 1938 for "corrupt[ing] the spiritual and moral worth of the German woman" and publishing essays "hostile to Germany."[13] There was no debate about her being Jewish. In 1902, Samuel Lublinksi's review of *Styx* calls the poet a late niece of "those ancient singers who once wrote the Psalms or the book of Job" (*MM* 40).[14] Peter Hille's 1904 review famously calls Else Lasker-Schüler "the black swan of Israel" (*MM* 47). As both Tino and Jussuf, the poet encourages this orientalization of her work, especially by placing Jussuf in Thebes and using the Arabic names *Jussuf* and *Malik* rather than the German or Hebrew forms for Joseph and king. In a 1922 letter she categorizes her work as "Arabian Jewish history."[15] In her prose, letters, and drawings, the Asian aspect of this mosaic identity receives full play; for example, she tells Bithell she will dress "as oriental" when she visits him in London, adding, "I will send you my picture as Arabian prince" and swearing "by Mohammed's belt."[16] In her poetry, Jewish elements arise most intensely in her 1913 and 1914 publications of *Hebräische Balladen (Hebrew Ballads)*, but many of the poems in this volume were written a decade or more earlier. The poet's exploration of an orientalist-Jewish heritage, in other words, dates from the beginning of her writing career.

Styx (1902) includes poems with multiple cultural and spiritual references—Hebrew Bible, Gypsy, Islamic, and fantastic. For example, one poem is titled "The Black Bhowanéh (Goddess of the Night) (Gypsy Song)" ("Die schwarze Bhowanéh [Die Göttin der Nacht.] [Zigeunerlied]") and speaks in the voice of an exotic, sensual, invented deity markedly un-German in her characteristics. Other poems are titled "Karma," "Orgie," "Eros," "Stars of Fatum," "Stars of Tartarus," and "Αθανατοι" ("The Immortals"). The keynote for the volume, however, appears in its third poem, "Flight from the World" ("Weltflucht"), which expresses the speaker's desire to flee all restrictive categories:

I want to go into boundlessness
  Back to me,
Already the timeless saffron of
  My soul blooms,
Maybe—it's already too late to
    go back!
Oh, I'm dying among you!
Because you suffocate me with
    your selves.
I'd like to pull threads around me—
End confusion!
  Misleading,
Bewildering you,
  To escape
    Mine-wards!

Ich will in das Grenzenlose
  Zu mir zurück,
Schon blüht die Herbstzeitlose
  Meiner Seele,
Vielleicht—ist's schon zu spät
    zurück!
O, ich sterbe unter Euch!
Da Ihr mich erstrickt mit Euch.
Fäden möchte ich um mich ziehn—
Wirrwarr endend!
  Beirrend
Euch verwirrend,
  Um zu entfliehn
    Meinwärts!

(*WB*, no. 37)

The *me* this speaker escapes toward is one without boundaries, where something like a cocoon of threads brings simultaneous escape for the speaker and labyrinthine confusion for others; the speaker is a caterpillar seeking transformation, Theseus/Ariadne escaping captivity, and a Minotaur threatening the ordered world with its labyrinth, simultaneously. This poem implies that "you" suffocate the poet because "you" impose "selves" that confuse. Because the you-plural *(Euch)* is never defined, neither is the direction of the speaker's flight except that it is toward "das Grenzenlose," and hence outside the dominant culture's boundaries.

The butterfly-like flight of individual consciousness in this poem is semantic and formal as well as psychological and social: the coinage "Meinwärts," with its echo of *Heimwärts,* or homewards, implies both the inadequacy and the flexibility of standard German, even for its alienated speakers. Similarly suggestive, until line 9, all the poem's rhymes are of repetition—suggesting the rut of the speaker's suffocation; she repeats *züruck, Euch,* and the suffix *-lose* at line ends, in an *abacbdd* pattern, where each rhyme is a repetition. Only when she begins wrapping herself in threads meant to bewilder "you" does the poem achieve aural variety: rhyme, after all, is based on difference as well as similarity—here, the sequence *ziehn, endend, Beirrend, verwirrend, entfliehn.* Such a rhyme pattern implies that even poetry is impossible without difference, or varied coexistence. The poem, then, argues thematically for the speaker's home within her own consciousness and structurally for a social context more homelike to a broader variety of people, including those who do not all sound alike.

There was good reason for Lasker-Schüler to feel alienated from Berlin's dominant German and Jewish populations around the turn of the century. In addition to the widespread masculinism and militarism of both communities before the war, nationalist identity was for both an overriding concern. The literature on Judaism and modernity refers repeatedly to the related concepts of cosmopolitanism and alienation—flip sides of the coin of Jewish life in the West at the turn of the century. German Jews especially identified with the cosmopolitanism of Western urban life as developed through the Enlightenment ideal that *Bildung,* or cultured education, provided individual access to a "universal" humanity.[17] Enlightenment philosophy "sought to neutralize the significance of personal background," declaring that such matters were overcome through education and culture; according to the popular phrase, Jews became "German by the grace of Goethe"—and indeed thousands of Jews proudly adopted German culture as their own, including both of Lasker-Schüler's parents.[18] *Bildung* was an end in itself, not a goal of mastering particular skills or a particular field of knowledge. As Europe experienced a dramatic increase in nationalist sentiment in the late nineteenth century, however, many Germans moved away from this ideal, developing instead a concept of themselves in their newly unified nation as a "people" or *Volksnation.* To the extent that Jews maintained the concept of *Bildung,* they adopted a different model for political and personal identity than other Germans (Mendes-Flohr, *German Jews* 14–15). Consequently, Jews were increasingly perceived by Christian Germans (and to some extent by themselves) as alien, outside dominant cultural beliefs and institutions, a racial rather than a religious group, and racially "Asian."

At the same time, as Mendes-Flohr persuasively argues, Jews struggled with the question of the logical end of cosmopolitanism: did *Bildung* mark the extinction of Judaism through its blending into other modern cultures? Kafka once quipped: "my people, provided I have one."[19] In 1871, Jews were granted German citizenship. In 1918, with the Weimar Republic, they received equal rights with Christians. In 1897, Austrian Theodor Herzl called the first international Zionist Congress; after Herzl's death in 1904, the Zionist leadership moved from Vienna to Berlin. Spurred by the atmosphere of increasing political and legal rights and by Zionism, Central European Jews engaged in what began to be called a Jewish Renaissance. In its celebration of things Jewish, this Renaissance put increasing pressure on secular and religious Germanic Jews to determine what it meant to be "modern" and "Jewish." Yet Goldstein's essay on the "German-Jewish Parnassus" demonstrated how ephemeral such a mixed heritage had become: Jews might consider themselves German, but other Germans did not hold the same view. In 1922, Alfred Wolfenstein contrasted the honor given Jewish works with the disparagement of Jews: "The honor does not carry over to the poet's living race. Their work is taken, their being oppressed and rejected."[20] Gershom Scholem coined the phrase "Männer aus der Fremde" to describe cosmopolitan German Jews—men not of foreign nationality but spiritually and psychologically "foreign" (Wohlfarth 19). Georg Simmel's 1908 "Der Fremde" singled out the European Jew as the "stranger" within, combining the familiar and the alien; this was to become the classic representation of the *Grenzjude* or border-Jew, "straddling the boundaries between cultures" (Mendes-Flohr, "The Berlin Jew" 21). In her persona Prince Jussuf, Lasker-Schüler similarly constitutes herself as "stranger," straddling boundaries, critiquing Jewish and German cultures from without and within.

Even while it moved legally toward full equality for Jews, Wilhelmine Germany experienced waves of anti-Semitism that underlined Jewish social marginality in the new nation. In particular, the social displacement caused by Germany's rapid industrialization in the 1870s and 1880s and the depression of the 1890s stimulated such a wave. In 1893, Adolf Stoecker's anti-Semitic party, centered in Berlin but stemming from Lasker-Schüler's native Westphalia and active during her youth, won several seats in the legislature (Kaplan, 16–17). As Jakob Hessing argues, and as one sees in Lasker-Schüler's play *Arthur Aronymous,* essay "Anti-Semitism," and sketches in *Concert,* the poet experienced anti-Semitism in her childhood; consequently, she was more sensitive to Jewish marginality than most assimilated Jews, especially those born too late to have experienced this 1890s wave themselves and growing up during the first two decades of the twentieth century.[21] At the same time, she identified too closely with German culture to feel comfortable with religious Judaism or Zionism. Lasker-Schüler's family identified proudly as Jewish but apparently celebrated only Yom Kippur; one of her brothers converted to Catholicism. Her stories of Jewish ritual from her childhood have primarily to do with pranks. For example, the poet claims to have dressed as a boy so she might attend synagogue with her father and drink from the *Kiddusch* cup—an escapade her father apparently found amusing.[22] Allegedly, she also sat on the men's side of the synagogue, offered a glass of wine to the rabbi during a prayer service, and climbed up a trellis to the second floor of a house to meet a rabbi who was only admitting men to his presence.[23] As Jussuf, Lasker-Schüler is a fully participatory Jewish male—although Jussuf is no more religious in his observance than his female author.

While Jewishness was always a topic in reviews of her work, the postwar rise of anti-Semitism increased attention to the poet as foreign.[24] In 1919 Eugen Höflich calls her "the poet of the entire race" of Jews; in 1922 Meïr Wiener writes that Else Lasker-Schüler is perceived "as especially Jewish" because her work is so "oriental."[25] In 1921, Ludwig Thoma accuses the press generally of corrupting the German "mother tongue" through the introduction of "Jewish swindler and criminal gibberish," which he later calls "language syphilis," and identifies with Lasker-Schüler.[26] Such linguistic racism was common at the time; even Jews who spoke flawless German were accused of speaking "Jewish," an insult meant to suggest impurity.[27] Lasker-Schüler may in part react against such diatribes in her regendering of German nouns and neologisms. In response to her winning the Kleist Prize in 1932, a headline called her the "daughter of a Bedouin sheik," and announced that the "pure Hebrew poetry of Lasker-Schüler doesn't suit us Germans" (*MM* 226–27). During her exile in Palestine, the poet was also torn by conflicting identities; as a German speaker, she was associated by Eastern European immigrants with the land of National Socialism. As Dagmar Lorenz summarizes, "Her desire for reconciliation among the religions and nations, her vision of a Jewish-Christian synthesis . . . and her love of the German language and . . . literature placed her in an outsider situation" among the Zionists.[28] Lasker-Schüler felt profoundly alienated as a German in Palestine, after a lifetime of marginality in Berlin.

In Berlin, Lasker-Schüler was both closely bound to a community and a loner. While Jews never constituted more than 4 percent of the population, they represented a high percentage of Expressionist writers, critics, editors, and reviewers.[29] For example, in Kurt Pinthus's 1920 anthology *Menschheitsdämmerung*, ten of the twenty-three authors included "have Jewish ancestors or identify themselves as Jews"; Hans Otto Horch also estimates that "half of those belonging to the circle of Expressionism are Jews or stem from Jewish ancestry."[30] In Berlin, these include not only Lasker-Schüler and Walden, but also major intellectual figures like Scholem, Benjamin, Buber, and Bloch, and writers Wolfenstein, Döblin, and Alfred Lichtenstein. With the exception of Lasker-Schüler, none of the canonized poets of Expressionism (Benn, Heym, Stadler, Trakl) was Jewish. In her identification as Jew, then, Lasker-Schüler would have felt herself both a distinct minority in Berlin and part of a significant population within Expressionist circles. As a celebrated Jewish female bohemian poet, she was one of a kind. As Prince Jussuf, Lasker-Schüler was more exotic but no more alien to the general population of Berlin.

Lasker-Schüler plays on the overlapping and contradictory definitions of Jewish and German identity in "Mein Volk" ("My People"; 1905), reprinted in 1914 as the first poem of *Hebrew Ballads:*

The rock decays	*Der Fels wird morsch,*
From which I spring	*Dem ich entspringe*
And sing my songs of God . . .	*Und meine Gotteslieder singe . . .*
Headlong I rush from the path	*Jäh stürz ich vom Weg*
And ripple wholly in me	*Und riesele ganz in mir*
Far away, alone on complaining stone	*Fernab, allein über Klagegestein*
To the sea.	*Dem Meer zu.*
Have streamed so far	*Hab mich so abgeströmt*
From my blood's	*Von meines Blutes*
Fermenting must.	*Mostvergorenheit.*
And yet again and again the echo	*Und immer, immer noch der Widerhall*
In me	

When, full of dread, toward East,	*In mir,*
The rotten rock-bone	*Wenn schauerlich gen Ost*
My people	*Das morsche Felsgebein*
To God cries.	*Mein Volk*
	Zu Gott schreit.

(*WB*, no. 209)

This speaker sings *Gotteslieder* that stem from and echo the crumbling rock of "Mein Volk" (also the biblical "Rock of Israel") even as she rushes away from it. At the end of the poem it is ambiguous whether this rock cries out the words "Mein Volk" or the rock is the people and what it cries remains unspoken. This syntactic ambiguity restates the poet's ambivalent positioning, since she (like the rock) literally cries "Mein Volk" (the poem) even while the rock metaphorically represents the people the poet flees. This speaker sings songs that echo those of a people to whom she does and does not belong. The other poems of *Hebrew Ballads* can be read as representing these echoes of the tradition she honors and flees—whether it is Hebrew as indicated by the volume's title, or German as suggested by the language and in reference to the overdetermined concept *Volk.* The volume's poems as a whole construct an ideal alternative ancestral past, apparently undecayed, to which the poet can give full allegiance—a pacifistic, creative, loving, erotic, and German Judaism.

Many of the poems of *Hebrew Ballads* portray biblical lovers as crossing lines of national, class, and spiritual hierarchy: Joseph, the Jewish slave in Egyptian exile, is the pharaoh's lover; David, the young shepherd's son, lives in the palace of his lover Jonathan's father, King Saul; Ruth begs as an alien in Boaz's field; Sulamith learns sensual "holinesses" from the angel Gabriel; and God communicates directly with and is loved playfully, sensually, or otherwise intimately by the speakers of various poems. By creating speakers who step unexpectedly across categorical lines of difference and social power to express love, these poems work in parallel with Lasker-Schüler's secular love poems in making love an instructional model for harmony among people and nations as well as between individuals.[31] Because the biblical speakers and protagonists of these poems belong to the most familiar cultural stories for Jewish and Christian readers, they foreground common religious and historical inheritance. Their revolutionary potential is based upon shared ground.

The reconciliation of religions and peoples became an increasingly prominent theme of Lasker-Schüler's writing as German anti-Semitism grew. Nor was she alone in turning to this theme. Benjamin, Buber, Leo

Beck, and others similarly regarded the Christian gospels as compatible with Judaism. While she is contradictory in her early work about her relation to Christianity—for example, writing Bithell in 1909 that she is "a Jew and foe to all Christianity," "throwing rocks at the Christian dogs" (*Br* I 45)—in *Concert* (1932), she repeatedly calls upon Christians to recognize their common past. A sketch called "Holy Communion" describes her and her friends ritually passing a glass of beer in a café: "Twelve people prepare themselves again and again on earth out of love. . . . They are the great, unsophisticated Jewish disciples of the Son of God, who climbed down to earth . . . to tell people that they should love each other" (*Concert* 67). In "The Day of Atonement," she writes, "The Messiah has already walked on earth," but "will come again at the end of the world . . . Because only the reconciliation of all people is able to uplift and deliver us" (133). In "The Lamas," Lasker-Schüler worships with Tibetan priests in the hotel where she lives. In the section "Concert," Lasker-Schüler proclaims "the miracle of the fakirs" with that of "all the saints, of the Baal Shem Tov and the other wonderful rabbis" (27, 29).[32] In "The Trees by Themselves," she writes, "World is in world as man is in man, animal in animal and tree in leaf and vice versa leaf again in tree and everything in everything and all in all and All in God. Amen" (13). Later she states, "There is only one faith, as there is only one God, one creation, one heaven. Religion . . . is simply accustomed to dressing differently. Thus one rests in St. Petron's blue words about the Heavenly Son as in Buddha's wise tranquility, but also in the lap of Abraham!" (79–80). As her multiple lists indicate, Lasker-Schüler attempts to unite religions through cumulative and metaphorical, not theological or philosophical, methods. She claims simultaneous characteristics and allegiances rather than expounding a similarity of doctrines. She is also at times naively optimistic about the possibilities for human transformation. In 1938, she believed that Mussolini would provide asylum for the Jews if she could obtain an audience to talk with him. Similarly, the poet sent flowers and stones from Jerusalem to the pope to persuade him to help the Jews (*WZ* 47). Emmy Hennings eulogized her friend in 1945 as "spanning the arc between the Old and the New Testament," and reported that, when asked if there were still Christian poets in Germany, some people had responded with the name Else Lasker-Schüler! Hennings herself, on the other hand, commented that if such a thing as "Jewish poetry" exists, it is "more radiant and purer" in Lasker-Schüler's work than anywhere.[33]

While Lasker-Schüler wrote to Martin Buber in 1942 that she was "no Zionist, no Jew, no Christian" but a "human," the speaker of "My

People" cries "toward East"—and indeed much of Lasker-Schüler's writing and self-performance was oriented toward both Judaism and the East.[34] Kasimir Edschmid finds "all Asia in the strange show" of her poems.[35] Orientalized by German culture as a Jew, Lasker-Schüler exaggerates this orientation, even inventing a language combining Turkish, Hebrew, and Arabic sounds that she called her "Ursprache," rediscovered from the time of Saul and the royal "wild" Jews. She was arrested once in Prague for "preaching a sermon" in this constructed "Asiatisch" in a church, and she translated poems into this language, printing a translated copy of "Weltflucht" in *Ich räume auf.* The first few lines read: "Min salihihi wali kinahu / Rahi hatiman / fi is bahi lahu fassun" (*WB* 4.1:59). She writes Bithell in December of 1910 about a reading she gave in "Arabic . . . even though [the poems] were written in the German language," and in March of 1910 she describes a reading she plans to give in London: "I present 3 or 4 of my Arabian tales in *Arabic* . . . by the curtain sits a 10-year-old Black boy in fire red fez, etc. and hands me each manuscript" while someone else translates the poems into English (*Br* I 45, 55–56).[36]

Lasker-Schüler radically defamiliarizes every aspect of her performance as poet and woman: dress, name, genre, and language. In a time of increasing anxiety about a pure German *Volk* and the purity of the German language, she flaunts foreignness. Robert Kern notes that romantic notions of "original language" were prevalent during the early modernist period and frequently associated with poetry.[37] Lasker-Schüler imagines poetic language as derived from Eden and the poet as "the true heir of the first people, before knowledge cuts him into two pieces, two heart-halves, a soul and two thoughts."[38] Her language experiments, however, do not seek a primitive originality; rather she wants simultaneous performance of languages—a language of pure sounds and the language of the country in which she performs, as well as the original German of her poems. Her readings anticipated Dada experiments with sound-poetry but stressed communication through multiple idioms: sound, semansis, visual effects, dance, music, staging properties, and the manner of her own dress and articulation.[39] Lasker-Schüler sought to construct not just a new kind of poetry but new modes to express the radical transformation required to establish meaningful communication among people who retain their differences.

Donna Heizer speculates that the general outpouring of orientalist literature among German Jews between 1900 and 1930 was the result of Jewish anxiety about questions of identity. For Jews to write about themselves as Jewish would be to mark themselves as non-German,

Heizer argues; writing orientalist narratives, however, allowed them to participate in a popular German stereotype while also indirectly imagining themselves.[40] This double identity, especially in Zionist thought, served as a double bridge, linking German intellectualism with the rich imaginative culture of Asia and bringing "superior" Western intellect to the Jews of the East and the Arabs of Palestine (Heizer 26–27). Such bridging, many turn-of-the-century German Jews believed, would spur a creative spiritual renewal in the East and West. Lasker-Schüler constructed herself as such a bridge: as Jussuf, she was German, Jewish, Asian, male, and female. Because Germans for the most part imagined Western categories as irrelevant in the East, Lasker-Schüler may have felt that her Jussuf persona freed her from the necessity of attending to those categories (Heizer 42).

The poet held primitivist stereotypes of the East but applied them also to German Jewish and Christian friends, and to herself.[41] Tibetan priests are "dear childlike people" whose "gentle velvet eyes are like the holy eyes of the cows that are their primal deities"; "hardly any European is capable of fathoming the depth of their being," but Christian "Saint" Peter Hille is similarly childlike in his superiority (*Concert* 43, 74). As previously mentioned, Lasker-Schüler characterized her knowledge as coming from nature, not books; she herself was primitive, an ancient "wild" Jew: untamed, passionate, and capable of loyal fellowship, great love, and great art—with the implication that modern Jews and Germans do not have these characteristics. Such categories had immediate political ramifications for German Jews, who generally regarded *Ostjuden,* Eastern European Jews, as religiously fundamentalist and culturally both Asian and primitive.[42]

With the rise of Zionism and following World War I, this primitivism was increasingly romanticized—in part because of wartime contact between German Jewish soldiers and traditional Jewish communities in Poland, Lithuania, and the Ukraine. As Robertson writes, this reevaluation of *Ostjuden* as the heirs of ancient Judaism provided educated Germanic Jews with a primal link to nature and sensuality in direct contrast to Western rationality and denigration of material being (187–88). Buber wrote extensively about Jewish orientalism in these terms, as did Theodor Lessing and Max Brod. In "Der Jude als Orientale" (1913), Jakob Wasserman writes that only as Oriental can the Jew be creative: "he is sure of himself . . . because a noble consciousness, blood-consciousness, connects him to the past."[43] In 1924, Abraham Suhl wrote, "Do we need Negroes and jazz bands in order to return to nature?—The primitive tone, the original nakedness, is still with us!

Shepherds sing new songs and they are the old psalms. David is still born out of our blood."[44] Such romanticization assumed cultural superiority, as did Lasker-Schüler's, to some extent. By making her persona explicitly Arabic rather than associated with Asiatic being through the "blood" of ancient Jews, however, Lasker-Schüler undercut assumptions of Western superiority. According to Valencia, Lasker-Schüler was also one of the few German Jews who entered Eastern European Jewish circles in Berlin; she was well known among the Yiddish speakers gathering in the huge Romanisches Café—described as a "parliament" for the "Jewish colony" of Russian émigrés.[45] In his memoir, Yiddish poet Abraham Stenzel describes meeting Lasker-Schüler when she sketched him on a napkin and sent the sketch to his café table with the note, "Hamid! I want to meet you! Prince Jussuf" (Valencia 84). Lasker-Schüler apparently saw herself as being like the *Ostjuden,* and ancient Jews; her poems were also "psalms" (*Concert* 32). Impatient with what seemed to her the bourgeoisie of Berlin's Jews, in 1913 she writes Buber with exaggerated scorn, "I hate the jews, because they misunderstand my speech, because their ears are deformed and they hearken to trivia"; yet in 1921, in response to an anti-Semitic parody, she writes the *Weltbühne* editor, "Through my prince's crown, I have placed an opal on the temple of judaism alone"; and in 1934, in a letter to Arthur Ruppin, she writes, "I have devoted a quarter of my life, indeed a whole life, to nothing but giving honor to all jews."[46]

Increased contact with *Ostjuden* during the 1920s did not alter Lasker-Schüler's orientalizations. For her, barriers between Germanness, Jewishness, and the Orient had long been permeable, although she emphasized the fluidity that allowed her release from the restrictions of bourgeois propriety rather than possibilities for immigrant assimilation.[47] Emmy Hennings described the poet as "more foreign to the world than a fairy tale."[48] Indeed Stenzel felt that his foreignness allowed him to understand Lasker-Schüler better than her fellow Germans, and he described her with the same primitivist metaphors of uninhibited spontaneity she used, linking her with "the first" Hebrew poets (Valencia 81). "With her tragic, hard life, how could she have continued to work without her prince illusions? Delusions? Isn't this what accompanies every real poet like a guardian?" Stenzel asks.[49] In "My Quiet Song" ("Mein stilles Lied"), Lasker-Schüler concludes:

I am the hieroglyph That stands under the creation.	*Ich bin der Hieroglyph,* *Der unter der Schöpfung steht.*
And I made myself resemble you,	*Und ich artete mich nach euch,*

Out of my longing for humanity.	*Der Sehnsucht nach dem Menschen wegen.*
I ripped the eternal glances from my eyes, The victorious light from my lips—	*Ich riß die ewigen Blicke von meinen Augen, Das siegende Licht von meinen Lippen—*
Do you know a graver prisoner, A more evil magician than myself.	*Weißt Du einen schwereren Gefangenen, Einen böseren Zauberer, denn ich.*
And my arms, that want to raise themselves Fall . . . . . .[50]	*Und meine Arme, die sich heben wollen, Sinken . . . . . .*

(*WB*, no. 122, ll. 43–52; ellipses Lasker-Schüler's)

As Egyptian hieroglyph, the poet underlies creation; she represents the undifferentiated, originary word of Jewish/Christian creation. Like Jesus, she becomes human, but through self-transformation and desire, and she is then both a prisoner in her human body and an evil magician, presumably heathen. Moreover, at the end of the poem the speaker resembles Moses, whose arms grew tired and sank as he watched the battle between Israel and the Amalek (Exod. 17:11). But where Moses had Aaron and Hur to support his hands on either side, thereby ensuring Israelite victory, this speaker stands alone. Consequently, if the victory of her people (however defined) depends upon her holding her hands high, that victory is lost: even Moses could not save the Jewish people without assistance. As frequently in her poems, here Lasker-Schüler does not divide good from evil or Judaism from other religions, and she addresses an audience that is both plural *(euch)* and singular *(du)*. Christine Reiß-Suckow comments that the poet is more interested in dialogue than in self-presentation, and one sees this desire to make contact with others even in the apparently most solipsistic of her poems: as hieroglyph she nonetheless repeatedly addresses the world, "out of my longing for humanity [*Menschen,* human beings]" (Reiß-Suckow 89).[51] For Buber as for Lasker-Schüler, the tensions of Judaism in Germany may have provoked intense awareness of the need for communication and bonding with that which is outside the self, a "you"—as he more famously articulates in *I and Thou* (1923). "Concert," the bringing of voices into harmony, is a primary metaphor of Lasker-Schüler's work—even before her publication of the volume of sketches by that name. Her poems validate feelings of difference and alienation, but seek to overcome them through contact with others.

In a more famous poem, "An Old Tibetan Carpet" ("Ein alter Tibetteppich," 1910), Lasker-Schüler temporarily achieves perfect communion through the figure of an Asian carpet:

Your soul, which loves mine Is woven with her into a Tibetan carpet	*Deine Seele, die die meine liebet* *Ist verwirkt mit ihr im Teppichtibet*
Light-beam by beam, colors in love, Stars courting each other throughout heaven.	*Strahl in Strahl, verliebte Farben,* *Sterne, die sich himmellang* *umwarben.*
Our feet rest on its preciousness Stitches-thousand-upon-thousand- dense.	*Unsere Füsse ruhen auf der* *Kostbarkeit* *Maschentausendabertausendweit.*
Sweet son of Lama on your musk throne How long has your mouth been kissing mine And your cheek my cheek, like brightly-knotted time.	*Süsser Lamasohn auf* *Moschuspflanzentron* *Wie lange küsst dein Mund den* *meinen wohl* *Und Wang die Wange buntgeknüpfte* *Zeiten schon*

(*WB*, no. 172)

Like the threads of an Asian carpet, the lovers' lives and souls are enmeshed in a dense fabric of love and time—as though the process of loving itself weaves a lasting product on which feet can "rest." Allusions to the East intensify communication for Lasker-Schüler. They provide a vocabulary for the erotic, emotional, and spiritual bonding that she desires but knows cannot be found more than fleetingly outside the structures of art. Through scenes of intense communion, however—as through her previously discussed renaming of friends—the poet seeks to nudge Berlin in the direction of her ideal.

In her prose and drama, Lasker-Schüler both intensifies stereotypic differences between West (as cold, rational, sober) and East (passionate, natural, sensual, sometimes cruel), and undercuts them. The Theban kingdom is hierarchical, complete with African servant; its enemies are Western, but they are also loved. For example, in *Der Malik,* part of the loosely structured plot involves the Prince's love for "Giselheer," a Christian "king" who has ceased to love him—or her, to the extent that the Prince represents the poet; Giselheer has raised a Christian army that the Prince must fight with his army of Muslims and Jews. Yet Jussuf also writes Giselheer a letter in the Hebrew alphabet, as though assuming he also knows this language. The novel includes battles, but Jussuf does not want to fight them, and they occur without clear point, representing the poet's ongoing cultural battle against repressive cultural codes more than events leading to a narrative conclusion. In a surprising twist at the end, Jussuf commits suicide, perhaps suggesting that even the fantasy of male royalty cannot prevent misunderstanding and isolation.

Lasker-Schüler's unpublished late drama *IchundIch* (*IandI*) explicitly raises questions of identity in a political context. The play begins with the blank-verse speech of an unseen female poet, who presents her splitting into two halves ("IandI") as a murder story. As it progresses, Faust and Mephistopheles (characters of the drama) represent some form of this split: each speaks poems written by Lasker-Schüler, and, in act 4, Mephistopheles takes on the *Dichterin*'s role, referring to his split *Ichgestalt* as *IchundIch.* Moreover, Faust and Mephistopheles refer to each other as brothers and, over a game of chess, express a devotion to each other that saves both: they ascend out of hell into heaven.[52] In the meantime Göring, Göbbels, several troops of Nazi soldiers, and finally Hitler himself fall into a lake of boiling lava, created by Mephistopheles in hell. In act 5, the poet dies quietly in a garden in Jerusalem; she is as "breathless and lifeless as this present time"—1941 (232). The Nazis have gotten rid of Christianity as well as Judaism, referring to Christ (in Göbbels's words) as a "dull" Jew ("der olle Jude"; 204), having no religion but their own power-hungry and destructive selfhood. Yet at the end of the play, an unseen voice asks, "Do you believe in God," and from behind the curtain the poet lightly sings, "I am so glad, I rejoice: God is 'there'" [Ich freu mich so, ich freu mich so: Gott ist "da"] (235). While the inset "there" is not explained, the play's whole structure of potential salvation and reintegration of the split self through love asserts belief in a living God.

This play is bewilderingly postmodern in its quick juxtapositions of scene, reference, and apparent time period, but its point is clear: the Nazis in their destructiveness are so horrific that they redefine hell and even devils shun them. Poetry and love, in contrast, bring everlasting life—even to one, like Faust, who has sold his soul to the devil. Moreover, Faust's continuous poetic being (manifested in his speech and his sympathy) transforms the devil who has corrupted him: Mephistopheles also speaks in verse, remembers his youth as "God's rascal" (quoting Lasker-Schüler's poem "In the Beginning" ["Im Anfang"]), and finally returns to a life in heaven. God lives through the combined beliefs and devotion of the two poets (the *Dichterin* and Faust, who stands for Goethe as poet more than for the scientist Faust) and Mephistopheles, the fallen angel. By implication, to kill Judaism is to kill Christianity, and to kill God. In contrast, the Christian Faust/Goethe and the Jewish Lasker-Schüler are aspects of each other in preserving creativity in all forms, part of the play's split but joined *IchundIch.* This coined word's lack of hyphens or spacing distinguishing *ich* from *und* from *ich* also leads in German to a pun at the word's end: *ich un[d] dich*—or I and you—a merger manifest in the plot by the Faust-Mephistopheles union, the return of the fallen angel to God, and the doubling of the poet in Faust and *Dichterin.* The capitalized "I" militates against reading the last four letters as *dich*/you, but the visual blending of I/you is still implied. Love grounds heaven, just as hatred characterizes the Nazi-filled hell.

In this play, Lasker-Schüler leaves behind all reference to Tino, Jussuf, and orientalism. The play is staged in Jerusalem and hell—perhaps representing East and West. Faust/Goethe must also represent the West, however, and the *Dichterin*'s split self combines Christian-German Faust/Goethe, Mephistopheles, and the Jewish-German exiled poet. In this conglomerate form, the poet performs her world's most destructive divisions and attempts to resolve them. In an age of massive Jewish suicide, especially by women, it is perhaps not surprising that Lasker-Schüler concludes two narratives of powerful self-construction with death: the suicide of Jussuf in *Der Malik* and the death of the poet in *IchundIch.*[53] It is also noteworthy that she restricts these deaths to her fictions while she herself lives (and continues writing) to the age of seventy-seven. Despite the despair of particular works and the paranoid unhappiness of much of her late life, the body of Lasker-Schüler's work is radically life- and spirit-affirming in times of difficulty and terror.

Moore's Ethical Poetic of (Protestant) Hebrew Prophecy

In contrast to Germany, in the United States orientalism is a more dominant trope than Judaism both for modernist writing and for recent critical understanding of the early twentieth century. As has been discussed by several scholars, U.S. orientalism also develops differently from that described by Edward Said in France and Britain. Zhaoming Qian argues that orientalizing poets like Pound and Williams did not assert Western cultural superiority; what attracted them to Eastern cultures was "the affinities (the Self in the Other) rather than the differences (the Otherness in the Other)" between the cultures.[54] Orientalism provided a justification for aesthetic principles poets had already

"Militants." Cartoon by Rodney Thomson in *Life,* March 27, 1913, 616.

rianne Moore and Her Mother, by rguerite Thompson Zorach. Oil canvas, 1925. National Portrait llery, Smithsonian Institution. urtesy of The Zorach Collection C.)

Marianne Moore, by Marguerite Thompson Zorach. Ink sketch, circa 1925. (Courtesy of The Zorach Collection LLC and the Brooklyn Museum of Art.)

Marianne Moore by Marjori Studio, 1922. Rosenbach Museum and Library, Philadelphia. (Courtesy of Marianne Craig Moore.)

Marianne Moore by Sarony Studio, 1924. Rosenbach Museum and Library, Philadelphia. (Courtesy of Marianne Craig Moore.)

Marianne Moore by Alice Boughton, mid-1920s. Rosenbach Museum and Library, Philadelphia. (Courtesy of Marianne Craig Moore.)

Mina Loy in New York City, 1920. Photograph by Man Ray. © 2004 Man Ray Trust / Artists Rights Society (ARS), New York / ADAGP, Paris. (Courtesy of Roger Conover for the Estate of Mina Loy.)

Mina Loy holding a Rodin sculpture. Photo by Stephen Haweis. Stephen Haweis Papers, Rare Book and Manuscript Library, Columbia University. (Courtesy of Roger Conover for the Estate of Mina Loy.)

Little Review Reunion, Paris, circa 1923: Jane Heap, Mina Loy, and Ezra Pound. National Archives and Records Administration, photo number 306-NT-328AA. (Courtesy of Roger Conover for the Estate of Mina Loy.)

Mina Loy, Paris, 1905. Photo by Stephen Haweis, inscribed "Ducy Haweis Stephen's Wife Mother of Giles." (Courtesy of Roger Conover for the Estate of Mina Loy.)

na Loy, fashion sketches, lated. Yale Collection of ıerican Literature, the necke Rare Book and nuscript Library. (Courtesy Roger Conover for the ate of Mina Loy.)

Self-portrait, 1905, by Mina Loy. Joella Bayer Collection. (Courtesy of Roger Conover for the Estate of Mina Loy.)

Else Lasker-Schüler, 1912. ullstein bild Berlin. The Else Lasker-Schüler Archive, the Jewish National and University Library, Jerusalem.

Else Lasker-Schüler, *Self-Portrait as Prince Jussuf*, circa 1913.
(Photo: © ARTOTHEK. Munich Bayerische Staatsgemäldesammlungen.)

Else Lasker-Schüler, *Laurencis Jussuf on the Path to Irsahab in Dance-Step*, from *Der Malik*, 1919. The Else Lasker-Schüler Archive, the Jewish National and University Library, Jerusalem.

Else Lasker-Schüler, *The Flute Player,* 1910. The Else Lasker-Schüler Archive, the Jewish National and University Library, Jerusalem.

Else Lasker-Schüler. Dedicated on back to René Schickele, February 9, 1906. Schiller-Nationalmuseum, Deutsches Literaturarchiv, Marbach. The Else Lasker-Schüler Archive, the Jewish National and University Library, Jerusalem.

begun to develop for themselves. As Qian argues, China and other Asian countries gave crucial authentication for ideas poets perceived as new to their own tradition, and hence enabled continued experimentation with new forms in English.[55] Moore studied oriental history at Bryn Mawr, visited the University of Pennsylvania Museum's extensive Asian archaeological holdings in 1909 and Lawrence Binyon's famous exhibit of Chinese art at the British Museum in 1911, and mentions Chinese art in early publications. As Qian argues, this art displayed Daoist sensibilities that both mirrored and challenged Moore's reverence for nature, non-mimetic detail in description, and her concerns with Western ego- and anthrocentrism (*Modernist Response* xvii, 65, 69, 72). Qian also sees Moore's "sensitivity to unusual combinations of colors and light" in early poems as stimulated by her early interest in Chinese art (32). Her study of ancient Hebrew poetry may have worked in conjunction with her study of Eastern cultures—and indeed her oriental history class included readings on the "civilization" of Egypt, Babylonia, Assyria, Phoenicia, the "Hebrews, Hittites, Sabaeans, and Persians" (31). This poetry, however, also contributed directly to Moore's linking of spiritual questions and political engagement to poetic form. Moore found in Hebrew prophetic poetry a model for addressing political injustice that acknowledged personal doubt or emotion as a part of public, ethical statement.

Writers in New York, like those in Berlin, must have been conscious of the city's Jewish presence. In 1910, 31 percent of the population of New York City was Jewish; by 1917, the city had approximately 1.4 million Jewish inhabitants, and Yiddish dominated a twenty-block square area of Manhattan, up to Fourteenth Street and bordering the Village.[56] Like Lasker-Schüler in Berlin, Moore and Loy would have heard Yiddish on the streets, and seen evidence of both a thriving Yiddish literary world and intersections between Anglo-American and Yiddish cultures.[57] Hutchins Hapgood published *Spirit of the Ghetto* in 1902; sixteen years later, Lola Ridge titled her first book *The Ghetto and Other Poems.* In 1918, New York's Yiddish theaters attracted an audience of two million people (Binder and Reimers 134). Many of the Jews emigrating from Eastern Europe to the United States were questioning traditional identities in ways similar to those of German Jews, although in reaction against the parochialism of their parents and home countries rather than against nationalism. In both cases, they turned to cosmopolitanism, stressing internationalism and a common humanity.

From a different historical background, many American Protestants were also rejecting American provincialism for international and cosmopolitan attitudes and questioning the relation of secular to religious culture. Such questioning arose in part from new German scholarship that interpreted the Bible as a historical and sociological as well as sacred document. As this scholarship spread to the United States, it set off an era of liberal Protestantism in tension with American fundamentalist understandings of religion. According to church historian Jerald C. Brauer, turn-of-the-century American clerical concern with the problems produced by immigration, rapid industrialization, and huge economic disparities produced a "Progressive Era" orientation that dominated especially northern Protestant denominations through the mid–twentieth century. The Federal Council of Churches, founded in 1908, convened around common desire for a "social gospel" of "applied Christianity": "Ignorance was to be overcome by knowledge, selfishness was to be conquered by service, and war was to be blotted out by fellowship."[58] "Modern" liberal Protestants, like their Jewish counterparts, sought to integrate religious and spiritual understanding with social and political concerns. While some parts of the U.S. population moved increasingly toward nationalist isolationism, religious fundamentalism, and xenophobia, cosmopolitanism provided an important meeting ground for other thinkers, writers, and artists.

In 1914, the first year Moore worked intently at developing a mature poetic, she also gave serious attention to a Bible study class taught by her Presbyterian minister and based on current scholarship.[59] Several of her poems written between 1914 and 1924 explore poetic prophecy as an aesthetic and ethical model. Significantly, Moore represents this verse as "Hebrew" rather than as "Old Testament" Christian. This insistence on the foreignness of ancient biblical poetry suggests a political and aesthetic stance that rejects the parochialisms of Protestant, Anglo-Saxon, and Victorian pieties. As she writes in the notebook she kept while taking the Bible study class: "Protestantism[:] a belief in no institution or creed which is not in a constant process of disintegr[ation?], reconstruction" (VII:08:03). An emphasis on shared rather than exclusive religious belief characterized liberal Protestantism and Moore's own deep faith. Just as Moore found principles of American art illuminated by observing Chinese forms, her spiritual and social values were illuminated through her understanding of Judaic history and scripture, where they were divorced for her from questions of nationalism, religious orthodoxies, and competing loyalties among Protestant sectarian creeds.

References to prophets occur in several of Moore's early poems exploring the ethical positioning of the poet. Most were not republished after *Observations* (1925). A 1915 poem called "Isaiah, Jeremiah, Ezekiel, Daniel" begins with an epigraph paraphrasing these four prophets: "*Bloodshed and Strife are not of God;* // What is war / For; / Is it not a sore / On this life's body?" (*EP* 360). By joining the prophets in speaking against war, Moore here implicitly also joins in the spirit of their prophecy. A 1924 poem takes its title from Isaiah 9:10: "The Bricks Are Fallen Down, We Will Build with Hewn Stones. The Sycamores Are Cut Down, We Will Change to Cedars," and admires Israelite resilience while, like Isaiah, condemning its pride. Perhaps indirectly addressing the United States, as the prophets do their people, Moore writes: "we have 'defeated ourselves / with false balances' and laid weapons in the scale." The central question of the poem, however, is "In what sense shall we be able to / secure to ourselves peace" (*EP* 66). The 1916 poem "Is Your Town Nineveh?" presents the speaker as Jonah and then questions whether readers are also Jonahs, having to choose between the duty of God-directed service to a community and personal desire. "Sojourn in the Whale" (1917) also presents the speaker, and women, as Jonah—temporarily captive but sure to "rise" above current prejudice and privation (*EP* 183). Moreover, as discussed in chapter 3, the faith required for such rising appears to be in large part faith in oneself, not in an external power, as suggested by the poem's lengthy opening reference to fairy tales and political grounding in the Irish Easter Rising.

In a poem best known as "The Past is the Present" (1915), Moore makes her most explicit claim for Hebrew prophecy as the model for her verse:[60]

If external action is effete
  And rhyme is outmoded,
    I shall revert to you,
  Habakkuk, as on a recent occasion I was goaded
      Into doing, by XY, who was speaking of unrhymed verse.
This man said—I think that I repeat
  His identical words:
    "Hebrew poetry is
  Prose with a sort of heightened consciousness. 'Ecstasy affords
    The occasion and expediency determines the form.'"

(*EP* 208)

Because rhyme had hardly been discarded in 1914 and because "external action" cannot in all cases be considered "effete" regardless of how one defines it, the opening "if" of the poem seems more like a hedge than a condition. Similarly, the speaker says, "I shall revert to you" as a future conditional event while already turning to Habakkuk in her poem. She states the opening conditions to prove her decision is right, but "revert[s]" to her Hebrew model whether or not they are fulfilled. Consequently, to the extent that the poem serves as a manifesto, its indirections also function as manifestations of principle.[61] According to George A. Smith's *Book of the Twelve Prophets,* Habakkuk introduced speculation into the field of Jewish prophecy, acknowledging that his "revelation is baffled by experience" and thereby initiating a model of address to, and questioning of, God as a part of the attempt to interpret God's will.[62] Moreover, Smith repeatedly praises Habakkuk's poetry as "exquisite" for its strong cadences, striking figures of speech, and forceful prosaic rhythms in parallel structure, translating the Hebrew into English verse more dynamic than that of the King James Bible (2:138, 149). In a notebook, Moore copied out several lines of Smith's translation, suggesting her own appreciation of his phrases of crescendoing intensity or unembarrassed bewilderment. Like Habakkuk, Moore combines the "ecstasy" of response to a current "occasion" with the "expediency" of unrhymed verse, combining prosaic syntax, colloquialism, patterns of syntactic intensity, and skeptical, speculative questioning.[63]

"Feed Me, Also, River God" (1916) articulates the stance of questioning prayer Smith attributes to Habakkuk. Unlike the Israelites who declared "'the bricks are fallen down, we will / Build with hewn stone,'" the speaker claims not to be "ambitious"; she cannot "match . . . their ability to catch // Up with arrested prosperity." "I am not like / Them, indefatigable," she bluntly concludes (*EP* 367). "Feed Me," she pleads, but not because she is one of a chosen people, or for individual worth, or for the barter of worship: in fact, the poem concludes, "if you may fulfill / None but prayers dressed / As gifts in return for your own gifts—disregard the request." According to Smith, the major prophets distinguished themselves from earlier prophets by rejecting ritualistic behavior (*Book of the Twelve* 1:23). Moore's speaker, too, refuses to participate in a ritual implying that one can exchange gifts with God and instead demands nourishment on the grounds of basic humanity, challenging: "if you are a god you will / Not discriminate against me." Moreover, she acknowledges that she fears her own "gluttony . . . close at hand— / On either side / Of me": if she is not "fed," she may fall prey to the "crocodile" of her own weakness, namely a desire to see God only as the instrument for satisfying her needs.[64]

Liberal Protestant scholarship was adamant about distinguishing prophecy from prediction. Smith calls such understanding "vulgar," "degenerated," and says "the first duty of every student" is to "get rid of this idea" (*Book of the Twelve* 1:11)—a conviction Moore repeats in her religion class notebook: "avoid the idea of prophecy as pre-diction" (VII:08:03). For her, prophecy voices the need for individual ethical decision-making in relation to world affairs, eschewing the egocentric narrowness of mere opinion or feeling while acknowledging historically and personally bound perspective. Consequently, while prophecy might seem to be an aggrandizing model for poetic speech, it is in Moore's view precisely the opposite. For her, the prophet has no hotline to truth but feels a compulsion to speak out about matters of public concern. As Smith writes, the prophet "starts from the facts of his own day and speaks first to his contemporaries." Prophets stress "justice and equity," enforcing religious observances "for social ends, or with regard to the interests of the poorer classes of the community"; they shape ethical awareness through insistence that religious duty demands not only love of God but also "of thy neighbour as thyself."[65]

Given her understanding of Hebrew prophetic poetry, Moore's poetic is closer to a Hebrew than an American Calvinist model, even though her faith was strongly Christian: her concern is with duty or relation to a community, not with the virtue of a speaker or "warfare between the forces of self-effacement and self-assertion with which the Puritans were obsessed" (Merrin 99). In effect, although never explicitly, her poetic rejects a fundamentalist Christian concept of religious ritual and duty. Indirectly, it also rejects the tradition of national religious exceptionalism outlined by Sacvan Bercovitch in *The American Jeremiad*. Although in Moore's verse the United States is at times analogous to Israel in that she (like biblical prophets) speaks to her country, she does not regard it as having a privileged covenant with God or in the light of millennialism; she understands prophecy to function as a brake on narrow loyalties rather than as a whip to encourage them.[66] Here again she follows Smith and other liberal theologians, noting that the prophets worshiped God not "out of a selfish passion for their own salvation like so many modern Christian fanatics; but in symp[athy] w. their nation's aspirations for freedom and her whole political life" (VII:01:01). The concept of direct address to a community may have encouraged the large number of illocutionary structures that play against the surface difficulty of Moore's poetic. It is also one of the characteristics distinguishing her poetic from that of Eliot and Pound, with their emphasis on individual learning and insight and with exclusive communities.[67]

Structurally, Moore's poetic is also closer to a Hebraic than a Calvinist model. According to Jonathan Barron, a Christian poetic privileges the symbol, with its ahistorical logocentrism; symbols of temptation, sacrifice, and redemption predominate. In contrast, a Jewish hermeneutic privileges history and allegory.[68] Moore favors historical and scientific over symbolic structures. Christian scholarship stereotyped Hebrew as a language of dynamic movement ("cinema"), and dynamism constitutes a primary characteristic of her own verse.[69] Like Hebrew poetry, it proceeds through a heightening or intensification of language—between metaphors and versets in Hebrew verse, and between listlike sequences of sentences, clauses, and descriptive units in Moore's poems (Alter 29). Moore also suggests dynamic movement through enjambment, breaking not just syntactic units but words between lines or stanzas: in "Black Earth," a line breaks at "sub- / Merged"; in "Sojourn in the Whale," a stanza breaks at the climactic conclusion "she will give // In." Such enjambment both syncopates the poem's syntactic flow and forces quick movement against traditional places of pause or rest. As Qian describes in his analysis of Pound's and William's orientalism, Moore finds in Hebrew poetry authorization for her own modernist ideas.

Moore also reads positively another common prejudicial portrayal of Hebrew, namely its "incapacity for abstraction"—a phrase she attributes to A. R. Gordon (VII:08:03). Moore already knew Pound's 1913 dictum "Go in fear of abstractions" and was, like other modernists, critical of "reason."[70] Moreover, she would have seen both the lack of abstraction in Hebrew verse and Pound's aesthetic as consonant with Christianity; in her religion notebook she cites Kellogg saying, "the Christian religion is not rational. It is dramatically opposed to the Greek idea 'all things in reason'" (RML VII:08:03). Later in "Poetry" (1919), Moore restates this idea in her own pragmatic terms: "things are important not because a // high sounding interpretation can be put upon them but because they are / useful" (*EP* 205). The biblical prophet does not philosophize but directs attention to the events of the world as he interprets them. The listener or reader then further interprets such text. Both interpretations—like traditional Jewish exegesis—occur within history. Hebrew prophecy offers Moore both a nonmetrical, highly rhythmic poetic and a self-positioning divorced from the self-examination of Calvinism and the righteousness of witness or exceptionalism, privileging not the individual's or nation's relation to God but the ethical imperative to speak publicly for what one believes is right. It coincides with her development of an aesthetic of contingency and knowledge that "'the barest glance at human history shows that mistakes have been the rule,'" yet belief in the possibilities of significant communication and change.[71]

Moore never called herself a prophet and did not think of herself as having a privileged perspective from which to judge contemporary events or her peers. She even rejected the title of "poet" as having too much authority for her "observations," as she titled the first book she arranged for publication. What she wrote could be called "poetry," she explained, only because "there is no other category in which to put" her "experiments in rhythm, or exercises in composition." When asked, "As a poet what distinguishes you . . . from an ordinary man," Moore responded "Nothing."[72] This stance is very different from that of Eliot's Prufrock, who exclaims, "I am no prophet" as an excuse for his inability to predict the future and hence act. For Moore, the analogy with prophecy is an explicit call to action, in a spirit of urgency.[73] "Nothing" distinguishes her from the people she speaks to except that she feels called upon to speak. As Michael Bell suggests generally for modernists, poetry for Moore provided an "active means of questioning and discovering fundamental values, truths, and understandings."[74] Although Bell sees this function of literature as substituting for religion, Moore saw the two as consonant.

By 1920, Moore's focus was less on establishing a prophetic model for her own poetic than on asserting the conjunction of various ancient and modernist American poetics. The 1920 poem "England" lists examples of "the flower and fruit of . . . superi- / ority," including "The sublimated wisdom / of China, Egyptian discernment, [and] the cataclysmic torrent of emotion compressed / in the verbs of the Hebrew language" (*EP* 278–79). The poem then concludes: "should one not have stumbled upon [that noted superiority] in America, must one imagine / that it is not there? It has never been confined to one locality." Superiority, Moore insists, can be found in every country, and presumably every language. In "When I Buy Pictures," the poet describes things "of which I may regard myself as the imaginary possessor," "fix[ing] upon what would give me pleasure in my average moments." As in "England," her references are far-flung: she admires a secular "medieval decorated hat-box," shades of blue in an artichoke, a "hieroglyphic," and a Blake drawing of "Michael taking Adam by the wrist."[75] Art, the poem concludes, must "be 'lit with piercing glances into the life of things'"—a phrase she quotes from Gordon's *Poets of the Old Testament:* "then I 'take it in hand as a savage would take a looking-glass.'" Art should have an inner life like that of Hebrew poetry and inspire primitive wonder, revealing that at our most receptive we are no less fundamentally "savage" than others more frequently called by that name.

"Novices" (1923) both represents "the unforced passion of the Hebrew language" and "the willowy wit, the transparent equation of Isaiah, Jeremiah, Ezekiel, Daniel" as ideals for modern verse and demonstrates that the superiority of ancient and foreign art may be wrought in English. In this poem, Moore manifests the "passion of Hebrew" in sixteen lines of extraordinary vigor and intensity, thereby proving that the Hebrew poet-prophets have taught her to write a poetry different from that of the "Novices" the poem condemns. Because of their grounding in Greek rationality ("Plato"), Moore claims, "Novices" see as "reiterative" and "stuffy" the texts that she regards as models of living language. The poem ends with an extraordinary mosaic of quotation and Moore's own phrases demonstrating her skills:

> "split like a glass against a wall"
> in this "precipitate of dazzling impressions,
> the spontaneous unforced passion of the Hebrew language—
> an abyss of verbs full of reverberation and tempestuous energy"
> in which action perpetuates action and angle is at variance with angle
> till submerged by the general action;
> obscured by fathomless suggestions of colour,
> by incessantly panting lines of green, white with concussion,
> in this drama of water against rocks—this "ocean of hurrying consonants"
> with its "great livid stains like long slabs of green marble,"
> its "flashing lances of perpendicular lightning" and "molten fires
> swallowed up,"
> "with foam on its barriers,"
> "crashing itself out in one long hiss of spray."
>
> (*EP* 279)

Here Moore undermines any literal base for the primitivist cliché that Hebrew functions like cinema by rewriting "Hebrew" action in English. What novices avoid is what Moore values: detailed language expressing the "transparent equation" of poetic speech striving for the highest truth and usefulness and that can be produced in any tongue. Lasker-Schüler similarly refused to allow the poems of *Hebraische Balladen* to be translated from German into Hebrew because, she claimed, "sie sind doch hebräisch geschrieben" [they are already written Hebrew].[76] As Heinz Politzer notes, "*Hebrew Ballads* are not Jewish visions in the German language . . . [but Lasker-Schüler's] attempt to write Hebrew poetry in German [*auf deutsch hebräisch zu dichten*]" (220).

In "Novices," Moore writes Hebrew poetry in English, as it were. Fifteen of the eighty-odd poems Moore published by 1924 make explicit reference to prophets or Jews; in several others she quotes from Smith, Gordon, Kellogg, or other theologians. Especially between 1914 and 1924, when she stopped writing poetry to edit the *Dial*, biblical reference or allusion permeated Moore's poems.

Moore's early poems participate in what she understands as both ancient Hebrew and contemporary Protestant questioning of what it means to pitch one's language beyond the merely personal, without losing sight of personal and historical positioning. God functions in such a reading of prophecy as the ethical spur to speech. As Moore writes in "Humility, Concentration, and Gusto," "The thing is to see the vision and not deny it," or in "Impact, Moral and Technical," "writing is difficult—at least it is for me . . . [but] 'our salvation is urgency. That saves us'"; "verbal felicity is the fruit of ardor, of diligence, and of refusing to be false" (*CPr* 426, 436, 437). It is also, for Moore, indivisible from her attitudes toward Jews and Judaism in her contemporary world.

Judaism was not foreign to Moore before her move to the Village. Bryn Mawr had at least some degree of religious diversity in its student population; Moore's entering class of 104 students included seven Jews, five Catholics, one Moravian, and four students listing their religious affiliation as "none."[77] In her first few months at Bryn Mawr, Moore mentions meeting "Lil," a "Jewess" from Arkansas, and quotes Dean Thomas as giving a "great Thanksgiving speech" saying that "the world should be thankful," among other things, for "the steps taken by [Israel] Zangwill and others to give the Jews their rights"; she also comments angrily to her family on the anti-Semitism of some of her classmates.[78] Mary Warner Moore relates a later incident in which Moore defends Jews to an anti-Semite by saying, "their writings were very great"; when asked to specify, "Rat quoted Ezekiel and Isaiah" and then brought "Pilate and Paul and the N. Test. Jews . . . forward" (April 6, 1921; VI.24.05). As this incident suggests, such attitudes were part of her upbringing and shared by her mother. Moore tells the story of her mother declaring, "I am a Jew" in response to someone "generalizing about the faults of the Jews."[79] Jacob Glatstein describes Mary Warner Moore speaking "of her 'Jewishness,' not only in the sense of the former pope who had said that 'spiritually, we are all Semites,' but with simplicity and feeling, like a Jewish woman."[80] In the 1930s and 1940s, Moore was active in attempts to publicize Jewish persecution in Europe, and she ends a 1944 review of a poem referring to concentration camps, by calling Jews "they, by way of whom all our moral advantages have come": "If we yet rescue them—those who are alive to be rescued—we are still in debt and need to ask ourselves who would have rescued whom" (*CPr* 403).[81]

Moore does not write any poems about specific contemporary Jews, as she later does about African Americans she admires. In an early poem, however, she identifies herself with Disraeli, the baptized Jew who was twice prime minister of Great Britain. Initially published as a companion piece to "Isaiah, Jeremiah, Ezekiel, Daniel," "To Disraeli on Conservatism" indirectly positions the poet in a world not receptive to her or her work by examining the politics of Disraeli's difference:

> You brilliant Jew,
> You bright particular chameleon, you
>   Regild a shabby fence.
>
> They understood
> Your stripes and particoloured mind, who could
>   Begrudge you prominence
>
> And call you cold!
> But when has Prejudice been glad to hold
>   A lizard in its hand,
>
> Or kindred thing?
> To flesh fed on a fine imagining,
>   Sound flesh is contraband.
>
> (*EP* 181; 1909)

While being cold-blooded would seem unattractive, the chameleon was a favorite animal of Moore's.[82] To call Disraeli a chameleon was to link him with herself, as Gator and Basilisk, and with that which she admired: the ability to change, figured intellectually as a "particoloured mind." The chameleon "regild[s]" what has become shabby because it could not change. Only prejudice can explain a failure to appreciate the "brilliant" qualities of such flexible responsiveness, whether in a lizard, a politician, or a woman working out her poetic alliances. As in its partner poem, where war is "a sore / on this life's body," here Moore uses a metaphor of health: reasonable adaptability equals "Sound flesh." In contrast to the stereotype of the Jew as diseased or polluting to Christian society, in these two poems Moore associates robust health with specific ancient and modern Jews.

The figure of the chameleon resonates multiply in the poem: with Disraeli's socially liberal but otherwise conservative politics, his Catholic religion but proudly professed Jewish heritage, with the Jewish diaspora's history of exile and partial assimilation, and with prejudicial stereotypes of Jews as alien, cold-blooded. It may also resonate, however, with Moore's genre-crossing prosaic poetry, and her female maleness—as Rat and prophet-poet, a calling historically male. She, too, is alien. Yet "Sound flesh" is not always warm; it may not correspond to popular assumptions about what is natural or right: a Jewish prime minister of Britain and a female modernist poet may make some as uncomfortable as holding a lizard in their hands. "To Disraeli" asserts Moore's opposition to prejudice by figuring the Jewish prime minister in one of her own marginalized shapes. Moore's decision not to republish the poem after 1924 may demonstrate her recognition that a general reader could not understand this identification and hence might read the poem as confirming the very stereotypes she intended to reject.

For Moore, the "Jew"—ancient or modern—was not an abstract category differentiable from people she knew, or from "America." In his 1947 essay, Jacob Glatstein defines Moore's Americanness as explicitly nonprejudicial and in contrast to "the snobbish anti-American rebels [who] fled from the Jews and the Negroes in order to be obsequious to Europe" (68). He sees her prosaic poetry, her American pluralism, and the "convincing sincerity of her poems . . . like the wine of religion" as all of a piece: the politics are inseparable from the poetic, with its permeating "ethical discipline" and "universal religion" (71, 73). As his translator Doris Vidauer comments, Glatstein highlights in Moore's verse principles characteristic of his own—a claim she follows by describing Glatstein's "conviction of the moral responsibility of the poet to the twofold culture in which he found himself, both as Jew and American."[83] The sequence of these statements suggests that both Vidauer and Glatstein saw Moore as responsible to a "twofold" America specifically inclusive of Jews. Similar concepts of pluralism were being developed by various writers and intellectuals in New York. In 1908, Zangwill's play *The Melting-Pot* was first performed; in 1915, Horace Kallen (the son of a rabbi) published his famous articulation of a model American cultural "orchestra," where each ethnic group or nationality maintains its own distinctive instrumentality in a unified harmony, and German Jewish immigrant Franz Boas was publishing frequent anthropological and polemical essays undermining popular racist assumptions.[84] In 1916, Protestant Randolph Bourne called for a "Trans-National America" in which the United States becomes "a cosmopolitan federation" of immigrants who adhere to their individual cultures but form alliances with those of others: "the eager Anglo-

Saxon . . . find[s] his true friends . . . among the acclimatized German or Austrian . . . Jew . . . Scandinavian or Italian. In them he finds the cosmopolitan note."[85] Together with colleagues at *The Seven Arts,* Bourne chose Stieglitz, son of an immigrant German Jew, as the "incarnation" of modernism "in American terms and on American soil."[86] Protestant theologian and philosopher Reinhold Niebuhr, whom Moore greatly admired, defined the self as in necessary dialogue with neighbor and God, a "condition which he denotes as 'the Hebrew rather than Hellenic description of . . . [the self's] reality.'"[87] When asked in 1929, "What is your world view?" Moore responds, "International fraternity" (*CPr* 673).

Writing not about America but Jewishness, Primo Levi celebrates "diversity" as an energizing principle. In *The Periodic Table,* thinking about zinc sulfate leads Levi to a "praise of impurity, which gives rise to changes, in other words, to life. . . . In order for the wheel to turn, for life to be lived, impurities are needed. . . . Dissension, diversity, the grain of salt and mustard are needed" (34). As a Jew, Levi concludes, "I am the grain of salt or mustard" (35).[88] While Moore does not use the word "impurity," which for her would have smacked of eugenics, she celebrates imperfection in multiple poems. In 1915, in "To Statecraft Embalmed," she exclaims over "Life's faulty excellence!"; in 1916, she begins "Critics and Connoisseurs" with the comment that she likes "a / mere childish attempt to make an imperfectly ballasted animal stand up" better than Ming porcelain (*EP* 203, 215). Moore delights in the ordinary and imperfect. Mina Loy, however, like Levi, sees herself as the "grain of salt" and impurity as key to her "mongrel" poetic.

Loy's "Mongrel" Poetics and Expatriation

Although orientalism was well established in the London of Loy's youth and Paris before 1910, Loy shows no interest in tropes of the East until around 1920, when religion and the relation of aesthetics to the spirit become central issues of her thought and art. At that point Loy, like Lasker-Schüler, formulates a self based on doubleness. Moore positions herself along continuums, erasing lines of distinction rather than juxtaposing contrasting categories. This is appropriate for a poet who structured her life along various lines of belonging: to a family, a church, a congregation, among coworkers, and with friends. Lasker-Schüler was forcefully reminded of her differences from mainstream German and Jewish communities at the same time that she intersected with significant elements of both populations; perhaps for this reason she positioned herself as simultaneously divided and uniting contrasts through the figure of doubleness: *IchundIch.* At the practical level, Loy enjoyed the potential for seamless integration into the mainstream population of every city she lived in: she was white, heterosexual, beautiful, a mother, femininely dressed, and (for the most part) identified as Christian. Nonetheless, because of her expatriation, her background, and her psychic construction, she felt fewer ties than Lasker-Schüler to any community. While Lasker-Schüler united contrasts to dismiss their significance, Loy constituted herself as conflicted, torn in contrary directions, like Levi—"impure." This construction had particularly pointed resonance during the 1920s, as fears of "race suicide" in Europe and the United States heightened, and as diatribes asserting the degenerative effects of miscegenation proliferated.[89] Loy was perhaps even more affected than Moore by the cosmopolitanism inclusive of and articulated by Jews in New York, because of her father's own Judaism and emigration out of Eastern Europe. Her better German would also have allowed her to understand more Yiddish than Moore. Whereas Moore's interests resonated with the liberal discourse of cultural pluralism, Loy was more sensitive to the prejudicial language of disease and mongrelism directed at immigrants and Jews, as indicated by her adoption of this language to articulate the principles of her poetic.

As mentioned previously, although Loy spent less than two and a half years in the United States before 1936, many critics have written about her as American. Most famous is Pound's 1917 reference to Moore's and Loy's verse as a "distinctly national product" of "le temperament de l'Americaine." In the first issue of *Contact* (1920), Robert McAlmon includes Loy among poets producing art that showed "essential contact between words and the locality that breeds them, in this case America," and *Broom* lists Loy among its "profoundly American" authors in a December 1922 issue on "the Oldest and the Newest Art of America." While there is no factual basis for these claims, Loy's brief residences in both the United States and Germany did shift the focus of her art. Here, Loy began to write about moments of religious and artistic epiphany in relation to Judaism.[90] Her experience of living in Greenwich Village in 1920–21, followed by a year in Berlin, provoked profound consideration of her Jewish heritage and its relation to her poetic.

According to her own autobiographical writing and to Burke's biography, Loy received no religious instruction in Judaism. Her closest young contact with other Jews was at the progressive school in Hampstead she attended briefly (*BM* 32). In Paris, Loy was apparently oblivious to the Marais, with its large Yiddish-speaking immigrant Jewish population, and seems to have regarded religion as a matter of little concern.[91] The Anglo-American community in Florence, where she lived between 1906 and 1916, was intensely interested in spiritual questions but, according to Burke, affiliation with Judaism "excited gossip"—something Loy at that point tried to avoid (*BM* 112). Loy attended Christian Science services, a religious affiliation Burke describes as "an acceptable alternative to traditional religions, especially among Jews"; the Stein family attended the same Christian Science church in Florence in 1911 (*BM* 129, 131).

When Loy arrived in New York in 1916, a few months after Moore, she encountered a racially and ethnically mixed world. Because this first year of Loy's in New York was dominated by her interaction with the French expatriates of the Arensberg circle and by her romance with Cravan, whom she met only a few months after arriving, this difference may not have struck her powerfully. When Loy returned to New York in 1920, however, she could not avoid daily contact with people from a variety of nations speaking various languages or inflections of English. As a native speaker of English yet a foreigner to the United States, Loy was extremely interested in this mix of peoples and idioms—different from those in the London of her youth. As she describes it in 1925, "it is inevitable that the renaissance of poetry should proceed out of America" because of the "composite" nature of its language; its English has been "enriched and variegated with the grammatical structure and voice-inflection of many races, in novel alloy with the fundamental time-is-money idiom of the United States . . . on the baser avenues of Manhattan every voice swings to the triple rhythm of its race, its citizenship, and its personality"; "the muse of modern literature arose" in America because "her tongue had been loosened in the melting pot" ("Modern Poetry," *LLB* 158–59). Loy hears the "time-is-money idiom" as an Englishwoman; it is foreign to her ear, as are the variegations of grammar, inflection, and idioms stemming from the racial and national diversity of New York's "baser avenues"—perhaps a reference to the Lower East Side, as Rachel Blau DuPlessis suggests (*Genders* 165). At the same time, this language matches her parallel desire to reject proprieties of form implying class, ideological, and national purity. Unlike conservative critics in the United States and Britain, she found in this "composite" language or mongrelism the generative energy of modern literature; it is noteworthy that she published "Modern Poetry" in the same year as she finished "Anglo-Mongrel and the Rose," the poem most fully articulating her new aesthetic.

Several critics use the term *mongrel* to describe Loy's aesthetic. Elisabeth Frost sees mongrelism in her feminist rejection of "a masculine tradition of heroic narrative"; Marjorie Perloff describes Loy as "mongreliz[ing]" linguistic registers through a combination of concrete and abstract nouns, puns, and "aggressive rhymes" that challenge the more conventional national idioms of Britain, France, Italy, and the United States.[92] Loy herself comments: "I left England at seventeen—& think in a subconscious muddle of foreign languages—Perhaps I have no notion of what pure English is."[93] Marisa Januzzi sees Loy's style as "deliberately abnormal": through "corrupt" mixing of linguistic registers, she chooses what she identified as an American, not a British, idiom; she "wrote herself out of one literary tradition and into another" ("Mongrel Rose" 431).

Loy would also have been likely to think in political terms about mixed language pools because of her multilingualism and because language was the focus of intense debate about cultural purity in England and the United States, as in Germany. In *The Dialect of Modernism*, Michael North explains that both the avant-garde and the rear guard were fascinated with manifestations of race in and as language: "the artist occupied the role of racial outsider because he or she spoke a language opposed to the standard. . . . dialect became the prototype for the most radical representational strategies of English-language modernism" (preface, n.p.). American modernists in particular attempted to root their artistic innovations in "American popular culture, . . . the multiracial heritage of the Americas"—that is, in precisely the argot Loy heard, and that Moore famously called "plain American which cats and dogs can read" ("England"; North 128).[94] These writers borrowed the idioms of jazz, popular song, modern slang, and various dialects as manifestations of the vitality of modern and American life, not its ruin. Critics, however, saw them as debasing the English language. As North describes it, the debate between the American Anglophilic academic establishment and innovative writers "linked language, literature, and race so closely together that aesthetic experimentation seemed racially alien to certain authorities even if it had nothing overtly to do with race" (131). Dreiser's English was described as "the mongrel sort to be expected from a miscegenation of the gutter," and Moore's was called a "disease" (North 132). Royal Cortissoz wrote, "The United States is invaded by aliens, thousands of whom constitute so many acute perils to the health of the body politic. Modernism is of precisely the same heterogeneous alien origin and is imperiling the republic of art in the same way" (1923; North 131). Loy was an invading "alien" in both senses—as (Jewish) Englishwoman, and as modernist poet.

Such criticism echoed the debates in England about how to maintain the purity of English, with its concomitant tradition of deploring the deterioration of English in the United States. Loy grew up among such debates, and within an educational system beginning to attend to the national development of "proper" English among the middle as well as the upper classes. As the daughter of an immigrant father and socially ambitious mother, the poet would have been highly conscious of the class implications of accent, dialect, and diction. In fact, her own linguistic alloy never includes lower-class speech or slang. During the years when she was beginning to write poetry, British little magazines increasingly emphasized "the proper values of poetry" as conveyed by "qualified" vocal interpretation and elocution.[95] Just as "purity of diction" alone could do justice to the English language and, by implication, British nation, "pure voice" became the desired standard for the poem, in opposition to the "artificiality" of verse depending on the spectacle of the page or on formulations not imaginable as part of ordinary speech (Morrisson 28, 37). The seeds of this movement were deeply rooted in middle-class English culture. Loy perhaps echoes and mocks this concept of purity in the 1930 letter quoted earlier, writing that she has "no idea what English is" and is "intensely aiming at pure language" (Januzzi 427). Loy's purity has nothing to do with that of the culture establishment.

When Loy began writing poetry, her fluency in German, French, and Italian provided extensive possibilities for conceptual distancing from her home culture. Similarly, the worlds of Parisian art school, Italian Catholicism, Futurism, and motherhood were apparently foreign, exotic, or absurd enough to her perspective that forays into non-Western cultures were unnecessary as spurs to the imagination or external vantage points. Burke also regards Loy as consumed with the desire to achieve secure social status among the Anglo-American residents of Paris and Florence. During her years there, she wrote nothing of Judaism, used no oriental or primitivist motifs, and saw herself as unquestionably English. In "Italian Pictures" (1914) she writes: "We English make a tepid blot / On the messiness / Of the passionate Italian life-traffic"—a poem elevating Italian street life above the "[in]disputably respectable" life of an Englishwoman's "prolonged invalidism . . . at the beck / Of a British practitioner" (*LLB* 9). Similarly, in a July

1915 letter to Carl Van Vechten she distinguishes "you" Americans from "we" British, after an initial inclusive "we": "I believe we'll get more 'wholesome sex' in American art—than English after all—though you *are* considered so suburban . . . we haven't had a Whitman" (B ZA Van Vechten). Later, rather than turning to non-Western cultures imaginable as either purer or more primitive, Loy portrays marginalized individuals in Vienna ("Der Blinde Junge") and New York ("Chiffon Velours," "Hot-Cross Bum").

Loy's engagement with Futurism in Florence encouraged her rejection of linguistic proprieties. Yet Futurism's concurrent rejection of religion and assumption of a monoracial culture must have been as alienating to Loy as its masculinism. Loy's poetic at this point was at its most cynical and disillusioned. In her early poems, there are no authors, objects, or cultural phenomena manifesting clear positive spiritual significance, as Joyce, Stein, Wyndham Lewis, Brancusi's sculpture, a blind youth, or even pigeons do in later poems. Her early poems constitute rebellious satires of the failed or repressive structures and relationships that prevent spiritual, intimate, and even sexual fulfillment. They explore the positioning of women in a Christian, masculinist, and chaotic world. As she writes of Catholicism in "The Black Virginity" (1915), "It is an old religion that put us in our places." "Baby Priests," in this poem, learn in their novitiate that women are "no less than the world flesh and devil" (*LLB* 442–43). In "Songs to Joannes" (1917), Loy's representation of religion is more complex. The speaker herself is a Christ-figure, martyred in "Crucifixion" (repeated three times) to her own desire for relationship despite her knowledge of the egotistic Joannes's "insolent isolation" (XXXI, *LLB* 67). Their failed affair is a "profane communion . . . Where wine is spill'd on promiscuous lips"; God is bypassed in the poem's claim that a "wanton duality" is responsible for her heterosexual desire (III, II); a "Wire-Puller" represents supreme power (VI). And yet references to the beloved's hair as "God's doormat" and to possible lights behind "God's eyes" suggest unironic potential for beauty or illumination, and the speaker's crucifixion suggests that she has attained knowledge and perhaps even a kind of elevation through her suffering.[96] Drafted in Florence, "Songs to Joannes" marks the high point of Loy's early verse and the cusp of her move from Europe to the United States, where the thirty-four-section poem was finished and published in 1917.

The shocking sexual explicitness of "Songs to Joannes" is matched by its attacks on propriety and poetic conventions, including those of spacing, capitalization, and punctuation—obvious only in a poem associated with the visual page, not speech. The "Songs" are "Spawn of Fantasies"; the speaker claims to be

Virginal   to the bellows
Of Experience
                    Coloured   glass

(*LLB* 53)

The poem's first two sections refer both to "Pig Cupid" and the male "skin-sack / In which a wanton duality / Packed / All the completion of my infructuous impulses." The extreme abstraction, mixture of categories of diction, and frank reference to sexuality seem directed against linguistic purity and prudery, as well as against patriarchal double standards and a world incapable of love. Loy's delight in the motley language of New York did not make her language colloquial; it remained dominated by a vocabulary of words uncommon to British and American speech. New York's linguistic mongrelism struck conceptual, not stylistic, chords.

Around 1919, Loy wrote a few poems combining an almost ecstatic vision of beauty with the desire to "clear the drifts of spring / of our forebear's excrements" ("O Hell," *LLB* 71).[97] During 1920 and 1921, her poetry increasingly focused on the ravaging beauties of modernist art. In "Poe," Loy writes of "a lyric elixir of death . . . corpses of poesy"; in "Joyce's Ulysses" of "lyrical hells," "Phoenix / of Irish fires / lighten the Occident"; in "Apology of Genius," "we forge the dusk of Chaos / to that imperious jewellery of the Universe / —the Beautiful—"; and "Brancusi's Golden Bird" stems from "immaculate conception."[98] Geniuses are "Ostracized . . . with God" ("Apology of Genius," *LLB* 77). Yet there is no complacency in this elevation, as she makes clear in "Lunar Baedeker" and "Der Blinde Junge," with its command that the "illuminati of the coloured earth" attend to the blind youth (*LLB* 84).

In these poems, labeled "1921–22" in Loy's first book, divinity is repeatedly manifest as both terrible or debased and "pure": "The voice and offal / of the image of God" ("Joyce's Ulysses" 88). In "'The Starry Sky' of Wyndham Lewis," the poet sees "the ghosts of the stars / perform the 'Presence'"; they are "Enviable immigrants / into the pure dimension / immune serene / devourers of the morning stars of Job" (91–92). In "Joyce's Ulysses," Joyce is a "rejector-recreator," "Master / of meteoric idiom / present / The word made flesh / and feeding upon itself / with erudite fangs" (*LLB* 90, 89). Art performs "Presence," allied with the incarnation of the divine—brutal or temporary as it may be. The secular and impure give body to the divine. In "The Dead"

(1919) she writes, "Our tissue is that which escapes you / Birth-Breaths and orgasms . . . The unsurpassable openness of the circle / Legerdemain of God"; paradoxically, it is "tissue" that defeats death and leads to God (*LLB* 73). The purity of divinity, like that of her own "pure language," depends upon impure elements.

As previously mentioned, Loy hopes that bearing witness to moments of "*extended* consciousness," like hers at the end of World War I, "may throw a more modern light on that Immortality promised by religion; and a little proof that the power called spiritual is indestructible."[99] The faith Loy expresses in reference to this moment may have influenced the turn of her poetic toward the possibility of at least "hells" of lyrical purity, and poets ostracized "with" a God-creator in the ignorant and hypocritical world she otherwise condemns. Loy was living in Mexico at the end of the war. The timing of this epiphany during her only period of fully satisfying sexual and romantic love but also most destabilizingly life circumstances—near starvation, without means of financial support, pregnant, in a racially heterogeneous, non-European culture—was probably not coincidental. It was apparently not, however, until her return to New York in 1920 that this epiphany began to take shape in multiple poems.

In poems and unpublished notes, Loy asserts the possibility of revelation, epiphany, or other manifestation of the divine. Especially in her late poems she suggests a mystical sensuality resembling Lasker-Schüler's in its striving to construct in language her experience of a knowable divinity. Despite her satirical bent, then, Loy counters assumptions of modernist hostility to religion and despair. For years, she mingled elevated and base registers of language, just as she juxtaposed vocabularies of religion, love, and carnality, mingling the linguistic and social spheres bourgeois culture strove to isolate. In "Anglo-Mongrels and the Rose," Loy constructs a mythic biography revealing the roots and implying the inevitability of this aesthetic of elevated impurity.

In "Anglo-Mongrels and the Rose," mongrelism is first and foremost hereditary, a result of the protagonist's Hungarian-Jewish father and English-Anglican mother. This poem's turn to Jewishness as a fundamental aspect of identity could not be anticipated by Loy's previous poems and seems to have been stimulated by her experiences of living among a culturally vital population of immigrant and assimilated Jews in New York and Berlin. Burke does not discuss Loy's contact with Jewish populations in either city or mention Jewishness as part of her experience there. DuPlessis emphasizes the strong Jewish presence in New

York but does not attribute Loy's interest in mongrelism or her own Jewishness to that presence. In fact, she speculates that Loy's "Anglo-Mongrels and the Rose" may be read "as a response to T.S. Eliot's anti-Semitic discourses of the early 1920s" and to the "loose, general anti-semitism in the British world in the 1920s and earlier" (*Genders* 160). I have found no evidence that Loy's responses to Jewishness in the teens and twenties are strongly influenced by British attitudes.

By the summer of 1922, Loy had moved to Berlin (stopping en route in Vienna to meet and sketch Sigmund Freud).[100] In Berlin, the overall Jewish population was much smaller than in New York, but Jews were more dominant culturally, as described earlier. Loy apparently spent time at the Romanisches Café—where she must have noticed the female prince of Thebes as well as the many Yiddish-speaking émigré writers.[101] She must also at least occasionally have read German papers, where she would have seen frequent discussion of the Jewish "crisis," in mainstream as well as specialized publications, like *Der Jude* or *Ost und West*.[102] Given the pressures of her childhood to rise above her Jewish and foreign ancestry (largely by denying it), Loy would certainly have been struck by the fact that one of the premier literary and political reviews published in Berlin was quite openly called *The Jew*. Moreover, although Burke describes the man with whom Loy lived in Berlin only as "a young Russian poet" who was "desperately poor" (*BM* 315), it is possible he was Jewish; as previously stated, "Russian" was at times a euphemism for Jewish at this time. Loy's year in Berlin coincided both with increasing anti-Semitism caused by increasing inflation, poverty, and political instability and with the continuing Jewish "Renaissance." Loy's class-consciousness and sensitivity to the rank of Jews on the British social ladder were products of her childhood. Her years in Paris and Florence encouraged little interest in acknowledgment of her Jewishness or identification with forms of social marginality. The environments of New York and Berlin, in contrast, apparently intensified such interest and identification. While living in Berlin, Loy began her only poem dealing specifically with purity of language and ethnic-religious inheritance, positioning its protagonist as the potential founder of a new people of "mongrel" writers.

Jewishness, in "Anglo-Mongrels and the Rose," has little to do with religious belief. Instead, it represents artistic and intellectual values in conflict with the repressive pieties of bourgeois British Protestantism and conventional art—hence functioning analogously to orientalism. Nonetheless, religion is more than a trope. The poem follows a roughly chronological narrative, beginning with "Exodus," the character representing her father, then "Ada," her mother, then moving to her own birth as Ova and those of her two husbands as Esau and Colossus. The clash of Judaism with Protestantism through the figures of Exodus and Ada dominates the first half of the poem; the social and psychological instability of the "mongrel" Ova dominates the second half. The mother and her Protestantism are savagely parodied: she is the English "Rose of arrested impulses," "wiping / its pink paralysis / across the dawn of reason" (*LLB82* 121, 122). Her "belligerent innocence" (123) comes from assumptions of imperial superiority played out in multiple wars: the figure of the woman acts as "storage / of British Empire–made pot-pourri / of dry dead men making a sweetened smell / among a shriveled collectivity" (122). While "an impenetrable pink curtain / hangs between [the Rose] and itself" (128), Exodus discovers the beat of his heart and experiences desire. He is an artist, "painting knowing not why / sunflowers turned sunwards" (115), "the wondering Jew" (117). Loy repeats the phrases "He paints / He feels his pulse"—implying that he, unlike the female storage pot of imperialism, has a capacity to express his vitality as part of a larger world. In a contrast echoing stereotypes of East and West, the Jew develops a relation to his own body, hence may experience beauty in nature and be an artist; the Protestant, in her militant self-repression, may not.

The child of this union, Ova, is the "composite / Anglo-Israelite" and receives Sleeping Beauty–like gifts from "Genii" called "racial birthrights"; all are, however, "Curses" until "the least godmother," named Survival, bestows upon her "The Jewish brain!" (130–32). After Ova's birth, negative stereotypes of Jews become pronounced: Judas is "the instinctive / murderer . . . of Jesus" (145) and in two incidents Exodus cruelly tricks his child. In Ova, "Jesus of Nazareth / becomes one-piece / with Judas Iscariot" (132), but the Christian piece seems to predominate. She regards the Jewish children she sees with a combination of fear and fascination, and repeats childish stereotypes: "the Jews killed Jesus / and are bound for Hades / with r-o-u-n-d noses" (158–60). The poem gives no hint of Jewish religious belief. In contrast, and despite Loy's savage parody of the Protestant mother, Ova "credulous[ly]" "loves the Gentle" Jesus (149).

The poem concludes, however, with a spiritual figure "greater than Jehovah" and implied to be Jewish as well as Christian—through the final section's title, "The Social Status of Exodus," and its blurred reference to both an ordinary "tailor" (like Exodus, and Loy's own father) and a singular "Tailor" (173).[103] It is hard to distinguish Exodus/tailor/father from Tailor/Jesus/Son, hence Jewish from Christian elements. "Man," we are told, "defied / the protoform of Who made him" (man defies God?) "but has not denied / Him" (Jesus—or a new divine being?); "man" also "obeyed / the tailor who remade him / and denies him" (man obeys Jesus, who in turn denies man?): "He is despised / this ostracized . . . weaver of fig-leaves . . . who staked the plot / of manhood in his nobler form." The poem's penultimate stanza alludes to Job's lament—"Man that is born of woman is of few days, and full of trouble" (Job 14:1)—and hypothesizes that the tailor may be despised because "he chose / an occupation all too feminine" (suggesting the iconography of a feminine Jesus, or stereotypes of emasculinized Jews?). In the secular skepticism of modern life, where "the tailor's concept of the man-made God . . . peoples the sod," "the cruciform scourge / of conscience / disappears" (174). Fashion triumphs over "the aboriginal / muscle-pattern" in "the image and likeness / of Deity" (172). God may have created people, but the tailor determines what they now look like, thereby also "fashioning" concepts of the God in whose image "men" were made. Earlier in the poem, Ova appeared as Christ-like, the victim of "unmentionable stigmata / stamped" by her mother's "inversion / of instinct," in which a child is nothing but proof that "'somebody' has sinned" (148, 147); there, God is "inattentive" or hidden (152, 157). At the conclusion, however, the poet declares that "Absurd / as it may seem / the 'unprintable word' / is impossible to erase from a vocabulary": the name of divinity, unprintable and unspeakable in Judaism, survives all "Spiritual drapers / Poles and fakirs and shakers" (173). God survives the ascendancy of theological squabble and secularism, and perhaps also the division of Christianity from Judaism. The poem ends without a closing period and without explanation of its composite tailor/Job/Jesus/new divinity or of this figure's relation to the rest of the poem—perhaps proposing a "mongrel Jew-Christian" divine (DuPlessis, *Genders* 164). For explanation, one must turn to the poem's aesthetic core.

Loy dramatizes her aesthetic of creation out of conflict, impurity, and miscomprehension in two sections of the poem, each couched in spiritual language. In the first, Ova has her first experience of poetic making, in which she assigns a pure sound to a vision. Having found "nothing objective new / and only words / mysterious," Ova attentively attaches "materialization" to what she hears—in this case the provocative sound of "iarrhea," identified only by the further phrase "It is quite green," as the nurses change her sister's diaper (139–40). Ova then visualizes "iarrhea" through a linguistic epiphany, in which "this fragmentary / simultaneity / of ideas / embodies / the word":

A
lucent
iris
shifts
its
irradiate
interstice

glooms and relumes
on an orb of verdigris

(*LLB*82 141)

"Iarrhea" is like a beautiful green ball, but even more like divinity manifest as both matter (object) and word. Ova makes "moon-flowers out of muck"; "the mongrel-girl . . . coerce[s] the shy / Spirit of Beauty / from excrements and physic" (143). Like the poet and protagonist, art is mongrel; an "irradiate interstice" can arise out of "fragmentary / simultaneity / of ideas" and other experiences of contradiction or confusion. In contrast to this modern artist of illuminated "interstice," Loy depicts her upper-class ex-husband Haweis as Esau, a privileged and conservative follower of rules. By implication, Ova is Jacob, who steals Esau's cultural birthright to pass on her own feminist and mongrel-Jewish art to future generations.[104] Not a patriarch, she will become the mother of a new people, namely, artists whose neediness and desire push them to find the "shy / Spirit of Beauty" particularly in moments of perception that break traditional boundaries of propriety, expectation, and form. The mongrel-daughter and rule-breaking Jacob implicitly combine to manifest the transgressive artist.

In the poem's second high point, Ova receives a literal revelation, which in the poem provides compensation for the suffering of her childhood. As she stands in the garden, "all [the] / steadfast light" of the "high skies" comes "shining out of her"—that is, she herself becomes transformed into that which illuminates even as she receives "Illumination," the title of the section. She becomes the "lucent iris" of the word, now "irradiate." This nonsectarian light is Christianized as a "saint's prize / this indissoluble bliss / to be carried like a forgetfulness / into the long nightmare" (163–64). Yet because revelation comes either literally out of the body or through the child/poet's unembarrassed appreciation for words as "materialization" of sound, it is associated with Jewishness in the poem. It is Exodus who lives in his body, not the Protestant Ada. In Loy's poem, Exodus (the East) furnishes accessibility to nature or sensuality as well as the contrasting "Jewish brain"; both are key to the child's spiritual and pragmatic "Survival."

These "gifts" are then illuminated through an epiphany conceived as Christian. The resulting art is perhaps possible only through the confusion, and hence greater than ordinary openness to revelation, stemming from the child's "mongrelism," which combines Jewish and Christian, Eastern and Western, psychic and cultural inheritance. What made childhood a psychic hell, she implies, also enables the "lyrical hells" and "immaculate conceptions" of modernist art—biographically hers, but suggestively her (especially Jewish?) generation's, with its similar experiences of disruption and complex inheritance.

In unpublished notes on Jews and in an unpublished prose manuscript, "Goy Israels," Loy is more specific about the categorical associations of "Anglo-Mongrels." "Goy Israels" describes its protagonist as "a wanderer infinitely more haunted than the eternal jew: a bi-spirited entity; to wander in opposite directions at once"—in short, a "Goy" with heightened Jewish characteristics hence even more displaced or marginal (B Box 2, folder 28). On a scrap of paper, Loy writes of Jews as mercenary, obsessed with counting, and "childlike," but more characteristic are other less-stereotyped and negative claims: "the jewish intellect used unconsciously during the stress of oppression—has remarked itself in the easy competition of occidental education—from a shield it has become a weapon—from a back door of escape it has become the front door of entry. A jew today wears his intellect as the Christian, his coronet—or as a courtesan her 'chien'" (B Box 2, folder 29; Box 7, folder 187). Loy sees Judaism both as leading inevitably to Christianity—"It was the task of Israel to establish a world-wide peace . . . upon which foundation Christianity might 'blossom'"—and as the savior of Christianity: "when the gentile world falls over itself it is usual for a jew to come to the rescue," giving the examples of Jesus and Freud. Loy does not see herself as coming "to the rescue" of Western culture, but she does see art as providing a kind of neutral ground on which she may wield imagination and intellect. Moreover, her understanding of Jewish contribution to Western spirituality and aesthetics affirms and enables her contribution as "mongrel" Jew.

Unlike Moore and Lasker-Schüler, Loy writes about stereotypes of Judaism and Christianity in relation to her art rather than finding in Judaism a model for her poetic. On the other hand, Loy's self-formulation as Jew corresponds to her development of an affirmative spirituality and an aesthetic that moves beyond rejection of repressive traditional structures and institutions. Like Moore's, Loy's identification with Judaism is consonant with her Christian faith. Loy writes as a guide, producer of "Baedekers," typically of "lunar" rather than earthly landscapes. As "lunar" implies, these guides are nonsectarian; they provide theoretical and spiritual rather than historical or ethical positioning. Once Loy has begun to articulate her poetic in these astrological terms, her puns and wordplays leave the concrete scenes of Florence, Paris, and bourgeois houses. The poem "Lunar Baedeker" imagines "oval oceans / in the oxidized Orient," punning on a westernized (occidized) East and on the molecular transformations of oxidation. It is from these nonexistent shores of transformed merger that "Onyx-eyed Odalisques / and ornithologists / observe / the flight / of Eros obsolete"—again a collapsing of East and West in the bird-watching of harem women and scientists, who witness Eros as an "obsolete" species. Neither culture is idealized or demonized; neither guarantees the return of love. Loy's poetry maps cultural decay, transformation, and mergers. For her as for Lasker-Schüler, the experiences of love, sexuality, art, and divinity provide crucial bridges between otherwise severed realms of being, often figured in her verse after 1920 as Jewish and Christian, or oriental and occidental.

The work of Loy, Lasker-Schüler, and Moore suggests that exploring representations of religion as analogous to those of orientalism might expand some of the narrow boundaries within which both categories are frequently understood, particularly in reference to Judaism. Moore's, Loy's, and Lasker-Schüler's various concepts of Judaism enable their individual constructions of new modes of poetry in English and German. All three writers have a quotidian contact with Jews and Judaism that Pound does not have with the Chinese, or Eliot and Lowell with Southeast Asians. Equally important, all three of these poets (as also Eliot) write out of active faith. Understanding their conceptions of religion in relation to other prominent patterns of thought in the early twentieth century enriches our perception of the influences on early modernism. Writers in London and Paris—let alone in cultural centers like Mexico City or Moscow—would construct Judaism and orientalism differently from those in New York or Berlin because of the different historical and immediate relation of these communities to large numbers of Asians and Jews. Yet the frequent traffic between, for example, New York, London, Paris, and Berlin might lead to speculations about the effect of Jewish (or conceptually "Oriental") paradigms there even for writers who, like Loy, spend little time among culturally significant Jewish communities.

Most importantly, examining the intersection of discourses of religion, Judaism, and orientalism in the works of Lasker-Schüler, Moore, and Loy reveals quite different political implications for the intermingling of these topics. Typically, discussions of modernist religious discourse have led to assertions of the isolation of religious belief from innovative art, and discussions of Judaism have led to representations of modernism as fascist, anti-Semitic, and xenophobic. Yet these poets grounded in different locations and proceeding from different constructions of faith see religion—particularly as it may be articulated through links with Judaism—as essential to the development and articulation of their aesthetics. Moreover, their uses of religious discourse reveal a variety of ways in which religious faith may subvert restrictive rationality, one-dimensional interpretation of sacred (and all other) language, and patriarchal authority through its belief in powers beyond the control of any single institution or subject and promotion of interfaith alliances. For these and other poets, religion was coincident with antiparochialism, antimaterialism, and active multiculturalism—movements that also intersected with the development of modernist poetics in the early decades of the twentieth century.

6 *Reading the Modernist Poem*

Literature and Location

This study has woven the threads of literary analysis, biography, social history, and gendered cultural studies to produce a fabric representing the difference that location makes to the details and patterns of women's self-performance and poetics in the early modernist period. Attending to these patterns in international comparison reveals the significance of gender and location to the study of this period's writers—including those who expatriate. Moreover, this study suggests that some patterns may have been more significant to women than to men, or may take more obvious form in the writings of women than of men. Modernist women made the performance of gender and sexuality significantly unstable and self-conscious—a performance affecting their choices of lyric form as well as their dress, names, and styles of living. At the same time, Moore's, Lasker-Schüler's, and Loy's individual poetics resemble those of the male peers with whom they allied themselves far more than they resemble each other's; the patterns of similarity among their performances of gender and sexuality are cultural and reactive, not structured or formal. Modernist women may also have articulated their continuum of sensual and sexual desire in closer conjunction to spiritual being and in more innovative ways than men, as makes sense given the social pressures against female articulation of sexuality and the inherent disadvantages of traditional heterosexuality for their financial and psychological independence. Similarly, modernist women may have manipulated the tropes of orientalism to different effect than men, given the primitivism and exoticism associated with dominant gender ideologies for women—as well as for non-Western peoples. Here a study of orientalism in the writing of African American, or a broader range of Jewish, women and men would be particularly illuminating for thinking about comparative patterns. Modernist women may also more openly have expressed belief, or more actively believed, in a divine spirit manifest in earthly forms or addressable through direct speech, although they were not more attached to formal worship than men. Moore, Loy, and Lasker-Schüler felt considerable flexibility in reinterpreting spiritual value and authority as consonant with a feminist, antitraditional poetic. Their poetry expresses dismay at social and political conditions or even at the human condition, but does not by and large share the angst or despair of those perceiving a world without God or a spirituality rarely manifest. Because this study does not compare male with female poets as its primary emphasis, these suggestions remain speculative. Nonetheless, the poets of my small sample suggest that traditional assumptions about modernism based primarily on the work of men are not accurate for a range of women.

Civilization was not, for these women, Pound's "old bitch / gone in the teeth" or Eliot's anemic typist awaiting a carbuncular young man. Instead, whatever its local impediments or flaws, it laid the ground for their opportunity to leave traditional repressions and restrictions behind. Women had even more cause than men for excitement at modernism's potential for change—if, that is, their educational, financial, and social background enabled them to perceive themselves as sharing in it. Women and men feared the effects of imperialism, nationalism, world wars, capitalist exploitation, materialism, and social instability. Women of confident self-assertion—often the product of education, financial independence, and some degree of cultural freedom—however, also relished their roles *as* women, and the specific modernity of those roles.

The generation of modernists coming of age in the first two decades of the twentieth century differed significantly from that coming of age in the twenties or later, particularly in its conception of art in relation to the public world and to concepts of gender and sexual fluidity. Like the men who began their careers in the early teens, women of this generation produced much of their best work after 1920 (one thinks of Woolf's great novels, or much of Loy's and Moore's poetry), but they were enabled by the conditions of earlier decades, just as their own writing, editing, and reviewing enabled that of younger women coming of age in the twenties and thirties.[1] Continuing comparative attention to women's writing will encourage greater attention in modernist studies to questions of gendered and sexual performance and self-formulation in relation to social politics, poetic structures, religious belief, ethical agency, and self-inclusive models of difference, like those of primitivism, orientalism, and alienation.

Location matters. Lasker-Schüler could not have been take ously as an Expressionist poet in Berlin had she adopted Moore's m nish decorousness and domestic seclusion, not to mention that the all-female higher education enabling Moore's self-confidence and strong female identification was not available to any German woman of the time. By the same token, Moore could not have adopted the radical fictions, dress, and bohemian manner of Lasker-Schüler's life and still have been offered the editorship of the *Dial*, maintained its authority as editor, or commanded the respect she did from peers like Pound, Eliot, Williams, and Stevens—all poets with advanced university degrees. It is perhaps not accidental that the most outrageously bohemian woman in New York was an expatriate German—the baroness Elsa von Freytag-Loringhoven. Neither Lasker-Schüler nor Moore could have seen Loy's modish femininity as anything but a distraction to her own goal of being taken seriously by the modernist circles of Berlin and New York, although this was a mode that Loy manipulated successfully. Femininity was a card Loy could play in every country with equal success, even in her older years when she was adored by the young men who were her fellow tenants (*BM* 410–16). Georgia O'Keeffe, Amy Lowell, H.D., Gertrude Stein, Virginia Woolf, Hannah Höch, Emmy Hennings, Jeanne Mammen, and many others may be seen as responding to similar gendered cultural restrictions or expectations in constructing their own equally idiosyncratic and representative life structures and modes of modernist art. Understanding how location shapes the lives of women also reveals more clearly how the women of particular places themselves shaped local modernisms.

To review briefly the conclusions of my previous chapters: Moore, in New York, was positioned among a sizable, relatively supportive community of feminist women controlling a good number of the infrastructural outlets for modernist exhibition and publication, and themselves publishing extensively. This environment enabled her to become the most influential female modernist poet in the United States and perhaps among Anglo-American writers: she was the only woman both widely acknowledged as a major experimentalist poet and playing a direct role in the editing and publication of modernist texts.[2] Among novelists in Anglo-American modernism, only Virginia Woolf had similar infrastructural influence and stature. Given her key role in the era, it is astonishing that Moore's life and work are so rarely discussed in the context of international modernism, and even more astonishing that studies of New York modernism typically all but ignore her presence.[3] Moore was not outrageous. She did not write manifestoes, drink multiple sexual partners, or participate in all-night the frequently told story of Loy's leaving the last Blind ;:00 A.M. for scrambled eggs at the Arensbergs, then ight chastely with four others in Duchamp's bed (*BM* e's lack of bohemian flare did not, however, make her ative of, or influential on, her time. Her feminism, faith in rogressive Era social politics, strong religious faith but ecumenical support of all religions, and rejection of racism, anti-Semitism, and normative heterosexuality were fully consonant with major trends of modernity in New York, whether or not these trends were shared by other now-canonical poets.

Moore thought and wrote seriously about the major intellectual issues of the early twentieth century. The topics of her reviews, poems, and letters provide an important link between literary modernism and U.S. cultural theorists like William James, John Dewey, Horace Kallen, Randolph Bourne, Kenneth Burke, and Reinhold Niebuhr.[4] Moreover, Moore's politics of social inclusion, interest in history, and concern with ethical agency place her work squarely within Anglo-American modernism and distance it from European-based formally innovative groups, with their greater emphasis on absurdity, antibourgeois and anti-institutional political stances, and rejection of literary and historical traditions. Moore described her political stance as "conservative," but defined conservatism as "opposed to regimentation" or, in another interview, "against fascism; against any suppression of freedom by tyranny masked as civilization" (*CPr* 674). In a *Partisan Review* interview called "Religion and the Intellectuals," Moore attributes "the helplessness of individuals and of society . . . to breakdown in the individual"; her remedy, as presented in several poems as well as in her voting record, is also primarily at the level of individual responsibility (*CPr* 676). This notion of individual agency, however, had liberal as well as conservative elements, and it grounded her poetic through all decades of her writing. Moore wrote in radical stanzaic, rhythmic, and rhyming forms; she juxtaposed wide-ranging scientific, historical, and cultural detail in an implied logical and ethical frame; and she made frequent recourse to a humor based more on the ironies of wit than on satire or concrete verbal play. All these elements of her verse contributed to the eclectic style of American modernism.

Lasker-Schüler entered bohemian Berlin with a background typical for women of her era and utterly different from that typical of women in American modernism, with her minimal formal education, scorn for book learning, and repudiated bourgeois past. To my knowledge, her name appears in no studies of international modernist poetry, yet she is accorded regular attention in studies dedicated to the Expressionist lyric, indicating that both during her lifetime and since, the concept of Expressionism has developed at least partly in response to her work.[5] As mentioned earlier, her name even served as a verb to describe her imitators, other poets who "lasker" in their writing. Her verse gave a new shape to the German lyric in its colloquialism, familiar address, extreme metaphorical layering and synaesthesia, and in her construction of radically unstable forms of individual, gender, and sexual embodiment.[6] Perhaps equally significant is that Lasker-Schüler was regarded by her peers as a major player in the negotiations of position determining who had symbolic capital among the experimentalists, during and after her marriage to Walden. People sought introductions to her and wrote in letters, journals, and memoirs about their encounters. The extravagance of her bearing and her disdain for bourgeois propriety offended some and inspired others. Without the slightest engagement in its formal infrastructures, she nonetheless influenced the directions and networks of the German avant-garde.

Lasker-Schüler was similarly a defining part of bohemian Berlin, asserting through her life structures the possibility for a female artist to live without inherited, bourgeois, or heterosexual means of support, and for a woman to take her independent artistic production as seriously as a man. She was the first female poet in Germany to function within a male literary community as a respected peer. Her work was frequently reviewed and discussed, in cities from Berlin to Prague, Zurich, and Vienna, and it deserves comparative analysis not just with her contemporary Jewish and German writers but with poets like Paul Celan and Emily Dickinson, with whom she has strong affinities, or with H.D., the Anglo-American modernist poet whose psychological, sexual, genre-crossing, and stylistic complexities may be closest to her own.

Although Loy lived among English and American expatriates in Paris and Florence, by 1912 her strongest professional relationships were with Americans, and she turned to the United States, not England, to begin publishing. Loy's lasting contacts with Americans, however, were primarily with those who expatriated, not those who first encouraged her move to the United States or stayed in New York. Like Anglo-American expatriates in Europe, Loy in the United States felt no compulsion to adhere to the strictures of local propriety or to heed gossip; for her, bohemianism and Dada mockery of middle-class standards had few social consequences. This was never true for Moore or Lasker-Schüler, both of whom felt responsible to multiple friends and family members and who orchestrated their lives in ways consonant with some dominant life-patterns in New York and Berlin, even while rejecting normative standards, to differing extremes. As a mother, Lasker-Schüler would have been particularly vulnerable to social criticism; she rejected bourgeois values in the entire constitution of her identity rather than through staged events.[7] As far as I can tell, Loy was indifferent to local cultural restriction of women's lives in Florence, New York, or Paris except as it gave her insight into the patterns of her own consciousness or contributed to her general analysis of gender and human relations.

Loy wrote and published poetry during relatively few of the years between her first publication in 1914 and her last in 1962; although her first book was published in 1923, a second did not appear until 1958.[8] Unlike Moore and Lasker-Schüler, Loy also apparently did not consider herself to be a part of a literary or artistic community: she participated only briefly in infrastructural work like editing, and there is no record of her trying to place manuscripts with journal or press editors for friends or helping to further other writers' careers. Conover claims that she was uninterested even in the process of seeing her own work into print: Loy depended on others to find publishers for her work, submitting manuscripts to editors only when invited (*LLB82* xxx). While her letters of the midteens urge Van Vechten and other friends to locate publishers for the work she sent them, Loy's passivity about her later publishing may be a sign of her general lack of perceived agency in the infrastructures of modernism. Loy's influence is based on the quality of her verse, the controversies it generated, and on the frequently admired force of her personal presence. Her unabashed reference to bodily functions, fluids, and sexuality was particularly groundbreaking, as was her general antisentimental treatment of gender relations. Loy's rejection of punctuation, use of white space to structure lines, satirical distance from her material, and ostentatiously artifice-ridden wordplay may well have pushed other writers toward more radical experimentation with language. Analysis of her bridging position between English, French, Italian, and U.S. modernisms and her influence on other poets in the period between 1914 and 1930 is long overdue.

Moore's "The Mind is an Enchanting Thing" makes no mention of the United States, New York, gender, sexuality, religion, orientalism, or any other of the primary topics of this study. By 1943, she had been living in Brooklyn for fifteen years, and the volume in which the poem was printed was her sixth.[9] In the guise of accumulating a collage of statements reflecting some aspect of the mind, the poem makes a political, historical, and ethical argument about human responsibility.

The Mind is an Enchanting Thing

is an enchanted thing
like the glaze on a
katydid-wing
subdivided by sun
till the nettings are legion.
Like Gieseking playing Scarlatti;

like the apteryx-awl
as a beak, or the
kiwi's rain shawl
of haired feathers, the mind
feeling its way as though blind,
walks along with its eyes on the ground.

It has memory's ear
that can hear without
having to hear.
Like the gyroscope's fall,
truly equivocal
because trued by regnant certainty,

it is a power of
strong enchantment. It
is like the dove-
neck animated by
sun; it is memory's eye;
it's conscientious inconsistency.

It tears off the veil; tears
the temptation, the
mist the heart wears,
from its eyes—if the heart
has a face; it takes apart
dejection. It's fire in the dove-neck's

iridescence; in the
inconsistencies
of Scarlatti.
Unconfusion submits
Its confusion to proof; it's
Not a Herod's oath that cannot change.

(*CPo* 134–35)

This poem makes no mention of the ongoing war. Its concluding line, however, reveals the thematic parallel that structures the poem.

Moore's thirty-six lines of definition build up to the poem's only use of negatives—both in the last line: the mind is "not a Herod's oath that cannot change." The mind, then, can change, and by changing, Moore implies, it can effect change. It is not oaths that determine history but minds, which at some level decide whether or not they will change. According to Christian scripture, Herod was the magistrate appointed by Rome who ordered all male Jewish infants to be killed, fearing rumors of a messiah who would be a military leader, "king of the Jews." While this policy was not genocidal, it forced many Jewish families into exile. With utterly characteristic indirection, Moore uses double negatives to assert that an oath like Herod's should be changed, hence any mind that makes such oaths and does not change them "is," by the terms of her definition, not a "mind." This chain of logic indirectly condemns the policies of Hitler as well, another leader whose name starts with H, has two syllables, and persecutes Jews—in addition to gays and lesbians, communists, Gypsies, and other communities denounced as marginal or antithetical to German nationalist mythology. A mind that "cannot change" is one that cannot learn, cannot admit mistakes; it ceases to think, to *be* a human mind. In a 1948 open letter to the *Quarterly Review,* Moore repeats: "The better the mind is, the more adaptable" (*CPr* 626).

Moore does not mention Hitler, instead referring to Herod as a kind of biblical type: her point is not to condemn a particular individual or society but to condemn a misuse of human judgment and ability.[10] From the time of World War I, she was conscious of the dangers of both nationalist militarism, like that of the Germans, and hysterical prejudicial response to it. "The Labours of Hercules" (1921) includes in its list of stereotypes requiring Herculean strength to combat not just "'that the negro is not brutal, / that the Jew is not greedy, / that the Oriental is not immoral," but also "that the German is not a Hun'" (*EP* 265). Moore makes a similar move in "The Mind is an Enchanting Thing" by using as her only contemporary referent Walter Gieseking, a gifted musician born in France of German parents, who was fabulously popular throughout Europe and North America before the war but after the war began was not permitted to reenter the United States until 1953, and then was given a full bodyguard on the assumption that he would need protection from Americans enraged at all Germans.[11] The enchantment of the human mind is embodied in the artistry of Gieseking playing music by Domenico Scarlatti, a composer of technically exquisite harpsichord sonatas, born in Italy but composing his most famous work in Spain, after a sojourn in Portugal. Just as a twentieth-century musician can powerfully render the music of a seventeenth-century composer, so can an American be enchanted by the artistry of a German playing music by an Italian written in Spain. Neither art nor the mind is limited by nationalisms or by petty understandings of difference as long as it remains capable of learning, open to change.

Moore's use of Herod as type at the end of this poem also cleverly inserts the politics of the poem into mainstream Christian discourse. For Christian readers, Herod is notorious as the governor who tried to kill Jesus and forced Jesus, Mary, and Joseph into exile. In effect, at the end of this poem, Moore reminds her readers that for Herod to kill Jews was potentially for him to have killed the Christian messiah—a fact that could not have been predicted by contemporaries at the time of Herod's decree. By analogy, for Hitler to kill Jews (or any targeted group) incurs the world's, not just Judaism's, risk of a similar loss: all lose terribly by any slaughter or genocide. That Moore's contemporaries would have been likely to hear the political resonance of this poem is perhaps suggested by Paul Celan's decision to translate it.

The belief that minds can change, that individuals affect history, and that one bears ethical and social responsibility for one's own acts characterizes Moore from her childhood in Carlisle, through her years at Bryn Mawr, and her years of living in both the Village and Brooklyn. While the poem says nothing about the particular targets of Hitler's persecution, by analogy it condemns any such targeting and thereby, as is also consistent with Moore's attitudes over the decades, condemns prejudice on the basis of race, religion, sexuality, and political affiliation. The poem proceeds not by logical steps but by association, in part through the formal structure of the poem. A series of variations on the formula "It [the mind] is a ———," the poem resembles both modernist collage and the rapid repetition of notes and patterns in Scarlatti's sonatas, repetitions extremely innovative in his day for their patterned inconsistencies. Moving from the trope of music to science, the mind is "truly equivocal," like the gyroscope, which appears to defy gravity in the tension of its spin. It is subject to two or more interpretations, uncertain, yet "trued" by physical laws of "certainty": the mind's directing certainty establishes precisely its defining equivocalness, just as the architecture of the poem appears confused while following a pattern of association mandating multiple perspectives of thought. Scarlatti's music again provides an analogy: the composer of secular, short forms for a single instrument in an age giving greatest prestige to sacred masses or other long and multiple-instrument compositions, Scarlatti provides a closer model than his contemporary Johannes Sebastian Bach for Moore's use of short forms and lack of epic grandeur.

Formally, "The Mind is an Enchanting Thing" follows a syllabic pattern of six-line stanzas, each containing lines of six, five, four, six, seven, and nine syllables. This pattern is broken only once, in line 24, the final line of the fourth stanza, where "it's conscientious inconsistency" has ten rather than nine syllables: the line itself is inconsistent, and Moore's word "conscientious" indicates that it is meaningfully so. The end of this fourth stanza also marks a change in the pacing of the poem. Up to line 20, the poem has consisted of five sentence-units, judging a unit as a full grammatical sequence, whether or not it includes end punctuation. The remaining sixteen lines of the poem contain ten sentence units, and lines 23 and 24 begin this quick succession with their presentation of two such units in seven words: "it is memory's eye; / it's conscientious inconsistency." The drama of the poem's conclusion is created in part by this crescendo of short statements. "Conscientious inconsistency" also marks the polysyllabic high-point of the poem, concluding one stanza with its coincidence of syntactic and stanzaic closure and introducing a stanza dominated by monosyllabic words with repeated *t* and long *a* sounds. The sound of the words "conscientious inconsistency" themselves also lend to the carefulness within variation that they signify, with their polysyllabic distinction of levels of accentual stress. The mind, this multiply marked line informs, is necessarily inconsistent. Its humanity inheres in its idiosyncrasies, its multifacetedness—an aspect Moore alludes to three times through references to sunlight making wing-glaze or feathers iridescent; its humanness lies in its inability to be, or hold, or believe only one thing. Yet at the same time the mind is, in the ideal ethical form Moore defines, "conscientious": it both has and exercises a conscience, admitting its errors and contradictions.

"The Mind is an Enchanting Thing" is also structured around repetitions. Not counting function words or *mind,* there are thirteen repeated words or word roots in this poem, including the play on the title: the mind is enchanting, enchanted, and "a power of strong enchantment." Here again Moore emphasizes change. The ethical or rightly structured mind of her definition is one not just capable of being enchanted but already in fact so: the mind lies under the power of other forces. It is vulnerable to the magic of things outside itself. This question of what it means to be enchanted long possessed Moore, and for her was directly related to questions of both faith and freedom. In 1941, in the poem

"Spenser's Ireland" she writes that "you're not free / until you've been made captive by / supreme belief." In an earlier draft of the poem she asks: "What is liberty? To succeed in being captive to the right thing" (RML I:04:21). Yet "supreme belief," she realizes, may not always be to "the right thing"; one must be responsible for one's beliefs as well as for one's actions. In "Humility, Concentration, and Gusto," Moore writes that "gusto thrives on freedom, and freedom in art, as in life, is the result of a discipline imposed by ourselves" (*CPr* 426). By calling the mind "a power of strong enchantment," Moore suggests that the mind's power, like its "gusto" and freedom, comes from its ability both to enchant and to be enchanted. The former alone does not suffice. For Moore, the mind is by definition interactive, responsive; it cannot remain human and stand alone.[12] Other repetitions in the poem make a similar point. The mind is "like the glaze on a / katydid wing / subdivided by sun," "like the dove- / neck animated by / sun," and like "fire in the dove-neck's // iridescence." As with the changes rung on the root "enchant," Moore varies the idea of light irradiating an object or animating its colors by shifting the focus slightly from one allusion to the next. Each comparison occurs so as to emphasize different words through rhyme, as syntactic subject, and by line placement. As these shifts indicate, how one states an idea and when and where it occurs in the structure, or temporal sequence, of one's speech, affects its emphasis or meaning.

Language, in this poem, is an ally. The apparent meanderings from one topic to the next then back to an earlier one suggest that the poet is enchanted by language play itself, by the sounds and rhythms of words in the mouth and on the page. Sound, syllabic construction, and sense repeatedly coincide, as in the line "conscientious inconsistency": following independent patterns, both sounds and syllabic shapes conjoin in the poem's climactic, if characteristically understated, conclusion. The speaker of this poem has a completely different relation to language than the skeptical distance of Loy's speakers. In the penultimate stanza, in the midst of multiple rhymes, the speaker lightly mocks her own metaphor: although the mind was "as though blind" and hears through memory, now it "tears off the veil . . . the / mist the heart wears / from its eyes." This mind will see without the "temptation" of its own self-perception or veil—"if the heart has a face," the speaker adds. This wry aside is pointed at the speaker's own inclination to anthropomorphize, not at the inability of language to communicate. Mildly poking fun at the extremity of her enthusiasm, the speaker acknowledges that the poem's conclusions are not objective or God-given but stem from the perspective of someone who can admit she gets carried away. Within the same sentence, the speaker returns to her serious point: the mind not only strives for the honesty of seeing without veils but "takes apart / dejection." Rhyming "heart" with "apart" emphasizes that the mind directs the heart in dismantling the emotions or beliefs that would incapacitate it: dejection, bitterness, depression. "Unconfusion" literally includes "confusion," but "submits its confusion" to the processes of this dissecting and denuding, yet enchanting, mind. Moreover, the long *a* sounds in "tears," "veil," "tears," "temptation," "wears," "face," and "takes" anticipates the final unrhyming word "change," which is the key to the mind's power and enchantment.

With its *abaccd* rhyme scheme, each stanza contains both rhyming and nonrhyming lines, another "conscientious inconsistency." This pattern is further varied by the fact that the final word of each stanza usually consists of a slant rhyme playing off one of the earlier rhyme units. In the first stanza, "Scarlatti" repeats the *i* of "thing" and "wing"; in stanza 2, "ground" repeats the monosyllabic *nd* ending of "mind" and "blind." "Inconsistency," in stanza 4, is a sight rhyme to "by" and "eye." At the end of the poem, "change" has no rhyme or even slant-rhyme words. It resonates partly in repeating the strong *a* vowels of the preceding stanza, but also partly in its distinctness, its difference. "Change"—the word and the event—cannot be predicted in its forms of occurrence. To demonstrate this conclusion, the poem works both through repetition and variance. Its patterns foreground the unrhymed, the unexpected, the concluding word of each structural unit. Without these disruptions, the poem itself might appear to be a "Herod's oath" kind of affair: a pattern that once begun must repeat itself mechanically. With them, the poem is distinctly syncopated. Moore's life of unfashionable but "markedly" decorous passing along a homosocial spectrum within the bounds of some understanding of social norms, simultaneous with aggressive assertion of what suits her and what she believes is right, manifests itself in the patterned inconsistencies and indirect political commentary of this poem.[13]

Else Lasker-Schüler's "Mein blaues Klavier" ("My Blue Piano") was first published in 1937, when the seventy-two-year-old poet was living in exile in Zurich. Like Moore's "The Mind is an Enchanting Thing," it makes no explicit reference to any of the primary topics of this study but reveals much about the poet's present and earlier locations.

I have at home a blue piano Yet can't play a note.	*Ich habe zu Hause ein blaues Klavier* *Und kenne doch keine Note.*

It stands in the dark of the cellar door, Since the world went to pot.	*Es steht im Dunkel der Kellertür,* *Seitdem die Welt verrohte.*
Starhands played, four, —The moon-woman sang in her boat— Now rats dance in the clatter.	*Es spielten Sternenhände vier* *—Die Mondfrau sang im Boote—* *Nun tanzen die Ratten im Geklirr.*
The keyboard is broken . . . . . I cry for the blue dead.	*Zerbrochen ist die Klaviatür. . . . .* *Ich beweine die blaue Tote.*
Oh dear angel open for me —I ate from bitter bread—— Me, living, already, heaven's gate— Even against the decree.	*Ach liebe Engel öffnet mir* *—Ich aß vom bitteren Brote—* *Mir lebend schon die Himmelstür—* *Auch wider dem Verbote.*

(*WB*, no. 377)[14]

Like "The Mind is an Enchanting Thing," this poem combines traditional and irregular or inconsistent structures, approaches its subject through description of an object—in this case a piano rather than the mind—and has to do with change. In an elegy for the "blue dead" of loss occasioned by the fact that the world "verrohte" (became raw, barbaric), the speaker pleads the laws of nature and divinity to alter for her, allowing her into heaven before death. On the one hand, such a request suggests despair: the keyboard of her life or art or world is "broken." On the other, the speaker does not consider suicide or seek death itself. Instead, she seeks heaven, with its implied succor. The sky is the literal source of the starhands that used to play the blue piano and the moon-woman who sang, as well as the possible resting place of the dead—whether the dead are people, ideals, or inspirations of art. The speaker implies that she has eaten bitterness enough to deserve a respite but wants this respite "living." In this sense, the speaker refuses to give way to despair even while admitting its causes.

This poem is enriched and illuminated by understanding Lasker-Schüler's years in Berlin. The color blue marking both the source of art and the dead she misses was the favored color of Expressionists, made famous in Kandinsky and Marc's *Der blaue Reiter Almanac.* As previously mentioned, not only did Lasker-Schüler call Marc her *blaue Reiter,* but she called herself the Blue Jaguar. For Expressionists, blue was not the color of longing or melancholy, as suggested by the American *blues,* but of spiritual creativity. In *Concerning the Spiritual in Art,* Kandinsky lays out a general "language" of form and color, associating blue with "rest, depth"; blue is a "typically heavenly color."[15] While others might assign slightly different associations, in all Expressionist color-spectrums blue is strongly positive, and color functions nonmimetically, as a system of energy contrasts. As Kandinsky writes, "Color is the keyboard, the eyes are the hammers, the soul is the piano with many strings. . . . *It is evident therefore that color harmony must rest ultimately on purposive playing upon the human soul; this is one of the guiding principles of internal necessity"* (45).[16] For him and for Marc, color manifested that "superordinated rhythm that determines Being and the world."[17] To have a blue piano is to possess the instrument or source of deep, passionate art and harmony. This is an emotional, spiritual, psychological sphere more than a color; as the poet writes in "An meine Freunde" (1943), to be "on earth with you" is to be "already in heaven. / To paint eternal life in all colors / on blue ground," punning on the word "ground" *(Grund)* as both the foundation on a canvas for oil painting and earth.[18] Art begins with blue "ground." As owner of a blue piano, Lasker-Schüler identifies herself as a maker of innovative art. Although she now cannot play, presumably earlier she had mastered the instrument.[19]

At the same time, the final stanza of the poem alludes to the poet's Judaism, echoing some of the complexities of earlier poems of alienation and identity like "Mein Volk" or "Heimweh." At Passover, one eats bitter herbs to remember the anguish of slavery, and unleavened bread to commemorate the quickly prepared food of the Jews fleeing Egypt. The eater of "bitter bread," the poet identifies herself both with the history of Jewish suffering and exile and, to the extent that the "blue dead" are the Jews already exterminated by a world increasingly "verrohte," with contemporary persecuted Jews. The poet may also allude to her own unpremeditated flight from Berlin to Zurich, after being beaten with an iron bar. Her bitter bread was not slavery or labor in a concentration camp or death but years of anti-Semitic experiences and exile.

Acknowledging the speaker as Jew also alters the resonance of the poem's discordant middle line. The poem begins with two-line stanzas; stanza 3 has three lines; the fourth stanza again has two lines, and the last stanza has four, combining two two-line units. The third line of stanza 3 is the only irregular line: "Nun tanzen die Ratten im Geklirr." In substance, the line is consonant with the poem's descriptions: the piano stands in the dark, its keyboard is broken, rats dance "im Geklirr"—a phrase suggesting that the rat's dance in a preexistent crash or jangle as well as themselves making a loud noise. In anti-Semitic Germany, however, rats carried a connotation out of harmony with this description. National Socialist propaganda, like decades of less formalized anti-Semitic mythmaking, associated Jews with rodents as dirty, disease-carrying, nonhuman. Art Spiegelman plays on this stereotype in his cartoon history of his father's holocaust experience, *Maus*.[20] In contrast, in Lasker-Schüler's poem, as in her life, Jews were among the music makers and artists, the Expressionists, her friends. For her, rats are not Jews but the creatures who dance at artistic and Jewish demise. While there is no single symbolic referent for rats, the poet disrupts the stereotype in which she and other Jews are the ratlike corrupters of German racial, linguistic, and cultural purity. Both the context of her image and her disgust that rats now dance where star-hands played demonstrate the distance between Lasker-Schüler's experience and Moore's delighted adoption of the English storybook "Rat" as her dominant familial name. I think this is more a matter of religious identification than location, however, since it seems unlikely that a Jew anywhere in Europe or the United States would have been comfortable with the nickname "Rat" by the 1930s. On the other hand, Jewish and lesbian Felice Schragenheim's chosen nickname Jaguar even into the 1940s in Berlin suggests how little right-wing and governmental propaganda affected at least some self-formulations.[21]

The speaker's appeal to the angel in the last stanza of "Mein blaues Klavier" is also consonant with her Judaism, and with the whole trajectory of her poems. Speaking with a request and in a tone suggesting a child pleading for special favors, the speaker begs for an extraordinary exception. To be admitted to heaven alive is even more radical than for Odysseus to communicate with the dead or Orpheus to enter Hades to bring back his wife. Those visits were temporary; Lasker-Schüler presumably asks to stay. She asks not on the basis of righteousness, faith, genius, hierarchies of value or suffering, or any other sign of special worth. Her bread was not necessarily more "bitter" than that of others. She just asks. While there is a long tradition of Christian mystics expressing loving familiarity with Jesus or God, there is a longer and broader tradition in Judaism whereby faith may be expressed through a range of kinds of familiarity, including playfulness, comradeship, and intimacy. Lasker-Schüler's early poem "Im Anfang" exemplifies this tradition: there her speaker remembers his youth, when a young God and the devil played tricks on each other, laughed boisterously together, and the speaker was God's "Schlingel"—rascal or scoundrel (*WB*, no. 225).[22] In "Mein blaues Klavier," the speaker adopts similar familiarity. The producer of several volumes of poems, stories, plays, and novels as well as hundreds of sketches or paintings speaks in sorrow as one wanting to be let in heaven's door just on the basis of asking.

This concluding plea also raises the question of where the "home" might be in which the speaker houses her blue piano. Presumably because of its current broken state and the speaker's alienation from its notes, the piano stands in Germany. Laws of mortality on the one hand and of an anti-Semitic, fascist state on the other prevent Lasker-Schüler from joining her friends, dead and living.[23] Perhaps she asks the "dear Angel" to be more lenient than the National Socialists in allowing her entrance to a new "home" despite the law that would forbid it. On the other hand, Lasker-Schüler had been considering the question of what constitutes a home for years. As Jean Snook points out, the unmistakable focus of *Concert* is the "types of homes that cannot be taken from her: the home of childhood memories, the home of being with friends, the home of living in harmony with nature, with herself, and ultimately the home of the spirit."[24] Max Reinhardt writes her from exile in the United States in 1936 with another definition of home, clearly assuming that the poet shares his view: "Things are going well there [in the United States], except that our real homeland is language and that it is fundamentally an incurable sorrow not to be able to work or be effective in it."[25]

In notes on a typescript, Lasker-Schüler indicates that she at one point considered calling her final volume of poems *Ich liebte dich* (I loved you) rather than *Mein blaues Klavier* (JNUL 2:18). The titular poem, as well as the volume as a whole, functions indirectly as a declaration of love, in the same sense that it functions to define "home." The poet loved her friends in Germany, loved Berlin, loved her life among artists and writers in Berlin's cafés. These are all topics she raises repeatedly in her Zurich journal, where she seems to be either drafting or repeating the ideas of "Mein blaues Klavier." On an early page, in the context of Berlin café life, she writes, "I've lost a pure fairyland—that's what it was once . . . // Oh love is dead—the angel guides some holy ones / 'living' today into paradise out of this world."[26] Yet later she insists, "Love is immortal, not from this world" and, referring to World War I, "In the World War, no matter how it raged, love itself was not injured" (JNUL 2:28, p. 29). Moreover, she hopefully understands Jews as responding to their persecution with love: Jews are the "children with whom God played in His youth and loved, in spite of their human mistakes. . . . Insomuch as you drive us out, you drive us—into—God's arms" (JNUL 2:28, 28). Although the "eternal Gates" seem to be closed against "us Jews," she questions: "shall—God Himself—open them for us?" (JNUL 2:28, 30).[27] The earth belongs to all people, and all people will eventually belong to heaven, "in a bright play of colors [*bunten Farbenspiel*]" (2:28, 8). At this moment of deep loss, however, the poet seeks more immediate comfort and inclusion.

The rhyme scheme and syntactic progression of the poem emphasize the personal aspect of the poem's final request. All thirteen lines use one of two basic rhymes: either *ir* (with the slant-rhyme variant *ür*) or the polysyllabic rhyme on *ote.* Seven lines use the first rhyme and six the second. Of the three repeated words in the poem, two participate in a related rhyme group: *tür* (door; in *Kellertür* and *Himmelstür*), and *mir.* The speaker asks to have heaven's door opened for her, repeating the word *mir* unnecessarily in this request, foregrounded by the word's positioning as line final and line initial in the last stanza. This request, then, seems to echo in the poem: both literally—door, me, me, door—and through the effect of the slant-rhymes on *ür* and *ir* throughout the poem.[28] Between these repeated and foregrounded references to *me,* the speaker interjects the second of two digressions. In the first, she describes the *Mondfrau* singing, implying that this music is like the harmony of four star-hands playing. These are by implication the days when the piano held an honored place and the speaker could play it or enjoy its music. Relevant here may be the fact that Herwarth Walden began his life in the avant-garde as a composer. Singing and music may evoke the poet's early days in Berlin's bohemia, when she could no more anticipate her divorce from Walden than World War I, far less her later persecution, exile in Switzerland and Palestine, and the horrors of National Socialism. The second digression, "I ate from bitter bread," refers presumably to a more recent past. Omitting this digression, the speaker's last sentence reads, "Oh dear angel, open for me—me, living, already heaven's door." The poem moves from allusion to the Western world's harmonic creativity at the beginning of the century to its barbarism, to the blue dead, to the speaker herself: "me—me, living." Here is in brief a history of Lasker-Schüler's life and of the twentieth century in Germany.

Lasker-Schüler could be seen as having lived most of her life outside the law, or at least outside the social norms that restrict behavior. She rejected conventions for bourgeois womanhood and capitalist accumulation, dressing strangely, dealing unpragmatically with money when she had any and, despite her poverty, sometimes refusing pay for a reading. She overthrew divisions between friendship and sexual love by using the language of passion and desire or even sexual contact for all kinds of loving, and she scorned the institution of marriage after having experienced its failure twice. She did not distinguish reality from fiction, and showed little concern for social rituals of politeness or hierarchy. All such rule-breaking behavior has to do with establishing or maintaining honest and open communication between individuals unhindered by the conventions that would, for example, keep women at home, keep friends at arm's length, or establish insurmountable barriers between those of different classes, genders, religions, or customs. In "Mein blaues Klavier," Lasker-Schüler asks to be admitted "wider dem Verbote," against or in spite of yet another law. If the poet could reject all other barriers, why not that between life and death?

Unlike Moore's poem, with its concluding indirect protest against oaths like Herod's/Hitler's, "Mein blaues Klavier" concludes with a direct plea to escape history. The change this speaker seeks is not social and political but personal, although it responds to the conditions of prejudice, genocide, and military nationalism that Moore also protests. Moore's poem celebrates the mind's enchanting, enchanted, enchantment by defining "mind" as that which can be celebrated. Lasker-Schüler describes a world in which the enchantment of "blue" harmony has been lost: rats dance on the broken keyboard that produced the art of her generation. Markus Hallensleben reads the "broken keyboard" even more extremely, as the destruction of the entire German "language canon," suggesting that the poem asks how a poet can write when language itself is broken.[29] To the extent that language is the instrument of Lasker-Schüler's art, this interpretation makes sense—and it echoes Reinhardt's claim to the poet that language is their true "Heimat." And yet Lasker-Schüler's poems foreground language as such far less than either Moore's or Loy's. It is the cumulative sounds, rhythms, overlapping metaphors, and often repeated phrases or exclamations that dominate one's sense of her poems rather than a sense of the harnessed or crafted word. Moreover, in many poems Lasker-Schüler turns thematically to kinds of communication not primarily language-based, depending instead on the body or spirit. One might even read the speaker's closing plea as requesting that the angel ignore language, the basis of all law: ignore the letter for the spirit, she cries, a plea calling into question the worth of all language-based art, like her own poetry.

To my mind, Lasker-Schüler had as deep a love of language as Moore, but in her world language functioned differently. Because of the persecutions of the German state in 1937, the abuses and dangers of language, especially in its relation to law, were as apparent as its riches. Lasker-Schüler breaks language rules; she distances the language of poetry from that of law, public institutions, political sloganeering. Just as Expressionist art wielded color extravagantly and at least partially to symbolic effect, German Expressionist poetry favored heightened articulations, languages of passion and grotesquery, not the languages of science, classics, or quotation toward which Anglo-American modernism leaned. Lasker-Schüler's deployment of fantasy is more direct and intimate than Moore's. Rather than referring to enchantment, she makes it integral to her poetic and life, where a speaker who owns a blue piano and addresses angels seems normal. While both Lasker-Schüler and Moore exercise vocabularies of extravagance in defiance of materialism, nationalism, fascism, and local gender and sexual codes, the extremity of Moore's poems lies in their accumulation of detail and in complex syntactic constructions that verge on chaos; in contrast, the extremity of Lasker-Schüler's poems lies in the activities and desires of the individuals she depicts and in their category-mixing metaphors. Moore expects readers to know the meaning and historical context of her words, and such knowledge illuminates the political stance of her poems. For Lasker-Schüler, language is more like the notes of a blue piano: it is a plastic tool for expressing the condition of the soul. Poetry consists less in the precise denotative and connotative values of what is said than in the spiritual energy that generates it and that it in turn generates—although of course this energy is constructed from language. Both poets reject the poem as icon, but where Moore presents a poem as material for observation and analysis among collaborative writer and reader, Lasker-Schüler presents the poem as performance, a medium for communication that comes as close to the sense of embodiment, of sensual experience, as possible within the bounds of language. Without her blue piano, the speaker loses not language itself but that aspect of language which communicates like music or like sexuality, subverbally, as rhythm, sound, form. Yet the poet's call to be remembered, "me . . . me living" at the end of the poem, and the fact that she writes even her despair in verse suggests that the blue keyboard represents a state of the world, or the possibility of creative living, more than language or the poet's ability to write poems. Even in this world descending into barbarity, Lasker-Schüler continues to write and expresses passionate connection to a wide circle of friends.

Loy published no poetry at all between 1931 and 1946 and began to write again only in 1941. What spurred her return to poetry is unknown, but on the basis of the poems themselves, one could speculate that it was a combination of her return to New York, her felt isolation, and the war in Europe, which the United States entered in 1941. Loy writes "Time-Bomb" in 1945. She had moved from Paris to New York in 1936 largely because of the exodus of many of her friends from

Paris, the brooding sense of European despair, and because her daughters were there. It took years for Loy to reestablish a sense of place in New York, and, according to Burke, she lived as if on a foreign planet, in a world of memory and fantasy (*BM* 402). She was financially dependent on her daughters and her son-in-law Julian Levy (until his divorce from Joella), and avoided contact with previous writer and artist friends, largely out of insecurity born of poverty and, according to Burke, her self-consciousness about aging (*BM* 399, 418).[30] Unlike Moore's "The Mind is an Enchanting Thing" and Lasker-Schüler's "Mein blaues Klavier," which approach the topic of World War II indirectly, "Time-Bomb" comments directly on a bombed-out world:

> The present moment
> is an explosion ,
> a scission
> of past and future
>
> leaving
> those valorous disreputables ,
> the ruins ,
>
> sentinels
> in an unknown dawn
> strewn with prophecy .
>
> Only the momentary
> goggle of death
> fixes the fugitive
> momentum .
>
> (*LLB* 123)

Words like "explosion," "valorous," "ruins," "sentinels," "strewn," and "death" (as well as the title's "bomb") echo reportage of the times and suggest that Loy sees every aspect of life as subsumed into this or some war. The poem gives no hint, however, of the nature of the conflict or who battles whom. The moment itself explodes. People are mere "disreputables," "ruins" that act as "sentinels" without having anything to look out for. They do nothing active. Moreover, both the fact that the sentinels are "ruins" and the reference to death in the next stanza suggest that the prophesied future contains little hope. We do not know when in 1945 Loy wrote "Time-Bomb," but it registers a shock like that felt by many when the United States dropped two atomic bombs on Japan in August, with its image of the "goggle"-eyed living or dead human "ruins," who look on in horror or appear to watch because death left them open-eyed. These strangely terrible beings look toward a dawn filtering through atomic fallout, "strewn" with prophetic comments like those Loy heard in Paris in the mid-1930s about the anticipated war's bringing the end of the world. The poem "Photo After Pogrom," also written in 1945, articulates far more direct emotional response: its "Arrangement by rage / of human rubble" expresses open shock. The speaker of "Time-Bomb" seems numb.

While this poem's title suggests cataclysmic motion through its references both to "time," which never ceases, and "bomb," which will at some moment explode, the poem projects stasis. It contains only one active verb—"fixes"—and that verb asserts a continuing state. The words suggesting movement or change occur in grammatical forms of substantive or participial event: explosion, leaving, strewn, goggle. The present does not cut past from future but "is" a scission; the ruins do not watch but are "sentinels"; the future does not move but has "momentary . . . fugitive / momentum." The most surprising word of the poem is "goggle," with its oddly colloquial and Anglo-Saxon ring among polysyllabic Latinate adjectives and nouns, but the "goggle" is of death. The landscape of this present is so lifeless that even death is not an event but a moment of staring with protuberant eyes, much like the "ruins" who serve as "sentinels." In 1926, Yvor Winters describes Loy's poems as moving "from deadly stasis to stasis," creating an "ominous grandeur, like that of a stone idol become animate and horribly aware"—a phrase anticipating the ruined "sentinels" in "Time-Bomb": frozen but aware (30).

The foreboding lifelessness of the poem seems consistent from beginning to end, yet the poem also suggests contrasts at odds with that pattern. The poem begins with an explosion that would seem to disrupt all momentum toward the future: the present divides what was previously conjoined, isolating past from future rather than linking them. In this sense, the present is unnatural. By making the poem's subject the abstract "present moment," rather than, for example, "August 1945," when the first atomic bombs were exploded, Loy also leaves ambiguous whether she speaks philosophically or historically: is it the particular present moment of time in the United States in 1945 to which she refers or all "present," a concept infinite in reference because every moment is by definition "present" rather than past or future? Consciousness occurs in the present. If each second, each present moment, explodes past from future, there can be little hope for knowledge or meaningful agency: time itself would seem to be destroyed in that one cannot understand life or time without a sense of sequence, a consciousness of the present in the context of both memory and anticipation or dread, past and future. Yet the poem's final stanza implies that the explosion of the present creates some kind of future momentum, or at least allows such momentum to proceed. It is "only the momentary / goggle of death" that "fixes" the movement of time. If one understands "fix" to mean make stationary, then the poem implies that the future does continue to move forward in at least a "fugitive" way despite the "momentary" interruptions of death and the "scission" between it and the past. On the other hand, if "fix" means to repair, then it is death that cures or puts back in order the future that is broken by the exploding present. In either case, the poem asserts "momentum" even while apparently denying it. That the sentinels watch "in an unknown dawn" also suggests a continuing future linked with the past at least by prophecy if not by more active and personal memory or narrative: dawn anticipates the coming of day, a new beginning, a world that goes on.

Again, Loy's notes on "*extended* consciousness" are suggestive here: she writes there both of "the intellectual consternation, stunning as an explosion, before the unprecedented inhumanities of Axis warfare" and of her conviction "that human existence is not the meaningless 'accident in bewilderment' it sometimes seems to me" (B Box 7, folder 187). Explosion can echo actual warfare or suggest the intellectual consternation of observers. According to these notes, a spiritual experience of consciousness can counteract the cataclysm of both event and confusion, persuading people that neither inhumane warfare nor death marks the end of life. In her poem, Loy provides no such reassurance, presenting instead the frozen moment of explosion.

The form of the poem, however, suggests momentum as well as stasis. As in some of her early poems, Loy here uses unconventional spacing, in this poem isolating every word and punctuation mark from every other. Words, commas, and periods are "strewn" across the page, blind sentinels, fixed in place. The stanzas occur in a chiasmic pattern: a four-line stanza, then two stanzas of three lines, then a final stanza of four. Most lines are approximately five syllables long, and each stanza contains one line of three syllables. The basic pattern from which the others vary seems to be set in stanzas 1 and 3: the first contains lines of five, five, three, and five syllables, and the third of three, five, and five syllables. The nine-syllable line "those valorous disreputables" most disrupts the syllabic order and provides another clue as to the cause of the present collapse. The disreputable are those without reputation, social standing, respect in the community: calling "disreputables" "valorous" indicates that the speaker disdains dominant social judgment of worth and finds the disrespected to be courageous, to have strength of mind and heart. In this reading, the explosion of the present isolates as "ruins" those who disregard social conventions or depart from popular beliefs, acting valorously according to their own lights. In some cataclysmic moment, the poem implies, values changed so radically that what once was valorous is now a ruin, and what once was unthinkable now occurs—including world war. Yet because these disreputables stand guard in a landscape containing prophecy (even if as litter), Loy's poem suggests consciousness of what they witness and perhaps some minimal spirit of protection. It could be their "momentum," a movement Loy associates with the future, that continues fugitively at the poem's end.

The poem's sound schemes also suggest connection in spite of exploded distance and difference. There is no rhyme scheme in the poem. From the first line on, however, words are paired by echoing sound patterns—as occurs in many of Loy's poems and becomes exaggerated in some (the "purposeless peace" of "Photo After Pogrom," or "lidded with unlisted likings" in "Faun Fare"—both poems also written in the midforties). The repeated *-ent* and trochaic two-syllable accentual pattern of "present" and "moment" in line 1 lead to the *-sion* unaccented rhyme of "explosion" and "scission" in lines 2 and 3, accented by the repeated *s* sounds initiated in "present" and "is." "Present" also prepares alliteratively for "past," just as "future" anticipates by alliteration and assonance the concluding stanza's "fugitive" momentum, and by assonance the second stanza's "disreputables." The second stanza foregrounds *l*s and *r*s; the third stanza abounds in *n*s, especially in the sequence "an unknown dawn / strewn"; and the final stanza repeats *m*s and *f*s: "momentary . . . momentum," and "fixes the fugitive." Nearly every grammatically significant word of the poem (and some of the function words as well) anticipates or echoes through soundplay some other word or grouping of words in the poem, suggesting tentacles of connection underlying the poem's exploded form. The sound echoes also create thematic rhymes, linking disrep*u*tables with the *fu*gitive *fu*ture, for example, or the *pr*esent with *pr*ophecy, and the *moment* with *moment*ary *moment*um. The ear can hear what the reader cannot see: language works through aural connections, sequences, patterns, even when apparently most disrupted. In fact, the syntax of the poem is relatively simple, belying the visual disruption of the words on the page.[31] Only the word "goggle" has no sound-partner in the poem, although the chiasmic placement of the present's explosion and death's goggle suggest that they may be analogous.

"Time-Bomb" suggests that World War II has had an effect on the structures and perception of time that no conclusion to the war can mend: the past has categorically disappeared; it has been vanquished, blown apart, divided forever from the present time with the force of the fission that divides atomic particles—perhaps an implied rhyme in Loy's "scission." Consequently, those like Loy, whose lives were by and large defined by the decades before this war, exist as "ruins," like the bombed-out cities of Europe Loy would have seen in newspaper photographs—cities where she had lived: Berlin, Paris, London. They commemorate a bygone era. These sentinels are perhaps like sentries, standing guard at the passageway between past and present, but their function seems to be merely to watch rather than to combat the incursions of an enemy. The poem's concluding stanza may imply that the war's casualties alone temporarily reinstate connections of past to present and future: the process of mourning necessarily involves memories of the prewar past and leads to the question of what kind of future can be born from so many deaths. Unlike Lasker-Schüler, however, Loy is not mourning the death of friends in this poem, and Burke does not mention that Loy suffers the loss of particular friends in the war. The conclusions and attitude of this poem in fact are found in Loy's earliest poems: the future is cut off from the past; most people are ignorant spectators, not agents, in the determination of their fate; conditions of being are static, not dynamic. The war does not provoke these conclusions, any more than it reshaped Moore's or Lasker-Schüler's perception of the world, or her place in it; the war confirmed or sharpened attitudes Loy had long held. Loy's is a poetry of castigation; catastrophe lurks in its revelations of the underbelly of the relations it observes. In "Der blinde Junge," written about World War I, Loy describes the youth as an "expressionless 'thing' / blow[ing] out damnation and concussive dark // Upon a mouth-organ" (*LLB* 84). And yet Loy believes in the powers of the spirit beyond those of destruction. Her call in "Der blinde Junge" to the "illuminati of the coloured earth" to "Listen!"—like her representation of "ruins" as sentinels in "Time-Bomb"—suggests that consciousness endures and that people can hear something new. As she writes in "Ephemerid," "The Eternal is sustained by serial metamorphosis, / even so Beauty is" (*LLB* 116). Although "Time-Bomb" depicts no moment of change, its "dawn" and mention of "momentum" suggest the possibility.

Where Lasker-Schüler's "Mein blaues Klavier" contrasts the present with the past through specific, albeit metaphorical, reference to what was lost and what occurs at present, Loy's poem presents only the present moment and that only through abstract assertions of division. There is no angel in this poem to whom the speaker can appeal for mercy, and no friends or place whose passing the speaker mourns. In fact, there is no acknowledged speaker. The isolated spacing of each word, as though language itself has been blown apart, and the abstract reference to event, make the poem resemble a proclamation of fact on the basis of some impersonal authority rather than an elegy, a political commentary on the state of modern warfare or inhumanity, or any other kind of personal expression. "Time-Bomb" does not even contain the momentary acknowledgment of idiosyncratic aesthetic perspective suggested in "Photo After Pogrom": there a woman's body is seen as "hacked to utter beauty / oddly by murder" (*LLB* 122). This is indeed an "odd" way to conceive the scene, as is the concluding assertion that "corpses are virgin." Like Moore's self-mocking aside ("if the heart has a face") in "The Mind is an Enchanting Thing," Loy's parenthetical phrase in "Photo After Pogrom" inserts a subjective presence into the poem. "Time-Bomb" contains no such phrases. Everything remains at arm's length from a particular consciousness. In a *View* questionnaire conducted during the 1940s, when asked, "What do you see in the stars," Moore answered with one word: "Hope." Responding to the same question, Loy said: "Our need of an instrument analogous to, yet the inverse of a telescope, which would reduce to our focus the forms of entities hitherto visually illimitable, of whose substance the astronomical illuminations are but the diamond atoms and electrons" (*BM* 394). While I am not sure what to make of this peculiarly abstruse response, it certainly does not relate immediately to the world war. In a 1965 interview with Paul Blackburn, Loy "chuckled at her fondness for 'long, long words'" and claimed that her early poems were written "for the sake of the sounds" (*BM* 437). Although the claim is disingenuous, there is no doubt that her poems foreground language as such and minimize its direct connection to audience or public agency.

In "Time-Bomb," language is disconnective, almost mechanical. The poem does not address an audience or trust its powers of communication. It lays out a design, as one would for a future age cut off from the present one and barely understanding its mode of communication. Loy's poetry suggests Constructivist event more than communication: it exposes the energies of making, the powers of craft, and the devastation or, sometimes, intense beauty of its isolated moment. And while it frequently critiques a modern world incapable of love, incapable of accepting "disreputables" (scything "immortelles" because it does not understand them, in "Apology of Genius"), or without sympathy for outcasts like "Der blinde Junge" or the woman of "Chiffon Velours," hers is not a poetry of sympathy.[32] When asked in a questionnaire to name her "weakest characteristics," Loy responded "Compassion" (*LLB82* 305–6). Lasker-Schüler's verse, one might say, shares some of the same targets as Loy's, but the German poet's critique is articulated through love stories, assertions of desire, fantasies of communication so intimate that bodies interpenetrate or dissolve. Loy's critique is articulated through distance, satire, language-play cut off from an immediately desiring or feeling body and distrusting the force of its own communications.

Reading a modernist poem requires engaging with language associatively, analytically, joining the poet in her or his construction of patterns that reveal reflections on modern life and the modern world, typically through implication and indirection. While no interesting poem is transparent in its significance, modernist interest in collage and the rejection of unifying vocal subjectivities, representational narrative, and logically sequential argument places particular demands on readers. Much has been written about the intentional difficulties and surface disruptions as well as the "negative dialectics" of modernist literature. My point in this chapter has been to demonstrate the ways that understanding a poet's primary location(s) may illuminate the implications of some of those difficulties—both formally and semantically—in reading individual poems. Locational-based study contributes to the reading of poems as well as to the understanding of poets.

Moore's witty extravagance in constructing broadly affirmative address to an audience on issues assumed to be of shared concern in apparently arbitrary forms cannot be directly attributed to her life in New York. To return briefly to Bourdieu, "There is nothing mechanical about the relationship between the field and the habitus" or in the production of a given work of art.[33] Her confident engagement as a woman of independent intelligence with ethical issues and the public structures of modernism over several decades, however, indeed has some base in her experience of the feminist, strongly female participatory institutions and atmosphere of her early years in the Village. Lasker-Schüler similarly benefits from Berlin's public and semipublic performances of Expressionism, to the extent that one cannot understand the resonance of her art without some knowledge of early-twentieth-century Berlin. As Paul Zweig writes in 1926, "In a bourgeois time like today's, she stands as a monstrosity, an abnormality: as a true poet"—using the unmarked *Dichter* rather than the female gendered *Dichterin* for his claim.[34] Loy would seem to be least dependent on particular scenes for an understanding of her poetic, but, as I have tried to demonstrate, the very distance suggested in the tones and attitudes of her poems reflects her lack of connection to place, family group, or community of fellow writers, artists, and friends. The extraordinary quality of Loy's work stems from the brutal directness this lack of connection perhaps liberates her to express. Pound describes her work as "without emotion." For me, the poems teem with anger, loss, bitterness, despair, longing, but they are without compunction: they pull no punches, soften no edges in their depiction of social institutions, moments of extreme pain or illumination (often the same moments), or relationship. Loy's is the tone most frequently associated with modernism. To understand it as "the" modernist tone, however, is to ignore the particularity from which it arises and the significant social, cultural, and political currents giving rise to other quite different, equally representative, and equally innovative tones.

Over a number of years, these three poets addressed many of the most pressing issues of their times and concerns of their communities in forms that pushed local and international conception of the modernist poem. Through reading, travel, correspondence with friends, or public discussion and through participation in local and international networks of modernist ideas, art, and literature, women like Moore, Lasker-Schüler, and Loy were both shaped by the contingencies of their time and place and helped to shape modernist literature in the communities in which they lived and wrote.

Appendix

Chronology of Else Lasker-Schüler, Mina Loy, and Marianne Moore

1869	Else Schüler born in Elberfelde, Germany.
1882	Mina Gertrude Lowy born in London.
1887	Marianne Craig Moore born in Kirkwood, Missouri.
1894	ELS marries Jonathan Berthold Lasker and moves to Berlin.
1896	MM moves to Carlisle, Pennsylvania.
1899	ELS gives birth to son Paul and publishes first poems; separates from Lasker and enters bohemian circles in Berlin.
	ML studies art with Angelo Jank in Munich until 1901, then returns to London.[1]
1902	ELS publishes *Styx.*
1903	ELS divorces Lasker and marries Georg Levin/ Herwarth Walden.
	ML moves to Paris, marries Stephen Haweis, and changes surname to Loy.
1904	Walden (with Lasker-Schüler) begins *Verein für Kunst.*
	ML gives birth to daughter Oda Janet, who dies 1905.
1905	ELS publishes *Der siebente Tag.*
	MM enters Bryn Mawr College.
1906	ELS publishes *Das Peter Hille-Buch.*
	ML elected a member of the Salon d'Automne, then moves to Florence.
1907	ELS publishes *Die Nächte Tino von Bagdads.*
	ML gives birth to daughter Joella.
1909	ELS publishes first play, *Die Wupper.*
	ML gives birth to son Giles and becomes a Christian Scientist.
	MM's first recorded trip to New York; graduates from Bryn Mawr.

1910	ELS separates from Walden; first issue of *Der Sturm.*
1911–14	MM teaches business English and math courses at the Carlisle Indian School.
1911	ELS publishes *Meine Wunder.*
1912	ELS publishes *Mein Herz.*
1913	ELS publishes book of essays *Gesichte* and first version of *Hebraische Balladen.*
	ML exhibits paintings in London; Carl Van Vechten becomes her literary agent (in New York).
1914	ELS publishes expanded *Hebraische Balladen* and an experimental novel, *Der Prinz von Theben,* and writes screenplay *Die morgendländische Komödie Plumm Pascha.*
	ML publishes first poems in little magazines and exhibits with Futurist art exhibit in Rome; has affairs with Marinetti and Papini.
	World War I begins.
1915	MM publishes her first poems in little magazines.
1916	MM moves to Chatham, New Jersey, in late summer and commutes regularly to New York.
	ML moves to New York in October, leaving children in Florence.
1917	ELS publishes *Gesammelte Gedichte.*
	ML guest-edits issue of *Others;* collaborates in writing *The Blind Man* and *RongWrong;* plays lead in *Lima Beans;* obtains divorce from Haweis; moves to Mexico City with Arthur Cravan.
	United States enters World War I.
1918	MM moves with mother to New York (Greenwich Village).
	ML marries Cravan, who disappears eleven months later; ML sails to Buenos Aires, then returns to England.
	World War I ends; revolution in Germany; Weimar Republic declared.
1919	ELS's *Die Wupper* performed at Max Reinhardt's Deutsche Theater in Berlin.
	ML gives birth to daughter Fabienne in England; travels to Switzerland, then Italy.
1920	ML leaves children in Italy and returns to New York in March.
1921	ELS publishes story "Die Wunderrabbiner von Barcelona."
	ML leaves New York for Paris in summer, then returns to Florence.

MM publishes *Poems* through agency of H.D. and Bryher.

1922 ML meets Freud in Vienna; in spring, settles in Berlin.

1923 ML returns to Paris in June, later joined by Fabi and Joella. Giles, in custody of Haweis, dies; ML publishes *Lunar Baedecker* and first sections of "Anglo-Mongrels and the Rose."

1924 MM publishes *Observations;* wins Dial Prize.

1925 ELS publishes *Ich räume auf! Meine Anklage gegen meine Verleger.*

1925–29 MM editor of the *Dial.*

1926 ML opens shop for self-designed lampshades and novelties, funded by Peggy Guggenheim.

1927 ELS's son Paul dies.

1929 Death of Gustav Stresemann; Wall Street stock market collapses; *Dial* closes.

1930 MM moves with mother to Brooklyn.

National Socialist party wins 6.5 million votes in Germany.

1931 ELS's drawings exhibited in Studiensaal der Nationalgalerie, Berlin.

ML becomes New York Julian Levy Gallery's art advisor and agent in Paris (through 1936).

1932 ELS wins Kleist Prize.

1933 ELS flees to Zurich after being beaten with an iron bar; suffers broken ribs.

Hitler becomes chancellor.

1935 MM publishes *Selected Poems.*

1936 *Arthur Aronymus und seine Vater* performed in Zurich Schauspielhaus.

MM publishes *The Pangolin and Other Verse.*

ML moves to New York.

1937 ELS publishes *Das Hebräerland.*

1939 ELS forced to leave Switzerland; goes to Palestine hoping to return, but reentry to Switzerland prohibited; ELS remains in Palestine.

Outbreak of World War II; Germany annexes Austria.

1941 ELS founds literary discussion group in Jerusalem, Der Kraal; first reading of *Ichundich.*

MM publishes *What Are Years.*

1943 ELS publishes *Mein blaues Klavier.*

1944 MM publishes *Nevertheless.*

1945 January 16, ELS has severe stroke; January 22, dies in Jerusalem and is buried on the Mount of Olives.

1946 ML becomes naturalized U.S. citizen.

1947 MM's mother dies.

ML moves to Bowery and starts making junk collages.

1951 MM publishes *Collected Poems;* awarded Pulitzer Prize and Gold Medal of the National Institute of Arts and Letters.

1952 MM awarded National Book Award.

1953 MM awarded Bollingen Prize.

ML moves to Aspen, Colorado.

1954 MM publishes *The Fables of La Fontaine.*

1955 MM elected to American Academy of Arts and Letters.

1956 MM publishes *Like a Bulwark.*

1958 ML publishes *Lunar Baedeker & Time-Tables.*

1959 ML exhibits "constructions" at Bodley Gallery, New York, and wins the Copley Foundation Award for Outstanding Achievement in Art.

MM publishes *O to Be a Dragon.*

1962 MM publishes *The Absentee: A Comedy in Four Acts Based on Maria Edgeworth's Novel of the Same Name.*

1966 ML dies of pneumonia on September 25, in Aspen.

MM publishes *Tell Me Tell Me.*

1967 MM publishes *Complete Poems;* receives Chevalier de l'Ordre des Arts et des Lettres, France, and the Gold Medal Award for Lifetime Achievement from the Poetry Society.

1972 MM dies in her sleep in New York.

Notes

CHAPTER ONE

"Paris, Capital of the Nineteenth Century," *Reflections,* trans. E. Jephcott (New York: Harcourt, Brace, Jovanovich, 1978); Baedeker quoted in David Frisby, "Deciphering the Hieroglyphics of Weimar Berlin: Siegfried Kracauer," *Berlin: Culture and Metropolis,* ed. Charles W. Haxthausen and Heidrun Suhr (Minneapolis: University of Minnesota Press, 1990), 152; Trotsky quoted in Christine Stansell, *American Moderns: Bohemian New York and the Creation of a New Century* (New York: Henry Holt, 2000), 6; Williams, *Spring and All,* 1923, in *Imaginations,* ed. Webster Schott (New York: New Directions, 1970).

1. Raymond Williams, *The Politics of Modernism* (London: Verso, 1989), 37. Williams elsewhere acknowledges the effect of diverse cultural environments (43).

2. Keith Tuma, *Fishing by Obstinate Isles: Modern and Postmodern British Poetry and American Readers* (Evanston, Ill.: Northwestern University Press, 1998), 9. Critics attentive to the peculiarities of place in modernism include Shari Benstock, *Women of the Left Bank: Paris, 1900–1940* (Austin: University of Texas Press, 1986); Susan Rubin Suleiman, "A Double Margin: Reflections on Women Writers and the Avant-Garde in France," *Yale French Studies* 75 (1988): 148–72; Peter Nicholls, *Modernisms: A Literary Guide* (Berkeley and Los Angeles: University of California Press, 1995); Rita Felski, *The Gender of Modernity* (Cambridge: Harvard University Press, 1995); Susan Stanford Friedman, *Mappings: Feminism and the Cultural Geographies of Encounter* (Princeton: Princeton University Press, 1998); Marsha Meskimmon, *We Weren't Modern Enough: Women Artists and the Limits of German Modernism* (Berkeley and Los Angeles: University of California Press, 1999); Deborah L. Parsons, *Streetwalking the Metropolis: Women, the City, and Modernity* (Oxford: Oxford University Press, 2000); and Alex Davis and Lee M. Jenkins, eds., *Locations of Literary Modernism: Region and Nation in British and American Modernist Poetry* (Cambridge: Cambridge University Press, 2000). In a similar vein, Rachel Blau DuPlessis develops a concept of "social philology" in *Genders, Races, and Religious Cultures in Modern American Poetry, 1908–1934* (Cambridge: Cambridge University Press, 2001).

3. In the "Author's Note," *Paterson* (New York: New Directions, 1963), n.p.

4. Pound's claim in "Patria Mia" is echoed by Hugh Kenner, "The Making of the Modernist Canon," *Canons,* ed. Robert von Hallberg (Chicago: University of Chicago Press, 1984), 363–76; and Williams, *The Politics of Modernism.*

5. Laurie Teal, "The Hollow Women: Modernism, the Prostitute, and Commodity Aesthetics," *Differences* 7.5 (1996): 80–108.

6. Virginia Woolf, *A Room of One's Own* (1929; reprinted, Cambridge: Cambridge University Press, 1995), 99, 117. Citations are to the 1995 edition.

7. Celeste Schenck, "Exiled by Genre: Modernism, Canonicity, and the Politics of Exclusion," *Women's Writing in Exile,* ed. Mary Lynn Broe and Angela Ingram (Chapel Hill: University of North Carolina Press, 1989), 226–50; 226.

8. According to Colin Holmes, *Anti-Semitism in British Society: 1876–1939* (New York: Holmes and Meier, 1979), by around 1880, "Jews had been freed from their former disabilities in [England and] every other major European country except Russia" (9).

9. Even Rachel Blau DuPlessis, who has written pioneering criticism on Loy, claims that Loy spent "many decades" in the United States before 1946, whereas she had spent only twelve and a half years there (*Genders* 27).

10. Michel de Certeau, Luce Giard, and Pierre Mayol, *The Practice of Everyday Life,* vol. 2, *Living and Cooking,* trans. Timothy J. Tomasik (Minneapolis: University of Minnesota Press, 1998), 142.

11. Interestingly, Moore's close friend Bryher does write Lasker-Schüler during her time in exile in Switzerland (the letter is dated June 24, no year); in ungrammatical German, Bryher writes: "Dear Mrs. Lasker-Schüler, Other writers and I from England have heard that you had difficulties crossing the border and we fear that you may have lost much because of events in Germany. If we can help, please write me. I have known your books for a long time. But please excuse me that, although I can read, I find it hard to write in German. Respectfully, W. Bryher" (JNUL Arc var 501, 5:90). There is no evidence that Lasker-Schüler responded. Unless otherwise noted, all translations from the German are mine.

12. Paul Rosenfeld, "Musical Chronicle," *Dial,* June 1927, 446.

13. For example, in "Seeing into Modernity," David Peters Corbett argues that the "art and thought of France" have been made to appear "central to the project of understanding modernism, and hence provide a norm upon which any definitions must explicitly or implicitly be built," but that this norm is inappropriate for discussion of English visual and musical art; *Modernism/Modernity* 7.2 (2000): 285–306; 285–86.

14. June Sochen, *The New Woman: Feminism in Greenwich Village, 1910–1920* (New York: Quadrangle Books, 1972), ix.

15. Carroll Smith-Rosenberg, *Disorderly Conduct: Visions of Gender in Victorian America* (New York: Oxford University Press, 1985), 255. Other quotations in this paragraph are from this text.

16. For related work on male modernists and college education, see Gail McDonald's *Learning to be Modern: Pound, Eliot, and the American University* (Oxford: Oxford University Press, 1993).

17. Curiously, wealthier American women were less likely to attend institutes of higher education: heiresses Edith Wharton, Amy Lowell, Peggy Guggenheim, and Natalie Barney did not attend college, despite strong bookish interests on the part of the former two, nor did upper-middle-class Sylvia Beach. Maria Jolas was awarded a scholarship to the University of Chicago, but her wealthy family derided such education, and she did not attend.

18. Jean V. Matthews, *Women's Struggle for Equality: The First Phase, 1828–1876* (Chicago: Ivan R. Dee, 1997). Earlier, the laws of "coverture" dictated that "the husband and wife are one person in law: that is, the very being

or legal existence of the woman is suspended during the marriage, or at least is incorporated . . . into that of the husband" (40).

19. Nancy Cott, *Public Vows: A History of Marriage and the Nation* (Cambridge: Harvard University Press, 2000), 55.

20. Helene Lange, *Higher Education of Women in Europe*, trans. L. R. Klemm (New York: D. Appleton, 1901), xxiv.

21. Ute Frevert, *Women in German History: From Bourgeois Emancipation to Sexual Liberation* (1986), trans. Stuart McKinnon-Evans with Terry Bond and Barbara Norden (Oxford: Berg, 1989), 317. On German women, see also Eva Kolinsky, *Women in 20th-Century Germany: A Reader* (Manchester: Manchester University Press, 1995); and Ute Gerhard, *Unerhört: Die Geschichte der deutschen Frauenbewegung* (Hamburg: Rowohlt, 1990). Kolinsky is more severe in her judgment of women's position at the turn of the century, writing that "a woman alone was unprotected and without rights" (19).

22. Reiß-Suckow, *"Wer wird mir Schöpfer sein!!" Else Lasker Schüler's Entwicklung als Künstlerin* (Constance: Hartung-Gorre Verlag, 1997), 24.

23. Benstock, *Left Bank* 67, 78. According to Robert von Hallberg, Pound was an exception in reading widely in contemporary French literature; "Ezra Pound in Paris," *On Modern Poetry: Essays Presented to Donald Davie*, ed. Vereen Bell and Laurence Lerner (Nashville: Vanderbilt University Press, 1988), 53–65; 57.

24. Norma Broude, "Edgar Degas and French Feminism, ca. 1880: 'The Young Spartans,' the Brothel Monotypes, and the Bathers Revisited," 1988, in *The Expanding Discourse: Feminism and Art History*, ed. Norma Broude and Mary D. Garrard (New York: Icon, 1992), 269–93; 273. See also Gill Perry, *Women Artists and the Parisian Avant-Garde* (Manchester: Manchester University Press, 1995), 22; James F. McMillan, *France and Women, 1789–1914: Gender, Society, and Politics* (Amherst: University of Massachusetts Press, 2000); and Dorothy McBride, *Women's Rights in France* (Westport, Conn.: Greenwood Press, 1987).

25. The French painters are Emilie Charmy, Marie Laurencin, Suzanne Valadon, Jacqueline Marval, and Suzanne Roger. Sonia Delaunay, Marevna, and Marie Vassiliev came from Russia; Alice Halicka and Mel Muter from Poland; Maria Blanchard from Spain; and Alice Bailly from Switzerland. Laurencin edited *391*, a Dada magazine, while living in Madrid during the war, but after the war turned to relatively conventional design and still life; Jeanne Hébuteine committed suicide after her lover Modigliani's death in 1920.

26. Perry 10. For example, Laurencin lived with Apollinaire from 1908 to 1912, her main period of exhibition with Cubism (60); Alice Halicka was married to Cubist artist Louis Marcoussis; Russian Sonia Delaunay married Robert in 1910, only a few years after moving to Paris; and Marevna was linked to Cubism in part through her involvement with Diego Rivera, even though he discouraged her use of Cubist techniques—as Marcoussis did Halicka's (73).

27. Suleiman, *Subversive Intent: Gender, Politics, and the Avant-Garde* (Cambridge: Harvard University Press, 1990), 20–24. Renée Riese Hubert comes to the same conclusion about women's absence at the inception of the movement, in *Magnifying Mirrors: Women, Surrealism, and Partnership* (Lincoln: University of Nebraska Press, 1994). In the twelve issues of *La Révolution Surréaliste*, only three women publish—two of whom are unknown as writers or artists (Fanny Beznos and Madame Savitsky); the third (Valentine Penrose) has a brief reply to an earlier essay in the last issue (Suleiman 29). The only native French writer

of the 1930s was Gisèle Prassinos, who was born in Turkey; Suleiman describes her as a "child prodigy" "discovered" by the group rather than a member (31).

28. Carolyn Burke proposes a candidate for a French avant-garde writer in her essay "Recollecting Dada: Juliette Roche," *Women in Dada: Essays on Sex, Gender, and Identity,* ed. Naomi Sawelson-Gorse (Cambridge: MIT Press, 1998), 546–77. Roche married Albert Gleizes in 1915, lived in New York briefly in 1915, then again from 1917 to 1919, and wrote a Dada novel commenting on the art scene in New York during these years; she published a book of free verse and prose poems in 1920 *(DemiCercle),* written during the teens. Burke does not say whether these poems were also written in New York.

CHAPTER TWO

Elizabeth Grosz, "Bodies-Cities," *Sexuality and Space,* ed. Beatriz Colomina and Jennifer Bloomer (New York: Princeton Architectural Press, 1992), 241–54; 243; Rowe, *Representing Berlin: Sexuality and the City in Imperial and Weimar Germany* (Hants: Ashgate, 2003), 7.

1. Betterton, "Women Artists, Modernity, and Suffrage Cultures in Britain and Germany, 1890–1920," *Women Artists and Modernism,* ed. Katie Deepwell (Manchester: Manchester University Press, 1998), 18–35; 24.

2. Williams, *Unreal City: Urban Experience in Modern European Literature and Art* (Manchester: Manchester University Press, 1985), 13.

3. Parsons, *Streetwalking the Metropolis* 226, 227. Janet Wolff writes that "the experience of anonymity in the city, the fleeting, impersonal contacts described by social commentators like Georg Simmel, the possibility of unmolested strolling and observation . . . analyzed by Walter Benjamin were entirely the experiences of men"; *Feminine Sentences: Essays on Women and Culture* (Cambridge: Polity Press, 1990), 58. Parsons, in contrast, distinguishes the flaneur as concept and as social manifestation, asserting that late-nineteenth-century women had some access to city streets as observers although they did not claim the concept of *flâneurie* (40–41). Jane Beckett and Deborah Cherry describe women's "street haunting" in London during the teens as having an explicitly feminine sense of risk; "Modern Women, Modern Spaces," 36–54; 44–45. See also Elizabeth Wilson, *The Sphinx in the City: Urban Life, the Control of Disorder, and Women* (Berkeley and Los Angeles: University of California Press, 1991).

4. "Nach meiner Heirat verliebte ich mich in Berlin: / Unter seinen Linden sass ich stundenlang. / Selbst Möbelwagenräder fuhren auf dem Asphalt wie Gesang. / Wo bist du Friedrichstrasse von Berlin? / Und du mein unvergessner Tauentzien? // Die Scheidung meiner Ehe mir begreiflicher, als meine Ausbürgerung gewaltsame Scheidung" (*WB,* no. 444).

5. "O wie mir die Scheidung nahe ging, / Von Berlin—viel näher wie ich wusste."

6. "Unsere Stadt Berlin ist stark und furchtbar, und ihre Flügel wissen, wohin sie wollen. Darum kehrt der Künstler—doch immer wieder zurück nach Berlin, *hier ist die Uhr der Kunst,* die nicht nach, noch vor geht" (*WB* 4.1: 26). All quotations from *Concert* use Jean M. Snook's translation (Lincoln: University of Nebraska Press, 1994), 40.

7. "In Berlin sahen wir damals den Mittelpunkt der Erde. Die Künstler und die Künste übten eine magnetische Kraft aus. Man kam aus aller Welt, um teilzunehmen an den geistigen Bewegungen, es war ein Glück, in jener Zeit zu leben"; Thilo Koch, *"Die 'Goldenen' Zwanziger Jahre 'Hoppla, Wir Leben,'"* in *Das*

Berlin Buch, ed. Heinz Ohff and Rainer Höynck (Berlin: Stapp Verlag, 1987), 127. Claims about Berlin's cultural prominence during the 1920s are romanticized because of the city's ensuing history. Koch and Gerhard Brunn provide an important corrective to this tendency, yet repeated accounts give credence to the reports of Berlin's intense vitality; Brunn, "Einleitung: Metropolis Berlin. Europäische Haupstädte in Vergleich," *Metropolis Berlin,* ed. Gerhard Brunn and Jürgen Reulecke (Bonn: Bouvier Verlag, 1992), 1–38.

8. Brunn 25, 31; Haxthausen and Suhr, introduction xiii. In 1899, Walter Rathenau regretted that "The culture of the Kingdom of Prussia no longer has a place in Imperial Berlin. Athens on the Spree is dead and Chicago on the Spree is emerging" (Lothar Müller, "The Beauty of the Metropolis: Toward an Aesthetic Urbanism in Turn-of-the-Century Berlin," in Haxthausen and Suhr 37–57; 40).

9. With this incorporation, Berlin encompassed sixty-two lakes, 127 other bodies of water, and almost one hundred square miles of undeveloped forest and agricultural land. Norbert Ritter, "Stadtentwicklung und Verkehr," in Ohff and Höynck 143–56. By the midtwenties, Berlin had the most advanced transportation system in Europe (151, 148).

10. Peter Jelavich claims that these groups never mingled entirely; "Modernity, Civic Identity, and Metropolitan Entertainment: Vaudeville, Cabaret, and Revue in Berlin, 1900–1933," Haxthausen and Suhr 95–110; 96.

11. According to Miles Carpenter, *Immigrants and Their Children* (Arno Press, 1969), in 1920 New York's immigrants stemmed primarily from the Russian empire, Italy, Ireland, Germany and Austria, in that order; two of New York's five and a half million inhabitants were immigrants (389–95). On internal migration, see William B. Scott and Peter M. Rutkoff, *New York Modern: The Arts and the City* (Baltimore: Johns Hopkins University Press, 1999), 17.

12. Andreas Huyssen, "Mass Culture as Woman, Modernism's Other," *Studies in Entertainment: Critical Approaches to Mass Culture,* ed. Tania Modleski (Bloomington: Indiana University Press, 1986),188–207; 191, 196.

13. See Benjamin, "On Some Motifs in Baudelaire," *Illuminations,* ed. Hannah Arendt, trans. Harry Zohn (New York: Schocken Books, 1968), 155–200; and Lloyd Spencer, "Allegory in the World of the Commodity: The Importance of *Central Park,*" *New German Critique* 34 (winter 1985): 59–77.

14. Teal, "The Hollow Women" 81–82.

15. David Weir, *Decadence and the Making of Modernism* (Amherst: University of Massachusetts Press, 1995), 19.

16. Similarly, Janet Wolff suggests that the extensive literature on the representative (male) modernist as flaneur is a remnant of mid-nineteenth-century Paris, not a figure of any twentieth-century metropolis. Wilson identifies the conditions of Paris in the 1830s and 1840s that encouraged writers of that period to link female prostitution with urbanity (55–56).

17. Wilson points out that "poets sometimes likened Paris to a prostitute, but more often sang her praises as a queen" (47). Molly Nesbitt agrees in "In the absence of the *parisienne* . . ." [ellipses Nesbitt's], *Sexuality and Space,* ed. Beatriz Colomina (Princeton: Princeton Architectural Press, 1992), 307–25; 308. Shari Benstock claims that Paris is typically described as prostitute, but she refers only to American expatriate descriptions; "Expatriate Modernism," in Broe and Ingram 20–40; 27.

18. Rowe 1; see also 89, 113, 122, 135–39.

19. Maria Tatar, *Lustmord: Sexual Murder in Weimar Germany* (Princeton: Princeton University Press, 1995), 54.

20. Patrice Petro, "Perceptions of Difference: Woman as Spectator and Spectacle," *Women in the Metropolis: Gender and Modernity in Weimar Culture,* ed. Katharina von Ankum (Berkeley and Los Angeles: University of California Press, 1997), 41–66; 42.

21. Charles W. Haxthausen, "'A New Beauty': Ernst Ludwig Kirchner's Images of Berlin," in Haxthausen and Suhr 58–94; 84.

22. Quotation from von Ankum's introduction, 1–11; 7.

23. Meskimmon, 60.

24. During the 1920s, women were a source of cheap, unskilled labor; the majority of women working outside the home between 1916 and 1929, however, continued to work in family shops (Petro 59 n. 4, 60). The percentage of women in the workforce remained constant between 1907 and 1925, but women working in industry were more visible than those in shops.

25. Renny Harrington, "The Stereotype of the Emancipated Woman in the Weimar Republic," *Women in German Symposium* (Oxford, Ohio: Miami University, 1977), 47–79; 47–48. By 1914 around half of all German women had had at least one abortion, and by 1930 abortions exceeded live births. Abortion was associated with and occurred most frequently in cities, especially Berlin (Beth Irwin Lewis, "Lustmord: Inside the Windows of the Metropolis," in von Ankum 202–32; 211).

26. Because *Sittenpolizei* (moral police) patrolled Berlin undercover, prostitutes had to be extremely circumspect; no visual markers distinguished prostitutes reliably from other women, and many women only occasionally solicited (Haxthausen 79).

27. This was underlined by a 2001 exhibit at the Neue Nationalgallerie in Berlin called "Potsdamer Platz: Ernst Ludwig Kirchner und der Untergang Preussens," which featured sections called "Prostitutes with Customers" and "The 'Sacred Whore.'" See also Rowe chap. 4.

28. Wolff describes brothel and bar scenes like Manet's *A Bar at the Folies-Bergère,* Picasso's *Demoiselles d'Avignon,* and Kirchner's *Strasse mit roter Kokotte* as key to visual modernism; the commercial exchange of (hetero)sexuality dominated the works seen as the "founding monuments of modern art" (59, 57; quoting Griselda Pollock). Tatar refers to men's representations of Berlin as "female" as a site where "German pathologies converge and flourish" (41).

29. See Meskimmon's analysis of this painting, 22–25.

30. See von Ankum's "Gendered Urban Spaces in Irmgard Keun's *Das kunstseidene Mädchen,*" in von Ankum 162–84.

31. Information in this paragraph comes from Timothy J. Gilfoyle, *City of Eros: New York City, Prostitution, and the Commercialization of Sex, 1790–1920* (New York: W. W. Norton, 1992), 306–9.

32. John Reed, *Collected Poems,* ed. Corliss Lamont (Westport, Conn.: Lawrence Hill, 1985), 37; Lola Ridge, *Sun-Up* (New York: B. W. Huebsh, 1920), 51. For other poems on the skyscraper, see John Timberman Newcomb's essay "The Footprint of the Twentieth Century: American Skyscrapers and Modernist Poems," *Modernism/Modernity* 10.1 (2003): 97–125.

33. Quoted in Shira Wolosky, "Santayana and Harvard Formalism," *Raritan* 18.4 (1999): 51–67; 53.

34. Carl Van Vechten, *Parties* (1930; Sun and Moon Press, 1993), 137, 142.

35. On this topic see Nancy Armstrong, "Modernism's Iconophobia and What It Did to Gender," *Modernism/Modernity* 5.2 (April 1998): 47–75, especially 52–53.

36. "Was immer in Deutschland nach oben strebte, saugte sie mit Tornado-Kräften in sich hinein. . . . Wer Berlin hatte, dem gehörte die Welt." Carl Zuckmayer, *Als wär's ein Stück von mir* (Frankfurt am Main: Fischer, 1966), 311.

37. "Trotzdem war bereits die unvergleichliche Intensität, . . . der Berlin in wenigen Jahren zur interresantesten, erregendsten Stadt Europas machte. . . Berlin schmeckte nach Zukunft" (Zuckmayer 313–14).

38. Jost Hermand,"Das Bild der 'großen Stadt' im Expressionismus," *Die Unwirklichkeit der Städte: Großstadtdarstellungen zwischen Moderne und Postmoderne,* ed. Klaus Scherpe (Reibeck bei Hamburg: Rowohlts Enzyklopädie, 1988). 65. Also see Haxthausen 60.

39. Richard Brinkmann, *Expressionismus: Internationale Forschung zu einem internationalen Phänomen* (Stuttgart: J. B. Metzler, 1980), 2. On Expressionism, see Peter Nicholls, "Cruel Structures: The Development of Expressionism," *Modernisms* 136–64; Silvio Vietta, "Großstadtwahrnehmung und ihre literarische Darstellung Expressionistischer Reihungsstil und Collage," *Deutsche Vierteljahrsschrift für Literatur wissenschaft und Geistesgeschichte* 48 (1974): 354–73; 361; Douglas Kellner, "Expression and Rebellion," in *Passion and Rebellion: The Expressionist Heritage,* ed. Stephen Bronner and Kellner (London: Croom Helm, 1983), 7; Richard Sheppard, "German Expressionism," *Modernism: A Guide to European Literature, 1890–1930,* ed. Malcolm Bradbury and James McFarlane (New York: Viking, 1991), 274–91; and McFarlane, "Berlin and the Rise of Modernism, 1886–96," in the same volume (96–104).

40. Reinhold Grimm and Henry J. Schmidt, "Foreign Influences on German Expressionist Poetry,"*Expressionism as an International Literary Phenomenon,* ed. Ulrich Weisstein (Paris: Didier, 1973), 69–78; 76.

41. Pierre Bourdieu, *The Field of Cultural Production: Essays on Art and Literature,* ed. Randal Johnson (Cambridge: Polity Press, 1993), 62.

42. See the appendix for a timeline of major events in all three poets' lives. The most thorough biography remains Sigrid Bauschinger's *Else Lasker Schüler: Ihr Werk und ihre Zeit;* on gender see Reiß-Suckow; Sonja Hedgepeth, *"Überall blicke ich nach einem heimatlichen Boden aus": Exil im Werk Else Lasker-Schülers* (Frankfurt am Main: Peter Lang, 1994); and Ulrike Müller, *Auch wider dem Verbote: Else Lasker-Schüler und ihr eigensinniger Umgang mit Weiblichkeit, Judentum und Mystik* (Frankfurt am Main: Peter Lang, 1997).

43. Helma Sanders-Brahms, *Gottfried Benn und Else Lasker-Schüler: Giselheer und Prinz Jussuf* (Hamburg: Rowohlt, 1997), 42.

44. Ingrid Heinrich-Jost calls Hille the most respected figure of bohemian Berlin and his gatherings the "ideal of the Cabaret as applied poetry"; "Das Berlin der Außenseiter," in Ohff and Höynek 157–64; 161.

45. On the changes in Berlin cabaret life before and after World War I, see Franz Matsche, "Grossstadt in der Malerei des Expressionismus am Beispiel E. L. Kirchners," *Die Modernität des Expressionismus,* ed. Thomas Anz and Michael Stark (Stuttgart: J. B. Metzler Verlag, 1994), 95–119; 95, 96, 106.

46. M. S. Jones argues that Lasker-Schüler and Alfred Döblin establish the literary importance of *Der Sturm* (*Der Sturm: A Focus of Expressionism* [Camden, N.J.: Camden House, 1984]). For the first two years of its publication, *Der Sturm* printed more work by Lasker-Schüler than by any other writer. Roy Allen similarly argues that Walden narrowly restricted his relationships whereas "because of her wide-ranging literary friendships," Lasker-Schüler initiated important contacts for him; *Literary Life in German Expressionism and the Berlin Circles* (Ann Arbor: UMI Research Press, 1983), 216–17, 218. As Markus Hal-

lensleben comments, until Walden's papers become accessible, such influence will be difficult to document precisely; *Else Lasker-Schüler. Avantgardismus und Kunstinszenierung* (Marburg: Francke Verlag, 2000), 29–42.

47. Bauschinger argues that the neutrality of the café also enabled the interaction of persons of diverse ethnic and national groups; "The Berlin Moderns: Else Lasker-Schüler and Café Culture," *Berlin Metropolis, Jews and the New Culture, 1890–1918,* ed. Emily D. Bilski (Berkeley and Los Angeles: University of California Press, 2000), 58–83; 59; Wilson makes this claim for cafés in Paris, although such freedom in Paris seems to have been enjoyed more easily by expatriates than by French women (63–64).

48. Alternative gathering places popular among Berlin writers were the Café Sezession, the Café Austria (site of *Die Aktion*'s recital evenings from 1911 to 1914), Das Gnu, and the Café Josty, also called the Zeitungscafé, where Walden shifted the *Sturm* circle after his remarriage.

49. There is, however, warm correspondence from Baum to Lasker-Schüler, after Baum's exile.

50. Dagmar Lorenz, "The Unspoken Bond: Else Lasker-Schüler and Gertrud Kolmar," *Seminar* 29.4 (1993): 349–69.

51. Brinkmann, *Expressionismus* 53. Among such publishers were Alfred Richard Meyer—with his publication of *Lyrische Flugblätter* (Lyric fly-sheets) from 1907 to 1923—Alex Juncker, Hermann Meister, Kurt Wolff, Paul Cassirer, and Wieland Herzfelde—with his Malik Press (1916–47), named after Lasker-Schüler's novel *Der Malik (The King).*

52. Peter Gay lists the lower number and John Willett the higher; *Weimar Culture: The Outsider as Insider* (New York: Harper and Row, 1968), 128, and *Art and Politics in the Weimar Period: The New Sobriety, 1817–1933* (New York: Pantheon, 1978), 74.

53. Zuckmayer claimed that the influence of Russia on Berlin's intellectual life was "more productive and stimulating than most of what came from the West" (334). Following World War I, Gorky, Ehrenburg, Kandinsky, Lissitzky, Mayakovsky, Moholy-Nagy, and Tsvetaeva lived at least briefly in Berlin. American and British writers and artists spending time there during the 1920s include Berenice Abbott, Djuna Barnes, Bryher, Malcolm Cowley, Lyonel Feininger, Marsden Hartley, Matthew Josephson, Loy, Kenneth MacPherson, McAlmon, Man Ray, and Thelma Wood.

54. Book titles in English are *The Seventh Day, My Wonder, The Peter Hille Book,* and *The Nights of Tino of Baghdad. Die Wupper* was staged twice in Berlin—in 1919 in Max Reinhardt's Deutschen Theater, director Heinz Herald with music by Friederich Holländer and Expressionist sets by Ernst Stern, and in 1927 by Leo Jeßner's Berlin Staatstheater, director Jürgen Fehling. See Calvin Jones, *The Literary Reputation of Else Lasker-Schüler: Criticism, 1901–1993* (Camden, N.J.: Camden House, 1994).

55. "Sie ist eine der größten Dichterinnen, weil sie zeitloser ist als alle, sie tritt dicht neben das Hohe Lied. . . . Die Lasker hat nichts um sich"; Kasimir Edschmid, "Expressionismus in der Dichtung," *Die neue Rundschau,* 1918, in Thomas Anz and Michael Stark, *Expressionismus: Manifeste und Dokumente zur deutschen Literatur 1910–1920* (Stuttgart: J. B. Metzler Verlag, 1982), 53.

56. Karl Kraus, "Ich halte Else Lasker-Schüler für eine große Dichterin. Ich halte alles, was um sie herum neugetönt wird, für eine Frechheit"; in "Gegen die Neutöner," *Die Fackel,* June 21, 1912, 53–54; Anz and Stark, *Expressionismus* 86.

57. She "paßt nirgendwo hin und gewiß nicht in das Milieu, in dem Sie sie sehen werden" (*WZ* 33).

58. "Ich habe doch schon empfunden, daß ich nur dem eine Leiter, dem eine Sensation, dem eine Warte, dem ein Ereigniß" [*sic*]; Abraham Stenzl, 1929, in Heather Valencia, *Else Lasker-Schüler und Abraham Nochem Stenzel: Eine Unbekannte Freundschaft* (Frankfurt am Main: Campus, 1995), 80.

59. Many of these appear in Lasker-Schüler's 1913 *Gesichte* (Faces). Letters also document her efforts to promote the work of Benn, Paul Boldt, Wieland Herzfelde, Paul Zech, and Hans Ehrenbaum-Degele, among others (*Br* I 79, 87–90, 92, 101).

60. Freud writes to thank her for taking part in the celebration of his eightieth birthday (JNUL Arc var 501). Einstein writes the poet in 1925, and later sends her a copy of his letter asking Louis Asher to find work for her son Paul in Chicago. In a third letter (May 23, 1933), Einstein writes, "Mrs. Else Lasker-Schüler also belongs to those noble natures that have been driven into foreign lands by blind hate" [Auch Frau Else Lasker-Schüler gehört zu den edlen Naturen, die blinder Hass in die Fremde verstossen hat] (JNUL 5:104).

61. See Bauschinger for an analysis of this "revolutionary" essay (*WZ* 158).

62. Ernst Bloch, *The Utopian Function of Art and Literature: Selected Essays*, trans. Jack Zipes and Frank Mecklenburg (Cambridge: MIT Press, 1988), 106, 107, 109. Although I know of no evidence that Lasker-Schüler knew Bloch, it is likely that they met during his years in Berlin (1908–11, and off and on between 1919 and 1933). Bloch was Jewish, associated with Expressionism, and married a sculptor, Else von Stritzky. The ideas of *The Spirit of Utopia* circulated among Expressionists long before the book's publication in 1918.

63. From "Something's Missing: A Discussion between Ernst Bloch and Theodor W. Adorno on the Contradictions of Utopian Longing" (Bloch 5, 4, 12).

64. Lasker-Schüler's and Moore's art might be described by Charles Altieri's speculation: "Countering realism entails treating art less as a mode of referring directly to the world than as an emphasis on the capacity of the artistic syntax to exemplify ways of feeling, thinking, and imaginatively projecting investments not bound to dominant social structures"; "What Is Living and What Is Dead in American Postmodernism," *Critical Inquiry* 22.4 (1996): 767.

65. Stieglitz's own art was influenced by his years in Berlin after his graduation from City College; according to Scott and Rutkoff, "Berlin became his cultural model" and spurred his interest in experimental photography; Stieglitz also took a course on photochemistry in Berlin (49–50).

66. See Arthur Frank Wertheim on little magazines in *The New York Little Renaissance: Iconoclasm, Modernism, and Nationalism in American Culture, 1908–1917* (New York: New York University Press, 1976); see Schulze for information on all magazines in which Moore published (*EP* 381–494).

67. Lloyd Morris, *Incredible New York: High Life and Low Life of the Last Hundred Years, 1850–1950* (New York: Random House, 1951), 310.

68. Janet Lyon describes a more divisive Village feminism, in which avant-garde aesthetics were opposed to social politics, in "Mina Loy's Pregnant Pauses: The Space of Possibility in the Florence Writing," *MLWP* 379–402. Indeed few formally innovative writers address issues of woman's desire, contraception, or maternity directly, but several address other feminist issues.

69. Kinnahan's *Poetics of the Feminine: Authority and Literary Tradition in William Carlos Williams, Mina Loy, Denise Levertov, and Kathleen Fraser* (Cambridge: Cambridge University Press, 1994) argues that Williams has been an

important precursor for later feminist poets in part because he was influenced by early-twentieth-century feminism (20).

70. According to Rebecca West, the writers of London changed their perspective during World War I: "Before the war . . . [t]he man in the street was anti-feminist but the writers of quality were pro-suffrage. Now the case is reversed. The man in the street accepts the emancipation of women. . . . But a very large number of the younger male writers adopt a [misogynistic] attitude"; in "Autumn and Virginia Woolf," *Ending in Earnest: A Literary Log* (New York: Doubleday, Doran, 1931), 212. Similarly, Kinnahan describes Dora Marsden's feminism as having less and less to do with social or psychological equality for women after 1914 (25).

71. Kathleen D. McCarthy provides multiple examples of the emergence of a virulent form of this myth; *Women's Culture: American Philanthropy and Art, 1830–1930* (Chicago: University of Chicago Press, 1991), 149. Ann Douglas's *Terrible Honesty: Mongrel Manhattan in the 1920s* (New York: Farrar, Straus and Giroux, 1995) takes the myth as true.

72. See Carol Duncan, *The Aesthetics of Power: Essays in Critical Art History* (Cambridge: Cambridge University Press, 1993), 172–73, on validating experimental arts.

73. Quoted in Wilson 77 and Nancy Berke, "Anything That Burns You: The Social Poetry of Lola Ridge, Genevieve Taggard, and Margaret Walker," *Revista Canaria de Estudios Ingleses* 37 (1998): 39–53; 39. Robert Crunden presents a masculinist version of this claim, writing that "competent, energetic women support[ed] socially backward, underfinanced, verbally fluent men" (107) and depended on these men for their sense of the avant-garde; *American Salons: Encounters with European Modernism, 1885–1917* (New York: Oxford University Press, 1993).

74. For women in New York, see Cristanne Miller, "Marianne Moore and the Women Modernizing New York," *Modern Philology* 98.2 (November 2000): 339–62.

75. McCarthy xi, xiii, 180, 196. On women's roles in music see Carol J. Oja, "Women Patrons and Activists for Modernist Music: New York in the 1920s," *Modernism/Modernity* 4.1 (1997): 129–55.

76. Dorothy Brown, *Setting a Course: American Women in the 1920s* (Boston, 1987), 205; Martin Green, *New York, 1913: The Armory Show and the Patterson Strike Pageant* (New York: Charles Scribner's Sons, 1988), 15; and McCarthy 196–239; 187–95.

77. See Jayne E. Marek, *Women Editing Modernism: "Little" Magazines and Literary History* (Lexington: University Press of Kentucky, 1995), 12.

78. Bennett also edited one of the three issues of the Philadelphia journal *Black Opals* and directed the Harlem Community Art Center.

79. Women involved with men in collaborative publishing ventures included Agnes Ernst, Katherine Rhoades, Louise Norton, Genevieve Taggard, Gwendolyn Bennett, Zora Neale Hurston, Maria Jolas, and Caresse Crosby—the last two in Paris. The presses and journals they cofounded and coedited include *291, Measure, Fire, transition,* and the Black Sun Press. Also in Paris, Sylvia Beach founded Shakespeare & Co. (1914–41), which published some books, and Gertrude Stein founded the Plain Edition Press.

80. Gillian Hanscombe and Virginia L. Smyers, *Writing for Their Lives: The Modernist Women, 1910–1940* (Boston: Northeastern University Press, 1988), 104.

81. Sawelson-Gorse, *Women in Dada* x–xiii.

82. See Marek 167–92.

83. Suzanne Churchill, "Making Space for *Others:* A History of a Modernist Little Magazine," *Journal of Modern Literature* 22.1 (fall 1998): 47–67; 63.

84. Douglas 61; Morris 317–22.

85. Biographical information on Moore comes from my reading in the Moore archives at the Rosenbach Museum and Library; Charles Molesworth, *Marianne Moore: A Literary Life* (New York: Atheneum, 1990); and Linda Leavell, *Marianne Moore and the Visual Arts: Prismatic Color* (Baton Rouge: Louisiana State University Press, 1995). Moore's father entered an asylum before her birth, and she never met him.

86. Leavell, *Marianne Moore* 11; Moore did help out briefly at the *Broom* (46).

87. On the importance of Moore's reviews in establishing her position, see Celeste Goodridge's *Hints and Disguises: Marianne Moore and Her Contemporaries* (Iowa City: University of Iowa Press, 1989).

88. Williams, "Marianne Moore" (1925), *Imaginations* 308–18; 309.

89. Yvor Winters, "Holiday and Day of Wrath," *Uncollected Essays and Reviews,* ed. Francis Murphy (London: Allen Lane, 1973), 26.

90. On the tendency of early Village radicals to avoid distinguishing movements, see Edward Abrahams, *The Lyrical Left: Randolph Bourne, Alfred Stieglitz, and the Origins of Cultural Radicalism in America* (Charlotte: University of Virginia Press, 1988).

91. Churchill 242.

92. *Marianne Moore Reader* (New York: Viking, 1961), 266; Leavell speculates that Moore preferred the *Dial* to other magazines because it had a policy of not taking sides (*Marianne Moore,* 47). Martin Green comments that inclusiveness characterized Mabel Dodge Luhan's salon in *New York, 1913* (59). Rudolf E. Kuenzli quotes Man Ray saying, "Pleasure and liberty were the words I used [in New York], as my goals," as evidence of "fiercely individualistic Americans' resistance to yet another European label"; *New York Dada,* ed. Rudolf E. Kuenzli (New York: Willis Locker and Owens, 1986), 5.

93. Scott and Rutkoff write that "New York dada was an attitude and a moment," not a "movement" (64, 65). Kuenzli similarly describes American Dadaists as uninterested in this European label; they used the name *Dada* only briefly in 1921, although art and events now considered "Dada" occurred there as early as 1915 (1).

94. The list of regular participants at the Arensbergs varies enormously. Amy Lowell, Alfred Kreymborg, and Williams are also mentioned as regulars. According to Scott and Rutkoff, the Arensbergs not only "provided the ambiance and the refreshments" but "determined [the] membership" of this group (66).

95. Mentioned in Thom Gunn's "Three Hard Women: HD, Marianne Moore, Mina Loy," in Bell and Lerner 37–52; 44, in the context of calling Moore "one of the chief innovators" of early modernism.

96. "Mutter" Ey owned and ran a gallery in Düsseldorf; in Hannover, Kate Steinitz and Kurt Schwitters founded the Aposs Press; in Munich Kathi Kobus founded the influential *Simplicissimus* in 1903, and in Berlin Rosa Valetti founded the Cabaret Größenwahn in 1920 and Trude Hesterberg the Wilde Bühne cabaret in 1921.

97. Because Jewish women were prevented from study of the Torah, the

most prestigious form of learning in the Jewish world, many turned to vernacular cultures and knowledge, well into the twentieth century. Jewish women were also frequently privately educated beyond the level typical of German women at the time.

98. Reiß-Suckow 88. Anti-intellectualism was also characteristic of Peter Hille and Die Neue Gemeinschaft's back-to-nature philosophy. Lasker-Schüler exaggerates accounts of her anti-intellectualism; her letters refer to people's work she has read, and a moving letter from Paul Zech when both are in exile mentions their last meeting at the Berlin Stadtbibliothek, the city's major library.

99. For biographical information about Loy I am indebted to Carolyn Burke's biography *Becoming Modern* and Roger Conover's introduction and timeline to *The Last Lunar Baedeker.* Shreiber and Tuma's collection of essays *Mina Loy: Woman and Poet* is also invaluable.

100. Mary E. Galvin speculates that Stein may have provided Loy a model of independence from heterosexual relationships; *Queer Poetics: Five Modernist Women Writers* (New York: Praeger, 1999), 155–56. As I speculate in "Feminist Location and Mina Loy's 'Anglo-Mongrels and the Rose,'" *Paideuma* 32.1–3 (2003): 75–94, Stein may also have been the first avant-garde Jewish writer Loy had met.

101. Pound, "Marianne Moore and Mina Loy," *Selected Prose, 1909–1965* (London: Faber and Faber, 1973), 394. For discussions of logopoeia in relation to Loy, see Carolyn Burke "Supposed Persons: Modernist Poetry and the Female Subject," *Feminist Studies* 7.1 (1985): 131–48; and Rachel Blau DuPlessis, "'Corpses of Poesy': some modern poets and some gender ideologies of lyric," in *Feminist Measures: Soundings in Poetry and Theory,* ed. Lynn Keller and Cristanne Miller (Ann Arbor: University of Michigan Press, 1994), 69–95.

102. Winters, "Mina Loy," *Uncollected Essays* 29.

103. Kadlec, *Mosaic Modernism: Anarchism, Pragmatism, Culture* (Johns Hopkins University Press, 2000), 156, 155.

CHAPTER THREE

Jeanette Winterson, *Oranges Are Not the Only Fruit* (New York: Atlantic Monthly, 1987), 170.

1. A tenet of the New Criticism was that the poet achieves a melding of "his" voice with the human condition and hence ceases to be personal; as Fiona Green puts it, the lyric voice "pours forth unhindered, the marks of place and time finding no purchase on its immaculate surface"; "Locating the Lyric: Moore and Bishop," in Davis and Jenkins 199–214; 200.

2. Eliot's "Tradition and the Individual Talent," in *Selected Prose of T. S. Eliot,* ed. Frank Kermode (New York: Harcourt Brace Jovanovich, 1975), 40.

3. Lisa Steinman, *Made in America: Science, Technology, and American Modernist Poets* (New Haven: Yale University Press, 1987).

4. McCabe, "'A Queer Lot' and the Lesbians of 1914: Amy Lowell, H.D., and Gertrude Stein," *Challenging Boundaries: Gender and Periodization,* ed. Joyce W. Warren and Margaret Dickie (Athens: University of Georgia Press, 2000), 62–90.

5. Quoted in Burke, "Supposed Persons" 136.

6. Emile Benveniste, *Problems in General Linguistics,* trans. Mary Elizabeth Meek (Coral Gables: University of Miami Press, 1971), 218.

7. Claire MacDonald, "Assumed Identities: Feminism, Autobiography,

and Performance Art," *The Uses of Autobiography,* ed. Julia Swindells (London: Taylor and Francis, 1995), 187–95; 189; Leigh Gilmore, *Autobiographics: A Feminist Theory of Women's Self-Representation* (Ithaca, N.Y.: Cornell University Press, 1994), 19.

8. Judith Butler, "Critically Queer," *GLQ* 1 (1993): 17–32; 17, 21.

9. Judith Butler, "Performative Acts and Gender Constitution: An Essay in Phemonology and Feminist Theory," *Performing Feminisms: Feminist Critical Theory and Theatre,* ed. Sue-Ellen Case (Baltimore: Johns Hopkins University Press, 1990), 270–82; 272. For a discussion of Butler's theory in relation to poetic productions of subjectivity see Suzanne Juhasz and Cristanne Miller, "Performances of Gender in Dickinson's Poetry," *Cambridge Companion to Emily Dickinson,* ed. Wendy Martin (Cambridge: Cambridge University Press, 2002), 107–28.

10. Antje Lindenmeyer, "'I Am Prince Jussuf': Else Lasker-Schüler's Autobiographical Performance," *Biography* 24.1 (2001): 25–34; 33.

11. Alex Goody, "Autobiography/Auto-mythology: Mina Loy's 'Anglo-Mongrels and the Rose,'" *Representing Lives: Women and Auto/Biography,* ed. Alison Donnell and Pauline Polkey (New York: St. Martin's Press, 2000), 270–79; 270.

12. Bonnie Costello, "The Feminine Language of Marianne Moore," *Marianne Moore,* ed. Harold Bloom (New York: Chelsea House, 1987); Leavell, *Marianne Moore* 126–30; Jeanne Heuving, *Omissions Are Not Accidents: Gender in the Art of Marianne Moore* (Detroit: Wayne State University Press, 1992), 149; and Miller, *Questions of Authority* 27–30, 35–36, 46–48, 87–89.

13. Because no manuscripts exist for many of Loy's poems, it is difficult to date their composition. I follow Roger Conover's notes *(LLB)* and Marissa Januzzi's "A Bibliography of Works by and about Mina Loy" (*MLWP* 507–606).

14. On Moore's political stance in this poem, see my "The Politics of Marianne Moore's Poetry of Ireland: 1917–1941," *Irish Journal of American Studies,* 11 (March 2003).

15. "Und sie wächst / Über die Welt hinaus / Ihren Anfang verlierend, / Über alle Zeit hinaus / Und zurück um dein Tausendherz." This is a sixty-three-line poem (*WB,* no. 103).

16. Sandra Gilbert and Susan Gubar's *No Man's Land,* vol. 3, *Letters from the Front* (New Haven: Yale University Press, 1994) discusses this topic, and I am indebted to their research for some of my examples. Their claim that the radical questioning of femininity occurs "from Rivière onward" (58), however, does not correspond with my study of the teens and twenties. Susan A. Glenn in *Female Spectacle: The Theatrical Roots of Modern Feminism* (Cambridge: Harvard University Press, 2000) also argues that the phenomenon of self-conscious costuming was at the heart of modernist public culture. In the 1880s and 1890s, women in theater in the United States were highly visible and self-consciously "demonstrated and encouraged new ways of acting female" (6). By 1900, 43 percent of the theatrical profession in the United States was female (13).

17. On U.S. women's movements, see Karen Manners Smith, "New Paths to Power: 1890–1920," *No Small Courage: A History of Women in the United States,* ed. Nancy Cott (Oxford: Oxford University Press, 2000), 353–412; and Eleanor Flexner's classic summary *Century of Struggle: The Woman's Rights Movement in the United States* (1959; rev. ed., Cambridge: Harvard University Press, 1975).

18. There is no U.S. analogy to Christabel Pankhurst's argument that no "spiritually developed woman" should mate with "men who in thought and conduct with regard to sex matters are their inferiors"; Sheila Jeffrey, *The Spin-*

ster and Her Enemies: Feminism and Sexuality, 1880–1930 (London: Routledge and Kegan Paul, 1985), 89. Similarly, the U.S. women's movement did not "denounce[] . . . Liberalism [and] . . . bourgeois individualism," instead seeing both as key to their own positioning; Edward P. Comentale, "Thesmophoria: Suffragettes, Sympathetic Magic, and H.D.'s Ritual Poetics," *Modernism/Modernity* 8.3 (2001): 471–92; 474.

19. Nancy Cott, *The Grounding of Modern Feminism* (New Haven: Yale University Press, 1987), 8, 49. Cott sees this as the point at which the "Woman movement" began to break into "feminism."

20. According to K. Smith, these discussions centered around the idea that behavior deemed appropriately feminine (submission, self-sacrifice, and the submergence of women into domestic life) was harmful as well as outmoded ("New Paths to Power" 399). On the feminism of the early Village, see also Brown's *Setting a Course.*

21. Moore went to Baltimore and Washington, D.C., to take a civil service exam and do some shopping, staying from February 23 to March 10. After the letter expressing her intention, Warner wrote strongly advising Moore not to march because it might hurt her standing at the Carlisle Indian School. The correspondence leaves unclear whether Moore received this letter by March 3, when she returned to D.C. (VI:10:04, February 23 and March 2). Her intent to march with the authors and artists, however, shows both her feminist and professional identification. Later, Moore did march in a New York suffrage parade.

22. Rayna Rapp and Ellen Ross, "The 1920s: Feminism, Consumerism, and Political Backlash in the United States," *Women in Culture and Politics: A Century of Change,* ed. Judith Friedlander, Blanche Wiesen Cook, Alice Kessler-Harris, and Carrol Smith-Rosenberg (Bloomington: Indiana University Press, 1986), 52–61. For emphasis on the liberatory effects of women's claim to nonreproductive sexual activity, see Mary Louise Roberts, "Samson and Delilah Revisited: The Politics of Women's Fashion in 1920s France," *American Historical Review* 97 (1993): 69–85; and John D'Emilio and Estelle Freedman, *Intimate Matters: A History of Sexuality in America* (New York: Harper and Row, 1988).

23. Women received the vote in New York state in 1917. See chapter 4 of *Questions of Authority* and "Women Modernizing New York" on Moore's feminism.

24. DuPlessis comes to a similar conclusion: "The issue is . . . individual reform of consciousness" (*Genders* 56).

25. This is my conclusion from Burke's description of people Loy knew in Florence (*BM* 105–64).

26. Stein's opposition to organized feminism may also have encouraged Loy's; they met in 1905. Stein repudiated women's movements and feminism while at Johns Hopkins, 1900–1903; Laura Behling, *The Masculine Woman in America* (Urbana: University of Illinois Press, 2001), 18.

27. Material in this paragraph comes from Frevert and Kolinsky.

28. Frevert notes that Jewish women were more apt than gentiles to join organizations; 20–25 percent of all Jewish women over thirty belonged to the Jüdischer Frauenbund (112). See also Marion Kaplan, *The Jewish Feminist Movement in Germany: The Campaigns of the Jüdischer Frauenbund, 1904–1938* (Westport, Conn.: Greenwood Press, 1979); and Paula E. Hyman, *Gender and Assimilation in Modern Jewish History: The Roles and Representation of Women* (Seattle: University of Washington Press, 1995), 167–68.

29. Nicola Brice, "The Autobiographical Voice in Lily Braun's Fiction," in Donnell and Polkey 260–69; 264.

30. "Ich bin immer wie ein Vogel frei—nicht frei im Sinne der Frauenrichtlerinnen" (*Br* I 52).

31. Von Ankum, introduction to *Women in the Metropolis,* 2. The "*neue Frau* of the 1920s was the popularised and depoliticised version of the New Woman . . . at the turn of the century" (Meskimmon 167). Because many of women's legal and educational gains of the first two decades of the century were taken for granted by younger women, the more radical conceptions of womanhood were easily usurped by the mainstream culture industry (168). See also Hilke Veth, "Literatur von Frauen," *Literatur der Weimarer Republik 1918–1933,* ed. Bernhard Weyergraf (Munich: Deutscher Taschenbuch Verlag, 1995); and Petro. All sources I have read indicate that while the Weimar Republic increased women's legal rights, a strong wave of antifeminist sentiment began in 1918 and built throughout the twenties.

32. Lynne Frame, "Gretchen, Girl, Garçonne? Weimar Science and Popular Culture in Search of the Ideal New Woman," in von Ankum 12–40; 14, 18.

33. Expressionists who studied philosophy include Johannes Becher, Gottfried Benn, Solomo Friedlaender, Kurt Hiller, Jakob van Hoddis, Oskar Kanehl, Rudolf Kayser, Robert Musil, Anselm Ruest, René Schickele, and Carl Sternheim; according to Wright, an even larger number studied law and literature. There were also more editorials, polemics, and commentaries published in Expressionist journals than works of fiction or poetry; Barbara Wright, "'New Man,' Eternal Woman: Expressionist Responses to German Feminism," *German Quarterly* 60.4 (1987): 582–99; 585, 583. See Felski on Simmel's importance in supporting the conception of woman as "overt object of nostalgic desire," outside history in her idealized form but therefore also a lower social and biological form than man (37–40).

34. Beth Lewis corroborates that avant-garde artists and writers in Germany were not receptive to women's professional aspirations on the principle that they would inhibit female sexuality (121, 122).

35. Gerald Izenberg, *Modernism and Masculinity: Mann, Wedekind, Kandinsky through World War I* (Chicago: University of Chicago Press, 2000), 10. Although Izenberg does not claim to describe Germany, his footnote mentions only Frevert's work—the source of many of his generalizations. Generally, Izenberg refers in his introductory chapter to German theory or cultural sources, chiefly Frankfurt school, Frevert, and historical analyses of German-language culture by Gay and by Jacque LeRider, *Modernity and Crises of Identity: Culture and Society in Fin-de-Siecle Vienna,* trans. Rosemary Morris (Cambridge: Polity Press, 1993).

36. Frevert 124; "Männerlichkeit eine der ersten Bedingungen der Kunst sei," in Birgit Schulte, "Die Emanzipation der Künstlerinnen um die Jahrhundertwende: Else Lasker-Schüler's Begegnungen mit Karl Ernst Osthaus und Milly Steger," *Prinz Jussuf ist Eine Frau* (Iserlohn: Evangelische Akademie, 1995), 83–97; 96.

37. Randal Johnson, introduction to Bourdieu 5.

38. Judith Butler, "Performativity's Social Magic," *Bourdieu: A Critical Reader,* ed. Richard Shusterman (Malden, Mass.: Blackwell, 1999), 113–28; 116.

39. Quoted in Elizabeth Meese, "Theorizing Lesbian: Writing—A Love Letter," *Lesbian Texts and Contexts: Radical Revisions,* ed. Karla Jay and Joanne Glasgow (London: Onlywoman Press, 1992), 70–87; 78, 79.

40. Bridget Elliott and Jo-Ann Wallace's vocabulary of "(im)positionings" works similarly to show women's negotiation of class and strategies of relationship; *Women Artists and Writers: Modernist (Im)positionings* (London: Routledge, 1994), 17.

41. Porter's pen name alters the name of her paternal grandmother—Catherine Anne Porter—with whom she and her siblings lived for nine years following the death of their mother.

42. Hanscombe and Smyers 97. I am indebted to this study's rich biographical information about Anglo-American female modernists, particularly for pseudonyms and nicknames.

43. "Ich selbst bin nie zu finden, also nicht zu zerstören als von mir selbst" (*Br* I 57; to Bithell, March 22, 1910).

44. Dickinson, *The Complete Poems,* ed. Ralph W. Franklin (Cambridge: Harvard University Press, 1998), poem 353; the misspellings are Dickinson's.

45. Vivian Liska's excellent review of gender criticism on Lasker-Schüler similarly indicates what is anachronistic and politically problematic in the trickster model of implied historical indeterminacy, although she also calls the poet a Cixous-like "medium of chaos and insanity . . . who proclaims the revaluation of fixed hierarchies"; *Die Dichterin und das schelmische Erhabene. Else Lasker Schülers Die Nächte Tino von Bagdads* (Marburg: Francke Verlag, 1998), 39, 50.

46. Susan Gilmore's "Imna, Ova, Mongrel, Spy: Anagram and Imposture in the Work of Mina Loy," *MLWP* 271–317, reviews information on Loy's nicknames and name changes. In British pronunciation, there would have been little difference between the names Lowy, Loy, and Loewe—presumably the initial spelling of Loy's family name.

47. Susan Gilmore 301 n. 30; B ZA Luhan. Loy titles a painting *Jemima* and uses this name in some autobiographical writing (*BM* 126). Haweis called Loy "Ducie," but Loy transforms the name to identify her self more closely with Dodge, through the visual and aural rhyme Doose/Moose.

48. Loy listed herself as Imna Oly on the playbill of a 1920–21 Provincetown Players performance. For "Hush Money" and "Goy Israels" see B MSS 6, Box 6, folder 160 and Box 2, folders 27–30.

49. Virginia Kouidis, *Mina Loy: American Modernist Poet* (Baton Rouge: Louisiana State University Press, 1980), 47.

50. According to Maeera Shreiber, as a modernist, Loy "inherits a radical distrust of the notion of the lyric subject"; "'Love is a Lyric / of Bodies': The Negative Aesthetics of Mina Loy's 'Love Songs to Joannes,'" *Genre* 27 (1994): 143–64; 143. See also Carolyn Burke's "Getting Spliced: Modernism and Sexual Difference," *American Quarterly* 39 (1987): 98–121.

51. Christine Poggi writes of the masculine bias, occasionally erupting into explicit misogyny, of Italian Futurism; "Dreams of Metallized Flesh: Futurism and the Masculine Body," *Modernism/Modernity* 4.3 (1997): 19–43. Lyon also notes the importance of seeing "the immediate context of [her early poems'] composition" as "Florence, where Futurism's attitude to virtually all forms of feminism was dismissive and contemptuous" (384).

52. "Aphorisms on Futurism," January 1914 (*LLB* 152, 150).

53. Robin Pickering-Iazzi, *Politics of the Visible: Writing Women, Culture, and Fascism* (Minneapolis: University of Minnesota Press, 1997), 207–9. Pickering-Iazzi does note, however, that from the midteens Futurists admitted women in their publishing, recordings, and photographs (207). Walter Adamson stresses this inclusion but admits that women attracted to Futurism before 1916 may

have cultivated their sense of being exceptional, hence shared Marinetti's much-debated "scorn for women"; "Futurism, Mass Culture, and Women: The Reshaping of the Artistic Vocation, 1909–1920," *Modernism/Modernity* 4.1 (January 1997): 89–114. Adamson's primary evidence stems from *L'Italia futurista,* which was published in Florence from June 1916 to February 1918—getting its start just as Loy was moving to New York (104–5). Burke does not mention Loy's interaction with any Futurist women.

54. On Loy's manifesto, see DuPlessis (*Genders* 52–57) and Jessica Burstein, "A Few Words about Dubuque: Modernism, Sentimentalism, and the Blasé," *American Literary History* 14.2 (2002): 227–54, especially the latter on the document's tonal allusiveness. Paul Peppis develops DuPlessis's argument that this manifesto makes "aesthetic production dependent on biological reproduction" by associating sex with the teleology of eugenic reproduction—although he also reads an implied radical politics in Loy's combined discourses of free love and racial purity; "Rewriting Sex: Mina Loy, Marie Stopes, and Sexology," *Modernism/Modernity* 9.4 (2002): 561–79; 573, 570.

55. The first four sections of this poem were published in 1915 as "Love Songs"; the thirty-four-part sequence appeared as a 1917 issue of *Others.* Loy abbreviated and changed the sequence for her 1923 *Lunar Baedecker.* I quote from Loy's 1917 version of this poem.

56. Shreiber reads this poem persuasively as an "anti-love lyric" mourning "a culture that is actively hostile to love" ("Love is a Lyric" 152, 144). DuPlessis reads it as allying the speaker with "Nature," arguing that Loy looks toward an evolution in which people leave behind "bourgeois individualism" (*Genders* 66). Like Shreiber, I see the invoked new breed of "sons and daughters" as commenting on the cultural loss of ability to feel emotion.

57. Von Hallberg 60, 64. Cocteau wrote: "Skepticism is a bad conductor of poetry. That is why poetry has no great hold in France, a country which is much too knowing" (von Hallberg 60). Von Hallberg argues that Dada interest in the "play of language" for its own sake and in art as absurd stands in contrast to the political coherence and presence of human character in poems by U.S. poets, including those who share some formal characteristics of the avant-garde.

58. Lyon 391, quoting Herbert Marcuse.

59. Conover describes Loy as "by action and temperament" more aligned with the avant-garde than modernism (*LLB82* xix, lxi); *LLB* includes two poems written between 1923 and 1927, although Loy also finishes "Anglo-Mongrels" after returning to Paris from Berlin.

60. Although Duchamp had returned to New York and Tristan Tzara had just listed Loy formally as a Dadaist ("Mina Lloyd"), other expatriates in the earlier Arensberg circle had left the city.

61. In a letter written from Florence and dated July 3, probably written in 1921, Loy tells Mabel Dodge, "I have so much accumulated that is bursting for expression" (B ZA Luhan).

62. Lyon makes this point in reading Loy's "Feminist Manifesto," although she argues that in "Parturition" Loy presents labor as "the primary carnal instantiation of the trope by which western metaphysicians . . . have . . . rendered the problematic of God, Universe, and Nature" (387–88).

63. To Marcet Haldeman, February 28, 1908; *SL* 38; to family March 18, 1908, RML VI:14:04.

64. Correspondence with Linda Leavell July 3 and October 10, 2003: Laura Benet calls Moore "Gillespie" after the hero of a ballad they liked; Moore called

Laura "Froggy." Moore also takes ungendered nicknames: with Bryher she is (Ptera)dactyl (*SL* 142), and with Katherine Jones and Marcia Chamberlain she is Baby Moore (RML V:31:05).

65. As I discuss in "Marianne Moore's Black Maternal Hero," *American Literary History,* (1989): 786–815, "we" are not all white either in Moore's poem.

66. Glenn 66, 63, 74. Eva Tanguay, the highest salaried actress of the early twentieth century, made her career playing off the cult of beauty, in part to reveal its artificiality. Like Moore, Tanguay "honed an image of gleeful eccentricity" (64). Sandra Gilbert remarks on Moore's comically unattractive self-portrayal in "Costumes of the Mind: Transvestism as Metaphor in Modern Literature," *Critical Inquiry* 7 (1980): 391–417.

67. H.D.'s "The Garden" also promotes full bloom rather than early-picked perfection, but Moore's poem makes this a matter of women's own choice: they can prevent themselves from being picked.

68. Moore writes her family on November 5, 1905, that her physician "is very much opposed to college for women for she thinks they are not strong enough and that there's too much strain. I took great satisfaction therefore in giving her the statistics in regard to the Freshman class's health" (RML VI:11a:11).

69. Randall Jarrell, "Her Shield," *Poetry and the Age* (New York: Knopf 1953), 166–81; 178.

70. DuPlessis comments that all Moore's early reviews "evince admiration for [the] erasure of gender binaries" (*Genders* 44); "Moore equalizes the genders while rejecting both" (51).

71. Victoria Bazin, "Marianne Moore, Kenneth Burke, and the Poetics of Literary Labour," *Journal of American Studies* 35.3 (2001): 433–52; 439.

72. As Bazin, "Moore, Kenneth Burke," points out, Burke and Moore corresponded frequently about history and social change during the 1930s. See also Moore's letters to Morton Zabel and Ronald Lane Latimer.

73. Robin Gail Schulze, *The Web of Friendship: Marianne Moore and Wallace Stevens* (Ann Arbor: University of Michigan Press, 1995), 97. Moore complained that "artists of her time seemed determined to avoid civic duties even while supposedly concerned with the state of the world," although she also felt she should do more (66).

74. I am grateful to Bazin for this connection; conversation July 8, 2002.

75. Bloch 5, 16. I know of no evidence that Moore knew Bloch's writing.

76. See "'What Is War For?' Moore's Development of an Ethical Poetry," *Critics and Poets on Marianne Moore: "A right good salvo of barks,"* ed. Linda Leavell, Cristanne Miller, and Robin Gail Schulze (Lewisburg, Pa.: Bucknell University Press, 2005).

77. Letters from Sally and Sina Grosshut begin "lieber Jussuf, liebe Tino" or "Liebe Tino-Jussuf!" (JNUL 5:129).

78. See November 30, 1931, to Hulda Pankok; December 18, 1932, to Ina Seidel; and October 4, 1933, to Heinrich Zimmer (DLA). On December 29, 1930, Carl Gebhart addresses the poet "Lieber blauer Jaguar" and on June 12, 1944, Paul Goldscheider changes the leopard's gender: "Liebe verehrte blaue Jaguarin" (JNUL 5:118).

79. To Elsa Asenijeff, a novelist and poet, Lasker-Schüler writes "You are a princess . . . I am a prince, Else. / Onit" (*Br* II 307); and August 21, 1933, to Heinrich Zimmer (DLA).

80. "ich mußte in seiner Begleitung stets keck und burschikos gekleidet

gehen. Die Füße in hohen Tresenstiefeln, und eine Knabenmütze gescheitelten, kurzgeschnittenen Haaren" (*WB* 5:79); "In his company I had to go dressed boyishly. Feet in high bar-boots and a boy's cap with parted short hair."

81. Markus Hallensleben compares *Die Nächte Tino* to work by Stein, Gabriel García Marquez, and Antonin Artaud, as well as pointing out similarities between this text and Expressionist drama—Oskar Kokoschka's *Murder, Hope of Women* (1910) and Franz Wedekind's *Pandora's Box* (1904)—with its excessive libidinal energy (54–56).

82. "die einzige männliche Erscheinung der heutigen deutschen Literatur" in Ernst Ginsberg, ed., *Else Lasker-Schüler: Dichtungen und Dokumente* (Munich: Kösel Verlag, 1951) 578; "die einzige nennenswerte Dichterin, die unter dem Einfluß des männlich 'Sublimen' steht" from *Geschichte der deutschen Literatur;* "strebt . . . ebenbürtig mit den ernsthaftesten männlichen Dichtern, nach einer großen, edlen Kunst" from *Deutsche Literaturgeschichte;* the latter two citations are quoted in Hedgepeth 83; see also 86–88.

83. "Ich bin gar keine Frau / wie die anderen" (*Br* I 135) to Hanns Hirt ca. 1915–17.

84. "Allzu männlich, allzu jünglinghaft die ganze Reihe, Werfel, Hasenclever, Ehrenstein, Wolfenstein, Becher, selbst Klemm. . . . Sie haben alle Leiden in Aufruhr gekehrt, das feminine Element, das im Grunde den Lyriker ausmacht, das Objektsein überwunden. Else Lasker-Schüler aber bleibt der einzige weibliche Lyriker von heute (nicht weil sie Weib ist, sondern trotzdem)"; from *Das Kunstblatt* (1919), quoted in Hedgepeth 86–87.

85. JNUL, "Tagebuchzeilen aus Zürich," 2:28, p. 19: "Der wahrer Dichter, lieber Leser, pflegt sich zu spalten. . . . Der Dichter in Urmensch zweiteiligen Zustand versetzt. . . . Adam und Eva waren ein Mensch in der Urstunde auf der heiligen Urkunde verzeichnet. Ihr Gemüt erlebe alle Dinge und Undinge verdoppelt und erst nach dem Sünderfalle schritten sie getrennt, von einander abgelöst." In *Bid Me to Live* H.D. makes the same claim indirectly, when the author-figure Julia Ashton calls the female artist a "man-woman" and male artist a "woman-man"; Diana Collecott, *H.D. and Sapphic Modernism, 1910–1950* (Cambridge: Cambridge University Press, 1999), 98.

86. On this topic, see Schulte 96–97.

87. As Christine Reiß-Suckow notes, there is no evidence that Lasker-Schüler gave Walden his name, but the claim is widely accepted (118). Thoreau's *Walden* (translated into German in 1898) was something of a cult book for German back-to-nature circles, including Die Neue Gemeinschaft, in which both Walden and Lasker-Schüler participated.

88. "Ich nannte sie den adeligen Strassenjungen. / Schelm der Russenstadt" (*WB,* no. 219).

89. Bauschinger also gives examples of places in her work where Lasker-Schüler plays with the grammatical gender of nouns and broken syntax (*WZ* 75–77, 110–12, 183–84).

90. "Keinen Glauben hab' ich mehr an Weib und Mann . . . Lernte meinen Leib, mein Herzblut und ihn hassen, / Nie so das Evablut kennen / Wie in Dir, Mann!" In a 1917 revision, the poet leaves out the line about not believing in "Woman and Man" and the last three lines of the poem.

91. Mary-Elizabeth O'Brien ("'Ich war verkleidet als Poet . . . ich bin Poetin!' The Masquerade of Gender in Else Lasker-Schüler's Work," *German Quarterly* 65 [1992]: 1–17) reads this and other poems where the speaker blends herself with a lover as evidence that for Lasker-Schüler the fulfillment of female

desire threatens the ego (4). Like Liska, I instead read such blendings as indicating her rejection of gender polarities.

92. *WB,* no. 182: "dein Angesicht ist mein Palmengarten. . . . In deinem Angesicht sind verzaubert / Alle die Bilder meines Blutes."

93. "Abels Angesicht ist ein goldener Garten, / Abels Augen sind Nachtigallen. . . . Aber durch Kains Leib führen die Gräben der Stadt."

94. In "An den Prinzen Benjamin," originally titled "Senna Hoy": "Wenn du sprichst, / Wacht mein buntes Herz auf. . . . Immerblau streut deine Stimme / Über den Weg."

95. "an deinem Herzen lauschen, / Mit deiner fernsten Nähe mich vertauschen"; "O, du Gottjüngling. / Du Dichter, / Ich trinke einsam von deinen Düften. // Mein erste Blüte Blut sehnte sich nach dir."

96. "Leise schwimmt der Mond durch mein Blut . . . / Schlummernde Töne sind die Augen des Tages" and "Ich kann deine Lippen nicht finden . . . / Wo bist du ferne Stadt / Mit den segnenden Düften?"

97. "Ich mich teilte in zwei Hälften kurz vor Tageslichte, / In zwei Teile: IchundIch!" (*WB* 2:188).

98. "Jedes wahre Gebet ist eine Konzentration . . . Ich und Ich. Und aus dieser Selbstverbindung entsteht doppelte Kraft" (*WB* 4.1: 215); *Concert* 162. Ellipses Lasker-Schüler's.

99. "Ich spreche überhaupt nicht mehr ohne Bezahlung, nur Bindewörter; könnt ich doch eins finden, das mich binden würde" (*WB* 3.1:235).

100. Meike Ningel, "Die Unzugänglichkeit des Eigenen: Zur Logic von Else Lasker-Schülers Umgang mit Sprache," *Die Fremdheit der Sprache. Studien zur Literatur der Moderne,* ed. Jochen C. Schütze, Hans-Ulrich Treichel, and Dietmar Voss, *Literatur im historischen Prozeß* 23 (1988): 103–16; "Ihre Maskeraden zeugen vom Bewußtsein, daß, wie Nietzsche bemerkte, jedes Wort eine Maske ist, und auch das 'Ich' nur eine, die andere verbirgt, von denen die ursprüngliche, die wiederum nur die Signatur der Uneigentlichkeit tragen könnte, nie aufzufinden ist" (111).

101. JNUL, "Tagebuchzeilen aus Zürich," 2:28, p. 19: "des Dichters Dichtung entspringt seinem tiefinnerlichsten uralten ewigen Gemüts der Doppel-Liebe seiner Seele."

CHAPTER FOUR

De Certeau, Girard, and Mayol 16; J. C. Flügel, *The Psychology of Clothes* (London: Hogarth Press, 1930), 15, 16; Moore conversation notebook, 1921–28, January 11, 1921 (RML VII.03.10).

1. George Chauncey, *Gay New York: Gender, Urban Culture, and the Making of the Gay Male World, 1890–1940* (New York: Basic Books, 1994), 13, 47–49.

2. Behling 4. The situation was much the same in Germany (Frame 19–20); see also Maude Lavin, *Cut with the Kitchen Knife: The Weimar Photomontages of Hannah Höch* (New Haven: Yale University Press, 1993), 185–204.

3. Although the connection of woman with the body is ancient, Alex Goody argues that by the late-nineteenth-century artists and writers associated certain constructions of beauty with particular aesthetics and politics; "Ladies of Fashion / Modern(ist) Women: Mina Loy and Djuna Barnes," *Women* 10.1 (1999): 266–82; 267.

4. Skirts reached their shortest around 1925. See Prudence Glynn, *In Fashion: Dress in the Twentieth Century* (London: George Allen and Unwin, 1978).

5. Sabine Hake, "In the Mirror of Fashion," in von Ankum 193. The

National Socialists associated international fashion with a conspiracy of French designers and Jewish control of the garment industry.

6. Like her daughter, Mary Warner Moore kept notebooks. This February 15, 1931, entry refers to a review of Flügel's book in the *Spectator*. There is no evidence that Moore read the review, but her mother would probably have shared the quoted line with her.

7. While Moore here copies someone else's words, she states in a January 18, 1935, draft of a letter to Bryher that everything in her notebooks is "in some way an expression of myself" (VII:03:11). Certainly the length and frequency of her notes on clothes suggest an intense interest.

8. Men were also gendered through their performance of identity in clothing. As Amelia Jones writes, "Clothing makes the body of the male artist both visible (allowing it to signify) and invisible (rendering it in the naturalized and so seemingly transparent codes of masculine genius)." "'Clothes Make the Man': The Male Artist as a Performative Function," *Oxford Art Journal* 18.2 (1995): 18–32; 19. In "The Stieglitz Circle Retraced," Robin Kelsey claims that in the Stieglitz group all painters were seen as embodied in their art; *Modernism/Modernity* 9.1 (2002): 177–84; 179.

9. Quoted in Hake 198.

10. Siegfried Kracauer, *The Salaried Masses: Duty and Distraction in Weimar Germany*, trans. Quintin Hoare (London: Verso, 1998), 38–39.

11. Leigh Gilmore 132.

12. Summarized by Butler, "Performativity's Social Magic" 115, 117.

13. Gilbert and Gubar, *Letters from the Front* 65, 66.

14. Jarrell 142.

15. Eliot, *The Waste Land: A Facsimile and Transcript of the Original Drafts Including the Annotations of Ezra Pound*, ed. Valerie Eliot (London: Faber, 1971), 26–27.

16. Maxwell Bodenheim, "The Decorative Straight-Jacket: Rhymed Verse," *Little Review*, December 1914, 22–23.

17. Quoted in Gilbert and Gubar, "Tradition and the Female Talent," *The Poetics of Gender*, ed. Nancy Miller (New York: Columbia University Press, 1986), 183–207; 200–201.

18. Nathanael West, *Miss Lonelyhearts* (London: Grey Walls Press, 1949), 47–48.

19. Robert McAlmon, *A Hasty Bunch: Short Stories* (Carbondale: Southern Illinois University Press, 1975), 275; *Post-Adolescence* (Paris: Contact Editions, 1923), 94.

20. In Hedgepeth 80; Remer's "Neue Frauendichtung" refers to the "hüllenlose Nacktheit der Seele und Sinne" in contrast to any who "hat wieder Schleier und Scham gefunden"; Klaiber writes, "Dichterinnen die sich in einer überhitzten Geschlechtlichkeit und mänadenhaften Perversität gefallen."

21. According to Svetlana Boym, the Russian avant-garde also saw the "poetess" as "a grotesque conglomeration of *lack* and *excess*"; *Death in Quotation Marks: Cultural Myths of the Modern Poet* (Cambridge: Harvard University Press, 1991), 194. Reviews of Tsvetaeva's work meshed response to the writing and body or dress of the poet (200–219).

22. Comments like these locate Flügel in the sexual politics of the late 1920s. Curt Moreck, author of the 1925 *Das Weib in der Kunst der neueren Zeit*, puts this even more strongly: "When the modern woman . . . strives fanatically toward equality with the man and uses the means of fashion to demonstrate

her masculinization by suppressing the female and imitating the male secondary sexual characteristics, the sexual instinct is bound to be irritated and enter the dangerous field of perversion"; clothing stimulated the "pathology" of the female body (quoted in Hake 195).

23. Bridget Elliott, "Performing the Picture or Painting the Other: Romaine Brooks, Gluck, and the Question of Decadence in 1923," in Deepwell 70–82; and Elliott and Wallace 51–53. See also Marjorie Garber's classic *Vested Interests and Cultural Anxiety* (New York: Routledge, 1992). Like Moore, Stein adopts unfeminine but not male clothing (Benstock, *Left Bank* 177–78).

24. Susan Fillin-Yeh, "Dandies, Marginality, and Modernism: Georgia O'Keeffe, Marcel Duchamp, and Other Cross-dressers," *Oxford Art Journal* 18:2 (1995): 33–44; 34, 35.

25. Chauncey 124. Similarly, in *Berlins Drittes Geschlecht: Schwule und Lesben um 1900,* 1904 (Berlin: Verlag Rosa Winkel, 1991), Magnus Hirschfeld asserts the frequency with which otherwise non-"inverted" men and women cross-dress, as does Curt Moreck in *Führer durch das "lasterhafte" Berlin,* 1931 (Berlin: Nicolaische Verlagsbuchhandlung, Beuermann, 1996).

26. According to Fillin-Yeh, Ewing posed for the hands (33).

27. Benstock asserts that efforts to invert patriarchy through cross-dressing inevitably failed, and that cross-dressers "could only proclaim themselves misfits" (*Left Bank* 469n; 180–81). Yet the vast range of female experimentation with dress, including transvestism, suggests to me that women experienced a pleasurably transgressive sense of loosening boundaries of culturally mandated femininity through self-fashioning. On the other hand, Benstock's critique of Gilbert and Gubar's liberatory readings of transvestism is useful. Miriam Hansen writes that *Hosenrolle* films dramatized women's "precarious social and economic status in terms of the patriarchal dilemma: women's access to the world of power, action, and wealth is gained either through a husband or transvestite clothing"; "Early Silent Cinema," *New German Critique* 29 (1983): 147–84; 184. According to James W. Jones, in fiction representing homosexuality in Germany, women frequently cross-dress and men do not; *"We of the Third Sex": Literary Representations of Homosexuality in Wilhelmine Germany* (Frankfurt am Main: Peter Lang, 1990), 297–98.

28. In the 1860s, Karl Ulrichs was the first openly "inverted" man to write on what he called the *Urning*—a being with a woman's spirit in a man's body; Leila J. Rupp, *A Desired Past: A Short History of Same-Sex Love in America* (Chicago: University of Chicago Press, 1999), 80.

29. See James W. Jones 2. Matti Bunzl's review essay "Sexual Modernity as Subject and Object" summarizes the history of sexology, with particular attention to Krafft-Ebing and the Viennese psychologists; *Modernism/Modernity* 9.1 (2002): 166–75.

30. In satirical response to Weininger, Ford Maddox Hueffer writes in "Men and Women" that around 1906, "in the men's clubs of England and in the cafés of France and Germany" one heard mutterings that "a new gospel had appeared" and it "spread through the serious male society of England as if it had been an epidemic"; *Little Review,* January 1918, 40, 42.

31. Otto Weininger, *Geschlecht und Charakter* (1903; reprinted, Munich: Matthes and Seitz, 1980), 217, 219.

32. Bunzl also makes the point that several early sexologists were Jewish: Ulrichs, Hirschfeld, Weininger, Freud, Karl Maria Kertbeny, Benedict Friedländer, Carl von Westphal, Albert Moll, and Havelock Ellis (172).

33. In Wright 590; according to Jacques LeRider, without the eager support of Kraus, Weininger's book would never have become the classic it did among the German-language avant-garde (114, 263). LeRider also mentions Kafka's enthusiasm for Weininger (91–92), and Kraus's support for homosexuality (262–64).

34. Richard Dyer, "Less and More than Women and Men: Lesbian and Gay Cinema in Weimar Germany," *New German Critique* 51 (fall 1990): 5–60; 24.

35. Quoted in Gay 129.

36. The film was a collaboration between Richard Oswald and Hirschfeld (*Other Than the Others [Anders als die Andern]*; Meskimmon 200. Dyer describes German films and fiction with homosexual content produced from 1910 to 1940. Moore admired the homoerotic *Mädchen in Uniform* (1931); and in *A Victorian in the Modern World* (New York: Harcourt, Brace, 1939), Hutchins Hapgood admires Berlin's progressive openness toward "sexual variations" (455).

37. According to James W. Jones, Hirschfeld played "the central role in the discussion about homosexuality which took place . . . throughout German (and European) society . . . through the early 1930s" (62); by 1903, he was so influential that theorists—including Weininger and Freud—felt they had to take a stand for or against his theory of natural homosexuality (63). In 1896, Hirschfeld published *Sappho und Sokrates;* in 1903 he conducted the first survey on male sexuality: of the 1696 Technische Hochschule students surveyed, 1.5 percent declared themselves homosexual and 4.5 bisexual; Manfred Baumgardt, "Die Homosexuellen-Bewegung bis zum Ende des Ersten Weltkrieges," *Eldorado: Homosexuelle Frauen und Männer in Berlin 1850–1950* (Berlin: Verlag rosa Winkel, 1992), 17–27; 20. His 1910 *The Transvestites: An Investigation of the Erotic Desire to Cross Dress* initiated the modern study of transgenderism, and in 1919, he founded the first institute dedicated to ending legal and social intolerance of gays. Americans were inspired by Hirschfeld to attempt to make gay life more open in New York (Chauncey 107, 144).

38. Moreck's *Führer* also argues that homosexuality is "natural": everyone seeks that love "for which nature has made them. If it isn't the right love, what can they do about it? . . . Nature does not make mistakes; she is wiser than we" (162).

39. According to Chauncey, there was a lively working-class gay subculture earlier than among professional men and artists.

40. Williams's poem "Transitional" is quoted in DuPlessis, *Genders* 31.

41. DuPlessis, *Genders* 32–33. See Steinman; Suzanne Clark's *Sentimental Modernism: Women Writers and the Revolution of the Word* (Bloomington: Indiana University Press, 1991) analyzes the attempt to masculinize modernism through rejection of "feminine" sentimentality.

42. Elliott and Wallace 51; Meskimmon 202; according to James W. Jones, lesbians were largely ignored by early literature on sexology (77). In "'The Cult of the Clitoris': Anatomy of a National Scandal," Jodie Mead argues that male homosexuality became a topic in Britain during Oscar Wilde's trial in 1895 but lesbianism did not until around 1918; *Modernism/Modernity* 9.1 (2002): 21–50; 24.

43. Chauncey 27; bourgeois women also do not begin to cross dress in any numbers until the late nineteenth century (Elliott and Wallace 53).

44. Also see Dyer on Berlin's lesbian journals *Die Freundin* and *Die Garçonne.* Aimée Duc's 1903 novel *Sind es Frauen (Are They Women?)* questioned whether inverted women constituted a third sex (Dyer 43, 45). Duc also edited

Berliner Modekorrespondenz and *Draisena, Blätter für Damenfahren* (James W. Jones, 146ff.).

45. According to Ina Schabert, comparable opportunities for female homosocial bonding are still unusual today; "No Room of One's Own: Women's Studies in English Departments in Germany," *MLA* 119.1 (2004): 69–79.

46. Kracauer refers to such women as "salaried bohemians" and says the type is common in Berlin: "girls who come to the big city in search of adventure and roam like comets through the world of salaried employees . . . even the best astronomer cannot determine whether they will end up on the street or in the marriage bed" (73).

47. This porousness continued through the middle of the century in some rural areas of the United States. For example, in Oklahoma during the early 1940s, my mother and her college roommate shared a bed. Other college women also rented rooms in town with one bed—practice evidently considered standard. In a review of Laura Doan's *Fashioning Sapphism: The Origins of a Modern English Lesbian Culture* (2001), Anne Herrmann states that in England sexual interpretive possibilities for women were also largely in flux until the 1928 trial of Hall's *The Well of Loneliness; Modernism/Modernity* 8.3 (2001): 530. The classic study of homosociality is Eve Kosofsky Sedgwick's *Between Men: English Literature and Male Homosocial Desire* (New York: Columbia University Press, 1985).

48. Nina Miller, *Making Love Modern: The Intimate Public Worlds of New York's Literary Women* (New York: Oxford University Press, 1999). Behling describes popular alarm about masculine women and inversion similarly to Miller.

49. Adrienne Rich, "Compulsory Heterosexuality and Lesbian Existence," *Blood, Bread, and Poetry: Selected Prose, 1979–1985* (New York: W. W. Norton, 1986), 51. Historians also provide conflicting accounts of women's colleges. Lilian Faderman sees women's colleges as fostering lifelong patterns of intense emotional engagement among women; Behling argues that colleges were under attack by the medical profession, sexologists, and popular media, and that college women themselves acknowledged homoerotic feelings to be temporary. In 1902, Havelock Ellis calls women's colleges "the great breeding ground" of female inversion (Behling 178, 187).

50. This is the primary argument of Hanscombe and Smyers; Katherine Mansfield gave enormous attention and encouragement to her husband but depended for such support on Ida Baker, whom she called her "wife" (245).

51. Lyon 382.

52. Women who lived in heterosexual relationships include Taggard, Alice Corbin Henderson, Georgia O'Keeffe, Edith Wharton, Dorothy Parker, and Katherine Ann Porter—although many of these relationships were unconventional or short-lived.

53. According to Hubert, the European avant-garde was more adamantly heterosexual than were the looser groupings of modernism. There was a "scarcity of gay and lesbian partnerships" in French Surrealism, and a "similar absence of homosexuals also characterized the even more revolutionary, but perhaps more sexist, Dadaist movement, to which so many Surrealists, including Breton and several members of his team, had belonged" (1).

54. See Meskimmon 181–83, 205–7, 216–18, 220–21.

55. See Höch's *Cut with the Kitchen Knife Dada through the Last Weimar Beer*

Belly Cultural Epoch of Germany (1919–20), *The Father*, 1920, *Love in the Bush* or *Tamer*, 1930, in Lavin.

56. Alfred Kreymborg, *Troubadour: An Autobiography* (New York: Boni and Liveright, 1925), 238–39.

57. Gilbert and Gubar, *Letters from the Front* 70.

58. Victoria Bazin, "Marianne Moore and the Arcadian Pleasures of Shopping," *Women* 12.2 (2001): 218–35; 236. William Carlos Williams, *Autobiography* (New York: Random House, 1951), 146. For quotations below see my *Questions of Authority* (19–21) and (for Blackmur) Bazin 218. As Bazin states, Moore was fetishized as exemplifying modernist resistance to capital and ideological immunity, "hermetically sealed off from its historical moment" (227).

59. Gaston Lachaise sculpts the poet's head in 1925. Loy draws more famous portraits of Joyce, Van Vechten, Stein, Marinetti, and Papini (*LLB82* xxiv).

60. Patricia C. Willis, "Images of Marianne," *Marianne Moore Newsletter* 3.2 (fall 1979): 22.

61. This sitting with Ulmann included Alyse Gregory, and several photos show the two women together, including one that shows them both as writers, sitting at a table with book and pen. Less typical are two late sketches made of Moore by her friend Hildegarde Watson, where the poet has shapely arms, an emphasized bust, and is presented with either sensually curving background trees (1962) or sensual patterns on a placket of her dress (1956; RML XII:12:27).

62. Stacy Hubbard discusses Moore's self-fashioning in photographs in "Mannerist Moore: Poetry, Painting, Photography," in Leavell et al.

63. Bonnie Costello, *Marianne Moore: Imaginary Possessions* (Cambridge: Harvard University Press, 1981), 246; see also Cynthia Hogue, "Another Postmodernism: Towards an Ethical Poetics," *How2* 1.7 (spring 2002): 6, www.departments/bucknell/edu/stadler_center/how2.

64. Molesworth (435–38) reviews Moore's essays on fashion. Stein was similarly interested in the "rhetoric of clothing" and published an article in *Vogue* about her favorite designer (Benstock, *Left Bank* 183).

65. Burke states that Moore had Loy in mind when writing this poem, but there is no hard evidence for this claim (*BM* 293). For readings of the poem, see Du Plessis, "Corpses of Poesy"; Heuving; Sabine Sielke, *Fashioning the Female Subject: The Intertextual Networking of Dickinson, Moore, and Rich* (Ann Arbor: University of Michigan Press, 1997); and my *Questions of Authority*.

66. According to Smith-Rosenberg, between 1870 and 1920, 40 to 60 percent of women who attended women's colleges did not marry (253).

67. The relation of Moore's life and poetics to queer theory has just begun to be explored. See John Emil Vincent, *Queer Lyrics (Difficulty and Closure in American Poetry)* (New York: Palgrave Macmillan, 2002); and Linda Leavell, "Marianne Moore, the James Family, and the Politics of Celibacy," *Twentieth-Century Literature* 49.2 (summer 2003): 219–45.

68. In *Scheming Women: Poetry, Privilege, and the Politics of Subjectivity* (Albany: SUNY Press, 1995), 79, Hogue links this description of Moore's poetic with her "transvestite" dress style and rejection of naturalness; the speaker "linguistically masquerades in the masculine position. Through such miming, she exposes the exploitation of the feminine in the symbolic order" (88).

69. In a reading notebook of 1921–22 Moore includes notes on a 1922 review by Horace Kallen that calls Freudianism largely "absurd" and on a 1922 essay by Maxwell Bodenheim in the *Nation:* "In this country, psychoanal. has

been widely accepted by critics & creators who were longing for a diagrammed excuse for their sensual admirations. . . . & it really grieves one to challenge this frank mirage created by Freud, Carpenter, Havelock Ellis, Weininger, [?], Krafft-Ebing & all the rest of those men who have been so eagerly seeking a scientific halo for the monotone of flesh. . . . I do not claim that they have not shrewdly penetrated & classified many of the causes & details of sex. I am simply attacking their contention that sex forms the whole of man's physical & intangible content. Man contains a far more plaintive interior than a sexologist dares to admit, & this mental & emotional sadness & confusion could not possibly spring fr[om] sexual longing alone" (RML VII:01:03).

70. In a 1964 interview, Moore describes her tennis playing, from childhood through her late sixties (*CPr* 681–88). Her enthusiasm for baseball and prizefighting is well known.

71. Bazin similarly argues that Moore's delight in display and consumption, and the sensuous immoderation of her language, contradict perceptions of her as chaste or unembodied ("Arcadian Pleasures" 228).

72. Kathryn R. Kent writes similarly that "Moore bases her poetics on a singular, queer, autoerotics of incorporation, what for her is an aggressive and appropriative, yet simultaneously dispersed and decentered, form of identification," asserting a "self-legitimating vision of poetic and queer power"; *Making Girls into Women: American Women's Writing and the Rise of Lesbian Identity* (Durham: Duke University Press, 2003), 209.

73. Marjorie Perloff, "English as a 'Second' Language," *MLWP* 134.

74. Susan E. Dunn, "Mina Loy, Fashion, and the Avant-Garde," *MLWP* 443–55; 443.

75. Dunn dates this photograph as probably taken in late 1917 and not developed or printed until 1918 or 1920.

76. Carolyn Burke, "'Accidental Aloofness': Barnes, Loy, and Modernism," *Silence and Power: A Reevaluation of Djuna Barnes*, ed. Mary Lynn Broe (Carbondale: Southern Illinois University Press, 1991), 67–79; 75.

77. Loy sold dress designs and modeled while in New York in 1917 (*LLB82* lvi); she also designed hats, theater sets, magazine covers, and jewelry.

78. Loy's designs were published in a range of magazines, from *Rogue* to *Playboy* (Dunne 446–47). Dunne compares Loy to the 1930s designers Sonia Delaunay and Elsa Schiaparelli; Loy also exhibited in Futurist shows in London and Italy with Russian Constructivist designers Luibov Popova and Alexandra Exter (446, 448).

79. Roberts describes Poiret as "wag[ing] war upon" the corset in his designs, using simple lines and fabric with modernist prints; his and Coco Chanel's clothes were a "visual fantasy of liberty" (666, 683).

80. Rita Felski, *The Gender of Modernity* (Cambridge: Harvard University Press, 1995) alludes to the rhetoric of decadence, in a discussion of aesthetes and dandies (95).

81. My reading is indebted to Shreiber's "'Love is a Lyric.'"

82. DuPlessis notes that of the poem's thirty-four sections, fourteen are "arguably centered on different occasions of acts of sexual intercourse, or may be said prominently to mention sex"—amounting to about 40 percent of the poem (*Genders* 53).

83. In *LLB82* xxxvii, and Kinnahan 53; from Kreymborg's 1929 *Our Singing Strength*.

84. Loy's poem may respond to a painting of Cunard hung "facing" portraits of George Moore and Princess Murat; Cunard was the subject of portraits by Ray, Wyndham Lewis, Cecil Beaton, Oscar Kokoschka, John Bannery, and Constantin Brancusi (Conover, *LLB* 205–6).

85. Burke quotes Loy as saying, "I was trying to make a foreign language because English had already been used"; later, however, Burke reports her comment that it "was a relief to find herself 'free to use a little plain English'" (*BM* 361).

86. In *That Kind of Woman,* ed. Bronte Adams and Trudi Tate (New York: Carroll and Graf, 1991), 42.

87. Conover also comments that the two sets of qualities ascribed to Loy by her peers—seductive beauty and charm plus distance and indifference—fit the "Femme Fatale Complex" attributed to media stars like Greta Garbo, with whom Loy was compared (*LLB82* xxxii).

88. Whitman was translated into German in 1868 and was popular among the avant-garde by the 1890s. Lasker-Schüler would have known of his work. See Grimm and Schmidt 69–78; and Walter Grünzweig, *Constructing the German Walt Whitman* (Iowa City: University of Iowa Press, 1995).

89. "Weite hosen, silberne Schuhe, eine Art weite Jacke, die Haare wie Seide, tiefschwarz, wild zuweilen, dann wieder sinnlich sanft. . . . Jussuf war so ganz Weib, sie war so schön . . ."; Wieland Herzfelde, "Else Lasker-Schüler: Begegnungen mit der Dichterin und Ihrem Werk," *Sinn und Form* 21.6 (1969): 1294–1325; 1307.

90. Quoted in Schulte 87: "Ihr Gesicht ist von einer orientalischen Sinnlichkeit, ihr Körper hat etwas Schlangenhaftes."

91. Quoted in U. Müller 68: "nicht der mindeste weibliche erotische Reiz ausging. Man empfand diese Wesen mit dem knabenhafte Körper . . . als geschlechtlos"; "Dazu kam, daß der kümmerliche Körper dieses armseligen Hascherls durch die Dämonie sexueller Abirrungen Folterqualen ausgeliefert war."

92. Quoted in Hallensleben 21–22: "Der Nebel des Symbolismus und Mystizismus und eine starke Sinnenlust flattern wirrdurch die Verszeilen. Der Hang zum Absonderlichen, Unnatülichen, ja Häßlichen wird die meisten abgestoßen haben." Benjamin quoted in *WZ* 124–25, 230, 324. Kafka had no patience for any bohemians and also criticized Lasker-Schüler, but attended at least one lecture on her poetry (*MM* 102, 125, 106).

93. *MM* 93. The *Marbacher Magazin* is the best source of photographs and images of the poet.

94. Least realistic is Rudolf Großmann's drawing of Lasker-Schüler as a stylized bug with human face, lying in the desert at sunset, accompanying Franz Blei's verbal portrait of the poet as a beetle in his *Bestiarium* (1922; *MM* 168). Emil Stumpp also painted Lasker-Schüler's portrait.

95. Reprinted in *Franz Marc–Else Lasker-Schüler: "Der Blaue Reiter präsentiert Eurer Hoheit sein Blaues Pferd": Karten und Briefe,* ed. Peter-Klaus Schuster (Prestel Verlag, 1987), fig. 3. Schuster reads the nude as Marc's response to Lasker-Schüler's poor health and depression.

96. Hallensleben speculates that the occasion for this Becker and Maas photograph was the poet's plan for a theatrical variety show, starring the "Arabian poet in Fakir dress," although she also describes the photo as her "boybild" (43, 46).

97. Richard Wagner initiated the policy of darkening a theater for performance, hence Lasker-Schüler's darkened room would still have been considered unconventional (Hallensleben 25).

98. "gleich gehe ich zum *Indianerfest*. . . . Mein Nägel sind met Hena gefärbt und meine Stirne habe ich *tätowiert* voll von Sternen. Rote Jacke Sammt, weißes Hemd, schwarze Hose mit Indianerfransen. 5 wilde Ketten, Federgurt, Federarmringe, Fußfederring." The poet indulges in repeated fantasy in letters to Bithell, so it is possible she never wore this costume.

99. Kaplan describes the self-discipline campaign from 1915 into the 1930s, encouraging "simplicity" in the appearance of women so they would not call attention to themselves (201).

100. "Else Lasker-Schüler als Prinz von Theben in Pluderhosen, Turban und mit langem schwarzen Haar, mit einer Zigarette in langer Spitze" (Schulte 87).

101. Ida Dehmel loved to dress in Asian clothing—although always feminine; Moreck describes clubs named Olala, Eldorado, and Monbijou, and a popular term for inverted women was Sapphists; one club advertised "Sapphic nights"; another decorated with Chinese lanterns on women-only nights (165). Graphics and advertisements in *Die Freundin* often featured orientalism. Reformer for gay rights Magnus Hirschfeld wrote the poet when both were in exile (JNUL Arc var 501; illegible). In 1919, the poet was condemned in Lucerne as a Communist sympathizer and for her association with Hirschfeld (*MM* 149); in 1939, she reminisces that Hirschfeld and Benn were both helpful in giving medical excuses to prevent people from being drafted (*MM* 294). That Hirschfeld was a political ally, if not also a personal friend, suggests at a minimum the poet's ease with gay politics.

102. Quoted in U. Müller 63: "Man konnte weder damals [1912] oder später mit ihr über die Straße gehen, ohne daß alle Welt stillstand und ihr nachsah: extravagante weite Röcke oder Hosen, unmögliche Obergewänder, Hals und Arme behängt mit auffallendem unechtem Schmuck, Ketten, Ohrringen. . . Dienstmädchenringe, immer in aller Blickpunkt."

103. Liska reviews criticism of the poet that sees the eroticism of early poems as disturbing and that presents her hostility to woman (37–38); Hedgepeth frequently repeats that Lasker-Schüler has no use for women or couldn't stand them (88, 130, 139).

104. She writes, for example, to both Franz and Maria Marc; Richard and both Paula and Ida Dehmel (continuing correspondence with Paula after her divorce from Richard, and with Ida after Richard's death), Paula and Martin Buber, Adele and Kurt Horwitz, Margarete and Leo Kestenberg, Kurt and Elisabeth Wolff, Grete and Leopold Krakauer, and Felix and Else Pinkus. She remains in contact with several childhood friends, especially Elvira Bachrach—whose daughter Charlotte, a dancer, also became a friend. The poet asks Elisabeth Wolff to influence her husband to publish a book by Herzfelde. In another instance, a business connection with Karl Ernst Osthaus leads to friendship with his wife Gertrud (Schulte 91–92).

105. "Ja, du bist die einzige wahre lebende Prinzessin im Lande und gleichst / meinen Schwestern darum liebe ich / dich" (U. Müller 148 n. 340).

106. "Meinen verlassenen Gespielinnen und treuen Freunde: / Elfrieda und Hedwig euch beiden Nachtigallen / Mariaquita und Wally und Elisabeth und Kete und Enja / und Margarete ich gedenke Eurer in Sehnsucht" (JNUL ms. 2.8).

107. Samuel Lublinksi, *Die Bilanz der Moderne* (Berlin: Siegfried Cronbach, 1904), 166–67.

108. There is no evidence that the two poets had an affair; Bauschinger suggests that Lasker-Schüler regarded being in love as an aspect of her playful relationship with the world: she was "in love with" Benn as poet (*WZ* 132–33). See also Hallensleben on the constructedness of this relationship.

109. "Spielprinz" is a coined word suggesting both playmate and musician or minstrel *(Spielmann)*. The lines quoted are "Sitz drauf wie auf einem Giebel. // Und in deines Kinnes Grube / Bau ich mir ein Raubnest— / Bis du much aufgefressen hast" (*WB*, no. 208).

110. "Ich trag dich immer herum / Zwischen meinen Zähnen . . . Ich kann nicht mehr sein / Ohne das Scalpspiel. // Rote Küsse malen deine Messer / Auf meine Brust—// Bis mein Haar an deinem Gürtel flatter" (*WB*, no. 198).

111. *WB*, no. 179. Lasker-Schüler's corrects "mein Herz" to read "dein Herz" (l. 17) in every version after the first printing of the poem (*WB* 1.2, no. 179).

112. "Ich raube in den Nächten / Die Rosen deines Mundes, / Daß keine Weibin Trinken findet."

113. "Ich glaube, wenn ich ein Mann wäre, wäre ich homosexuell" (*MM* 355); Werner Kraft interprets this pronouncement to be proof of the poet's "special play of heterosexuality"; *Else Lasker-Schüler: Eine Einführung in ihr Werk und eine Auswahl* (Wiesbaden: Steiner, 1951).

114. "In deinem goldenen Schoß . . . Dein goldenes Spielzeug sein"; "O, du meine goldene Nacht— / Goldsyrinxe. . . . . ." [*sic*]; "Ein Lied aus Gold" (*WB*, no. 408). Syrinx was an Arcadian river-nymph pursued by Pan. To escape him, she asked the gods to turn her into a reed; Pan then cut the reed into different lengths to make his pipes. In this poem the poet-speaker would seem to be in the position of Pan, and the poem is clearly a love song.

115. "Die Liebe zu Dir ist das Bildnis / Das man sich von Gott machen darf" (*WB*, no. 317).

116. "ich bin voll Traurigkeit. . . . . / Nimm mein Herz in deine Hände" ("Gebet," *WB*, no. 378; ellipses are Lasker-Schüler's).

117. "Nicht die tote Ruhe— / So ich liebe im Odem sein. . . . . ! / Auf Erden mit euch im Himmel schon" (*WB*, no. 373; ellipses are Lasker-Schüler's).

118. Loy's frequently repeated claim that her "conceptions of life evolved while . . . stirring baby food on spirit lamps—and my best drawings behind a stove to the accompaniment of a line of children's clothes hanging round it to dry" (*LLB82* lxvi) is misleading. Oda lived one year; Joella was not born until after Loy moved to Florence, where she had a cook and a nursemaid. Loy's conceptions of life may have developed during her year of motherhood in Paris, but after that point she had regular domestic help. Most letters of her years in Florence don't mention her children, let alone housework, and Burke's description of her life there gives scant evidence of Loy's involvement in the minutiae of mothering.

CHAPTER FIVE

Tsvetayeva, "Poem of the End" (1924), *Selected Poems*, trans. Elaine Feinstein (Oxford: Oxford University Press, 1971). H.D.'s "I Sing Democracy" is quoted in Celena E. Kusch, "How the West Was One: American Modernism's Song of Itself," *American Literature* 74.3 (2002): 517–38; 529.

1. Andrew Kappel, "Notes on the Presbyterian Poetry of Marianne Moore," *Marianne Moore: Woman and Poet*, ed. Patricia C. Willis (Orono, Maine: National Poetry Foundation, 1990), 39–51; 44. Kappel depicts Moore as a

"devout" believer, "crying in the wilderness" of a sinful world and writing a poetry of inner Calvinist "struggle as the means to salvation," thereby inventing "modern religious verse" (41, 45, 40).

2. See Leon Surette, *The Birth of Modernism: Ezra Pound, T. S. Eliot, W. B. Yeats, and the Occult* (Toronto: McGill-Queen's University Press, 1993); and Helen Sword, *Ghostwriting Modernism* (Ithaca, N.Y.: Cornell University Press, 2002).

3. Betterton makes this argument with reference to Käthe Kollwitz and Cornelia Pacczka Wagner in Germany and Mary Lowndes and Sylvia Pankhurst in England.

4. Rathenau, "Höre, Israel," *Die Zukunft* (1897), 454, in Ritchie Robertson, "'*Urheimat Asien*': The Re-orientation of German and Austrian Jews, 1900–1925," *German Life and Letters* 49.2 (1996): 182–92; 184. Sombart published *Die Juden und das Wirtschaftsleben* (*Jews and Modern Capitalism*) in 1911 (Paul Mendes-Flohr, "The Berlin Jew as Cosmopolitan," in Bilski 14–31;17–18).

5. Moritz Goldstein, "German-Jewish Parnassus," quoted in Mendes-Flohr, "The Berlin Jew" 20.

6. In *Raiding the Icebox: Reflections on Twentieth-Century Culture* (Bloomington: Indiana University Press, 1993), Peter Wollen explains that prewar Parisian enthusiasm for the "oriental" changed almost overnight into distrust: France became the standard bearer of classical reason and values, as opposed to "the wave of supposed unreason and irrationalist Kultur represented by Germany" (21). In *Légitime défense,* André Breton cites "a series of examples of anti-orientalist rhetoric of the day, which linked the spell of the East . . . to 'Germanism,' and more generally, to monstrosity, madness and hysteria" (Wollen 24).

7. Malini Johar Schueller, *U.S. Orientalisms: Race, Nation, and Gender in Literature, 1790–1890* (Ann Arbor: University of Michigan Press, 1998).

8. In Gottfried Benn, "Bekenntnis zum Expressionismus," *Expressionismus: Der Kampf um eine literarische Bewegung,* ed. Paul Raabe (Zurich: Arche Verlag, 1987), 235–46.

9. Jonathan Freedman, *The Temple of Culture: Assimilation and Anti-Semitism in Literary Anglo-America* (Oxford: Oxford University Press, 2000), 16.

10. James Longenbach, "Modern Poetry," *Cambridge Companion to Modernism,* ed. Michael Levenson (Cambridge: Cambridge University Press, 1999), 100–129; 102, 109. Longenbach falsely characterizes Moore, however, as desiring "to limit poetry's terrain" by depicting "a strategically circumscribed world" (103).

11. Mark S. Morrisson, *The Public Face of Modernism: Little Magazines, Audiences, and Reception, 1905–1920* (Madison: University of Wisconsin Press, 2001), 7, 6.

12. Churchill's review of Morrisson, in *Modernism/Modernity* 8:3 (September 2001): 531–33.

13. *MM* 298, from an internal memo to the chief of the SS and German police, July 14, 1938. See my "Reading the Politics of Else Lasker-Schüler's 1914 *Hebrew Ballads,*" *Modernism/Modernity* 6.2 (1999): 135–59.

14. "jener uralten Sänger, die einst die Psalmen oder das Buch Hiob gedichtet haben" (*MM* 40).

15. Quoted in Hedgepeth 153. Lasker-Schüler also characterized herself as American "Indian" (*Concert* 16, 37, 50).

16. "Ich verkleide mich als Orientale. . . . Ich schick Ihnen im Januar mein Bild als arabischer Prinz" (November 6, 1909, *Br* I 40).

17. In *German Jews: A Dual Identity* (New Haven: Yale University Press, 1999), Paul Mendes-Flohr notes that Jews had "hugely disproportionate numbers within the ranks of the *Bildungbürgertum*" (6). I am indebted to his work in the following paragraphs.

18. Mendes-Flohr, *German Jews* 37, 5. Lasker-Schüler writes at length about her mother's love of Goethe and both her parents' love of literature in *Concert.*

19. In Irving Wohlfarth, "'Männer aus der Fremde': Walter Benjamin and the 'German-Jewish Parnassus,'" *New German Critique* 70 (winter 1997): 3–86; 4.

20. Alfred Wolfenstein, "Jüdisches Wesen und Dichtertum," *Der Jude* 6 (1922): 428–40; 428.

21. Jakob Hessing, *Else Lasker-Schüler: Biographie einer deutsch-jüdischen Dichterin* (Karlsruhe: von Loeper Verlag, 1985), 32–34.

22. This story is told by Abraham Stenzel, in Valencia 105.

23. These stories come from *WZ* 166, and from "Erinnerungen" (Memories), a manuscript by Olga Lieblich (DLA); Lieblich provides no date for the story about the poet climbing the trellis but states that the incident took place on the Baltic Sea, the poet was wearing trousers, and the rabbi smiled to see her, sending his other disciples away so that they might talk.

24. Calvin Jones mentions both several admiring reviewers in this period, who follow Hille's lead in calling her "the" Jewish "poetess," and hostile critics already expressing "views typical of explicit Nazi judgements," condemning her as unhealthy and erotic (24–27).

25. Meïr Wiener, "Else Lasker-Schüler," *Juden in der Deutschen Literatur: Essays über zeitgenösische Schriftsteller,* ed. Gustav Krojanken (Berlin: Welt-Verlag, 1922), 179–92; 179. The poet comments to Bithell on November 6, 1909, that people assume she is Russian—perhaps a euphemism for Jewish and Asian; many Russian immigrants were Jews (*Br* I 41).

26. From "Unsere Muttersprache," *Miesbacher Anzeiger* (1921); in *MM* 166.

27. See LeRider 266.

28. Dagmar Lorenz, "Jewish Women Authors and the Exile Experience: Claire Goll, Veza Canetti, Else Lasker-Schüler, Nelly Sachs, Cordelia Edvardson," *German Life and Letters* 51:2 (April 1998): 225–39; 235.

29. Emily Bilski notes that where museum directors (state officials, under Wilhelm II) tended to be gentile, private collectors and small gallery owners tended to be Jewish (5). The modernist period coincides with the high point of Jewish assimilation into German society and was certainly influenced by Jewish German writers, artists, critics, buyers, and readers.

30. "Rechnet man alle Autoren, Kritiker, Regisseure, Verleger und sonst am Literatur- und Theaterbetrieb Beteiligten zusammen—knapp die Hälfte der zum Umkreis des Expressionismus Zählenden Juden sind oder von jüdischen Vorfahren abstammen"; Hans Otto Horch, "Expressionismus und Judentum: Zu einer Debatte in Martin Bubers Zeitschrift 'Der Jude,'" in Anz and Stark, *Die Modernität* 120–41; 136 n. 4. Pinthus was also Jewish. According to Horch, Jews may have been attracted to Expressionism because its utopianism resembled Jewish messianic thought—a connection frequently commented on in journals like Buber's *Der Jude.* Gottfried Benn claimed that "The overflowing plenty of stimuli of artistic, scientific, commercial improvisations which placed the Berlin of 1918 to 1933 in the class of Paris stemmed for the most part from the talents of [the Jewish] sector of the population" (Gay 131–32).

31. According to Wohlfahrt, early-twentieth-century Jews turned logically to the indirections of literature to voice critique because "the German Jew has

no credible political voice." Whatever an individual's personal credentials, real authority requires "authentication . . . furnished, or at least recognized, by the public authorities" (31). German Jews had no such platform from which to speak, so their commentary had to be indirect. Ulrike Müller argues that the poet sees the "inability to love as a social problem" of patriarchy (90, 98).

32. *Wunderrabbiner* is a common description of Hasidic ("miracle-working") rabbis.

33. Ginsberg 604–6; 605.

34. *Br* I 128: "ich bin keine Zionistin, keine Jüdin, keine Christin; ich glaube aber ein Mensch." This letter is dated December 23, 1942, and signed "Ihr Prinz Jussuf (E L-Sch.)." Hallensleben provides the most detailed account of orientalism in Lasker-Schüler's writing in relation to cultural orientalism in Berlin (chap. 5).

35. "Man glaubt, ganz Asien sei in der seltsamen Schau ihres Gedichts Lyrik geworden" (Edschmid 53).

36. Lasker-Schüler wrote about a fakir variety evening to several people during this period; it is unclear whether such an evening ever occurred, but she had it planned to the smallest detail: she would play bagpipes, a flute, and drums as well as reading, interspersed with dance and a theatrical performance starring her friend Kete Parsenow. She planned to take this act on the road to Munich, Cologne, Dusseldorf, Berlin, Paris, London, Brussels, and Istanbul.

37. Robert Kern, *Orientalism, Modernism, and the American Poem* (Cambridge: Cambridge University Press, 1996), chap. 2.

38. JNUL, "Tagebuchzeilen aus Zürich," 2:28, p. 19.

39. Hallensleben notes that Lasker-Schüler's poems were read in the Zurich Cabaret Voltaire in 1916; Hugo Ball's "Karawane" may take both its name and concept from her "Asian" experiments (65–71). Stefan Georg also constructed a language of his own (*WZ* 104).

40. Donna Heizer, *Jewish-German Identity in the Orientalist Literature of Else Lasker-Schüler, Friedrich Wolf, und Franz Werfel* (Camden, N.J.: Camden House, 1996), 8, 1.

41. Lasker-Schüler's assignment of servant status to black people participates in similarly problematic racism that could be explored in relation to orientalism. Hallensleben links the poet's reference to a black servant in her performance scenarios to the popular anthropological exhibitions occurring in European cities at the beginning of the century, often including the display of whole villages of "primitives" (47). Her use of "primitives" manipulates popular conceptions of the dramatic, mixing popular and high art. Hallensleben, however, sees the poet's representation of Africans as assigning them more than common respect and authority (51).

42. According to Valencia, Berlin was a center for Jews from all over the world: there were over two hundred thousand Jews living in the city, and Berlin was the home of the most important Jewish aid organizations and an important publishing center for Yiddish (48, 62, 66–68). In addition, before 1933 Berlin was the most important communication and trade center between the five million Jews in the Americas and the ten million Jews in Eastern Europe (62–63).

43. Quoted in Robertson 188: "Der Jude hingegen, den ich den Orientalen nenne. . . . Er ist seiner selbst sicher, . . . da ihn ein edles Bewußtein, Blutbewußtsein, an die Vergangenheit knüpf."

44. Quoted in Valencia 69: "Brauchen wir Neger und Jazzband, um zur

Natur zurückzukehren?—Noch ist der primitive Urklang, die erste Nacktheit unter uns! Hirten singen neue Lieder und es sind die alten Psalmen. Immer noch wird David aus unserem Blute geboren."

45. Valencia 63, 64. Valencia states that Lasker-Schüler could both read and understand Yiddish (73). In "Abraham Stenzel," Lasker-Schüler romanticizes Yiddish: "Hamid is the poet of jargon / Of the ghetto-dialect. // When he speaks it, helplessly and movingly, / The song of our young people beats in my heart" [Der Hamid ist der Dichter des Jargons / Des Ghettoplatts. // Wenn er es spricht, hilflos und rührend, / Pocht an mein Herz das Jugendvolkslied] (*WB*, no. 413).

46. To Buber: "ich *hasse* die Juden, da ich David war oder Joseph—ich hasse die Juden, weil sie meine Sprache mißachten, weil ihre Ohren verwachsen sind und sie nach Zwergerei horchen" (*Br* I 117); "Ich habe durch die Prinzenkrone nur dem judentum einen Opal in die Schläfe gesetzt"; "Ich habe ein Viertel Leben, ja ein ganzes nichts getan als allen juden Ehre gemacht" (*MM* 164, 246). Lasker-Schüler characteristically writes *Jew* and *Judaism* without capitals.

47. Angelika Koch interprets the Jussuf figure as a kind of imaginative "inner emigration" that allowed the poet escape into a foreign realm, parallel to the emigration of *Ostjuden* although in the reverse direction; *Die Bedeutung des Spiels bei Else Lasker-Schüler* (Bonn: Bouview, 1971).

48. "Sie war weltfremder als ein Märchen," in Ginsberg 605.

49. "Bei ihrem tragishen, schweren Leben, wie hätte sie fortfahren können zu arbeiten, ohne ihre Prinz-Illusion? 'Größenwahn'? . . . Begleitet er nicht jeder echten Dichter wie ein Leibwächter?" (1926; Valencia 111).

50. This is the conclusion to the 1905 first printing of the poem; most of these lines were later omitted.

51. Hallensleben also writes about dialogic aspects of Lasker-Schüler's art in relation to performance art and to a public audience (22–24).

52. In her Zurich journal the poet anticipates this scene in a description of her father playing chess (JNUL 2:28, p. 8): "Interessanter noch den Männern zuzuschauen, / Die mit lebenden Figuren spielen Schach. / Auf des Suez Bette, / Auf Europas Brette, / Unter Bombenkrach! / Bis kein Mensch mehr unter Dach" [More interesting to watch men / Who play chess with living figures / On the board of Suez / Europe / Under bombardment! / Until no one remains under shelter]; see also *WB*, no. 431.

53. On Jewish women's suicide, see Darcy Buerkle, in *Reading Charlotte Salomon*, ed. Michael Steinberg and Monica Bohm-Duchen (Ithaca, N.Y.: Cornell University Press, 2005).

54. Zhaoming Qian, *Orientalism and Modernism: The Legacy of China in Pound and Williams* (Durham: Duke University Press, 1995), 2; Qian's *The Modernist Response to Chinese Art: Pound, Moore, Stevens* (Charlottesville: University of Virginia Press, 2003) argues that Pound, Moore, and Stevens also distinguish the "Orient" from orientalism. Cynthia Stamy discusses U.S. orientalism as part of its historical project to distinguish itself from Europe; *Marianne Moore and China: Orientalism and a Writing of America* (Oxford: Oxford University Press, 1999).

55. Robert Kern similarly claims that Pound writes "English-as-Chinese" (chap. 6).

56. Frederick M. Binder and David M. Reimers, *All the Nations under Heaven* (New York: Columbia University Press, 1995), 115, 134.

57. Unlike in Berlin, in New York Jews did not represent a high percentage of those involved in English-language avant-garde literature or arts; Nathan Glazer, "The National Influence of Jewish New York," *Capital of the American City: The National and International Influence of New York City*, ed. Martin Shefter (New York: Russell Sage Foundation, 1993), 167–92; 170. According to Binder and Reimers, there were twenty Yiddish theaters in New York (134).

58. Jerald Brauer, *Protestantism in America: A Narrative History* (London: SCM Press, 1966), 250. Neither all denominations nor all congregations participated in this liberal turn, and some churches became more fundamentalist in response.

59. For greater detail on Moore's interest in Hebrew poetic prophecy, see my "Marianne Moore and a Poetry of Hebrew (Protestant) Prophecy," *Sources* 12 (spring 2002): 29–47. Previous scholarship on Moore and religion focuses on the poet in relation to American Calvinism and sees Moore as continuing her mother's rhetoric of Christian battle and exceptionalism—regarding the family as "a people *set apart* . . . [with] a mission in the world"; Jeredith Merrin, "Sites of Struggle: Marianne Moore and American Calvinism," *The Calvinist Roots of the Modern Era*, ed. Aliki Barnstone, Michael T. Manson, and Carol J. Singley (Lebanon, N.H.: University Press of New England, 1997), 91–106. See also Andrew J. Kappel, "The World Is an Orphan's Home: Marianne Moore on God and Family," *Reform and Counterreform: Dialectics of the Word in Western Christianity since Luther*, ed. John C. Hawley (Berlin: Mouton de Gruyter, 1994), 173–92; and Kappel, "Presbyterian Poetry." While Moore adopts the language of armor and battle, I argue that she uses them to different effect from her mother and brother.

60. First published *Others* (1915), under the title "So far as the future is concerned, 'Shall not one say, with the Russian philosopher, "How is one to know what one doesn't know?"' So far as the present is concerned" (*EP* 208–9).

61. According to John Slatin, Moore here posits her relation to poetic tradition on a par with Pound's and Eliot's; *The Savage's Romance: The Poetry of Marianne Moore* (State College: Pennsylvania State University Press, 1986), 30–32. Cynthia Hogue reads the poem in gendered terms in "Another Postmodernism" 6–8.

62. George Adam Smith, *The Book of the Twelve Prophets Commonly Called the Minor* (London: Hodder and Stoughton, 1898), 2:131.

63. Moore frequently uses questions to articulate her views, and often ends poems with questions. "Black Earth" and "Those Various Scalpels" exemplify this practice. Darlene Williams Erickson claims that most major characteristics of Moore's verse are parallel to Hebrew, including her syllabics, prose rhythms, rhyme, and "unusual parallels of thought"; *Illusion Is More Precise Than Precision: The Poetry of Marianne Moore* (Tuscaloosa: University of Alabama Press, 1992), 23. She also speculates that Moore writes "The Past is the Present" in "irritated reaction against" Marcel Duchamp's claim, "We must learn to forget the past" (67).

64. Dale Miller identified the biblical allusions of this poem for me, to Isa. 8:6–8, 8:18–22, and 9:8–12. In the first passage, Isaiah describes the Assyrian conquest as a God-given flood of "waters of the River," hence the "River God" of Moore's poem. The phrase "crocodile of gluttony" is a lovely instance of Moore's humor; she uses the image of gluttony in Isa. 9:12, where the Syrians "devour Israel with open mouth," to construct a play on her own nickname as "gator": to become "food for crocodiles" in the poem is quite literally to fall prey to herself and her own desires.

65. George Adam Smith, *Modern Criticism and the Preaching of the Old Testament* (London: Hodder and Stoughton, 1901), 217, 217, 272, 274.

66. George Adam Smith emphasizes that the form of prophecy represented by the major biblical prophets arose in a period when the Israelites were developing an increasingly commercial and urban culture, giving rise to what he calls a "new civilization" of international awareness, similar to that of the modern Western world: Smith, *Book of the Twelve Prophets* 1:30; and *Modern Criticism* 267–74.

67. Kinnahan argues that William Carlos Williams also develops a poetic of "relatedness or connectedness" in distinction to "ideas of the expatriate modernists at a very early stage in the movement's development" (36).

68. Jonathan Barron, "New Jerusalems: Contemporary Jewish American Poets and the Puritan Tradition," in Barnstone et al. 231–49. Wohlfahrt also points to Benjamin's distinction between symbol and allegory as linking the (German Romantic) symbol with "an immediate redemptive transfiguration of reality," whereas allegory more closely resembles a Jewish interpretive strategy in calling attention to its arbitrariness and hence to "unredeemed traits of the historical world" (40). See also Harold Bloom, "The Sorrows of American Jewish Poetry," *Figures of Capable Imagination* (New York: Seabury Press, 1975), 247–62.

69. Eastern languages were said to be uninflected, based on pictorial characters, hence implicitly less developed than European languages. Moore quotes Gordon's description of Hebrew as a "lang[uage] of action & picture—very little inflection. Every word has in it a picture and often a picture of motion—'movies.'" (VII.08.03). George Adam Smith uses similar language in *The Early Poetry of Israel in Its Physical and Social Origins* (London: Oxford University Press, 1912), 7–9, as does Robert Alter in *The Art of Biblical Poetry* (New York: Basic Books, 1985), 10, 39.

70. Ezra Pound, "A Few Don'ts by an Imagiste," *Poetry*, March 1913, 200–206; 201.

71. This quotation from Moore's reading notebook 1250/2 comes from Kadlec 166.

72. *Marianne Moore Reader* 258, and interview in *New Verse* (1934; *CPr* 674).

73. Murray Roston's discussion of Eliot is useful for identifying differences between his poetic and Moore's: where Eliot sees the modern world's "triviality, aimlessness, sordidness" as "redeemed by its allusion to a lost mythical world" that in turn validates the rituals of Christianity, Moore turns away from abstraction, the universal, and myth; *Modernist Patterns in Literature and the Visual Arts* (New York: New York University Press, 2000), 70, 73, 77. On the other hand, both share with other contemporaries a "yearning for . . . truths that would answer the needs of the soul" (64).

74. Michael Bell, "The Metaphysics of Modernism," in Levenson 9–32; 29. Kadlec writes that Moore's poetic of "contingency showed her that ethical positions could be powerfully significant not when they were written in stone but when they were adopted as choices" (155).

75. I quote here from the *Dial* version. Moore did not know that H.D. and Bryher were bringing out a volume of her poems so could not send them the revisions she submitted to the *Dial,* where the poem appeared a few weeks before *Poems* (1921) was published (*EP* 253–54).

76. Heinz Politzer, "Else Lasker-Schüler," *Expressionismus als Literatur: Gesammelte Studien*, ed. Wolfgang Rothe (Bern: Franke Verlag, 1969), 215–31; 219.

77. These figures were provided by Lorett Treese, the Bryn Mawr College archivist, and remain more or less constant during Moore's four years at the college.

78. November 23 and December 4, 1905; RML VI.11b.11 and 12. Moore took notes on Zangwill's *Children of the Ghetto* and a 1914 sermon in her reading notebook for 1907–15, RML VII:01:01; for comments on anti-Semitism, see October 7 and 22, 1906; RML VI.12.11.

79. In a letter to Hildegarde Watson, August 17, 1954. In this same letter, Moore reports that "much of my professional progress is through the magnanimity (and benevolence with money,) of Jews—the Guggenheims, the Times newspaper, Lincoln Kirstein, Harry Levin, the Helen Haire Levinsons—I could go on and on," concluding with an apology for her "diatribe": "I am really impassioned about injustice—the root of every current world sin as I see it." I am indebted to Linda Leavell for this reference.

80. Jacob Glatstein, "Marianne Moore," 1947, *Yiddish* 6.1 (1985): 67–73, translated by Doris Vidauer.

81. Moore's letters to Bryher reveal her concern on behalf of European Jews in the 1930s. Bryher worked in the European resistance, passing on documents that Moore tried to get published.

82. When asked in a survey whether she was part of the "American tradition," Moore calls herself "an American chameleon on an American leaf" (*CPr* 675). DuPlessis notes that in the index of *Observations,* Moore highlights her attempt to be nonprejudicial by including the categories "Jew, brilliant, 16; not greedy, 64" but reads "To Disraeli" as substantiating stereotypes of Jews, perhaps because she does not see Moore's self-reference to lizards in the poem (*Genders* 158).

83. Opening comment in "Translator's Note," Glatstein 67.

84. There is no evidence that Moore knew the 1915 essay "Democracy versus the Melting-Pot," but she probably read Kallen's "Value in Existence," in John Dewey's anthology *Creative Intelligence: Essays in the Pragmatic Attitude;* during 1916, Moore read most or all of this volume (my correspondence with Robin Schulze, December 1, 2001).

85. Bourne 173, 175–76.

86. Michael North, *The Dialect of Modernism: Race, Language, and Twentieth-Century Literature* (Oxford: Oxford University Press, 1994), 148.

87. Quoted from Jennifer Leader's "A House Not Made with Hands," Ph.D. diss., Claremont Graduate University, September 2002, 44. Leader points out that Niebuhr revises Martin Buber's "*Ich-Du*" theory of self-formulation. Moore corresponded with Niebuhr and his wife from 1952 to 1962 and quotes him in essays and letters.

88. Primo Levi, *The Periodic Table,* trans. Raymond Rosenthal (1984; reprinted, London: Time Warner UK, Abacus, 1986).

89. See Kadlec (156–58) and North on this discourse in the United States. DuPlessis points out that much of the rhetoric regarding race suicide was pointed against Jews (*Genders* 137, 138).

90. For a more detailed account of the effects of location on Loy's writing see my "Feminist Location and Mina Loy's 'Anglo-Mongrels and the Rose,'" *Paideuma* 32.1–3 (2003): 75–94. Maeera Shreiber comes to the same conclusion, although not making Judaism her focus; "Divine Women, Fallen Angels: The Late Devotional Poetry of Mina Loy," *MLWP* 467–83; 471.

91. *BM* 112. On Jews in Paris around the turn of the century, see Nancy L.

Green, *The Pletzl of Paris: Jewish Immigrant Workers in the Belle Epoque* (New York: Holmes and Meier, 1986).

92. Elizabeth Frost, "Mina Loy's 'Mongrel' Poetics," *MLWP* 149–79; 151; Perloff 140, 145, 133.

93. Letter ca. 1930, quoted in Marissa Januzzi, "Mongrel Rose: The 'Unerring Esperanto' of Loy's Poetry," *MLWP* 403–41; 427. In the next quotation, Januzzi quotes from Arthur Symons (418).

94. Kadlec reads "England" as responding directly to notions of genetic and linguistic purity through her assertion that only ignorance imagines all "mushrooms" to be "poisonous toadstools" just because the latter also exist (160–63).

95. Mark Morrisson, "Performing the Pure Voice: Elocution, Verse Recitation, and Modernist Poetry in Prewar London," *Modernism/Modernity* 3.3 (1996): 25–50; 38.

96. Shreiber argues that "Love Songs" critiques the secularism of modernism by representing sex as divine: the poet-lover is an "inversion of the canonical Christ" ("'Love is a Lyric'" 150).

97. Published in 1920, "O Hell" precedes Eliot's "Waste Land" with its similar opening reference to the cruelty of spring and sense of a wasted or hellish land.

98. *LLB* 76, 88; 78, 80. DuPlessis, "Corpses of Poesy," argues that Loy criticizes Poe's claim that the death of a beautiful woman is the most poetic subject through her phrase "corpses of poesy," but Loy also mixes images of death with ecstatic art, perhaps even seeing her own loss of Cravan as analogous to that which Poe describes, even while it reverses his gender assumptions .

99. B Box 7, folder 187. Loy writes two versions of this long passage, neither titled.

100. According to Roger Conover, Loy moved to Berlin in the spring of 1922 and left on June 13, 1923 (*LLB82* lxxi, and correspondence April 22, 2003); Burke states that Isadora Duncan was in Berlin when Loy arrived, which would place her "spring" arrival in May or June (*BM* 315).

101. Burke implies that, at least during the first part of her stay in Berlin, Loy was part of the "international crowd gathered each night" at the Romanisches Café (*BM* 314).

102. On *Der Jude,* see Mendes-Flohr, "The Berlin Jew" 25–27; and Inka Bertz, "Jewish Renaissance—Jewish Modernism," in Bilski 165–87. The journal was widely read by secular Jews and gentiles.

103. Around the turn of the century, many immigrant Jewish workers were employed in the garment industry, and Jews were consequently often stereotyped as tailors. I am indebted to Keith Tuma's and DuPlessis's readings for my interpretation of the poem's conclusion (Tuma 146, 163; *Genders* 163–64). Tuma, however, I believe, misreads the conclusion as specifically Christian—perhaps in part due to his claim that Loy wrote the poem in Paris.

104. Frost and Gilmore also interpret Ova/Loy as a Jacob figure in this poem, *MLWP* 167, 291.

CHAPTER SIX

1. Woolf is an interesting case because she published no experimental fiction until 1921, when she was already thirty-nine; she finished her first novel in 1913, however, and had published both it and a second novel by 1919.

2. Stein's break from lyric and narrative traditions is more radical than Moore's, and many regard Stein as the most influential woman writing in this period. Yet she took no active part in editing, publishing, reviewing, or promoting the work of others. Both Michael North's *The Dialect of Modernism* (25–26) and Thom Gunn's "Three Hard Women" provide useful reminders of how shocking Moore's verse seemed to contemporary audiences; Gunn calls Moore's "experiments in poetic structure" "extraordinarily bold" (43).

3. For example, in Douglas, and Scott and Rutkoff. Loy receives twice the number of mentions as Moore in the latter, although both appear primarily as names in lists.

4. On Moore's relation to contemporary philosophers, see Kadlec; on Moore and contemporary science, see Robin Schulze's essays "Textual Darwinism: Marianne Moore, the Text of Evolution, and the Evolving Text," *Text* 11 (1998): 270–305; and "Marianne Moore's 'Imperious Ox, Imperial Dish' and the Poetry of the Natural World," *Twentieth Century Literature* 44.1 (1998):1–33. On Moore and Kenneth Burke, see Bazin, "Moore, Kenneth Burke"; on Moore's ethical agency, see Hogue, "Another Postmodernism."

5. See, for example, Pinthus's *Menschheitsdämmerung* and Heinrich Eduard Jacob's "Zur Geschichte der deutschen Lyrik seit 1910" (1924), in Raabe, *Expressionismus* 194–217; or more recently Brinkmann's *Expressionismus;* Allen's *Literary Life in German Expressionism;* and Hans Esselborn in "Die expressionisticsche Lyrik," *Die Literarische Moderne in Europa,* vol. 2, ed. Hans Joachim Piechotta, Ralph-Rainer Wuthenow, and Sabine Rothemann (Opladen: Westdeutscher Verlag, 1994).

6. On what is significantly innovative in Lasker-Schüler's development as a poet, see *WZ* 75–77, 110–12, 183–84, 312.

7. Lasker-Schüler's son also spent much of his school time in boarding schools in the country, which Lasker-Schüler found healthier for him than urban life, and which freed her from daily maternal care once Paul was school age. I know of no accounts that fault her for lack of attention or devotion to her son, and she spent most of her income on his schooling and support, or later on his medication and treatment, before he died of tuberculosis.

8. According to Conover, Loy's last new publication before her death was of "Faun Fare," composed in 1948 and published in 1962. She also composed poems in 1949 (*LLB* 213–14).

9. First published in *The Nation,* 1943. During the 1940s, Moore published several poems in this left-leaning political magazine, an indication of the context in which she wanted them to be read.

10. On Moore's innovative use of typology, see Leader.

11. I do not know whether Moore heard Gieseking's first concert in the United States, in 1926. In 1944, she would not, of course, have known that Gieseking would return to the United States in 1953.

12. I discuss Moore's concepts of freedom and duty or responsibility in relation to both a concept of community and illocutionary elements of her poetry in *Questions of Authority,* chaps. 2 and 6.

13. Cynthia Hogue analyzes Moore's distinction between "decorum" and "marked decorum" for women stepping outside the norm of feminine sexuality; "decorum" is not enough to protect the radical woman from popular attack. Moore's own decorum was indeed "marked," revealing the extent to which she knew herself to be overstepping boundaries of feminine behavior and authority; *Scheming Women* 74–75.

14. In line 5, Lasker-Schüler printed the past-tense *spielten* in all but her 1943 first edition of the volume *Mein blaues Klavier*, where it appeared in the present tense.

15. Kandinsky, *Concerning the Spiritual in Art* (1912), trans. Michael Sadleir (London, 1914), 58. In "The Meaning of Colour in Else Lasker-Schüler's Poetry," G. Guder claims that for the poet blue signifies "the divine, the sublime, the eternal"; *German Life and Letters* 14–15 (1960–62): 175–87; 176.

16. Lasker-Schüler may not have associated this metaphor of color as a keyboard with Kandinsky's theories; concepts of color harmony were extremely popular during the time, as was the linking of all arts to music. On color theory see Charles A. Riley II, *Color Codes: Modern Theories of Color in Philosophy, Painting, Architecture, Literature, Music, and Psychology* (Hanover, N.H.: University Press of New England, 1995), 147.

17. Paul Vogt, "The *Blaue Reiter*," in *Expressionism: A German Intuition, 1905–1920*, ed. Vogt et al. (New York: Solomon R. Guggenheim Museum, 1980), 192–237; 185.

18. "Auf Erden mit euch im Himmel schon. / Allfarbig malen auf blauem Grund / Das ewige Leben" (*WB*, no. 373).

19. In her Zurich journal, Lasker-Schüler mentions having had a blue "doll piano" as a child (JNUL 2:28, p. 16). This claim initiates what may be a first draft of "Mein blaues Klavier."

20. Art Spiegelman, *Maus: A Survivor's Tale* (New York: Random House, 1986).

21. Erica Fischer, *Aimée und Jaguar: Eine Liebesgeschichte, Berlin 1943* (Berlin: DTV, 1998).

22. See Miller, "The Politics of Else Lasker-Schüler" for my translation of this poem.

23. Lasker-Schüler's implied concept of heaven combines aspects of traditional Jewish and early-twentieth-century popular Christian belief, as would have been typical for a relatively assimilated Jew in Germany.

24. Jean M. Snook, "The Concept of Home in Else Lasker-Schüler's Concert," *Else Lasker-Schüler. Ansichten und Perspektiven*, ed. Ernst Schürer and Sonja M. Hedgepeth (Marburg: Francke Verlag, 1999), 219–27; 227.

25. August 13, 1936: "Es geht mir gut dort, nur daß unsere eigentliche Heimat die Sprache ist und daß es im Grunde ein unheilbares Leid ist, in ihr nicht mehr werken und wirken zu können" (JNUL 5:144).

26. "Ich hab rein Märchenland—es war einmal—verloren. . . . // Ach die Liebe ist gestorben—manch Heiligen führt der Engel / 'lebend' heute in das Paradies von dieser Welt"; printed as "Ich glaube wir sind all für einand' gestorben" (I think we are all dead to each other), *WB*, no. 427.

27. "Die Liebe ist unsterblich, nicht von dieser Welt"; "Im Weltkriege, wie er auch wütete, der Liebe selbst geschah kein Leid." "Kinder mit denen noch Gott spielte in Seiner Jugendewigkeit und lieb gewann, trotz ihrer menschlichen Fehler, die jeden Wolk behafte. Indem Ihr uns vertreibt, treibt Ihr uns—in—Gottes Arme." "Wir Juden sind gewillt mit dem Preis unseres Lebens ungezählter roter Tropfen unserer Herzen in die Stadt Gottes zu ziehen . . . Verschliesst uns nicht die verbrämten ewigen Tore, unserer Gottheimat . . . . Oder—soll sie uns—Gott Selbst öffnen?"

28. The effect of the repetition is lost in translation because the English idiom is heaven's *gate* rather than *door*.

29. "[D]ie zerbrochenen Klaviatür des alten Sprachkanons," 19. Such a

question anticipates Adorno's later and more despairing assertion that there can be no poetry "after Auschwitz."

30. Burke also sees Joella's separation from Julian Levy as a blow to Loy, particularly because of Loy's own unacknowledged attraction to Levy and dependence on his emotional as well as financial support. Throughout her daughter's separation and divorce proceedings, Loy took Julian's rather than Joella's side, even to the extent of mouthing platitudes, for example, that a woman should do everything to avoid divorce, in complete contradiction to her own life choices (*BM* 389). Although such behavior continues Loy's pattern of preferred dependence on men, it is also a sign, I think, of her increasing instability. Important exceptions to Loy's isolation in New York were her attendance at Frances Steloff's informal gatherings at the Gotham Book Mart and her friendships with Clarence John Laughlin and Joseph Cornell (*BM* 399–400, 404–8).

31. Kenneth Rexroth was the first to comment on this aspect of Loy's poetic (*LLB82* xxxi).

32. Perloff writes that in Loy's verse "structures of voice and address take precedence over the 'contestation of fact,' as Pound called it, of the Image" (144). Certainly, many of Loy's poems are charged with emotion, but they do not seem to me structured as address: illocutionary features are almost absent in Loy's poems, and the presence of an interlocutor seems a matter of indifference. In this sense, all Loy's poems are more like manifestoes; Moore's and Lasker-Schüler's, in contrast, are typically pointed at some "you" with whom communication is desired.

33. Bourdieu 65.

34. Zweig, "In einer bourgeoisen Zeit wie der heutigen steht sie als Monstrum, als eine Abnormität: als ein wirklicher Dichter" (*Jüdischer Rundschau*; *MM* 199).

APPENDIX

1. Many dates for Loy's movement are not precise. Burke lists her time in Munich as a single year; Conover lists it as extending from 1899 to ca. 1901–2 in his 1982 time line (*LLB82*). Neither gives even approximate dates for her departure from or return to London. ML refers to her "year" in Munich in an autobiographical manuscript, "Islands in the Air" (B MSS 6; Mina Loy Papers Box 4, folder 69), but there is no evidence as to the degree she fictionalizes such narratives. Where there is no existing counterevidence, Burke tends to read them as factual.

Works Cited

Abrahams, Edward. *The Lyrical Left: Randolph Bourne, Alfred Stieglitz, and the Origins of Cultural Radicalism in America.* Charlottesville: University of Virginia Press, 1988.

Adams, Bronte, and Trudi Tate. *That Kind of Woman.* New York: Caroll and Graf, 1992.

Adamson, Walter. "Futurism, Mass Culture, and Women: The Reshaping of the Artistic Vocation, 1909–1920." *Modernism/Modernity* 4.1 (1997): 89–114.

Allen, Roy F. *Literary Life in German Expressionism and the Berlin Circles.* Ann Arbor: UMI Research Press, 1983.

Alter, Robert. *The Art of Biblical Poetry.* New York: Basic Books, 1985.

Altieri, Charles. "What Is Living and What Is Dead in American Postmodernism." *Critical Inquiry* 22.4 (1996): 764–89.

Anz, Thomas, and Michael Stark, eds. *Die Modernität des Expressionismus.* Stuttgart: J. B. Metzler Verlag, 1994.

———, eds. *Expressionismus: Manifeste und Dokumente zur deutschen Literatur 1910–1920.* Stuttgart: J. B. Metzler Verlag, 1982.

Armstrong, Nancy. "Modernism's Iconophobia and What It Did to Gender." *Modernism/Modernity* 5.2 (1998): 47–75.

Baedeker, Karl. *Berlin and Its Environs.* 5th edition. Leipzig, 1912.

Barash, Carol. "Dora Marsden's Feminism, the *Freewoman,* and the Gender Politics of Early Modernism." *Princeton University Library Chronicle* 49.1 (1987): 31–56.

Barnstone, Aliki, Michael T. Manson, and Carol J. Singley, eds. *The Calvinist Roots of the Modern Era.* Lebanon, N.H.: University Press of New England, 1997.

Barron, Jonathan. "New Jerusalems: Contemporary Jewish American Poets and the Puritan Tradition." In Barnstone et al., 231–49.

Baumgardt, Manfred. "Die Homosexuellen-Bewegung bis zum Ende des Ersten Weltkrieges." *Eldorado: Homosexuelle Frauen und Männer in Berlin 1850–1950.* Berlin: Verlag rosa Winkel, 1992: 17–27.

Bauschinger, Sigrid. "The Berlin Moderns: Else Lasker-Schüler and Café Culture." In Bilski, 58–83.

———. *Else Lasker Schüler: Ihr Werk und ihre Zeit.* Heidelberg: Stiehm, 1980.

Bazin, Victoria. "Marianne Moore, Kenneth Burke, and the Poetics of Literary Labour." *Journal of American Studies* 35.3 (2001): 433–52.

———. "Marianne Moore and the Arcadian Pleasures of Shopping." *Women* 12.2 (2001): 218–35.

Beckett, Jane, and Deborah Cherry. "Modern Women, Modern Spaces: Women, Metropolitan Culture, and Vorticism." In Deepwell, 36–54.

Behling, Laura. *The Masculine Woman in America.* Urbana: University of Illinois Press, 2001.

Bell, Michael. "The Metaphysics of Modernism." In Levenson, 9–32.

Bell, Vereen, and Laurence Lerner, eds. *On Modern Poetry: Essays Presented to Donald Davie.* Nashville: Vanderbilt University Press, 1988.

Benjamin, Walter. *Illuminations.* Ed. Hannah Arendt, trans. Harry Zohn. New York: Schocken Books, 1968.

———. "Paris, Capital of the Nineteenth Century." *Reflections.* Trans. E. Jephcott. New York: Harcourt, Brace, Jovanovich, 1978: 146–62.

Benn, Gottfried. "Bekenntnis zum Expressionismus." In Raabe, 235–46.

Benstock, Shari. "Expatriate Modernism." In Broe and Ingram, 20–40.

———. *Women of the Left Bank: Paris, 1900–1940.* Austin: University of Texas Press, 1986.

Benveniste, Emile. *Problems in General Linguistics.* Trans. Mary Elizabeth Meek. Coral Gables: University of Miami Press, 1971.

Berke, Nancy. "Anything That Burns You: The Social Poetry of Lola Ridge, Genevieve Taggard, and Margaret Walker." *Revista Canariade Estudios Ingleses* 37 (1998): 39–53.

Bertz, Inka. "Jewish Renaissance—Jewish Modernism." In Bilski, 165–87.

Betterton, Rosemary. "Women Artists, Modernity, and Suffrage Cultures in Britain and Germany, 1890–1920." In Deepwell, 18–35.

Bilski, Emily D., ed. *Berlin Metropolis: Jews and the New Culture, 1890–1918.* Berkeley and Los Angeles: University of California Press, 1999.

Binder, Frederick M., and David M. Reimers. *All the Nations under Heaven.* New York: Columbia University Press, 1995.

Bloch, Ernst. *The Utopian Function of Art and Literature: Selected Essays.* Trans. Jack Zipes and Frank Mecklenburg. Cambridge: MIT Press, 1988.

Bloom, Harold. *Figures of Capable Imagination.* New York: Seabury Press, 1975.

Bodenheim, Maxwell. "The Decorative Straight-Jacket: Rhymed Verse." *Little Review,* December 1914, 22–23.

Bourdieu, Pierre. *The Field of Cultural Production: Essays on Art and Literature.* Ed. Randal Johnson. Cambridge: Polity Press, 1993.

Bourne, Randolph. "Trans-national America." *American Intellectual Tradition.* 4th ed. 2 vols. Ed. David Hollinger and Charles Capper. Oxford: Oxford University Press, 2001: 170–80.

Boym, Svetlana. *Death in Quotation Marks: Cultural Myths of the Modern Poet.* Cambridge: Harvard University Press, 1991.

Bradbury, Malcolm, and James McFarlane, eds. *Modernism: A Guide to European Literature, 1890–1930.* New York: Viking 1976; 1991.

Brauer, Jerald. *Protestantism in America: A Narrative History.* London: SCM Press, 1966.

Brice, Nicola. "The Autobiographical Voice in Lily Braun's Fiction." In Donnell and Polkey, 260–69.

Brinkmann, Richard. *Expressionismus: Internationale Forschung zu einem internationalen Phänomen.* Stuttgart: J. B. Metzler Verlag, 1980.

Broe, Mary Lynn, and Angela Ingram, eds. *Women's Writing in Exile.* Chapel Hill: University of North Carolina Press, 1989.

Bronner, Stephen, and Douglas Kellner, eds. *Passion and Rebellion: The Expressionist Heritage.* London: Croom Helm, 1983.

Broude, Norma. "Edgar Degas and French Feminism, ca. 1880: 'The Young Spartans,' the Brothel Monotypes, and the Bathers Revisited." *The Expanding Discourse: Feminism and Art History.* Ed. Norma Broude and Mary D. Garrard. New York: Icon Editions, 1992: 269–93.

Brown, Dorothy. *Setting a Course: American Women in the 1920s.* Boston: Twayne, 1987.

Brunn, Gerhard. "Einleitung: Metropolis Berlin: Europäische Hauptstädte in Vergleich." *Metropolis Berlin.* Ed. Gerhard Brunn and Jürgen Reulecke. Bonn: Bouvier, 1992: 1–38.

Buerkle, Darcy. "Facing Charlotte Salomon." *Reading Charlotte Salomon.* Ed. Michael Steinberg and Monica Bohm-Duchen. Ithaca, N.Y.: Cornell University Press, 2005.

Bunzl, Matti. "Sexual Modernity as Subject and Object." *Modernism/Modernity* 9.1 (2002):166–75.

Burke, Carolyn. "'Accidental Aloofness': Barnes, Loy, and Modernism." *Silence and Power: A Reevaluation of Djuna Barnes.* Ed. Mary Lynn Broe. Carbondale: Southern Illinois University Press, 1991: 67–79.

———. *Becoming Modern: The Life of Mina Loy.* New York: Farrar, Straus and Giroux, 1996.

———. "Getting Spliced: Modernism and Sexual Difference." *American Quarterly* 39.1 (1987): 98–121.

———. "Recollecting Dada: Juliette Roche." In Sawelson-Gorse, 546–77.

———. "Supposed Persons: Modernist Poetry and the Female Subject." *Feminist Studies* 7.1 (1985): 131–48.

Burstein, Jessica. "A Few Words about Dubuque: Modernism, Sentimentalism, and the Blasé." *American Literary History* 14.2 (2002): 227–54.

Butler, Judith. "Critically Queer." *GLQ* 1.1 (1993): 17–32.

———. "Performativity's Social Magic." *Bourdieu: A Critical Reader.* Ed. Richard Shusterman. Oxford: Blackwell, 1999: 113–28.

Carpenter, Miles. *Immigrants and Their Children.* New York: Arno Press, 1969.

Chauncey, George. *Gay New York: Gender, Urban Culture, and the Making of the Gay Male World, 1890–1940.* New York: Basic Books, 1994.

Churchill, Suzanne. "Making Space for *Others:* A History of a Modernist Little Magazine." *Journal of Modern Literature* 22.1 (1998): 47–67.

———. Review of *The Public Face of Modernism,* by Mark Morrison. *Modernism/Modernity* 8.3 (2001): 531–33.

Clark, Suzanne. *Sentimental Modernism: Women Writers and the Revolution of the Word.* Bloomington: Indiana University Press, 1991.

Collecott, Diana. *H.D. and Sapphic Modernism.* Cambridge: Cambridge University Press, 1999.

Comentale, Edward P. "Thesmophoria: Suffragettes, Sympathetic Magic, and H.D.'s Ritual Poetics." *Modernism/Modernity* 8.3 (2001): 471–92.

Corbett, David Peters. "Seeing into Modernity." *Modernism/Modernity* 7.2 (2000): 285–306.

Costello, Bonnie. "The Feminine Language of Marianne Moore." *Marianne Moore.* Ed. Harold Bloom. New York: Chelsea House, 1987: 89–106.

———. *Marianne Moore: Imaginary Possessions.* Cambridge: Harvard University Press, 1981.

Cott, Nancy. *The Grounding of Modern Feminism.* New Haven: Yale University Press, 1987.

———. *Public Vows: A History of Marriage and the Nation.* Cambridge: Harvard University Press, 2000.

Crunden, Robert N. *American Salons: Encounters with European Modernism, 1885–1917.* New York: Oxford University Press, 1993.

Davis, Alex, and Lee M. Jenkins, eds. *Locations of Literary Modernism: Region and Nation in British and American Modernist Poetry.* Cambridge: Cambridge University Press, 2000.

de Certeau, Michel, Luce Giard, and Pierre Payol. *The Practice of Everyday Life.* Vol. 2: *Living and Cooking.* Minneapolis: University of Minnesota Press, 1998.

Deepwell, Katie, ed. *Women Artists and Modernism.* Manchester: Manchester University Press, 1998.

D'Emilio, John, and Estelle Freedman. *Intimate Matters: A History of Sexuality in America.* New York: Harper and Row, 1988.

Dickinson, Emily. *The Poems of Emily Dickinson.* 3 vols. Ed. Ralph W. Franklin. Cambridge: Harvard University Press, the Belknap Press, 1998.

Donnell, Alison, and Pauline Polkey, eds. *Representing Lives: Women and Auto/Biography.* New York: St. Martin's Press, 2000.

Douglas, Ann. *Terrible Honesty: Mongrel Manhattan in the 1920s.* New York: Farrar, Straus, and Giroux, 1995.

Duncan, Carol. *The Aesthetics of Power: Essays in Critical Art History.* Cambridge: Cambridge University Press, 1993.

Dunn, Susan E. "Mina Loy, Fashion, and the Avant-Garde." In Shreiber and Tuma, 443–55.

DuPlessis, Rachel Blau. "'Corpses of Poesy': Some Modern Poets and Some Gender Ideologies of Lyric." *Feminist Measures: Soundings in Poetry and Theory.* Ed. Lynn Keller and Cristanne Miller. Ann Arbor: University of Michigan Press, 1994: 69–95.

———. *Genders, Races, and Religious Cultures in Modern American Poetry, 1908–1934.* Cambridge: Cambridge University Press, 2001.

Dyer, Richard. "Less and More than Women and Men: Lesbian and Gay Cinema in Weimar Germany." *New German Critique* 51 (1990): 5–60.

Edschmid, Kasimir. "Expressionismus in der Dichtung." 1918. In Anz and Stark, *Expressionismus: Manifeste und Dokumente* 53.

Eliot, T. S. "Tradition and the Individual Talent." *Selected Prose of T. S. Eliot.* Ed. Frank Kermode. New York: Harcourt Brace Jovanovich, 1975: 37–44.

———. *The Waste Land: A Facsimile and Transcript of the Original Drafts Including the Annotations of Ezra Pound.* Ed. Valerie Eliot. London: Faber, 1971.

Elliott, Bridget. "Performing the Picture or Painting the Other: Romaine Brooks, Gluck, and the Question of Decadence in 1923." In Deepwell, 70–82.

Elliott, Bridget, and Jo-Ann Wallace. *Women Artists and Writers: Modernist (Im)positionings.* London: Routledge, 1994.

Erickson, Darlene Williams. *Illusion Is More Precise Than Precision: The Poetry of Marianne Moore.* Tuscaloosa: University of Alabama Press, 1992.

Esselborn, Hans. "Die expressionistische Lyrik." *Die Literarisiche Moderne in Europe.* Vol. 2. Ed. Hans Joachim Piechotta, Ralph-Rainer Wuthenow, and Sabine Rothemann. Opladen: Westdeutscher Verlag, 1994: 204–13.

Felski, Rita. *The Gender of Modernity.* Cambridge: Harvard University Press, 1995.

Fillin-Yeh, Susan. "Dandies, Marginality, and Modernism: Georgia O'Keeffe, Marcel Duchamp, and Other Cross-dressers." *Oxford Art Journal* 18.2 (1995): 33–44.

Fischer, Erica. *Aimée und Jaguar: Eine Liebesgeschichte, Berlin 1943*. Berlin: DTV, 1998.
Fitzgerald, F. Scott. "My Lost City." 1932. *The Bodley Head Scott Fitzgerald*. Vol. 3. London: Bodley Head, 1971: 339–49.
Flexner, Eleanor. *Century of Struggle: The Woman's Rights Movement in the United States*. Rev. ed. Cambridge: Harvard University Press, 1975.
Flügel, J. C. *The Psychology of Clothes*. London: Hogarth Press, 1930.
Frame, Lynne. "Gretchen, Girl, Garçonne? Weimar Science and Popular Culture in Search of the Ideal New Woman." In von Ankum, 12–40.
Freedman, Jonathan. *The Temple of Culture: Assimilation and Anti-Semitism in Literary Anglo-America*. New York: Oxford University Press, 2000.
Frevert, Ute. *Women in German History: From Bourgeois Emancipation to Sexual Liberation*. Trans. Stuart McKinnon-Evans with Terry Bond and Barbara Norden. New York: Berg, 1989.
Friedman, Susan Stanford. *Mappings: Feminism and the Cultural Geographies of Encounter*. Princeton: Princeton University Press, 1998.
Frisby, David. "Deciphering the Hieroglyphics of Weimar Berlin: Siegfried Kracauer." In Haxthausen and Suhr, 152–65.
Frost, Elizabeth. Frost, "Mina Loy's 'Mongrel' Poetics." In Shreiber and Tuma, 149–79.
Galvin, Mary E. *Queer Poetics: Five Modernist Women Writers*. New York: Praeger, 1999.
Garber, Marjorie. *Vested Interests and Cultural Anxiety*. New York: Routledge, 1992.
Gay, Peter. *Weimar Culture: The Outsider as Insider*. New York: Harper and Row, 1968.
Gerhard, Ute. *Unerhört: Die Geschichte der deutschen Frauenbewegung*. Hamburg: Rowohlt, 1990.
Gilbert, Sandra. "Costumes of the Mind: Transvestism as Metaphor in Modern Literature." *Critical Inquiry* 7.2 (1980): 391–417.
Gilbert, Sandra, and Susan Gubar. *No Man's Land*. Vol. 3: *Letters from the Front*. New Haven: Yale University Press, 1994.
———. "Tradition and the Female Talent." *The Poetics of Gender*. Ed. Nancy Miller. New York: Columbia University Press, 1986: 183–207.
Gilfoyle, Timothy J. *City of Eros: New York City, Prostitution, and the Commercialization of Sex, 1890–1920*. New York: W. W. Norton, 1992.
Gilmore, Leigh. *Autobiographics: A Feminist Theory of Women's Self-Representation*. Ithaca, N.Y.: Cornell University Press, 1994.
Gilmore, Susan. "Imna, Ova, Mongrel, Spy: Anagram and Imposture in the Work of Mina Loy." In Shreiber and Tuma, 271–317.
Ginsberg, Ernst, ed. *Else Lasker-Schüler: Dichtungen und Dokumente*. Munich: Kösel Verlag, 1951.
Glatstein, Jacob. "Marianne Moore." 1947. Trans. Doris Vidauer. *Yiddish* 6.1 (1985): 67–73.
Glazer, Nathan. "The National Influence of Jewish New York." *Capital of the American City: The National and International Influence of New York City*. Ed. Martin Shefter. New York: Russell Sage Foundation, 1993: 167–92.
Glenn, Susan. *Female Spectacle: The Theatrical Roots of Modern Feminism*. Cambridge: Harvard University Press, 2000.
Glynn, Prudence. *In Fashion: Dress in the Twentieth Century*. London: George Allen and Unwin, 1978.

Goodridge, Celeste. *Hints and Disguises: Marianne Moore and Her Contemporaries.* Iowa City: University of Iowa Press, 1989.

Goody, Alex. "Autobiography/Auto-mythology: Mina Loy's 'Anglo-Mongrels and the Rose.'" In Donnell and Polkey, 270–79.

———. "Ladies of Fashion/Modern(ist) Women: Mina Loy and Djuna Barnes." *Women* 10.1 (1999): 266–82.

Green, Fiona. "Locating the Lyric: Moore and Bishop." In Davis and Jenkins, 199–214.

Green, Martin. *New York, 1913: The Armory Show and the Paterson Strike Pageant.* New York: Charles Scribner's Sons, 1988.

Green, Nancy L. *The Pletzl of Paris: Jewish Immigrant Workers in the Belle Epoque.* New York: Holmes and Meier, 1986.

Grimm, Reinhold, and Henry J. Schmidt. "Foreign Influences on German Expressionist Poetry." *Expressionism as an International Literary Phenomenon.* Ed. Ulrich Weisstein. Paris: Didier, 1973: 69–78.

Grosz, Elizabeth. "Bodies-Cities." *Sexuality and Space.* Ed. Beatriz Colomina and Jennifer Bloomer. Princeton: Princeton Architectural Press, 1992: 241–54.

Grünzweig, Walter. *Constructing the German Walt Whitman.* Iowa City: University of Iowa Press, 1995.

Guder, G. "The Meaning of Colour in Else Lasker-Schüler's Poetry." *German Life and Letters* 14–15 (1960–62): 175–87.

Gunn, Thom. "Three Hard Women: HD, Marianne Moore, Mina Loy." In Bell and Lerner, 37–52.

Hake, Sabine. "In the Mirror of Fashion." In von Ankum, 185–201.

Hallensleben, Markus. *Else Lasker-Schüler. Avantgardismus und Kunstinszenierung.* Marburg: Francke Verlag, 2000.

Hanscombe, Gillian, and Virginia L. Smyers. *Writing for Their Lives: The Modernist Women 1910–1940.* Boston: Northeastern University Press, 1988.

Hansen, Miriam. "Early Silent Cinema." *New German Critique* 29 (1983): 147–84.

Hapgood, Hutchins. *A Victorian in the Modern World.* New York: Harcourt, Brace, 1939.

Harrington, Renny. "The Stereotype of the Emancipated Woman in the Weimar Republic." *Women in German Symposium.* Oxford, Ohio: Miami University, 1977: 47–79.

Haxthausen, Charles W. "'A New Beauty': Ernst Ludwig Kirchner's Images of Berlin." In Haxthausen and Suhr, 58–94.

Haxthausen, Charles W., and Heidrun Suhr, eds. *Berlin: Culture and Metropolis.* Minneapolis: University of Minnesota Press, 1990.

Hedgepeth, Sonia. *"Überall blicke ich nach einem heimatlichen Boden aus": Exil im Werk Else Lasker-Schülers.* Frankfurt am Main: Peter Lang, 1994.

Heinrich-Jost, Ingrid. "Das Berlin der Außenseiter." In Ohff and Höynek, 157–64.

Heizer, Donna. *Jewish-German Identity in the Orientalist Literature of Else Lasker-Schüler, Friedrich Wolf, and Franz Werfel.* Columbia, S.C.: Camden House, 1996.

Hermand, Jost. "Das Bild der 'großen Stadt' im Expressionismus." *Die Unwirklichkeit der Städte: Großstadtdarstellungen zwischen Moderne und Postmoderne.* Ed. Klaus Scherpe. Reinbek bei Hamburg: Rowohlts Enzyklopädie, 1988.

Herrmann, Anne. Review of *Fashioning Sapphism: The Origins of a Modern English Lesbian Culture,* by Laura Dean. *Modernism/Modernity* 8.3 (2001): 530.

Herzfelde, Wieland. "Else Lasker-Schüler: Begegnungen mit der Dichterin und Ihrem Werk." *Sinn und Form* 21.6 (1969): 1294–1325.

Hessing, Jakob. *Else Lasker-Schüler: Biographie einer deutsch-jüdischen Dichterin.* Karlsruhe: von Loeper Verlag, 1985.

Heuving, Jeanne. *Omissions Are Not Accidents: Gender in the Art of Marianne Moore.* Detroit: Wayne State University Press, 1992.

Hirschfeld, Magnus. *Berlins Drittes Geschlecht: Schwule und Lesben um 1900.* 1904. Berlin: Verlag Rosa Winkel, 1991.

Hogue, Cynthia. "Another Postmodernism: Towards an Ethical Poetics." *How2* 1.7 (2002), 6. www.departments.bucknell.edu/stadler_center/how2.

———. *Scheming Women: Poetry, Privilege, and the Politics of Subjectivity.* Albany: State University of New York Press, 1995.

Holmes, Colin. *Anti-Semitism in British Society: 1876–1939.* New York: Holmes and Meier, 1979.

Horch, Hans Otto. "Expressionismus und Judentum: Zu einer Debatte in Martin Bubers Zeitschrift 'Der Jude.'" In Anz and Stark, *Die Modernität,* 120–41.

Hubbard, Stacy. "Mannerist Moore: Poetry, Painting, Photography." In Leavell et al.

Hubert, Renée Riese. *Magnifying Mirrors: Women, Surrealism, and Partnership.* Lincoln: University of Nebraska Press, 1994.

Hueffer, Ford Maddox. "Men and Women." Part 1. *Little Review,* January 1918: 17–31.

Huyssen, Andreas. "Mass Culture as Woman, Modernism's Other." *Studies in Entertainment: Critical Approaches to Mass Culture.* Ed. Tania Modleski. Bloomington: Indiana University Press, 1986: 188–207.

Hyman, Paula E. *Gender and Assimilation in Modern Jewish History: The Roles and Representation of Women.* Seattle: University of Washington Press, 1995.

Izenberg, Gerald. *Modernism and Masculinity: Mann, Wedekind, Kandinsky through World War I.* Chicago: University of Chicago Press, 2000.

Jacob, Heinrich Eduard. "Zur Geschichte der deutschen Lyrik seit 1910." 1924. In Raabe, 194–217.

Januzzi, Marissa. "A Bibliography of Works by and about Mina Loy." In Shreiber and Tuma, 507–606.

———. "Mongrel Rose: The 'Unerring Esperanto' of Loy's Poetry." In Shreiber and Tuma, 403–41.

Jarrell, Randall. *Poetry and the Age.* 1953. London: Faber and Faber, 1955.

Jeffrey, Sheila. *The Spinster and Her Enemies: Feminism and Sexuality, 1880–1930.* London: Routledge and Kegan Paul, 1985.

Jelavich, Peter. "Modernity, Civic Identity, and Metropolitan Entertainment: Vaudeville, Cabaret, and Revue in Berlin, 1900–1933." In Haxthausen and Suhr, 95–110.

Johnson, Randal. Introduction to *The Field of Cultural Production: Essays on Art and Literature,* by Pierre Bourdieu. Ed. Randal Johnson. Cambridge: Polity Press, 1993.

Jones, Amelia. "'Clothes Make the Man': The Male Artist as a Performative Function." *Oxford Art Journal* 18.2 (1995): 18–32.

Jones, Calvin. *The Literary Reputation of Else Lasker-Schüler: Criticism, 1901–1993.* Columbia, S.C.: Camden House, 1994.

Jones, James W. *"We of the Third Sex": Literary Representations of Homosexuality in Wilhelmine Germany.* Frankfurt am Main: Peter Lang, 1990.

Jones, M. S. *Der Sturm: A Focus of Expressionism.* Camden, N.J.: Camden House, 1984.

Juhasz, Suzanne, and Cristanne Miller. "Performances of Gender in Dickinson's Poetry." *Cambridge Companion to Emily Dickinson.* Ed. Wendy Martin. Cambridge: Cambridge University Press, 2002: 107–28.

Kadlec, David. *Mosaic Modernism: Anarchism, Pragmatism, Culture.* Baltimore: Johns Hopkins University Press, 2000.

Kandinsky, Wassily. *Concerning the Spiritual in Art.* 1912. Trans. Michael Sadleir. London, 1914.

Kaplan, Marion. *The Jewish Feminist Movement in Germany: The Campaigns of the Jüdischer Frauenbund, 1904–1938.* Westport, Conn.: Greenwood Press, 1979.

Kappel, Andrew. "Notes on the Presbyterian Poetry of Marianne Moore." *Marianne Moore: Woman and Poet.* Ed. Patricia C. Willis. Orono, Maine: National Poetry Foundation, 1990: 39–51.

———. "The World Is an Orphan's Home: Marianne Moore on God and Family." *Reform and Counterreform: Dialectics of the Word in Western Christianity since Luther.* Ed. John C. Hawley. Berlin: Mouton de Gruyter, 1994: 173–92.

Kellner, Douglas. "Expression and Rebellion." In Bronner and Kellner, 3–40.

Kelly, Catriona. *A History of Russian Women's Writing.* Gloucestershire: Clarendon Press, 1994.

Kent, Kathryn R. *Making Girls into Women: American Women's Writing and the Rise of Lesbian Identity.* Durham: Duke University Press, 2003.

Kern, Robert. *Orientalism, Modernism, and the American Poem.* Cambridge: Cambridge University Press, 1996.

Kinnahan, Linda. *Poetics of the Feminine: Authority and Literary Tradition in William Carlos Williams, Mina Loy, Denise Levertov, and Kathleen Fraser.* Cambridge: Cambridge University Press, 1994.

Koch, Angelika. *Die Bedeutung des Spiels bei Else Lasker-Schüler.* Bonn: Bouview, 1971.

Koch, Thilo. "Die 'Goldenen' Zwanziger Jahre 'Hoppla, Wir Leben.'" In Ohff and Höynck, 165–78.

Kolinsky, Eva. *Women in 20th-Century Germany: A Reader.* Manchester: Manchester University Press, 1995.

Kouidis, Virginia. *Mina Loy: American Modernist Poet.* Baton Rouge: Louisiana State University Press, 1980.

Kracauer, Siegfried. *The Salaried Masses: Duty and Distraction in Weimar Germany.* 1930. Trans. Quintin Hoare. London: Verso, 1998.

Kraft, Werner, ed. *Else Lasker-Schüler: Eine Einführung in ihr Werk und eine Auswahl.* Wiesbaden: Steiner, 1951.

Kraus, Karl. "Gegen die Neutöner." *Die Fackel,* June 21, 1912, 53–54. In Anz and Stark, *Expressionismus: Manifeste und Dokumente* 86.

Kreymborg, Alfred. *Troubadour: An Autobiography.* New York: Boni and Liveright, 1925.

Kuenzli, Rudolf E., ed. *New York Dada.* New York: Willis Locker and Owens, 1986.

Kusch, Celena E. "How the West Was One: American Modernism's Song of Itself." *American Literature* 74.3 (2002): 517–38.

Lange, Helene. *Higher Education of Women in Europe.* Trans. L. R. Klemm. New York: D. Appleton, 1901.

Lasker-Schüler, Else. *Briefe von Else Lasker-Schüler.* 2 vols. Ed. Margarete Kupper. Munich: Kösel Verlag, 1969.

———. *Concert.* Trans. Jean M. Snook. Lincoln: University of Nebraska Press, 1994.

———. *Else Lasker-Schüler Werke und Briefe: Kritische Ausgabe.* 5 vols. Ed. Norbert Oellers, Heinz Rölleke, and Itta Shedletzky. Frankfurt am Main: Suhrkamp Jüdischer Verlag, 1996.

———. *Hebrew Ballads and Other Poems.* Trans. Audri Durchslag and Jeanette Litman-Demeestere. New York: Jewish Publication Society of America, 1980.

———. *Inside This Deathly Solitude.* Trans. Ruth Schwertfeger. New York: Berg, 1991.

———. *Star in My Forehead: Selected Poems by Else Lasker-Schüler.* Trans. Janine Canan. Duluth, Minn.: Holy Cow! Press, 2000.

Lavin, Maude. *Cut with the kitchen knife: The Weimar Photomontages of Hannah Höch.* New Haven: Yale University Press, 1993.

LeRider, Jacques. *Modernity and Crises of Identity: Culture and Society in Fin-de-Siecle Vienna.* Trans. Rosemary Morris. Cambridge: Polity Press, 1993.

Leader, Jennifer. "A House Not Made with Hands: Natural Typology in the Works of Jonathan Edwards, Emily Dickinson, and Marianne Moore." Ph.D., diss., Claremont Graduate University, September 2002.

Leavell, Linda. "Marianne Moore, Her Family, and Their Language." *Proceedings of the American Philological Society* 147.1 (2003): 140–49.

———. "Marianne Moore, the James Family, and the Politics of Celibacy." *Twentieth-Century Literature* 49.2 (summer 2003): 219–45.

———. *Marianne Moore and the Visual Arts: Prismatic Color.* Baton Rouge: Louisiana State University Press, 1995.

Leavell, Linda, Cristanne Miller, and Robin Gail Schulze, eds. *Critics and Poets on Marianne Moore: "A right good salvo of barks."* Lewisburg, Pa.: Bucknell Press, 2005.

Levenson, Michael, ed. *Cambridge Companion to Modernism.* Cambridge: Cambridge University Press, 1999.

Levi, Primo. *The Periodic Table.* Trans. Raymond Rosenthal. London: Time Warner UK, Abacus, 1986.

Lewis, Beth Irwin. "Lustmord: Inside the Windows of the Metropolis." In von Ankum, 202–32.

Lindenmeyer, Antje. "'I Am Prince Jussuf': Else Lasker-Schüler's Autobiographical Performance." *Biography* 24.1 (2001): 25–34.

Liska, Vivian. *Die Dichterin und das schelmische Erhabene. Else Lasker Schülers Die Nächte Tino von Bagdads.* Marburg: Francke Verlag, 1998.

Longenbach, James. "Modern Poetry." In Levenson, 100–129.

Lorenz, Dagmar. "Jewish Women Authors and the Exile Experience: Claire Goll, Veza Canetti, Else Lasker-Schüler, Nelly Sachs, Cordelia Edvardson." *German Life and Letters* 51 (1998): 225–39.

———. "The Unspoken Bond: Else Lasker-Schüler and Gertrud Kolmar." *Seminar: A Journal of Germanic Studies* 29.4 (1993): 349–69.

Loy, Mina. *The Last Lunar Baedeker.* Ed. Roger L. Conover. Highlands: Jargon Society, 1982.

———. *The Lost Lunar Baedeker.* Ed. Roger L. Conover. New York: Farrar, Straus and Giroux, 1996.

———. "Street Sister." *That Kind of Woman.* Ed. Bronte Adams and Trudi Tate. New York: Carroll and Graf, 1991: 41–42.

Lublinksi, Samuel. *Die Bilanz der Moderne.* Berlin: Siegfried Cronbach, 1904.

Lyon, Janet. "Mina Loy's Pregnant Pauses: The Space of Possibility in the Florence Writing." In Shreiber and Tuma, 379–402.

MacDonald, Claire. "Assumed Identities: Feminism, Autobiography, and Performance Art." *The Uses of Autobiography.* Ed. Julia Swindells. London: Taylor and Francis, 1995: 187–95.

McAlmon, Robert. *A Hasty Bunch: Short Stories.* 1922. Carbondale: Southern Illinois University Press, 1975.

———. *Post-Adolescence.* Paris: Contact Editions, 1923.

McDonald, Gail. *Learning to be Modern: Pound, Eliot, and the American University.* New York: Oxford University Press, 1993.

Marek, Jayne E. *Women Editing Modernism: "Little" Magazines and Literary History.* Lexington: University Press of Kentucky, 1995.

Matsche, Franz. "Grossstadt in der Malerei des Expressionismus am Beispiel E.L. Kirchners." In Anz and Stark, *Die Modernität,* 95–119.

Matthews, Jean V. *Women's Struggle for Equality: The First Phase, 1828–1876.* Chicago: Ivan R. Dee, 1997.

McBride, Dorothy. *Women's Rights in France.* Westport, Conn.: Greenwood Press, 1987.

McCabe, Susan. "'A Queer Lot' and the Lesbians of 1914: Amy Lowell, H.D., and Gertrude Stein." *Challenging Boundaries: Gender and Periodization.* Ed. Joyce W. Warren and Margaret Dickie. Athens: University of Georgia Press, 2000: 62–90.

McCarthy, Kathleen D. *Women's Culture: American Philanthropy and Art, 1830–1930.* Chicago: University of Chicago Press, 1991.

McFarlane, James. "Berlin and the Rise of Modernism, 1886–96." In Bradbury and McFarlane, 96–104.

McMillan, James F. *France and Women, 1789–1914: Gender, Society, and Politics.* Amherst: University of Massachusetts Press, 2000.

Mead, Jodie. "'The Cult of the Clitoris': Anatomy of a National Scandal." *Modernism/Modernity* 9.1 (2002): 21–50.

Meese, Elizabeth. "Theorizing Lesbian: Writing—a Love Letter." *Lesbian Texts and Contexts: Radical Revisions.* Ed. Karla Jay and Joanne Glasgow. London: Onlywoman Press, 1992: 70–87.

Mendes-Flohr, Paul. "The Berlin Jew as Cosmopolitan." In Bilski, 14–31.

———. *German Jews: A Dual Identity.* New Haven: Yale University Press, 1999.

Merrin, Jeredith. "Sites of Struggle: Marianne Moore and American Calvinism." In Barnstone et al., 91–106.

Meskimmon, Marsha. *We Weren't Modern Enough: Women Artists and the Limits of German Modernism.* Berkeley and Los Angeles: University of California Press, 1999.

Miller, Cristanne. "Feminist Location and Mina Loy's 'Anglo-Mongrels and the Rose.'" *Paideuma* 32.1–3 (2003): 75–94.

———. *Marianne Moore: Questions of Authority.* Cambridge: Harvard University Press, 1995.

———. "Marianne Moore and a Poetry of Hebrew (Protestant) Prophecy." *Sources* 12 (2002): 29–47.

———. "Marianne Moore and the Women Modernizing New York." *Modern Philology* 98.2 (2000): 339–62.

———."Marianne Moore's Black Maternal Hero." *American Literary History* 1.4 (1989): 786–815.

———. "The Politics of Marianne Moore's Poetry of Ireland: 1917–1941," *Irish Journal of American Studies* 11 (December 2004): 1–14.

———. "Reading the Politics of Else Lasker-Schüler's 1914 *Hebrew Ballads.*" *Modernism/Modernity* 6.2 (1999): 135–59.

———. "'What Is War For?' Moore's Development of an Ethical Poetry." In Leavell et al., 56–73.

Miller, Nina. *Making Love Modern: The Intimate Public Worlds of New York's Literary Women.* New York: Oxford University Press, 1999.

Molesworth, Charles. *Marianne Moore: A Literary Life.* New York: Atheneum, 1990.

Moore, Marianne. *Becoming Marianne Moore: The Early Poems, 1907–1924.* Ed. Robin Gail Schulze. Berkeley and Los Angeles: University of California Press, 2002.

———. *The Complete Poems of Marianne Moore.* New York: Macmillan, Viking, 1981.

———. *The Complete Prose of Marianne Moore.* Ed. Patricia C. Willis. New York: Viking, 1986.

———. *Marianne Moore Reader.* New York: Viking Press, 1961.

———. *Selected Letters of Marianne Moore.* Ed. Bonnie Costello, Celeste Goodridge, and Cristanne Miller. New York: Knopf, 1997.

Moreck, Curt. *Führer durch das "lasterhafte" Berlin.* 1931. Berlin: Nicolaische Verlagsbuchhandlung, Beuermann, 1996.

Morris, Lloyd. *Incredible New York: High Life and Low Life of the Last Hundred Years, 1850–1950.* New York: Random House, 1951.

Morrisson, Mark S. "Performing the Pure Voice: Elocution, Verse Recitation, and Modernist Poetry in Prewar London." *Modernism/Modernity* 3.3 (1996): 25–50.

———. *The Public Face of Modernism: Little Magazines, Audiences, and Reception, 1905–1920.* Madison: University of Wisconsin Press, 2001.

Müller, Lothar. "The Beauty of the Metropolis: Toward an Aesthetic Urbanism in Turn-of-the-Century Berlin." In Haxthausen and Suhr, 37–57.

Müller, Ulrike. *Auch wider dem Verbote: Else Lasker-Schüler und ihr eigensinniger Umgang mit Weiblichkeit, Judentum und Mystik.* Frankfurt am Main: Peter Lang, 1997.

Nesbitt, Molly. "In the absence of the *parisienne* . . ." In *Sexuality and Space.* Ed. Beatriz Colomina. New York: Princeton Architectural Press, 1992: 307–25.

Newcomb, John Timberman. "The Footprint of the Twentieth Century: American Skyscrapers and Modernist Poems." *Modernism/Modernity* 10.1 (2003): 97–125.

Nicholls, Peter. "Cruel Structures: The Development of Expressionism." In Nicholls, 136–64.

———, ed. *Modernism: A Literary Guide.* Berkeley and Los Angeles: University of California Press, 1995.

Ningel, Meike. "Die Unzugänglichkeit des Eigenen: Zur Logic von Else Lasker-Schülers Umgang mit Sprache." *Die Fremdheit der Sprache. Studien zur Literatur der Moderne.* Ed. Jochen C. Schütze, Hans-Ulrich Treichel, and Dietmar Voss. *Literatur im historischen Prozeß* 23 (1988): 103–16.

North, Michael. *The Dialect of Modernism: Race, Language, and Twentieth-Century Literature.* Oxford: Oxford University Press, 1994.

O'Brien, Mary-Elizabeth. "'Ich war verkleidet als Poet . . . ich bin Poetin!' The

Masquerade of Gender in Else Lasker-Schüler's Work." *German Quarterly* 65 (1992): 1–17.

Ohff, Heinz, and Rainer Höynek, eds. *Das Berlin Buch.* Berlin: Stapp Verlag, 1987.

Oja, Carol J. "On Women Patrons and Activists for Modernist Music: New York in the 1920s." *Modernism/Modernity* 4.1 (1997): 129–55.

Parsons, Deborah L. *Streetwalking the Metropolis: Women, the City, and Modernity.* Oxford: Oxford University Press, 2000.

Peppis, Paul. "Rewriting Sex: Mina Loy, Marie Stopes, and Sexology." *Modernism/Modernity* 9.4 (2002): 561–79.

Perloff, Marjorie. "English as a 'Second' Language." In Shreiber and Tuma, 31–148.

Perry, Gill. *Women Artists and the Parisian Avant-Garde.* Manchester: Manchester University Press, 1995.

Petro, Patrice. "Perceptions of Difference: Woman as Spectator and Spectacle." In von Ankum, 41–66.

Pickering-Iazzi, Robin. *Politics of the Visible: Writing Women, Culture, and Fascism.* Minneapolis: University of Minnesota Press, 1997.

Poggi, Christine. "Dreams of Metallized Flesh: Futurism and the Masculine Body." *Modernism/Modernity* 4.3 (1997): 19–43.

Politzer, Heinz. "Else Lasker-Schüler." In Rothe, 215–31.

Pound, Ezra. "A Few Don'ts by an Imagiste." *Poetry,* March 1913: 200–206.

———. "Marianne Moore and Mina Loy." *Selected Prose, 1909–1965.* Ed. William Cookson. London: Faber and Faber, 1973: 424–25.

Qian, Zhaoming. *The Modernist Response to Chinese Art: Pound, Moore, Stevens.* Charlottesville: University of Virginia Press, 2003.

———. *Orientalism and Modernism: The Legacy of China in Pound and Williams.* Durham: Duke University Press, 1995.

Raabe, Paul, ed. *Expressionismus: Der Kampf um eine literarische Bewegung.* Zurich: Arche Verlag, 1987.

Rapp, Rayna, and Ellen Ross. "The 1920s: Feminism, Consumerism, and Political Backlash in the United States." *Women in Culture and Politics: A Century of Change.* Ed. Judith Friedlander, Blanche Wiesen Cook, Alice Kessler-Harris, and Carrol Smith-Rosenberg. Bloomington: University of Indiana Press, 1986: 52–61.

Reiß-Suckow, Christine. *"Wer wird mir Schöpfer sein!" Die Entwicklung Else Lasker-Schüler als Künstlerin.* Constance: Hartung-Gorre, 1997.

Rich, Adrienne. *Blood, Bread, and Poetry: Selected Prose, 1979–1985.* New York: W. W. Norton, 1986.

Ridge, Lola. *Sun-Up.* New York: B. W. Huebsch, 1920.

Riley, Charles A., II. *Color Codes: Modern Theories of Color in Philosophy, Painting, Architecture, Literature, Music, and Psychology.* Hanover, N.H.: University Press of New England, 1995.

Ritter, Norbert. "Stadtentwicklung und Verkehr." In Ohff and Höynck, 143–56.

Roberts, Mary Louise. "Samson and Delilah Revisited: The Politics of Women's Fashion in 1920s France." *American Historical Review* 97 (1993): 69–85.

Robertson, Ritchie. "'Urheimat Asien': The Re-orientation of German and Austrian Jews, 1900–1925." *German Life and Letters* 49.2 (1996): 182–92.

Rosenfeld, Paul. "Musical Chronicle." *Dial,* June 1927, 446.

Roston, Murray. *Modernist Patterns in Literature and the Visual Arts.* New York: New York University Press, 2000.

Rothe, Wolfgang, ed. *Expressionismus als Literatur: Gesammelte Studien.* Bern: A. Francke Verlag, 1969.

Rowe, Dorothy. *Representing Berlin: Sexuality and the City in Imperial and Weimar Germany.* Hants: Ashgate, 2003.

Rupp, Leila J. *A Desired Past: A Short History of Same-Sex Love in America.* Chicago: University of Chicago Press, 1999.

Sanders-Brahms, Helma. *Gottfried Benn und Else Lasker-Schüler: Giselheer und Prinz Jussuf.* Hamburg: Rowohlt, 1997.

Sawelson-Gorse, Naomi, ed. *Women in Dada: Essays on Sex, Gender, and Identity.* Cambridge: MIT Press, 1998.

Schabert, Ina. "No Room of One's Own: Women's Studies in English Departments in Germany." *MLA* 119.1 (2004): 69–79.

Schenck, Celeste. "Exiled by Genre: Modernism, Canonicity, and the Politics of Exclusion." In Broe and Ingram, 226–50.

Schueller, Malini Johar. *U.S. Orientalisms: Race, Nation, and Gender in Literature, 1790–1890.* Ann Arbor: University of Michigan Press, 1998.

Schulte, Birgit. "Die Emanzipation der Künstlerinnen um die Jahrhundertwende: Else Lasker-Schüler's Begegnungen mit Karl Ernst Osthaus und Milly Steger." *Prinz Jussuf ist Eine Frau.* Iserlohn: Evangelische Akademie Iserlohn, 1995: 83–97.

Schulze, Robin Gail. "Marianne Moore's 'Imperious Ox, Imperial Dish' and the Poetry of the Natural World." *Twentieth Century Literature* 44.1 (1998): 1–33.

———. "Textual Darwinism: Marianne Moore, the Text of Evolution, and the Evolving Text." *Text* 11 (1998): 270–305.

———. *The Web of Friendship: Marianne Moore and Wallace Stevens.* Ann Arbor: University of Michigan Press, 1995.

Schuster, Peter-Klaus. *Franz Marc-Else Lasker-Schüler: "Der Blaue Reiter präsentiert Eurer Hoheit sein Blaues Pferd": Karten und Briefe.* Munich: Prestel Verlag, 1987.

Scott, William B., and Peter M. Rutkoff. *New York Modern: The Arts and the City.* Baltimore: Johns Hopkins University Press, 1999.

Sedgwick, Eve. *Between Men: English Literature and Male Homosocial Desire.* New York: Columbia University Press, 1985.

Sheppard, Richard. "German Expressionism." In Bradbury and McFarlane, 274–91.

———. "German Expressionist Poetry." In Bradbury and McFarlane, 383–92.

Shreiber, Maeera. "Divine Women, Fallen Angels: The Late Devotional Poetry of Mina Loy." In Shreiber and Tuma, 467–83.

———. "'Love is a Lyric / of Bodies': The Negative Aesthetics of Mina Loy's 'Love Songs to Joannes.'" *Genre* 27 (spring–summer 1994): 143–64.

Shreiber, Maeera, and Keith Tuma, eds. *Mina Loy: Woman and Poet.* Orono, Maine: National Poetry Foundation, 1998.

Sielke, Sabine. *Fashioning the Female Subject: The Intertextual Networking of Dickinson, Moore, and Rich.* Ann Arbor: University of Michigan Press, 1997.

Slatin, John. *The Savage's Romance: The Poetry of Marianne Moore.* State College: Pennsylvania State University Press, 1986.

Smith, George Adam. *The Book of the Twelve Prophets Commonly Called the Minor.* London: Hodder and Stoughton, 1898.

———. *The Early Poetry of Israel in Its Physical and Social Origins.* London: Oxford University Press, 1912.

———. *Modern Criticism and the Preaching of the Old Testament.* London: Hodder and Stoughton, 1901.

Smith, Karen Manners. "New Paths to Power: 1890–1920." *No Small Courage: A History of Women in the United States.* Ed. Nancy Cott. Oxford: Oxford University Press, 2000: 353–412.

Smith-Rosenberg, Carroll. *Disorderly Conduct: Visions of Gender in Victorian America.* New York: Oxford University Press, 1985.

Snook, Jean M. "The Concept of Home in Else Lasker-Schüler's *Concert.*" *Else Lasker-Schüler. Ansichten und Perspektiven.* Ed. Ernst Schürer und Sonja M. Hedgepeth. Marburg: Francke Verlag, 1999: 219–27.

Sochen, June. *The New Woman: Feminism in Greenwich Village, 1910–1920.* New York: Quadrangle Books, 1972.

Spencer, Lloyd. "Allegory in the World of the Commodity: The Importance of *Central Park.*" *New German Critique* 34 (winter 1985): 59–77.

Spiegelman, Art. *Maus: A Survivor's Tale.* New York: Pantheon, 1986.

Stamy, Cynthia. *Marianne Moore and China: Orientalism and a Writing of America.* Oxford: Oxford University Press, 1999.

Stansell, Christine. *American Moderns: Bohemian New York and the Creation of a New Century.* Henry Holt, 2000.

Steinman, Lisa. *Made in America: Science, Technology, and American Modernist Poets.* New Haven: Yale University Press, 1987.

Suleiman, Susan Rubin. "A Double Margin: Reflections on Women Writers and the Avant-Garde in France." *Yale French Studies* 75 (1988): 148–72.

———. *Subversive Intent: Gender, Politics, and the Avant-Garde.* Cambridge: Harvard University Press, 1990.

Surette, Leon. *The Birth of Modernism: Ezra Pound, T. S. Eliot, W. B. Yeats, and the Occult.* Toronto: McGill-Queen's University Press, 1993.

Sword, Helen. *Ghostwriting Modernism.* Ithaca, N.Y.: Cornell University Press, 2002.

Tatar, Maria. *Lustmord: Sexual Murder in Weimar Germany.* Princeton: Princeton University Press, 1995.

Teal, Laurie. "The Hollow Women: Modernism, the Prostitute, and Commodity Aesthetics." *Differences* 7.5 (1996): 80–108.

Tsvetayeva, Marina. *Selected Poems.* Trans. Elaine Feinstein. Oxford: Oxford University Press, 1971.

Tuma, Keith. *Fishing in Obstinate Isles: Modern British Poetry and American Readers.* Evanston, Ill.: Northwestern University Press, 1998.

Valencia, Heather. *Else Lasker-Schüler und Abraham Nochem Stenzel: Eine Unbekannte Freundschaft.* Frankfurt am Main: Campus Verlag, 1995.

Van Vechten, Carl. *Parties.* 1930. Los Angeles: Sun and Moon Press, 1993.

Veth, Hilke. "Literatur von Frauen." *Literatur der Weimarer Republik 1918–1933.* Ed. Bernhard Weyergraf. Munich: Deutscher Taschenbuch Verlag, 1995: 446–82.

Vietta, Silvio. "Großstadtwahrnehmung und ihre literarische Darstellung: Expressionistischer Reihungsstil und Collage." *Deutsche Vierteljarhrsschrift für Literaturwissenschaft und Geistesgeschichte* 48 (1974): 354–73.

Vincent, John Emil. *Queer Lyrics (Difficulty and Closure in American Poetry).* New York: Palgrave Macmillan, 2002.

Vogt, Paul. "The *Blaue Reiter.*" In *Expressionism: A German Intuition, 1905–1920.* Ed. Paul Vogt et al. New York: Solomon R. Guggenheim Museum, 1980: 192–237.

von Ankum, Katharina. "Gendered Urban Spaces in Irmgard Keun's *Das kunstseidene Mädchen.*" In von Ankum, 162–84.

———, ed. *Women in the Metropolis: Gender and Modernity in Weimar Culture.* Berkeley and Los Angeles: University of California Press, 1997.

von Hallberg, Robert. "Ezra Pound in Paris." In Bell and Lerner, 53–65.

Weininger, Otto. *Geschlecht und Charakter.* Munich: Matthes and Seitz, 1980.

Weir, David. *Decadence and the Making of Modernism.* Amherst: University of Massachusetts Press, 1995.

Wertheim, Arthur Frank. *The New York Little Renaissance: Iconoclasm, Modernism, and Nationalism in American Culture, 1908–1917.* New York: New York University Press, 1976.

West, Nathaniel. *Miss Lonelyhearts.* London: Grey Walls Press, 1949.

Wiener, Meïr. "Else Lasker-Schüler." *Juden in der Deutschen Literature: Essays über zeitgenösische Schriftsteller.* Ed. Gustav Krojanken. Berlin: Welt-Verlag, 1922: 179–92.

Willett, John. *Art and Politics in the Weimar Period: The New Sobriety, 1817–1933.* New York: Pantheon, 1978.

Williams, William Carlos. *Autobiography.* New York: Random House, 1951.

———. "Marianne Moore." 1925. *Imaginations.* Ed. Webster Schott. New York: New Directions, 1970: 310–19.

———. *Paterson.* New York: New Directions, 1963.

Williams, Raymond. *The Politics of Modernism.* London: Verso, 1989.

———. *Unreal City: Urban Experience in Modern European Literature and Art.* Manchester: Manchester University Press, 1985.

Willis, Patricia C. "Images of Marianne." *Marianne Moore Newsletter* 3.2 (fall 1979): 20–24.

Wilson, Elizabeth. *The Sphinx in the City: Urban Life, the Control of Disorder, and Women.* Berkeley and Los Angeles: University of California Press, 1991.

Winters, Yvor. "Holiday and Day of Wrath" and "Mina Loy." *Uncollected Essays and Reviews.* Ed. Francis Murphy. London: Allen Lane, 1973: 22–26; 27–31.

Winterson, Jeanette. *Oranges Are Not the Only Fruit.* New York: Atlantic Monthly, 1987.

Wohlfahrt, Irving. "'*Männer aus der Fremde*': Walter Benjamin and the 'German-Jewish Parnassus.'" *New German Critique* 70 (1997): 3–86.

Wolfenstein, Alfred. "Jüdisches Wesen und Dichtertum." *Der Jude* 6 (1922): 428–40.

Wolff, Janet. *Feminine Sentences: Essays on Women and Culture.* Cambridge: Polity Press, 1990.

Wollen, Peter. *Raiding the Icebox: Reflections on Twentieth-Century Culture.* Bloomington: Indiana University Press, 1993.

Wolosky, Shira. "Santayana and Harvard Formalism." *Raritan* 18.4 (1999): 51–67.

Woolf, Virginia. *A Room of One's Own.* Cambridge: Cambridge University Press, 1995.

Wright, Barbara. "'New Man,' Eternal Woman: Expressionist Responses to German Feminism." *German Quarterly* 60.4 (1987): 582–99.

Zuckmayer, Carl. *Als wär's ein Stück von mir.* Frankfurt am Main: Fischer, 1966.

Index

- Rachel Blau DuPlessis: Genders, Races + Religious Cultures in Mod. American Poetry 1908–34 (Cambridge 2001)
- Women's Writing in Exile; Eds M.L. Broe, Angela Ingram (1989)
- Cynthia Hogue, "Another Postmodernism: Toward an Ethical Poetics." 20th C Lit

---

Chpt. 3

✓– paradoxical approach to self: poetic simultaneously ren[illegible] fictitious + reveals desired/perceived aspects of poetic/se[illegible] b[illegible]
52

✓ gender as performance/artifice (relate to racial perform[illegible] of dialect?)
57, 66 ⊛

- language change → social change 64, 66

✓ 1920's "heterosexual revolution"; commodification of heterosexuality concomitant demonization of female-centered activity.

✓– MM: naming patterns reveal how self-referential her poems [illegible] w[illegible]
74

✓– MM: "chooses not to be one thing, but to choose." 75

✓– MM: "♀ + ♂ are not polarities but modes to combine" 79

Chpt. 1

- Cristanne Miller's main argument: insistence at once on general + local 2
- situates both theory and historical overviews 5

Chpt. 2

25, 26, 38–9 (NYC + feminism)